**AA**

# GUIDE TO
# NEW ZEALAND

**AA**

# GUIDE TO
# NEW
# ZEALAND

**WELDON**
PUBLISHING

SYDNEY · HONG KONG · CHICAGO · LONDON

**Text**
Allan Eadie
Wendy Simons

**Maps**
Automobile Association (Auckland) Inc
Department of Survey and Land Information
Licence No 1989/56
Crown Copyright Reserved

**Publishing Manager**
Robin Burgess

**Designer**
Kathie Baxter Smith

**Project Co-ordinator**
Claire Craig

**Distributed by:**
Beckett Sterling
28 Poland Road
Glenfield
Auckland
New Zealand

Typeset by Savage Type, Brisbane, Australia
Printed in Hong Kong by Everbest Printing Co Ltd

Published by Weldon Publishing New Zealand,
a division of Weldon International Pty Ltd.
372 Eastern Valley Way, Willoughby, NSW 2068, Australia.

© Automobile Association (Auckland) Inc
  AA Centre
  99 Albert St, Auckland, New Zealand

National Library CIP
1. New Zealand — Description and travel — 1981 — Guide-books.
2. Automobile travel — New Zealand — Guide-books. 3. New Zealand — Road
maps. I. Automobile Association (N.Z.). II. Title: Guide to New Zealand.
ISBN 1 86 302 067 5

# ACKNOWLEDGEMENTS

Auckland Public Library
Auckland Tourist and Publicity
Automobile Association
Department of Statistics
Ministry of Transport
New Zealand Railways Corporation

*Sheep gather in the morning mist, Central North Island.*

# PHOTOGRAPHIC ACKNOWLEDGMENTS

Photographs have been credited by page number. References have been abbreviated as follows:

BE     Brian Enting
CP     Craig Potton
CS     Conrad Sims
FC     Fotocentre Ltd, Oamaru
FT     Fiordland Travel Ltd
GM     Geoff Mason
RJ     Ray Joyce
RM     Robin Morrison
SR     Stephen Robinson
TS     Tim Steele

## Acknowledgments

**6–7**: CP   **9**: FT   **10**: GM   **12**: GM   **17**: SR   **23**: GM   **26**: GM
**31**: TS   **33**: RJ   **36**: CP   **39**: CP   **42**: GM   **45**: SR
**48–49**: RJ   **51**: GM   **56–57**: GM   **59**: CP   **61**: GM
**65**: CP   **67**: GM   **69**: GM   **71**: CP   **75**: CP   **78–79**: RM
**80–81**: CP   **84–85**: GM   **88–89**: CP   **92–93**: CP   **97**: TS
**98–99**: GM   **100–101**: TS   **104–108**: GM   **108–109**: GM
**112–113**: RM   **114–115**: GM   **117**: SR   **120–121**: CP
**126–127**: RJ   **130–131**: RJ   **134–135**: CP
**136–137**: GM   **139**: RM   **140–141**: GM   **144–145**: GM
**147**: GM   **150–151**: GM   **152–153**: BE   **154–155**: GM
**157**: BE   **160–161**: CP   **166–167**: GM   **168–169**: RM
**174–175**: GM   **178–179**: GM   **180–181**: GM   **183**: GM
**187**: GM   **190–191**: CP   **192**: FT   **193**: GM
**196–197**: RJ   **198**: GM   **200–201**: GM   **204–205**: GM
**206–207**: CP   **209**: CP   **211**: CP   **212–213**: RJ   **214**: RJ
**217**: GM   **221**: GM   **223**: GM   **228–229**: GM   **231**: GM
**232–233**: CP   **236**: GM   **238–239**: CP   **244–245**: GM
**248–249**: GM   **253**: CP   **254**: CP   **255**: GM
**256–257**: CP   **258–259**: CP   **262–263**: RM
**268–269**: CP   **274–275**: CP   **276**: BE   **283**: RJ
**288–289**: GM   **295**: GM   **297**: CP   **299**: RJ   **300**: FC
**302–303**: CP   **307**: TS   **310–311**: CP   **317**: CP
**320–321**: CS   **322–323**: RJ   **326–327**: CP   **332–333**: TS
**334–335**: RJ   **336–337**: GM   **339**: BE   **340**: CP
**342**: RJ   **344–345**: GM   **348–349**: GM   **351**: RJ
**355**: RJ   **358–359**: GM   **357**: CP

# REFERENCES

*AA Guide to Bushwalks and Tramping*
*AA Guide to Day Tours*
*AA Guide to Walkways — North Island*
*AA Guide to Walkways — South Island*
*AA Road Atlas*
*Cycle Touring in the North Island*
*Cycle Touring in the South Island*
*Mobil NZ Travel Guide — North Island*
*Mobil NZ Travel Guide — South Island*
*NZ Census of Population 1986*
*NZ Railway and Tramway Atlas*
*Wises New Zealand Guide*

*A pohutukawa tree at sunset, Bland Bay.*

*Carey's Bay, Otago Harbour, Dunedin.*

# CONTENTS

*An old stackstone cottage near Roxburgh, Central Otago.*

# INTRODUCTION

Welcome to New Zealand! Most readers of this introduction will probably be New Zealanders, but some will be tourists from overseas. Regardless, we welcome your interest in finding out more about this wonderful country.

It is too easy to travel from one place to another without realising the things to see and do on the way, or when you get there. This book gives you a range of options to allow you to plan your sightseeing. Do not arrive back home lamenting unseen sights with the cry 'if only I'd known'. With this guide you can know in advance, and select your time and opportunities accordingly.

The first section of this book describes New Zealand's major touring routes. We have followed the format previously used by the Automobile Association's loose-leaf itinerary sheets. In order to save duplication, these routes are described in one direction only; that is, the direction seemingly used most by tourist travellers. Generally, we describe those routes through the west and the centre of each island in a southbound direction, while eastern routes are described in a northbound direction.

In these itineraries, places printed in bold type are described under their own heading in the second section of the book, while places marked with an asterisk are listed under a larger place's heading. For example, Matakohe* is listed under **Maungaturoto**. An index at the back of the book refers to the listings in our A–Z section.

Although this book is written mainly for road travellers, we also describe some of the rail routes for train passengers and also the inter-island ferry service between Wellington and Picton.

The central section of the book describes major destinations in alphabetical order. We give a brief synopsis of each destination's history and geography and under 'Environs and Attractions', we list those local features and sights in the downtown or central part of the area. Under the heading 'Local Touring' we list those options that are out of the centre or in a neighbouring area. Some of the places listed will probably be passed by you on the way into a town, so read ahead about your next destination. To help you in that respect, each heading has a 'see also' line that enables you to look ahead to the next heading in the direction you intend travelling.

The final section of the book is intended to give tourists from overseas a brief insight into New Zealand's culture and characteristics.

We have deliberately chosen not to go into too much detail in the sections of this book. It is for the 'casual' as opposed to the 'specialist' tourist', because it would be impossible to cover all topics to the complete satisfaction of, for example, speleologists, train enthusiasts, or Maori historians. If you are particularly interested in a specific subject then other texts, or local advice, can usually be found to lead you further into that topic.

This is especially the case with the many walking tracks that are listed in this book. We list them to draw them to your attention, but many will require further reference to determine the exact route, or whether they are suitable for your walking ability. The *AA Guide to Tramping and Bushwalking* and the *AA Guide to Walkways* (North and South Islands) will provide you with further information on walking in New Zealand.

This book is also *not* a substitute for a road atlas. Most bookshops sell the *AA Road Atlas* and members of Automobile Associations in New Zealand, as well as members of associated overseas motoring clubs, will be able to receive a selection of excellent maps if they present their membership card to an AA office.

You have already taken two positive steps towards enjoying a great New Zealand holiday. First, by buying this publication, and secondly by reading this introduction. These steps should help you to have a satisfying journey! Our best wishes to you.

# North and South Island Itineraries

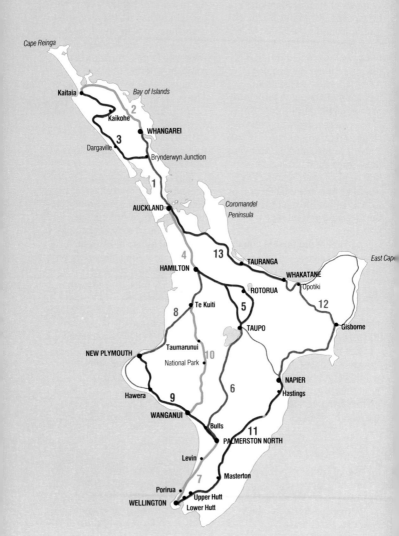

Cape Reinga

Bay of Islands

Kaitaia

2

Kaikohe

3

WHANGAREI

Dargaville

Brynderwyn Junction

1

AUCKLAND

Coromandel
Peninsula

4

13

TAURANGA

East Cape

HAMILTON

WHAKATANE

Opotiki

ROTORUA

8

Te Kuiti

5

12

TAUPO

Gisborne

NEW PLYMOUTH

Taumarunui

10

National Park

9

NAPIER

6

Hastings

Hawera

WANGANUI

Bulls

11

PALMERSTON NORTH

Levin

7

Masterton

Porirua

Upper Hutt

WELLINGTON

Lower Hutt

Farewell Spit

Collingwood

Picton

NELSON

15

BLENHEIM

WESTPORT

Murchison

14

Lewis Pass

Kaikoura

GREYMOUTH

16

Hanmer
Springs

Hokitika

18

Arthur's Pass

Waipara

17

Franz Josef Glacier
Fox Glacier

CHRISTCHURCH

Mt Cook

20

Banks Peninsula

Haast

Tekapo

Geraldine

Ashburton

19

Twizel

Fairlie

Omarama

Timaru

Lake Hawea
Wanaka

21

Milford Sound

QUEENSTOWN

Cromwell

26

Oamaru

Alexandra

Te Anau

23

22

24

Lumsden

Gore

DUNEDIN

Milton

25

Balclutha

INVERCARGILL

Stewart Island

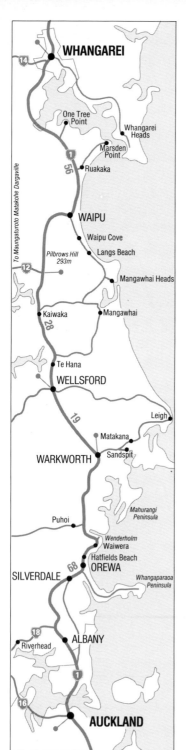

# AUCKLAND– WHANGAREI
**via Warkworth and Wellsford**
*171 km (3 hr)*

A comfortable run that takes you through predominantly hilly country.

From downtown **Auckland** follow Custom Street West and Fanshawe Street on to the northbound motorway and the Auckland Harbour Bridge. Take careful note of lane control arrows on the bridge, and follow signs for Route 1 and Whangarei. Cyclists are forbidden on the bridge.

*Southbound* motorists should note that the left lane leads to the suburb of Ponsonby. Avoid this lane if heading for downtown Auckland or further south. Also note ½ km after crossing bridge, two left lanes go to downtown Auckland, and two other lanes continue to the south.

In due course the motorway reverts to normal road formation, continuing through light industrial and residential areas, then into open area. Follow through Albany, pass the Riverhead (Route 18)Road junction, the East Coast Bays Road junction, drop down to Silverdale, rise up to the Whangaparaoa Peninsula* junction, and down to the seaside town of Orewa*. The route climbs a headland to Hatfields Beach, and then another headland to Waiwera* (accessed on side road).

From Waiwera the road follows through predominantly hilly country. It passes the Wenderholm turn-off, climbs steeply up and over a razorback, passes the side road to Puhoi*, and then rises again through to a broken plateau. On the descent, the high Pohuehue viaduct is

*The Auckland Harbour Bridge at sunset.*

crossed, before passing a junction to the satellite communications station on the right, and entering **Warkworth** (68 km from Auckland). The main road by-passes the business area, which is accessible by two roads on the right. The second of these junctions also links Mahurangi Peninsula*, Sandspit*, Matakana and Leigh.

Northwards from Warkworth Route 1 continues across a flat area, then goes up and over the Dome Hill. In due course it leads directly into the main street of **Wellsford** (88 km from Auckland). Route 16, an alternative western route from (or to) Auckland also joins here.

Onward through the Lower North, it is comfortable travelling through the small towns of Te Hana and Kaiwaka. From the latter an eastbound road, partially unsealed, leads to Mangawhai, Mangawhai Heads, Langs Beach and Waipu Cove*. But Route 1 strikes north, with a steep rise up and over

the Brynderwyn deviation at Pilbrows Hill (293 m).

Just after commencing the ascent, Route 12 to **Maunga-turoto** and **Dargaville** swings away. This route is described southbound in itinerary 3.

From the top of Pilbrows Hill you can see a vast panorama that includes Waipu, Marsden Point and the Whangarei Heads. Be careful if you stop to enjoy the view, as there are few pull-off areas. From here Route 1 drops down to **Waipu**. Waipu provides alternative access to Waipu Cove* and Langs Beach. Proceed north over flat ground, past the turn-off for Ruakaka*, Marsden Point* (oil refinery) and One Tree Point. Portland Cement Works is off to the right before entering **Whangarei**. If travelling directly north of Whangarei, follow the western by-pass as indicated. If travelling to downtown Whangarei, watch out for one-way streets. Part of the main shopping area (Cameron Street) is closed to through traffic.

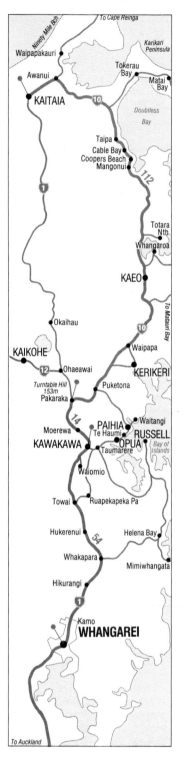

# WHANGAREI – KAITAIA
### via Bay of Islands and Mangonui

*Whangarei – Paihia 68 km (1 hr 15 min)*
*Paihia – Kaitaia 94 km (2 hr 15 min)*

An interesting drive through many historic parts of New Zealand.

From **Whangarei** drive up Bank Street and Kamo Road, through the northern suburb of Kamo. The western by-pass from the south intersects here. Proceed through open country bypassing Hikurangi (note the peculiar limestone rocks cropping up on the right). At Whakapara, 22 km from Whangarei, the coastal road to Helena Bay, Mimiwhangata, Oakura and Russell branches away to the right. This is a secondary route to the Bay of Islands — scenic, hilly and partially unsealed.

Route 1 continues north over partially developed hill-lands through the tiny localities of Hukerenui and Towai. A road on the right north of Towai leads 5 km to the Ruapekapeka Pa* Historic Reserve, site of the final battle between British troops and Hone Heke's Maori warriors, the defeat of whom, in 1864, brought an end to the Northern War. Further on, another road to the right leads 1 km to the Waiomio Caves*.

**Kawakawa** is a commercial centre noted for the railway line running down its main street. Here our route divides. The main road north does not go via the **Bay of Islands**, and access to Paihia*, Waitangi* and Russell* is by connecting roads from Kawakawa or Puketona. The more direct route to Paihia swings away to the right as you enter Kawakawa. It proceeds a short distance to the Taumarere junction where the road from Russell intersects. This is the other end of the coast road to Russell; either way, however, this route is narrow, winding, and partially unsealed, and tourists wishing to take their cars to Russell should consider using the vehicular ferry service from Opua.

The road to Paihia is hilly, but sealed. 11 km from Kawakawa, a hilltop crossroad leads down to Opua*. Proceed on through Te Haumi to arrive in Paihia. Drive along the waterfront to the wharf, where passenger ferries operate to Russell, which is in sight across the Bay. This road also continues around the Bay to Waitangi. The alternative route from Kawakawa via Moerewa and the Puketona corner is at the Waitangi end of Paihia. This route also connects Kaikohe, Kerikeri, and other points north.

At the Puketona corner (which provides the alternative access to the Bay of Islands), continue north to the gardening and orchard district of **Kerikeri**. The town itself is on a side road. The way north follows Route 10, but there is also an alternative route via Kerikeri: turn right down this side road, going through Kerikeri, past its inlet and then turn left for Waipapa, where you would rejoin Route 10. This alternative route is only an extra 5 km.

Continuing north from Waipapa, the route becomes reasonably hilly. Note the road to the right, which leads to Matauri Bay*. Proceed round a bluff and then descend to the town of

**Kaeo**. Just past Kaeo, Route 10 turns left, while the road ahead leads a short distance to the Whangaroa Harbour* wharf.

Route 10 passes mangrove swamps, and the junction for Totara North (a sawmilling community on the north side of Whangaroa Harbour), before rising through broken country, and proceeding up and over to Mangonui Harbour.

From the little town of **Mangonui** it is pleasant travelling just around the corner to Coopers Beach*, Cable Bay* and Taipa*. These nice beaches face on to Doubtless Bay. Drive past the junction on the right, which leads to Tokerau Bay and Matai Bay* on the Karikari Peninsula*. Easy running continues to Awanui. The road to the right leads to Waipapakauri, Ninety Mile Beach* and **Cape Reinga**. The road to the left (Route 1 again) leads directly to the main street of **Kaitaia**.

## 2A KAITAIA – CAPE REINGA
*114 km*

From Kaitaia follow Route 1 to Awanui, and then continue north passing the old World War II base at Waipapakauri. Note the side road to the west, which gives access to Ninety Mile Beach. Continue north. Houhora Heads is on a side road. The road continues over barren undulating country north to Waitaki Landing, then over the Te Paki station to Cape Reinga. At the time of compiling this book, the last 16 km remains unsealed.

Bypassing the Bay of Islands, Route 1 proceeds through Kawakawa to Moerewa, then up the Turntable Hill to the Pakaraka junction. From here Route 1 continues inland to Ohaeawai, Okaihau and eventually Kaitaia. This route, however, is described southbound in itinerary 3, as our preferred northbound route diverts to Route 10 at this junction.

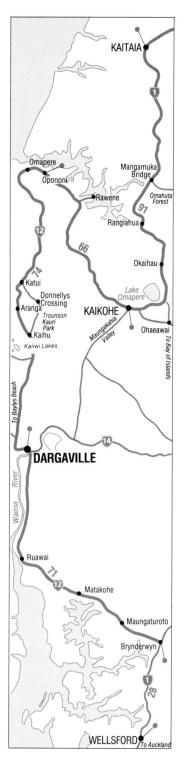

# KAITAIA – DARGAVILLE
**via Kaikohe and Opononi connecting south to Auckland.**

*Kaitaia – Kaikohe 91 km (2 hr)*
*Kaikohe – Dargaville 140 km (2¾ hr)*
*Dargaville – Auckland 185 km (3 hr)*

This southbound itinerary follows a more westerly course than the northbound ones described in the previous two itineraries. The Bay of Islands may easily be added if desired. The last 100 km of the Dargaville – Auckland section is on the same road as that used northbound in itinerary 1.

From **Kaitaia** the direct route south is on Route 1. From the main street, proceed over flat farming country before ascending sharply through the forest-clad ranges of the Mangamukas. After crossing the summit (350 m), the road winds down a long grade in to the Mangamuka Gorge. In due course the road re-enters open country and proceeds to the locality of Mangamuka Bridge. A side road from there gives access to the Omahuta State Forest and Kauri Sanctuary.

Route 1 continues southbound over undulating countryside with easy grades, before rising to the settlement of Okaihau. A short-cut side road to **Kaikohe** is soon signposted, which leads around Lake Omapere, and joins up with Route 12 in to the town.

There are two routes from Kaikohe to Dargaville. The more direct route strikes south through open country via the Maungakahia Valley, and also provides an alternative access to Whangarei. Our preferred route, however, is via Route 12, around the Hokianga Harbour and down through the Waipoua Forest.

At first, Route 12 proceeds westward over undulating countryside, then becomes hilly around the Hokianga Harbour area. 36 km out of Kaikohe, a side road leads down to **Rawene**. Continue through Whirinaki settlement, and on to Opononi* and Omapere. The road then leaves the harbour, winds around, climbs over a headland, then climbs again to enter the **Waipoua Kauri Forest**.

Through here, the road is unsealed, but surrounded by great forest scenery. Shortly after reaching open country again, Route 12 leads on through the districts of Katui, Aranga and Kaihu. Forest lovers might consider an alternative link between Katui and Kaihu, via Donnelleys Crossing and the Trounson Kauri Park*.

Soon another side road gives access to the Taharoa Domain and the Kaiiwi Lakes*. Follow on through flatter country, eventually noting a side road to Baylys Beach* before turning in to **Dargaville**. Route 12 parallels the main street, which is one block away.

Southbound from Dargaville on Route 12, cross the Wairoa River, proceed along the Ruawai Flats, and through the town of Ruawai. Continue on into more undulating countryside, noting side roads to Matakohe* — one of which is sealed. Rolling countryside leads on to the sprawling community of **Maungaturoto**, and eventually the road joins up with Route 1 at the Brynderwyn junction.

Continue south on Route 1 to **Wellsford**, **Warkworth** and **Auckland** on the same roads described northbound in itinerary 1.

### 3A DARGAVILLE – WHANGAREI
*Route 14, 58 km*

From **Dargaville** it is an easy travelling road, following the Wairoa River valley across rolling farmland, and down in to **Whangarei** past farm paddocks with old stone walls.

### 3B WELLSFORD – HELENSVILLE – AUCKLAND
*Route 16, 108 km*

An alternative to Route 1, this is a lightly travelled route through rolling farmland from **Wellsford** to **Helensville**, which becomes progressively busier as it approaches **Auckland**. The final 17 km are motorway standard.

### 3C RIVERHEAD – ALBANY
*Route 18, 14 km*

A short link road to enable motorists to go around the top of the **Auckland** (Waitemata) Harbour. This route links Route 16 with Route 1, north of Albany. Rolling farmland, with a gentle hill at the Albany end.

If you wish to travel directly south to Auckland, stay on Route 1 to Ohaeawai, Kawakawa, and points south — do not take the bypass road to Kaikohe. If you prefer to detour via the **Bay of Islands**, follow the signs leading off from Route 1 via Waimate North* and the Puketona corner, or via Pakaraka junction and **Kawakawa**.

# AUCKLAND – HAMILTON
## via Huntly and Ngaruawahia
*127 km (2 hr)*

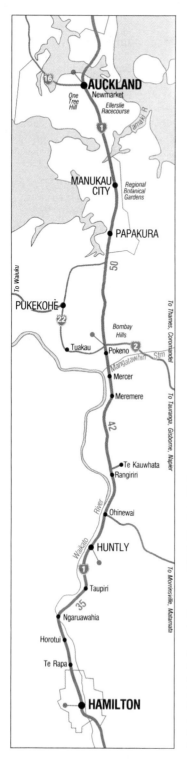

This is an easy, though heavily travelled route, over excellent roads from New Zealand's largest city to the rich farming lands of the Waikato.

From downtown **Auckland**, Hobson Street leads on to the southbound motorway Route 1. Watch your lanes here, as Hobson Street also feeds north-western Route 16, as well as other city streets. The route is of motorway standard for 45 km, out through the southern suburbs. Mt Eden*, Newmarket, One Tree Hill*, Ellerslie racecourse*, the Tamaki River, Manukau City* centre and the Regional Botanical Gardens* can all be seen from the motorway. Beyond Papakura the motorway crosses open country. Route 22 to **Pukekohe** (also **Waiuku** and **Tuakau**) branches off after 35 km.

Northbound motorists in to Auckland should carefully determine in advance what part of the city, and what off-ramp to use, as the number of divergent lanes can be quite confusing to newcomers. The central business district can be reached via Wellesley Street East and Nelson Street exits.

When the motorway ends, rise up to the Bombay crossroads (watch for traffic lights) and then down the southern slopes of the Bombay Hills. There is a view over the northern Waikato district, which includes the chimneys of the power stations at Meremere and Huntly. Watch for opposing uphill traffic. After 50 km, Route 2 branches off eastward. This route serves the east coast of the North Island, including Tauranga, Gisborne and Napier, and is covered northbound in itineraries 11, 12 and 13. This route also provides access to Thames and the Coromandel Peninsula.

Continuing south, drive through the small town of Pokeno and cross the unobtrusive Mangatawhiri stream, the historical boundary of the Waikato area. (The crossing of this stream by General Cameron and British troops in 1863 was interpreted as an act of war by the Waikato Maoris.) Meet up with the Waikato River* and pass the small community of **Mercer** and the Meremere* power station.

The well-formed road continues over open country. Side roads lead to Te Kauwhata* and travel on past **Rangiriri**. The road here almost bisects a battleground site of the Waikato Wars. Pass alternative routes to Morrinsville and Matamata at Ohinewai, and drive in to **Huntly** (94 km from Auckland). A rest area overlooks the power station. The main road avoids the town centre.

Continuing past Huntly, the road runs parallel to the river and railway, passing Taupiri Mountain*. It goes through the town of Taupiri, and crosses the Waikato River to enter **Ngaruawahia** (108 km from Auckland). The flat road continues past Horotiu freezing (meat) works, and enters the light industrial area of Te Rapa on the northern outskirts of **Hamilton**.

Route 1 leads through the main street of the city, however, various by-passes are signposted, and can be identified by numbers on inverted shields.

## 4A **AUCKLAND (DRURY) – RAGLAN (TE UKU)**
*Route 22, 110 km*

This road branches off the **Auckland** southern motorway

*A dairy farm.*

(Route 1) at Drury, 35 km south, travelling over mainly flat farmland to **Pukekohe** and **Tuakau**. After crossing the Waikato River, the route is hillier. Note the turn-off to Waingaro* thermal pools. From here the route is unsealed until the junction of Route 22, which leads in to **Raglan**.

## 4B **HAMILTON – RAGLAN**
*Route 23, 47 km*

From **Hamilton**, cross flat farmland before climbing up and over a range of hills. During the descent to Raglan, watch for views of its large harbour. The road is sealed, and the route is well defined.

## 4C **RAGLAN – KAWHIA**
*40 km*

This is a link road connecting Route 23 on the outskirts of Raglan with Route 31 on the outskirts of **Kawhia**. The road is hilly, and partly unsealed. En route, take the short walk to the Bridal Veil Falls*.

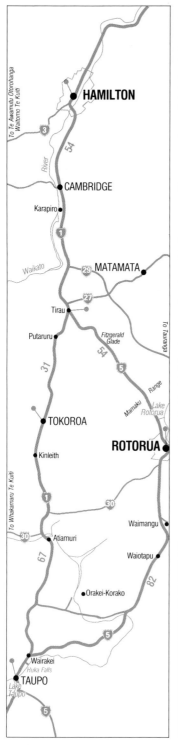

## 5

### HAMILTON – TAUPO
**with optional routes via Waitomo and Rotorua.**
*Hamilton – Rotorua 108 km (1¾ hr)*
*Rotorua – Taupo 82 km (1¼ hr)*
*Hamilton – Taupo 152 km (2 hr)*

A combination of forests, thermal activity and cultural heritage are present in these popular routings.

At the southern end of Victoria Street, the main street of Hamilton, Route 1 turns in to Bridge Street, and follows on to a road of almost motorway standard. You will soon come to a junction from which Route 3 diverges; this route leads directly south to Te Awamutu, Otorohanga, Waitomo and Te Kuiti, and is described in itinerary 8. However, Route 1 continues ahead at that intersection, crosses the Waikato River*, and leads south-easterly through suburbs before striking open country. The road is clearly defined over flat farming areas, and after 24 km arrives at **Cambridge**. Again Route 1 leads through the main street, but a by-pass is signposted.

Continuing from Cambridge, this route passes the side road to Karapiro Dam*, and follows along the terraces above the Waikato River. After the road leaves the river, links to Matamata and

If tourists travelling to Rotorua want to visit the **Waitomo Caves** on the way, they should take the Route 3 junction mentioned above at Hamilton, and follow southbound as described in itinerary 8. After visiting the Caves, they should retrace their path northbound back to Te Awamutu, where a cross-country road to Cambridge is signposted at the northern end of the town. This detour adds about 119 km.

If you are travelling directly to Taupo and bypassing Rotorua, you will follow Route 1 through the timber town of **Putaruru**. As the road continues to **Tokoroa**, you will start entering 'the largest man-made forest in the World'. The trees are radiata pine, and grow well on the pumice soils of the region. Tokoroa is the commercial centre for the region, and lies out on the west side of Route 1. 7 km further on, is the giant pulp and paper mill of Kinleith.*

The road continues through the forest, rising on to the 'volcanic plateau' of the central North Island. Route 30, an alternative link to Rotorua, swings in from the left, and 5 km on, swings away to the right to Whakamaru and Te Kuiti at the **Atiamuri** bridge over the Waikato River. There are several hydro-electric power stations in the vicinity.

Route 1 continues through forest and eventually intersects Route 5 — the route via Rotorua — at Wairakei*.

Tauranga (Routes 29 and 27) branch off. The country gets hillier towards the approach to Tirau, and almost immediately after leaving Tirau, the route divides. Travellers to Rotorua should connect straight ahead on to Route 5; while Route 1, which bypasses Rotorua, swings away towards Taupo.

From Tirau junction, the Rotorua road — now Route 5 — winds on to hillier forest-clad country as it ascends the Mamaku Range. Of particular note is Fitzgerald Glade where the trees overhang the road. After a while Lake Rotorua can be seen in the distance, and the road gently descends towards it. At the bottom of the hill turn right and follow the road round in to **Rotorua**.

Route 5 leads in along Old Taupo Road, turning in to Pukuatua Street, and curving around on Amohau Street; then it leads out to the south along Fenton Street. This route fringes the central business district. An alternative route is to take Lake Road and follow around near the lake shore in to the main shopping street, Tutaneki Street. This street is partially closed as a parking precinct and pedestrian

mall. Fenton Street runs parallel one block further over. If you prefer to avoid central Rotorua entirely, a by-pass via Old Taupo Road is signposted.

Southbound out of Rotorua, Fenton Street leads to the Whakarewarewa* thermal area, intersects with Old Taupo Road by-pass, and leaves the city behind as the road skirts pine forest. Route 30 to Atiamuri and Te Kuiti swings away to the west as the road meanders south towards Waimangu* and Waiotapu*. After the Route 38 junction (for Waikaremoana and Wairoa), Route 5 passes through open country. In due course pass the turn-off to Orakei-Korako*, cross the Waikato River, and re-enter pine forest.

Route 5 meets up with Route 1 again at **Wairakei**; and the direct Hamilton–Taupo route, which bypasses Rotorua (described above), intersects here. Wairakei is noted for its geothermal power operation, and at times hot steam drifts across the roadway. Side roads lead to the Huka Falls*. Descend towards Lake Taupo, New Zealand's largest lake, with a great view across the lake towards the peaks of the Tongariro National Park in the distance. The

Waikato River, which flows out of Lake Taupo, is crossed again, before entering the main street of **Taupo**.

## 5A MANGATARATA – THAMES
*Route 25, 30 km*

From **Auckland** it is a little more than an hour's drive via Routes 1 and 2 to the start of Route 25 on the Hauraki Plains. From there proceed across the flat lowlands and over the Waihou River bridge to the Kopu corner. Then it is 6 km north to **Thames**.

## 5B HAMILTON – THAMES (Kopu)
*Route 26, 107 km*

Leave Route 1 on the south-east side of **Hamilton**, and cross rolling farmland to **Morrinsville**. Then cross Route 27 and travel north to **Te Aroha** and **Paeroa**. Here there is a staggered or 'dog-leg' intersection with Route 2. Route 26 continues north along

the foot of the Kaimai Range. The route terminates at its intersection with Route 25 at Kopu. **Thames** is 6 km further on.

## 5C THAMES (Kopu) – TAIRUA (Hikuai)
*Route 25a, 29 km*

From its Kopu intersection south of **Thames**, the road climbs steeply up and over the Coromandel Range, and slices down the other side. At its intersection with Route 25 on the east coast, turn north for **Tairua** and **Whitianga**; turn south for **Whangamata** and **Waihi**.

## 5D MANGATARATA – TIRAU
*Route 27, 95 km*

From **Auckland** it is a little more than one hour's drive via Routes 1 and 2 to the beginning of Route 27 on the Hauraki Plains. This road offers a fast and flat alternative to Route 1, bypassing Hamilton and Cambridge. It

*Lady Knox geyser at Rotorua.*

crosses Route 26, passes **Matamata**, and towards its **Tirau** end gives access to **Tauranga** by Route 29, **Tokoroa** and **Taupo** by Route 1, and **Rotorua** by Route 5.

## 5E TIRAU – TAURANGA
*Route 29, 76 km*

This road branches off Route 1, 11 km on the **Cambridge** side of **Tirau**. Alternatively take Route 27 from Tirau, as the two roads intersect. (If connecting from Rotorua northbound on Route 5, a signposted short-cut leads off from Tapapa, and links in turn to Routes 27 and 29.) A triangle of roads allows alternative accesses before starting a steep curving climb up the Kaimai Range. There are good views from the lookout on the top and a longer undulating descent on the other side. Cameron Road, which leads to the city of **Tauranga**, branches off at a roundabout. Route 29, however, continues to meet with Route 2, in the suburb of Maungatapu, and then continues to Mt Maunganui*.

## 5F TE KUITI – ROTORUA
*Route 30, 147 km*

This route provides an alternative for travellers from the **Waitomo Caves** to **Rotorua** and offers a cross-section of North Island scenery. Follow the road straight out from the southern end of **Te Kuiti**. The route follows the main trunk railway line, passing the Waiteti viaduct, winding and climbing around to Mangapehi. After Benneydale the road enters bush, skirting the Pureora Forest, passing high country sheep farms, and drops down to the Waikato River valley, near Mangakino*, to Whakamaru*. Route 32 intersects before crossing the dam. Then follow the river past pine plantations to **Atiamuri**. Here

the route coincides with Route 1 for 5 km, before striking eastward through rolling countryside to enter **Rotorua** from the south via Route 5. (Route 30 continues to Whakatane.)

## 5G ROTORUA – WAIROA
*Route 38, 222 km*

This road branches off Route 5, 26 km south of **Rotorua**, and proceeds over gradual slopes through the Kaingaroa pine forests to Murupara. The route is mainly unsealed from here as it winds and climbs through the mountainous country of the Urewera National Park*. The through route is not considered suitable for caravans (that is, between Ruatahuna and **Waikaremoana**). The road passes around bluffs above Lake Waikaremoana, and then drops down steeply through mainly open country to **Wairoa** on Route 2. This route is reasonably rugged.

## 5H TAUPO – NAPIER
*Route 5, 143 km*

Route 5 coincides with Route 1 for 2½ km south out of **Taupo**. It then branches to the south-east, passing the historic site of Opepe*, and rises gently from the Lake Taupo basin through pine plantations to the Rangitaiki plains. Then the road rises and falls three times crossing hills towards the coast. Note the two waterfalls on the Waipunga River, pass Tarawera hot springs, and cross the Mohaka River bridge. In due course descend through Te Pohue to Eskdale* in the Esk valley. The road meets Route 2 for the final 14 km in to **Napier**. Despite the topography, this route is now a reasonably easy 2½ hr drive, but beware of logging trucks.

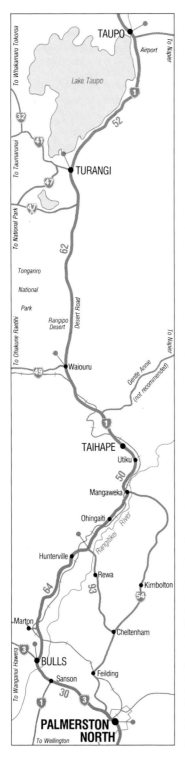

## 6

# TAUPO – BULLS and PALMERSTON NORTH
**via Waiouru and Taihape**
*258 km (3½ hr)*

This 'Desert Road' route crosses the volcanic plateau, in sight of the North Island's highest peak.

From the main street of **Taupo**, Route 1 follows Lake Terrace, skirting Lake Taupo. Route 5 also follows this road for 2½ km until it turns eastward for Napier.

Continuing south, Route 1 skirts the lake shore, passes Taupo airport, and eventually rises up through 'earthquake gully', to cross over a headland. Over the other side, the road hugs the lake, and passes through fishing resorts, eventually coming in to **Turangi** at the southern end of the lake. From Turangi connecting roads lead to Taumarunui (Route 41), the 'west Taupo' route up to Whakamaru and Tokoroa (Routes 41 and 32), and also to **National Park** (Route 47, or 10 km further south to Route 47A).

Southbound from Turangi, Route 1 crosses the Rangipo Desert, and is known as the 'Desert Road'. The road undulates, dropping for stream crossings, as it crosses this tussock-covered plateau to the east of the mountains of the Tongariro National Park*, to an altitude of 1074 m. The mountains seem to create a local weather zone, and the road is sometimes closed by adverse conditions. Part of the area is used for army training, so you should take heed of the notices warning 'keep out'. 62 km from Turangi, arrive at **Waiouru**, an important army training centre. A connecting road to and from **Ohakune** and **Raetihi** intersects here. The main Auckland–Wellington railway line also joins this route here.

Heading south from Waiouru, Route 1 winds through broken hill country, as it descends from the volcanic plateau, towards the valleys of the Rangitikei River, and the plains of the Manawatu. This country was once bush-covered and with the removal of the bush the blanket-like folds of the countryside can be seen. A difficult side road, known as the 'Gentle Annie' route to Napier leads eastward — but is not recommended — before reaching **Taihape**. The road (and rail) now winds down along the terraces above the Rangitikei River through the communities of Utiku, Mangaweka, Ohingaiti and Hunterville. The town of **Marton**, a railway junction, is on a side road while Route 1 goes directly to **Bulls**, where Route 3, from the western side of the North Island (including Wanganui and Hawera) also meets.

From Bulls, Routes 1 and 3 coincide for 6 km to Sanson, where Route 1 strikes directly south to Wellington, bypassing Palmerston North. The continuation of this route is described in itinerary 7. Otherwise follow Route 3 past side roads for **Feilding**, and eventually arrive in the central square of **Palmerston North**.

## 6A WHAKAMARU – KURATAU (TURANGI)
*Route 32, 67 km*

This 'west Taupo' route branches off Route 30, 21 km west of **Atiamuri**. A connection from

**Tokoroa**, through pine forests to Whakamaru*, is often used as a connecting road. Route 32 crosses rolling high country to terminate at its intersection with Route 41. This latter route connects **Taumarunui** with Tokaanu* and **Turangi**.

## 6B TAUMARUNUI – TURANGI
*Route 41, 59 km*

The turn-off for this route is south of **Taumarunui**. There is a long climb through bush to the Waituhi Saddle, from which there is a grand view. Then the road descends to the intersection of the 'west Taupo' Route 32 at Kuratau junction. Travel down again past Waihi Village* (on side road), and across the flat to Tokaanu* and **Turangi**.

## 6C MANGAWEKA – PALMERSTON NORTH
*Route 54, 90 km*

See itinerary 6. This is a short cut that eliminates Hunterville and Marton. A bit hilly and at time of printing, still partially unsealed. The route goes via Feilding. Also consider another alternative route via Vinegar Hill.

## 6D TAIHAPE – NAPIER
*157 km*

This has been known as the Inland Patea Route over the 'Blowhard' and 'Gentle Annie'. It is one of the North Island's most rugged and desolate roads and is not recommended for tourists.

While travellers bound directly for Wellington should follow the route via Bulls and Sanson as described, those who want to travel to or via Palmerston North, may consider either of two short-cuts. From Mangaweka, Route 54 follows a reasonably hilly course via Kimbolton and Cheltenham. The other route diverges after Ohingaiti from Vinegar Hill via Rewa to Cheltenham; then both alternatives follow Route 54 to Feilding and on to Palmerston North.

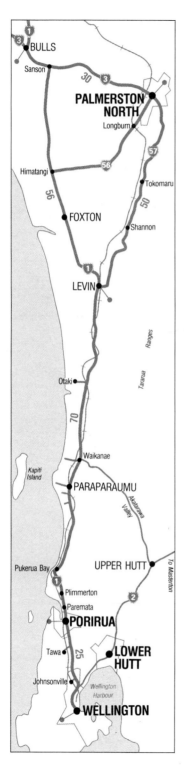

# BULLS and PALMERSTON NORTH – WELLINGTON

*151 km (2 hr)*

A mostly flat route from the Manawatu region to New Zealand's capital city.

In the township of **Bulls**, Routes 1 and 3 combine for 6 km to Sanson. Here Route 3 swings across to Palmerston North, while Route 1 strikes south on an easy travelling highway over pleasant and comparatively flat country, to Himatangi, **Foxton** and **Levin**.

If proceeding south from **Palmerston North** you do not need to travel via Sanson as there are two short cuts available. From Palmerston North's central square you can choose either Route 56 via Longburn to the Himatangi intersection with Route 1; or alternatively Route 57 via Tokomaru* and Shannon, to intersect with Route 1 at the southern end of Levin.

From Levin the road follows the railway, passing a side road to **Otaki**, and continues to **Waikanae**. Western side roads give access to beaches along the coast, but to the east the Tararua Ranges come closer and the plain narrows. From Waikanae there is a side road over the ranges and through the Akatarawa valley to Upper Hutt.

At Paraparaumu* we enter the northern suburbs and commuter belt of Wellington. Although Route 1 stays on the flat at Paekakariki*, you might consider going a short way up the Hill Road to see the view over the Kapiti coast, with visibility stretching from Mt Egmont to the South Island on clear days.

Route 1 now hugs the coast to Pukerua Bay, and rises to pass Plimmerton, then crosses Porirua Harbour to Paremata. The road

Northbound motorists out of Wellington should clearly check motorway signs to ensure they have the correct one – Route 1 to the Ngauranga Gorge, Kapiti Coast, Manawatu and points north; and Route 2 for the Hutt valley, the Rimutakas, Masterton and the Wairarapa. Travellers from the Picton ferry not stopping in Wellington, should do a U-turn after exiting the terminal, and follow signs along Hutt Road to join Route 1 at the Ngauranga interchange.

changes to motorway standard, and passes exits to Porirua*, Tawa and Johnsonville.

Now descend through the Ngauranga Gorge. Travellers for Lower Hutt*, Upper Hutt* and the Picton ferry should watch for off-ramps that anticipate the junction ahead. When you reach Wellington Harbour, turn right and join the route in to Wellington from the Hutt Valley. Consider in advance whether you require to exit at Aotea Quay, Thornton Quay, Hawkestone Street or Ghuznee Street.

The cable car in Wellington.

## 7A PALMERSTON NORTH – HIMATANGI
*Route 56, 29 km*

A flat, easy-going link road connecting **Palmerston North** with Route 1, via Longburn.

## 7B PALMERSTON NORTH – LEVIN
*Route 57, 50 km*

Leaves **Palmerston North** via the Manawatu River and passes through Tokomaru* and Shannon to join Route 1 at **Levin**. A convenient connection between Palmerston North and Wellington If proceeding from Woodville and the Manawatu Gorge there is a direct connection (Route 57A) bypassing Palmerston North, just after leaving the Gorge.

## 7C PAREMATA – LOWER HUTT
*Route 58, 16 km*

A steady climb out of Paremata* and a steep drop in to Lower

Hutt*. The Paekakariki* hill road, with good views before dropping in to the Horokiri Valley, provides an alternative link to Route 58 from Paekakariki further north.

## 7D WAIKANAE – UPPER HUTT
*35 km*

Also known as the Akatarawa Valley Road, this is a link from Route 1 at Waikanae*. It is reasonably quiet and narrow, with a steep climb up to the Akatarawa Gorge and an equally steep dip down into the Upper Hutt* area.

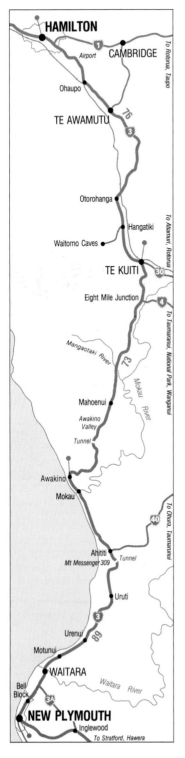

# HAMILTON – NEW PLYMOUTH
### via Waitomo and Te Kuiti
*Hamilton – Te Kuiti 76 km (1 ¼ hr)*
*Te Kuiti – New Plymouth 162 km (3 hr)*

This is a reasonably hilly route via a seemingly remote part of the North Island.

At the southern end of the main street of Hamilton, Victoria Street, Route 1 runs into Bridge Street, and follows on to a roadway of almost motorway standard. Soon you will come to a junction from which Route 3 diverges — take it. (The Route 1 road straight ahead goes towards Rotorua and Taupo, and is described in itinerary 5.)

Route 3 passes through southern suburbs and then in to open country. The road is well defined and of a good standard as it rolls across undulating countryside past Hamilton's airport, and on to Ohaupo and **Te Awamutu**. At the northern end of Te Awamutu note the intersection of a cross-country road to Cambridge.

Watch for signs indicating the route through Te Awamutu, and proceed on through rolling country to **Otorohanga**. 8 km south of Otorohanga, at the Hangatiki corner, note the side road leading 8 km to the **Waitomo Caves**.

Back on Route 3, follow the road through to **Te Kuiti**. Cross the railway to enter the main road through the town. At the southern end, the road ahead is Route 30 cutting across to Atiamuri and Rotorua. But Route 3 turns right up and over a hill 12 km to 'Eight Mile Junction', where Route 4 branches off to Taumarunui, National Park and Wanganui.

Route 3 continues in a south-westerly direction following the valley of the Mokau River. The country is undulating for a time, and then becomes very broken.

*The coast at North Tongaporutu, Taranaki.*

Drop down beside the Mangaotaki River, then rise up and overlook the Mangaotaki Gorge. Then descend again to comparatively flat country to Mahoenui, and enter the pleasant Awakino Valley. After a time pass through a road tunnel, and continue down the valley to **Awakino** on the coast. This indeed seems to be a remote area of the North Island.

Continuing south, Route 3 follows the coast for a short distance to pass **Mokau** and the big Mokau River — the historical boundary between the Waikato and Taranaki. The road parallels the coast, then moves inland to a junction at Ahititi with Route 40 — a fairly rugged link from Ohura (and Taumarunui).

The road now winds through bush up Mt Messenger, at the top of which is a short tunnel with a right-angle approach — watch for opposing traffic. Descend through Uruti, and then proceed over flatter, more open country through Urenui and Motunui* — noting the synthetic fuel plant at the latter.

Route 3 crosses the Waitara River — the town of **Waitara** is down side roads to the right. Keep on to intersection with Route 3A.

If proceeding directly south to Stratford and Hawera and bypassing New Plymouth, take the turn-off for Route 3A to Inglewood. Route 3 continues straight ahead to New Plymouth, then angles back to Inglewood by another road.

Route 3 leads through Bell Block, and then in to Devon Street, the main street of **New Plymouth**. Just before entering the central business district, Devon Street becomes a mall and parking precinct, and through traffic is not permitted. At this point Route 3 turns to the south in order to leave the city again, while access to the central business district and beyond is by two adjacent one-way streets. Watch for signs.

## 8A NGARUWAHIA – OTOROHANGA
*70 km*

A succession of back roads is becoming an alternative for traffic bypassing Hamilton and Te Awamutu, and heading for Te Kuiti or further south. The road angles out from **Ngaruwahia**, crosses Route 23, passes Pirongia*, and uses Route 31 to enter **Otorohanga**.

## 8B OTOROHANGA – KAWHIA
*Route 31, 57 km*

From **Otorohanga**, the road crosses rolling farmland, and becomes steeper over some ranges, before dropping down to **Kawhia**. There are views of its large harbour on the way down. The road is sealed and the route is well defined.

## 8C KAWHIA – WAITOMO CAVES
*77 km*

Branching off from Route 31, 10 km out of **Kawhia**, the route winds through hills around the Kawhia Harbour, and crosses a range to Te Anga; turn inland here. Note a ten-minute walking track to Marokopa Falls*, and later another ten-minute walk to Mangapohue Natural Bridge*. The road continues to **Waitomo Caves**. The Route 3 junction is a further 8 km.

## 8D MANGATUPOTO – AHITITI
*Route 40, 95 km*

This route branches off unobtrusively from Route 4, 26 km north of **Taumarunui**. Note, however, an alternative 'river road' connection directly from Taumarunui to Ohura*. Between Ohura and Ahititi the road is reasonably rugged, partially unsealed, and narrow in places. Ahititi is situated on Route 3 south of **Awakino** and **Mokau**.

## 8E TAUMARUNUI (OHURA) – STRATFORD
*Route 43, 121 km*

Route 43 commences at Ohura* at its junction with Route 40. There is a connection from **Taumarunui** via the 'river road' that intersects Route 43, 10 km south of Ohura. This river road is quite scenic, as it skirts round the bluffs on the Wanganui River, and it also gives access to other side roads that offer more river views and historic sites. Then Route 43, which is mainly sealed, passes through a gorge and travels over saddles through a remote but rugged part of the North Island. The countryside opens out before reaching **Stratford**.

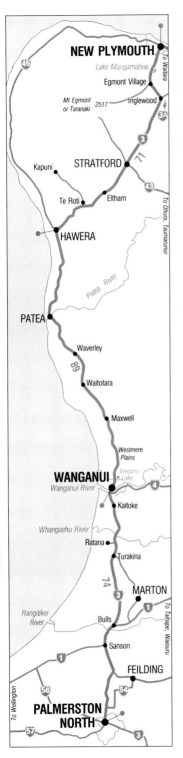

# NEW PLYMOUTH – BULLS and PALMERSTON NORTH
## via Stratford and Wanganui

*New Plymouth – Wanganui 160 km (2¼ hr)*
*Wanganui – Bulls 43 km (¾ hr)*
*Bulls – Palmerston North 29 km (½ hr)*

An easy drive across flat and rolling countryside from the Taranaki region to the Manawatu.

Route 3 enters **New Plymouth** from the north along Devon Street, then turns to leave the city via Eliot Street and Coronation Drive. The route improves for a stretch to motorway standard. Near Lake Mangamahoe* you should see good views of Mt Egmont (2517 m). The road continues to **Inglewood**.

Northbound travellers from Stratford and Hawera heading for Te Kuiti and Hamilton need not travel via the city of New Plymouth. Although Route 3 goes from Inglewood in to New Plymouth and out to Waitara, Route 3A offers a direct connection from Inglewood towards Waitara.

South from Inglewood, Route 3 is an easy travelling road across rich Taranaki dairy country with uninterrupted views of Mt Egmont. Access to Egmont National Park is available from a side road near Egmont Village, and more popularly from side roads near **Stratford**, where there is also a junction with Route 43 from Ohura (and Taumarunui). Continuing there is a clear run to **Eltham**. Side roads near Te Roti lead to **Kapuni**. In due course the route enters **Hawera**. The 'round the mountain' Route 45 joins here.

Route 3 now strikes south-east over undulating country through to **Patea**. The road turns and dips to cross the Patea River. Go on

*Mt Taranaki rises behind the city of New Plymouth.*

through Waverley*, and continue through the communities of Waitotara and Maxwell.

The route then becomes more hilly, and rises to run over the Westmere Plains. It then descends gradually past Virginia Lake*, and down St John's Hill. The main road leads in to the main street of **Wanganui** (Victoria Street), but loops around a section of parking

precinct closed to through traffic. You then have a choice of taking the city bridge across the Wanganui River, or following Route 3 a kilometre further west to cross over on the Cobham Bridge. Alternatively a by-pass that avoids the city centre completely is signposted.

On the south side of the river, Route 4 from Te Kuiti, National

from your left. Routes 1 and 3 coincide for 6 km to Sanson, where Route 1 turns south for Wellington. Travellers taking this direct route should refer to itinerary 7.

For Palmerston North continue straight ahead on Route 3. Pause for views over Mt Stewart. Note the side roads to **Feilding**. Follow ahead, and shortly arrive in the central square of **Palmerston North**.

### 9A NEW PLYMOUTH – HAWERA
*Route 45, 70 km*

This route parallels the coast around Mt Egmont from **New Plymouth**. An interesting option is to travel via the Pukeiti Rhododendron Trust*, then drop down to Route 45 at Okato*. The road is mostly flat, and crosses farm lands. Note the on-shore Maui gas production station at Oaonui*. The route continues via **Opunake** and Manaia*; alternatively you can loop around via Kapuni*. At **Hawera**, Route 45 meets up (again) with Route 3.

### 9B PALMERSTON NORTH – WOODVILLE
*Route 3, 27 km*

This continuation of Route 3 from **Palmerston North** traverses the spectacular Manawatu Gorge*. There is a continuing program to upgrade this road over the next few years. Route 3 terminates at **Woodville** where it meets Route 2. There is an alternative saddle road from Ashurst to the north of the Gorge (steep climb), and also an alternative — the Pahiatua track (a longer climb with views) connecting Aokautere and Pahiatua — south of the Gorge. We suggest using the Gorge road unless it is closed due to slips or reconstruction.

Park and Raetihi intersects. This route is described in itinerary 10. Southbound, Route 3 rises over higher country through Kaitoke, and drops down to cross the Whangaehu River. Pass Ratana* and Turakina and note the side road to **Marton**. Continue ahead and soon pass through **Bulls**.

At Bulls, Route 1 from Taihape, Waiouru and points north, enters

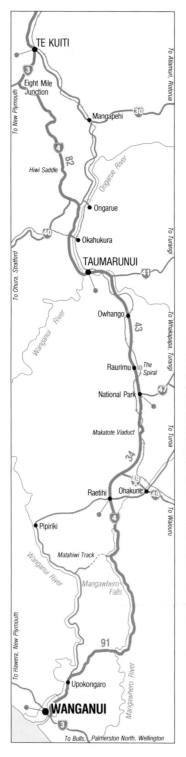

## TE KUITI – WANGANUI
### via Taumarunui and National Park
*Te Kuiti – Taumarunui 82 km (1½ hr)*
*Taumarunui – Wanganui 168 km (2¼ hr)*

This is a striking route that takes you via the Waimarino Plateau and the peaks of the Tongariro National Park.

At the southern end of the main road through **Te Kuiti** turn right across the railway line. (The road straight ahead is Route 30 cutting across to Atiamuri and Rotorua, with back country connections following the main trunk railway line to Taumarunui via Mangapehi and Ongarue.) Route 3 goes up and over a hill 12 km to 'Eight Mile Junction'. Here Route 3 continues on towards New Plymouth, but this

itinerary turns on to Route 4.

The road is well defined but crosses hilly country with limestone outcrops. In due course it rises up and over the Hiwi Saddle. Route 40 to Ohura and Stratford branches off just before the side road to Ongarue. Continue to follow the Ongarue River. Note a side road with a double-decker rail and road bridge across the river to Okahukura railway junction. Keep following the river, then cross it to enter the main street of **Taumarunui**.

Route 4 continues through the town, rising to cross over the railway, and then the Wanganui River at the southern end. Route 41 from Turangi intersects 6 km past Taumarunui. The road follows rail and river before rising up to an over-look. Continue over rolling country, passing Owhango, as the road climbs up to the volcanic plateau of the central North Island. Note the signs indicating the mid-point between Auckland and Wellington on this routing, and also the lookout for the Raurimu* railway spiral.

The route then ascends to **National Park**, the community serving the Tongariro National Park*. You should get splendid views of Mt Ruapehu and Mt Ngauruhoe. Route 47 towards the Whakapapa ski-field and Turangi cuts across the tussock plateau to the left.

Route 4 continues south, fringing pine forests, and

*Mt Tongariro in the Tongariro National Park.*

dropping down and up at the Makatote railway viaduct. In due course note the junction for Route 49A to **Ohakune**, the Turoa ski-field* and **Waiouru**. 8 km further enter **Raetihi** where Route 49 gives alternative access to Ohakune, Turoa and Waiouru; the rough 'river road' to **Pipiriki** and Wanganui intersects here.

Route 4 continues south and winds through the Parapara Ranges as it descends from the volcanic plateau. Note the access to the Matahiwi track before you pass the Mangawhero Falls. After some time the road drops down towards the Wanganui River valley, the river road from Pipiriki intersects, and you pass Upokongaro. The road follows the true left bank of the river to **Wanganui**. You can use the Dublin Street bridge to cross and link with Route 3 north to Hawera and Taranaki, or take the city bridge for access to the central business district. Otherwise continue to the 'T' intersection with Route 3 on the same side of the river; turn left for Bulls, Palmerston North and Wellington (in which case, refer to itinerary 9).

## 10A TURANGI – NATIONAL PARK
*Route 47, 46 km*

There are two alternative routes from **Turangi**. Choose either Route 41 in the direction of Tokaanu*, but branch off steeply up and over the Te Ponanga saddle road (note the lookout with a view back over Lake Taupo); or travel south 10 km from Turangi along Route 1 in the direction of the Desert Road, to pick up Route 47A. Both routes link, and pass the slopes of Mt Tongariro (1968 m), Mt Ngauruhoe (2290 m) and Mt Ruapehu (2796 m), in the Tongariro National Park*. The road terminates at **National Park**, where it intersects Route 4.

40

## 10B NATIONAL PARK – 'THE CHATEAU'
*Route 48, 7 km*

Route 48 branches off Route 47, 9 km out of **National Park**. It then leads up to the Chateau Tongariro* in the Tongariro National Park*. From the Chateau, which is at 1127 m altitude, the Bruce Road winds up 6 km to 1622 m to serve the Whakapapa ski-field*. Although this unsealed road is easily negotiable in summer, in winter you should ensure your vehicle is using 'anti-freeze' and that you are carrying chains. It may be better to use the mountain buses at such times. If you do drive, however, beware of changeable weather.

## 10C RAETIHI – WAIOURU
*Route 49, 38 km*

An easy road across the southern part of the volcanic plateau linking Raetihi on Route 4 with **Waiouru** on Route 1. If approaching from the north you may use link road 49A, which bypasses Raetihi.

## 10D RAETIHI – PIPIRIKI – WANGANUI
*106 km*

This river road is a slower and rugged alternative to the main road on Route 4. From **Raetihi** the road winds over hilly farming country (look back for a view of Mt Ruapehu) and when the seal stops, the road descends steeply and sharply to the settlement of **Pipiriki** (28 km) on the Wanganui River. The road is then narrow and rough on high bluffs above the river, through Jerusalem*, Ranana, Matahiwi and Koriniti*. Pass the Skyline walk at Atene before rising up over the Aramoana ridge — look back for a river view. The road meets up with Route 4 again for the final 14 km riverside drive into **Wanganui**. Note that petrol is not available on the river road.

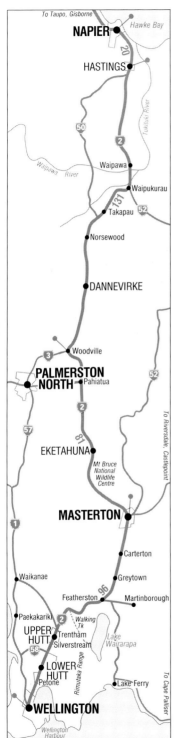

# WELLINGTON – NAPIER
## via Masterton and Hastings
*Wellington – Woodville 177 km (3 hr)*
*Woodville – Napier 151 km (2½ hr)*

A climb over the Rimutaka hill, then flat to undulating country through the Wairarapa and Hawke's Bay.

Northbound from **Wellington** on the Wellington Urban motorway follow signs for Route 2 to the Hutt Valley and Masterton. Keep ahead at the Ngauranga interchange where Route 1 (for Porirua, Kapiti Coast and Levin) swings away to the left. Travellers from the Picton ferry should make a U-turn after exiting the terminal, and follow along Hutt Road to join Route 2 at this interchange.

Southbound travellers for the Picton ferry should exit at the Ngauranga interchange, and follow signs along Hutt Road to the terminal. Motorists heading for Wellington city should consider in advance whether to exit at Aotea Quay, Thornton Quay, Hawkestone Street, or Ghuznee Street.

Route 2 continues along the western shore of Wellington Harbour (Port Nicholson) and then along the western edge of the Hutt Valley, passing turn-offs for Petone*, Lower Hutt*, Silverstream*, Trentham and Upper Hutt*. Also note Route 58 cutting across to Porirua Harbour (and connecting to 'the hill road' to Paekakariki). Later also note the Akatarawa Valley road to Waikanae and the Kapiti Coast.

Route 2 then rises over a small hill, passes the entrance to the Rimutaka Incline walking track* (over the route of the old Fell railway), and then starts the long, winding climb up and over the Rimutaka Range. Although this

41

*Farmland near Hastings.*

road is now in good condition, it can be subject to high winds, and motorists with caravans should not attempt it in blustery conditions.

Down the other side note a lookout over Lake Wairarapa* and proceed through **Featherston**. Note side roads to Martinborough*, Lake Ferry* and Cape Palliser*. Route 2 continues over flat Wairarapa countryside through **Greytown** and Carterton* to **Masterton**. From here there are side roads to Riversdale Beach* and Castlepoint*. Also from this point, Route 52 branches away to provide an alternative route north via the eastern Hawke's Bay area.

The main road now proceeds to gently rolling country, passing the Mt Bruce National Wildlife Centre*, and is well defined through Eketahuna* and

Pahiatua*. From the latter the road known as the Pahiatua Track* cuts over the hills to Palmerston North. An easier route to Palmerston North, however, is through **Woodville** — the next point on Route 2. Route 3 also intersects here.

This itinerary turns right at Woodville and continues along Route 2 through the rolling sheeplands of the Hawkes Bay district. Pass **Danniverke**, Norsewood* and Takapau. Note that the junction of Route 50 provides an alternative route to Napier. Continue on Route 2 through **Waipukurau**, cross the Tukituki River, and pass Waipawa*. Then gently descend to **Hastings**. The main road passes through the centre of the city (note one-way streets), but there is a signposted by-pass that offers a direct route to Napier.

of the southern Wairarapa to **Martinborough**.

## 11B MASTERTON – WAIPUKURAU
*Route 52, 163 km*

This route is a series of back roads winding through the eastern hill country of Wairarapa and Hawke's Bay. From **Masterton** this route gives access to roads to Riversdale Beach*, Castlepoint*, and Cape Turnagain. There are three unsealed sections on Route 52, which eventually intersects Route 2 again at **Waipukurau**.

## 11C TAKAPAU – NAPIER
*Route 50, 90 km*

This is a sealed road leaving Route 2 near Takapau north of **Dannevirke**, and then winding around some Hawkes Bay uplands before descending to the flatter areas of the Heretaunga Plains.

This route terminates in **Napier**, but also connects with roads to **Hastings**. However, it remains a secondary route.

## 11D FEATHERSTON – LAKE FERRY
*44 km*

From **Featherston** take Route 53, 6 km towards Martinborough, and then travel southwards across the southern Wairarapa flatlands. Lake Ferry* faces on to Palliser Bay at the southern end of the North Island. The road is sealed. However, the continuation of this road, a further 38 km to the southern tip at Cape Palliser, is not sealed, has some open waterways, and is generally more rugged — especially when a southerly is blowing!

However, the Hastings area deserves some of your attention before following Route 2 out to the coast, and entering **Napier** along the foreshore. Route 2 through Napier angles away from the foreshore to fringe the central business district; alternatively continue ahead along the Marine Parade to lead directly in to the central area of the city.

## 11A FEATHERSTON – MARTINBOROUGH
*Route 53, 19 km*

Branching off Route 2 at **Featherston** this road provides easy travelling over the flat lands

En route to Waipukurau the road passes New Zealand's longest placename — a hill called Taumatawhakatangihangakoauauotamateapokaiwhenuakitanatahu.

43

# NAPIER – WHAKATANE
## via Wairoa and Gisborne
*Napier – Gisborne 215 km (3½ hr)*
*Gisborne – Whakatane 201 km*
*(3½ hr)*

This is a hilly route, mostly inland but with some coastal views, to Gisborne, which then turns inland over Traffords Hill and the Waioeka Gorge.

Route 2 out of **Napier** fringes the central business district and leads out across the Westshore flats (prior to the 1931 earthquake these flats were under the sea). The road parallels the coast, passing the Route 5 junction for Taupo, and the Whirinaki* power plant and pulp mill.

The road then moves inland through hilly country, passing Lake Tutira*. It continues over hills, dropping to cross streams, passes under the Matahorua railway viaduct, and in due course passes under the Mohaka railway viaduct — New Zealand's highest viaduct. The countryside flattens out as you enter **Wairoa**. Note Route 38, which branches out via Waikaremoana to Rotorua; 7 km along Route 38 is Route 36, an alternative road via an inland routing to Gisborne.

The main road, Route 2, takes a more coastal routing, rising over a hill directly after leaving Wairoa. It follows through to Nuhaka, where a side road leads to Opoutama, Beach Loop and the Mahia Peninsula*. It rises over another hill to Morere Hot Springs*; and from yet another hill there is a lookout towards the Poverty Bay flats. Route 2 swings away from **Gisborne** 6 km out of the city, so you must continue on Route 35 to get to the central business district.

Route 35 is the road around East Cape, but as this itinerary follows Route 2, you must back-track 6 km from Gisborne to the

Makaraka junction, and follow out through the vineyards and cornfields in a north-westerly direction. It is flat going to Te Karaka, where you gradually start climbing to Matawai. You may notice earthworks from the old railway line to Motuhora. Matawai is on the headwaters of the Motu River, a waterway that further down becomes a testing 'ground' for white-water rafters. The road via Motu is a rugged alternative to the main road to Opotiki.

From Matawai, Route 2 climbs up Traffords Hill, and then begins a seemingly endless descent (actually 58 km) down and through the Waioeka Gorge. Eventually leave the mountains behind and pass by the town of **Opotiki** on the Bay of Plenty. The central part of the town is on a side road. Route 35, which follows around the East Cape, also starts (or finishes) here.

From Opotiki, Route 2 loops inland through the Waimana Gorge, past the railway terminus at Taneatua to lead in to **Whakatane**. Again, the downtown area is on a side road. Alternatively, 20 km from Opotiki, you can take a branch road that leads to Ohope Beach*, and from there to Whakatane.

## 12A WAIROA – GISBORNE
*Route 36, 98 km*

This routing follows Route 38 — the Waikaremoana Road — for the first 7 km out of **Wairoa**, and then turns north-east at Frasertown to follow an inland route over some hilly country. The road is partly unsealed, but gives access to the Tiniroto Lakes* and Te Reinga* falls. After passing through rugged country it crosses over a 'Gentle Annie' hill, and terminates 11 km south of **Gisborne**. Entry to the city is via Routes 2 and 35.

*North Island Coastline.*

## 12B GISBORNE – OPOTIKI
*Route 35, 339 km*

This routing follows around the East Cape. From **Gisborne** the road passes Wainui Beach* and then moves a little inland until it reaches **Tolaga Bay**. Then, on to **Tokomaru Bay**. Inland again the road passes Te Puia Springs*, and hilly conditions continue to **Ruatoria** (entry on side road) and Tikitiki*. From **Te Araroa** a narrow, metalled side road (13 km) gives access to the East Cape* lighthouse. Route 35 then provides magnificent coastal scenery for 115 km down in to the Bay of Plenty from Cape Runaway. The road passes **Waihau Bay** and **Te Kaha**, crosses the Motu River, passes the road junction to Motu, and eventually reaches **Opotiki**, where it meets up again with Route 2. The route is now sealed throughout.

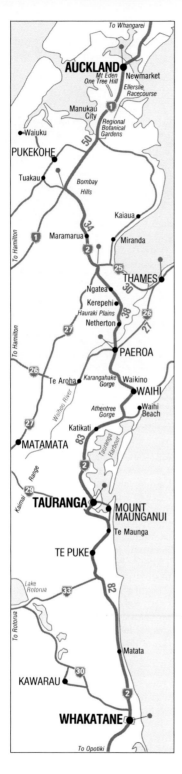

# 13

# WHAKATANE – AUCKLAND
## via Tauranga and Waihi

*Whakatane – Tauranga 82 km (¾–1 hr)*
*Tauranga – Auckland 205 km (3¼ hr)*

An easy-going routing, mostly flat, but passing through two short hilly sections.

Downtown **Whakatane** is on a side road so proceed to Route 2, which parallels the Bay of Plenty coast. Note a side road, Route 30, towards Kawarau and Rotorua. The road is close to the coast through Matata, and then moves inland again to meet the junction of Route 33 (to Rotorua).

Route 2 then continues through the main street of Te Puke. When you reach Te Maunga, the route turns left across the railway tracks to cross an arm of Tauranga Harbour and enter **Tauranga**. Route 2 'dog-legs' through the city, but the central business and shopping area are on side roads — for which you must follow the signs. Alternatively, the road straight ahead at the Te Maunga junction goes to Mt Maunganui*. You may carry on to the road's end at 'The Mount', noting side roads to the beach on the right, to the port on the left, and also from the port area by toll bridge ($1 per car) across the harbour to Tauranga.

From Tauranga, Route 2 skirts north over undulating country between Tauranga Harbour and the Kaimai Range. Pass through **Katikati** and then descend to the Athenree Gorge. Note side roads to Waihi Beach* before reaching **Waihi**. Route 25, which goes around the Coromandel Peninsula, branches off here.

From Waihi, Route 2 leads to Waikino* and the picturesque Karangahake Gorge*. Note the historical gold mining remains, and accesses for the

Karangahake walkway.
Proceed to **Paeroa** where
Route 26, which leads north to
Thames and south to Te
Aroha, intersects.

Route 2 crosses the Waihou
River and traverses the Hauraki
Plains, passing the small
communities of Netherton and
Kerepehi, and the town of Ngatea.
The road then junctions with
Route 27 (from Matamata, and an
alternative routing from
Tauranga) and Route 25 (from
Thames, and around the
Coromandel Peninsula from
Waihi). Side roads to Miranda*
and Kaiaua provide an alternative
entry to Auckland. Route 2,
however, continues over
undulating farm lands, through
Maramarua, to terminate at its
junction with Route 1, 50 km
south of Auckland.

Turn right on to Route 1,
immediately rising up the
Bombay Hills (watch for traffic
lights at the top). The road then
becomes motorway standard for
the remaining 45 km to central
**Auckland**.

Route 22 to Pukekohe (also
Waiuku and Tuakau) branches
off, and then Route 1 enters
Auckland's southern suburbs. The
Regional Botanical Gardens*,
Manukau City* centre, the
Tamaki River, Ellerslie
racecourse*, One Tree Hill*,
Newmarket and Mt Eden* can all
be seen from the motorway.

Motorists in to Auckland should
decide in advance which part of
the city they are heading for and
which off-ramp to use; the
number of divergent lanes can be
quite confusing to newcomers.
The central business district can
be reached via Wellesley Street
East and Nelson Street exits. The
Route 1 motorway, however,
continues over the Auckland
Harbour Bridge and through to
the northern suburbs.

## 13A WHAKATANE – ROTORUA
*Route 30, 85 km*

Route 30 branches off Route 2,
5 km west of **Whakatane**. After a
period of flat travelling, note side
roads to **Kawerau**. Route 30 then
enters a bush section and passes
the Rotorua lakes of Rotoma* and
Rotoehu*; later it passes the
Hongi's Track bush section, Lake
Rotoiti* and the side road to Lake
Okataina*. Then it junctions with
the Route 33 road from Te Puke,
and leads in past the airport to
**Rotorua**. Route 30 then angles
out to the south to continue to
Atiamuri and Te Kuiti.

## 13B ROTORUA – TE PUKE
*Route 33, 56 km*

This link road leaves **Rotorua** on
Route 30 heading north, and after
passing the airport, keeps ahead
on to Route 33 when Route 30
turns to the east. It passes over
the Ohau Channel (note road to
the left around the top of Lake
Rotorua*), skirts Lake Rotoiti*,
and then winds through hilly
country. Eventually descend to
the Route 2 junction at Paengaroa,
and follow Route 2 over open
country in to **Te Puke**.

## 13C WAIHI – COROMANDEL
*Route 25, 158 km*

This road goes up the eastern side
of the Coromandel Peninsula,
mainly inland from the coast, and
has numerous side roads to beach
resorts. From **Waihi**, travel north
to **Whangamata**, and later note
Route 25A — a direct road to
Thames. Route 25 follows through
**Tairua** to Coroglen (junction of
unsealed Tapu Road to the
western coast of Peninsula —
caravans should avoid), and
**Whitianga**. The road continues,
partly unsealed, past beaches and
over hills to **Coromandel**.

Another road called the '309' is a narrow, winding alternative between Whitianga and Coromandel.

## 13D THAMES – COROMANDEL
*Route 25, 54 km*

Route 25 actually branches off Route 2 near Mangatarata, 30 km west of **Thames**, and follows a flat route to Kopu (intersection of Route 26 from Paeroa and close by intersection of Route 25A from Hikuai) and Thames. From Thames the road is scenic and sealed up to the picturesque Firth of Thames coast to **Coromandel**. En route pass the junction for the rugged Tapu–Coroglen unsealed road to the east coast (avoid for caravans) and later the rugged unsealed 309 road to Whitianga.

## 13E KOPU – HIKUAI
*Route 25A, 29 km*

A newer, sealed road slicing over the Coromandel Range from the western side south of **Thames** to the eastern side between **Whangamata** and **Tairua**.

## 13F WAITAKARURU – CLEVEDON
*54 km*

This is a less travelled alternative from the Hauraki Plains to Auckland. Waitakaruru is on Route 25, 6 km back from its western terminus with Route 2 (14 km north-west from Ngatea). The road crosses flat coastal country through Miranda and Kaiaua, and passes the Waharau* Regional Reserve. Then there is a short hilly section, which passes a side road to Orere Point and Kawakawa Bay before arriving in Clevedon*. From here choose between travelling 15 km to Papakura and Route 1; or take the longer way around via Maraeta and Auckland's eastern suburbs.

*Limestone Bluff, Cathedral Caves, north Hahei.*

# 14

# CHRISTCHURCH – PICTON

**via Kaikoura and Blenheim**
*Christchurch – Blenheim 312 km (4½ hr)*
*Blenheim – Picton 28 km (½ hr)*

A scenic route offering vistas of both hill country and spectacular coastal scenery.

Central **Christchurch** has a one-way street system, and from Cathedral Square you must move two blocks east to follow Route 1 out, northbound on Madras Street (southbound traffic is one block further over on Barbadoes Street). The route then turns west on to Bealey Avenue, and north again on Sherborne Street, leading on to Cranford Street, and the Main North Road. Near Belfast a signposted by-pass route joins from the south.

Southbound travellers, wishing to bypass central Christchurch, should take the signposted alternative, via the outer suburbs of Harewood (Christchurch Airport) and Yaldhurst (for the Arthur's Pass Route 73 to the west coast) to rejoin Route 1 south of the city at Templeton.

After Belfast take the motorway across the Waimakariri River, bypassing Kaiapoi. After rejoining the Main North Road, note side Route 72 on the left to Rangiora and Oxford, and side roads to Woodend and Waikuku beaches on the right. Cross the Ashley River and follow the road through to Leithfield and Amberley.

After crossing the Waipara River, Route 7 from Waipara to Hanmer Springs and the Lewis Pass route to the west coast branches off (refer itinerary 16). Northbound, Route 1 enters open hill country over the Omihi saddle. Pass Centre Hill and

Pendle Hill, and cross the Hurunui River. Proceed through Domett and Cheviot to cross the Waiau River. The road continues through sparse country, follows and crosses the Conway River, before dropping to sea level for a scenic run along the coast, including two short tunnels, to **Kaikoura**. Part of the town and a lookout are on a side road, on the peninsula. Route 70 from Culverden intersects 5 km south of the town.

Continuing north, road and rail hug the seashore at the base of the seaward Kaikoura Range. Cross the Clarence River and the Ure River. Route 1 then moves inland through Ward, and rises over open grades to **Lake Grassmere** and Seddon. It crosses the Awatere River, and after rising again over the Dashwood Pass, descends to the Wairau plains and the town of **Blenheim**. Follow the signs through the town streets (note restricted pedestrian mall) to the intersection of Route 6 to Nelson and the west coast.

Continue straight on to Spring Creek, cross the Wairau River, and then rise up a valley, and drop down in to **Picton**. Route 1 leads to the inter-island ferry terminal, with the Grove road (Queen Charlotte Drive) to Havelock leading off to the left, and the main street to the right.

*Sheep on a South Island farm.*

gently sloping except for the drop to cross the Waimakariri River Gorge*. Note also the side roads to Ashley Gorge*.

## 14B KAIKOURA – CULVERDEN
*Route 70, 107 km*

This is a secondary link (still unsealed) over undulating country with steady grades and sharp bends. It serves as a link between **Hanmer Springs** and the Lewis Pass route with the Kaikoura coast, and intersects Route 1, 5 km south of **Kaikoura**. It is not suitable for caravans. There is an alternative link between Waiau and the Leader River bridge near Parnassus, which is sealed, but still hilly and winding.

## 14A WOODEND/RANGIORA – SHEFFIELD
*Route 72, 61 km*

This road branches off Route 1 at Woodend, north of Christchurch, and travels via **Rangiora** and **Oxford** to intercept Route 73 near Sheffield. It is therefore a link road for motorists wishing to travel between Arthur's Pass and the Kaikoura coast, bypassing Christchurch. Its countryside is

## 14C SEDDON – MOLESWORTH
*93 km*

This road up the Awatere Valley leads to Molesworth, New Zealand's largest sheep station. It is unsealed, with some narrow sections. The road climbs to approximately 900 m and is subject to snow in winter. The road beyond Molesworth, towards Hanmer Springs, is not open to the public.

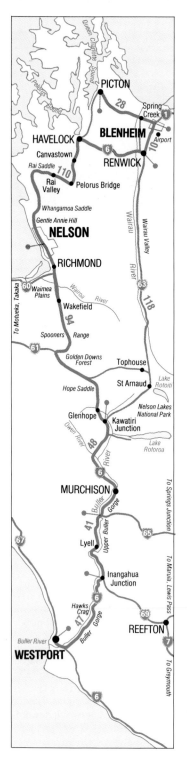

# 15

# PICTON – WESTPORT
**via Blenheim and Nelson with optional route via St Arnaud**

*Picton – Blenheim 28 km (½ hr)*
*Blenheim – Nelson 120 km (1¾ hr)*
*Nelson – Westport 230 km (3¾ hr)*

From the delightful Marlborough Sounds to the South Island's rugged west coast, via the beautiful Buller River.

Route 1 leads away from the inter-island ferry wharf at **Picton**, with the main streets to the left, and Queen Charlotte Drive (also known as the Grove road) accessible to the right. The main road rises through the town, over a hill and down a valley to Spring Creek, where there are signposted roads bypassing the town of Blenheim (and saving 8 km).

The main road, however, continues in to **Blenheim**, where you should turn on to Route 6. Proceed past the Woodbourne airport, and veer to the right at Renwick. (The road ahead, Route 63, is a direct link to St Arnaud, Kawatiri Junction, and the West Coast — described below).

After Renwick, pass the by-pass from Spring Creek, and cross the Wairau River. Route 6 continues through rolling country to **Havelock**. Just before entering Havelock, note the exit of the Grove road from Picton.

The 'Grove road' is a picturesque short cut between Picton and Havelock. The road is winding and narrow in places, but provides attractive views of the Queen Charlotte and Pelorus Sounds. It is unsuitable for caravans.

Route 6 continues through Canvastown to the Pelorus Bridge Reserve*, and enters the Rai Valley. Rise through forest over the Rai saddle and descend; then rise again over the Whangamoa saddle (357 m). There is a steady descent, before rising over Gentle Annie Hill, and descending beside the waters of Nelson Haven. The main road leads in to Trafalgar Street, the main street of **Nelson**.

Route 6 runs off Trafalgar Street in to Halifax Street, follows Haven Road around past Port Nelson, and then on past Tahunanui Beach*. The main road is well defined through the suburb of Stoke, and satellite town of Richmond. Just south of Richmond, Route 60 to Motueka and Takaka branches off.

Continue across the Waimea Plains and Wairoa River and gently rise to Wakefield. The country is now broken, and the road rises on easy grades over Spooners Range (464 m). Descend through the Golden Downs forestry plantation. At river level, note side road Route 61, an alternative link from Motueka; and shortly afterwards an alternative road, via Tophouse, to **St Arnaud** and the Nelson Lakes National Park*. The latter road intersects Route 63, the direct route from Blenheim, and meets up again with Route 6 at Kawitiri Junction*, making an interesting detour.

After these turn-offs, Route 6 rises sharply up and over the Hope Saddle (634 m). The road drops down to Glenhope, then reaches a meeting of roads and rivers (the Hope and the Buller) at Kawatiri Junction. There are no commercial facilities here — only the remains of a railway that was never completed!

From Kawatiri Junction Route 6 follows the Buller River to the sea. Shortly after the junction, note the side road to Lake Rotoroa*. There is rugged, rolling bush country down to the Owen River after which the country opens up to **Murchison**.

Continuing downriver, Route 6 follows the beech-clad upper Buller Gorge and soon reaches the corner of Route 65, which leads to Maruia Springs Junction and the Lewis Pass (an alternative road link from Murchison to intersect Route 65 via the Maruia Saddle is not recommended). Almost 5 km after the Route 65 junction, note signs pointing to the fault line of the 1929 Inangahua earthquake. However, following the later 1968 earthquake, and subsequent road realignment, the upthrust is not readily visible.

Follow through picturesque river scenery and beech forest, and note the information about the gold mining days at the Lyell* rest area. Then cross the Buller River and proceed to the **Inangahua Junction**. Here Route 69 links through to Route 7

The direct route from Blenheim to Kawatiri Junction bypasses Havelock and Nelson, but has its own attractions. Leave Blenheim and travel for 10 km on Route 6. At Renwick, join Route 63. Then follow the river up the Wairau valley.

The road steadily rises, crosses the river, and keeps rising to the Tophouse side road (this is where the detour from the Golden Downs meets Route 63). Soon enter the community of **St Arnaud**, and note the short side road to Lake Rotoiti*, in the Nelson Lakes National Park*. The Buller River flows out of Lake Rotoiti, and Route 63 follows the river to its junction with Route 6 at Kawatiri. From Blenheim to Kawatiri the distance is 128 km, while via Nelson it is 214 km.

at Reefton, and offers a more direct inland access to Greymouth.

Route 6 continues downriver, through the Lower Buller Gorge and its fine scenery. The gorge road is narrow in places (especially at Hawks Crag where the cliff face overhangs the road), and follows close to the river for much of the distance. A railway line hugs the other river bank.

In due course the mountains are left behind, and Route 6 turns south down the west coast. **Westport** is 6 km straight ahead on Route 67. Cross over the Buller River to enter the town.

## 15A NELSON – COLLINGWOOD
*Route 60, 140 km*

Leave **Nelson** on Route 6, and turn off after Richmond, on to Route 60. Drive past farming and orchard lands to **Motueka** (55 km from Nelson). After leaving Motueka, note side road to popular Kaiteriteri* beach. Soon start the long, steady, winding climb, via a marble quarry and the Ngarua caves*, over Takaka hill (790 m). Drop down again to **Takaka**, noting side road to Totaranui* and the Abel Tasman National Park*. The Pupu Springs* are also nearby. The route remains well defined on to **Collingwood** where Farewell Spit* and the Heaphy Track* are accessed. Return to Motueka via the same route. An alternative link between Motueka and Richmond, via Moutere, could be considered for the return journey to Nelson.

## 15B MOTUEKA – GOLDEN DOWNS
*Route 61, 58 km*

This is a link road from Motueka to the south, eliminating the return trip to Richmond, for those seeking Route 6 southbound.

Route 61 branches off Route 60, 2½ km east of Motueka, crosses a tobacco-growing area, then rises over a hill to Motupiko junction on Route 6. Part of this road remains unsealed. Provides access to Wangapeka Track*.

## 15C MURCHINSON – (MARUIA) SPRINGS JUNCTION
*Route 65, 83 km*

This link road branches off Route 6, 11 km west of **Murchison**, and rises through rugged country over the Shenandoah Saddle (500 m). The road intercepts Route 7 (the Lewis Pass road), 15 km west of Maruia Springs*. An alternative link road, which leads directly out of Murchison over the Maruia Saddle is not recommended.

## 15D INANGAHUA – REEFTON
*Route 69, 33 km*

**Inangahua** is a junction for river and road — but not for railway, even though that was once mooted. The road is sealed, and rises slightly to **Reefton**. Parallel to Route 65, but flatter, this route provides a link between Routes 6 and 7, that is, between the Buller Gorge and the Lewis Pass.

## 15E WESTPORT – KARAMEA
*Route 67, 97 km*

From **Westport**, follow through the coal towns of Denniston*, Granity* and Ngakawau*. There is also access to Seddonville, the Charming Creek* walkway and the Chasm Creek* walkway. Rise over the long, winding Karamea Bluff and 'Four Mile Saddle', then drop down again. Note access to the Wangapeka Track*, and continue to **Karamea**. There is access from here to the Heaphy Track*. The return journey is via the same route.

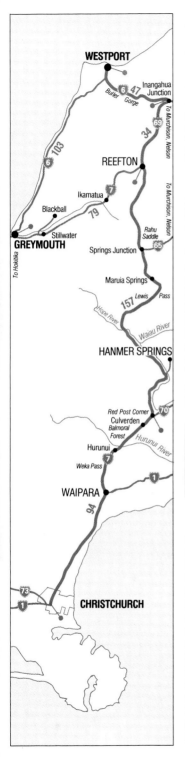

## CHRISTCHURCH – WESTPORT/ GREYMOUTH
### via Lewis Pass (Hanmer Springs and Reefton)

*Christchurch – Westport 332 km (3 hr)*
*Christchurch – Greymouth 330 km 4¾ hr*

The 'Lewis Pass' route from **Christchurch** to the west coast commences by travelling north on Route 1 to Waipara*. Please refer to itinerary 14 for a description of this section.

At Waipara Junction take Route 7 and head west on easy grades over Weka Pass. Continue over undulating country through Hurunui*. Cross the Hurunui River, and pass through the Balmoral Forest pine plantation to Culverden. At 'Red Post Corner' note Route 70 to Waiau branching off. Continue westward on Route 7, gradually rising over open country to the Hanmer Springs junction.

> The resort of **Hanmer Springs** is 10 km up the side road. The road crosses three bridges to the gardens, forest and thermal pools that make up this spa.

From Hanmer junction, Route 7 drops down to follow the wide shingle riverbed of the Waiau and Hope rivers. The valley gradually narrows and after a time the road rises above the river and crosses it. The road predominantly rises as it passes round high bluffs and enters picturesque birch forest, to cross the Lewis Pass (940 m). Proceed downhill to **Maruia Springs**. The road continues through bush, and before long the valley widens out, and you reach the Springs Junction intersection of Route 65 (north to Murchison and Nelson).

*Cape Foulwind lighthouse and seal colony near Westport.*

Route 7 proceeds with a winding climb through birch forest to the Rahu saddle (676 m). The descent is on easy grades through shady woodlands following the widening Inangahua River. As the forests recede, enter a cleared valley and proceed to **Reefton**. Swing right on to Route 69 northwards for Inangahua and Westport, or follow Route 7 to the south for Greymouth and Hokitika.

Leaving Reefton, Route 7 rises to cross the Reefton Saddle, and then starts a gradual descent down the valley of the Grey River. The area has a history of gold, coal, and timber — the working remains of which are still visible at Ikamatua and Blackball* (on side road). After Stillwater*, note the footbridge over the river to the

Brunner* historic industrial site. The road continues to **Greymouth**. Route 7 terminates at its intersection with Route 6 — north across the river to Punakaiki and Westport; south through the town for **Hokitika**. Refer to itinerary 18.

Route 69 links north on an easy travelling route down the valley of the Inangahua River following the railway line. In due course the river junctions with the Buller, and the road junctions with Route 6 at Inangahua Junction. Turn right upriver for Murchison and Nelson; turn left downriver for **Westport**. This road, on Route 6 through the Lower Buller Gorge, is described in itinerary 15.

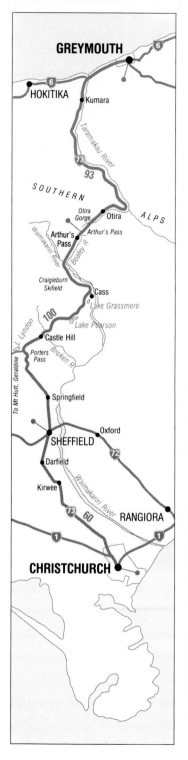

# 17

# CHRISTCHURCH – GREYMOUTH/ HOKITIKA
### via Arthur's Pass
*Christchurch – Greymouth 253 km (4 hr)*
*Christchurch – Hokitika 257 km (4 hr)*

This Arthur's Pass route is a striking trans-alpine connection from coast to coast, but also note its restrictions.

Downtown **Christchurch** has a one-way street system, and north/south traffic on Route 1 is carried on separate streets to the east of Cathedral Square. Over Moorhouse Avenue, these separate ways link up to join an arterial route heading west. Route 1 then turns along Blenheim Road, but this itinerary picks up Route 73 along Curletts Road, and Peer Street, before turning in to West Coast Road. (West Coast Road branches off Riccarton Road and this may be a more direct route for those familiar with the city).

As the suburbs clear, it is comfortable travelling over closely settled flat farming country. Proceed south-westerly, with the mountains getting closer, through Kirwee and Darfield, then turn to the west through Sheffield and Springfield.

Near Sheffield, Route 72 crosses. This route provides access for travellers wishing to bypass Christchurch to or from the north via Oxford and Rangiora; to or from the south via Mt Hutt and Geraldine.

After Springfield, you are in the mountains, and Route 73 commences a steep ascent to the summit of Porters Pass (944 m). It then drops down to the Lake Lyndon junction (for Lake Coleridge*). Route 73 continues descending past Castle Hill, crosses Broken River and passes Lakes Pearson and Grassmere. Side

*The steep, winding road of Arthur's Pass.*

roads provide access to Craigieburn ski-field, and Cass railway station. Soon the Waimakariri River can be seen, and the road descends to cross it. The road follows the Bealey River up a narrowing valley and eventually arrives at the settlement of **Arthur's Pass**.

The next 15 km over the Pass is steep, as the road winds through the main divide of the Southern Alps. Caravans, trailers and vehicles over 13 m long are prohibited. Arthur's Pass (920 m) is not as high as Porters Pass, but it can be windy, and there is a steep zigzag descent on the west coast side. At the end of the Otira Gorge, the road reaches the declining railway town of Otira*.

Route 73 descends steadily beside the Otira and Taramakau Rivers through scenic country. After a while it enters **Kumara**, and finally ends with the intersection of Route 6 at Kumara junction. Turn right (north) for **Greymouth**, and left (south) for **Hokitika**. These sections of Route 6 are described in more detail in itinerary 18.

### 17A SHEFFIELD– GERALDINE
*Route 72, 129 km*

This road through the back country of Canterbury is a continuation of the Route 72 link

from Woodend. From **Sheffield** on the Arthur's Pass road, the route has undulating conditions, windy in parts, down to the bridges at Rakaia Gorge*. Note side road here to Lake Coleridge*, Lake Ida and Algidus sheep station. Also note Mt Hutt*, and the side road to **Methven** and Ashburton on Route 77. The road continues to undulate, and crosses the Ashburton River near Mt Somers, and the Rangitata River; note side roads to Erewhon* and Mesopotamia* sheep stations. At **Geraldine**, Route 79 crosses to Fairlie and Route 8; while Route 72 carries on a further 11 km to intersect with Route 1 at Winchester, 25 km north of Timaru.

### 17B LAKE LYNDON – RAKAIA GORGE
*42 km*

This is a fine-weather short cut from the Arthur's Pass road, Route 73, to the Rakaia Gorge*, where it joins Route 72, for onward travel to **Methven** or **Geraldine**. It branches off at Lake Lyndon, and therefore avoids Porters Pass. The first 14 km are narrow and winding. Note side roads leading to Lake Ida, Lake Coleridge* and Algidus sheep station.

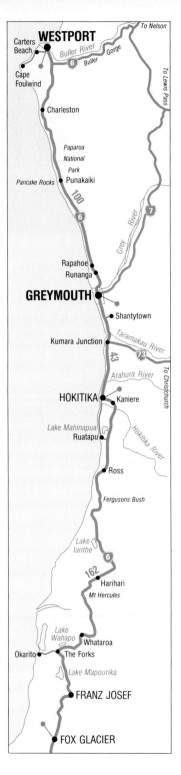

# 18

# WESTPORT – FOX GLACIER
## via Greymouth and Hokitika

*Westport – Greymouth 100 km (1¾ hr)*
*Greymouth – Hokitika 43 km (¾ hr)*
*Hokitika – Fox Glacier 162 km (3 hr)*

Route 6, arguably the South Island's most scenic highway, offers magnificent mountain, bush, and coastal scenery, down through Westland.

Southbound from **Westport**, follow Route 67 out of the main street (Palmerston Street) across the Buller River towards its intersection 6 km later with Route 6. Note the side road to Carters Beach* and Cape Foulwind*. Route 6 comes down the Buller Gorge from Nelson, Kawatiri Junction and Inangahua before it swings south down to the west coast.

Route 6 proceeds through a scrubby landscape, with mountain backdrop, and passes Charleston*. In due course the road is squeezed between mountains and sea, and you arrive at **Punakaiki**, the site of the famous Pancake Rocks* and the new Paparoa National Park*.

The road parallels the coast to the coal mining area of Rapahoe*, and then turns inland to Runanga*. Soon it crosses the Grey River; note the junction of Route 7 to and from the Lewis Pass. Follow Route 6 behind the railway yards. For the central business district of **Greymouth**, turn over the rail tracks.

Route 6 is clearly defined leading out to the south, following the railway (and crossing it several times) in sight of the coast. Note the side road to Shantytown*, and then a combined road-rail bridge over the Taramakau River. At Kumara Junction, note Route 73 branching eastwards to and from

*Pancake Rocks and blowholes at Punakaiki.*

Christchurch; this is the restricted route via Arthur's Pass previously described in itinerary 17.

Soon Route 6 crosses another combined bridge over the Arahura River, and then follows a straight run in to **Hokitika**. The central business district is towards the end and to the right of the street you will follow in, that is, Fitzherbert Street. Route 6 to the south, however, turns left in to Stafford Street and moves further inland to Kaniere* to cross the Hokitika River. After crossing the river note the side road to Lake Mahinapua and Ruatapu.

From Ross onwards, Route 6 offers magnificent bush, mountain and river scenery. Rise through Fergusons Bush and pass Lake Ianthe. In due course the road re-enters open country to pass Harihari.

Soon re-enter bush to ascend forest-clad Mt Hercules. Cleared areas of farmland, clumps of bush, swift-flowing creeks and snow-capped mountains combine to present delightful scenes as the road continues to Whataroa. Pass Lake Wahapo, and 'The Forks' junction (the road on the right leads to Okarito). Continue through the bush, pass Lake Mapourika, and then enter the settlement of **Franz Josef**.

Route 6 then climbs up and down three times through a mountainous section of road, before eventually entering the **Fox Glacier** area.

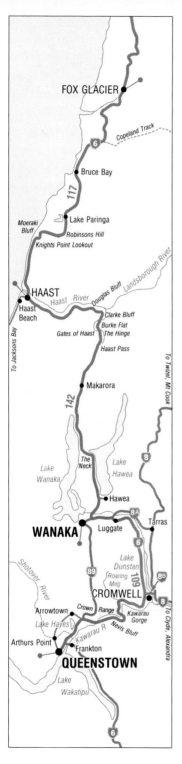

**FOX GLACIER**

Copeland Track

6

117

Bruce Bay

Moeraki
Bluff          Lake Paringa
          Robinsons Hill
Knights Point Lookout

**HAAST**     Haast  River      Douglas Bluff     Landsborough River
Haast
Beach                    Clarke Bluff
                         Burke Flat
        Gates of Haast   The Hinge
                         Haast Pass

To Jacksons Bay

142                Makarora

To Twizel, Mt Cook

        The
        Neck     Lake
Lake             Hawea            8
Wanaka

                Hawea
                        8A
**WANAKA**  Luggate     Tarras
                        6
              Lake
              Dunstan   109
Shotover River  89  Roaring
                    Meg          8B
              **CROMWELL**
Arrowtown   Crown  Range  Kawarau    To Clyde, Alexandra
Lake Hayes         Nevis Bluff Gorge
          Kawarau R
Arthurs Point        8
            Frankton
**QUEENSTOWN**
        Lake
        Wakatipu
                    6

# 19

# FOX GLACIER – QUEENSTOWN
## via Haast and Wanaka

*Fox Glacier – Haast 117 km (2 hr)*
*Haast – Wanaka 142 km (3¼ hr)*
*Wanaka – Queenstown 109 km (1¾ hr)*

More magnificent scenery along Route 6, from the rugged west coast, via the Haast Pass, to the beauty of the Southern Lakes district.

From the **Fox Glacier** area, Route 6 continues southbound through patches of farmland and bush, passing the entrance to Copeland Track*. It touches the coast at Bruce Bay, then moves inland again to Lake Paringa.

Continue crossing creeks and tributaries, rise up Robinsons Hill, and proceed around Moeraki Bluff. Climb up to the Knights Point Lookout. The road runs high along the coast, and after a series of ridges descends to sea level to traverse swamps and forested sand dunes. Cross the Haast River bridge to the locality of **Haast**. Haast beach is 4 km down the side road, which leads on to Jacksons Bay* (49 km).

Route 6 now turns inland up the valley of the Haast River. It is a scenic route with magnificent views of rivers, valleys, mountains and forests — and later of lakes. As the valley narrows, proceed around Douglas Bluff and Clarke Bluff, and note the confluence of the Haast and Landsborough Rivers.

After crossing Burke Flat, start a steep winding ascent, cross the Gates of Haast* chasm and 'The Hinge', to the summit (563 m) of the Haast Pass. The descent is more gradual and the road partially unsealed. Cross a number of flats to reach Makarora*. Proceed through open valley and soon follow the shores of Lake Wanaka. The road winds around a bluff above the lake, before rising up and over 'The Neck', to descend by Lake **Hawea** and dam. Soon you will reach Wanaka junction where Route 6 turns, but also note the side road to **Wanaka** (2 km).

Route 89, a secondary road via the Crown Range to Arrowtown and Queenstown, continues on from here, but this itinerary describes the main road via Cromwell.

If you have gone in to Wanaka, backtrack to Wanaka junction, and continue on Route 6. At Luggate junction, note the side road Route 8A leading over the Clutha River to Tarras, where it links up with the Lindis Pass route to Twizel and Mt Cook (Route 8). Both Route 8 and Route 6 come down the Clutha valley towards **Cromwell**. Note Lake Dunstan (a result of the Clyde dam further downstream) and also note the link road Route 8B, which again connects Routes 6 and 8 near the newer part of the town. (Route 8 carries on to Clyde, Alexandra and Roxburgh.) At the time of printing, the Clyde dam remains unfinished and Lake Dunstan is yet to be filled.

After Cromwell, Route 6 turns in to the Kawarau Gorge, and follows the Kawarau River. Then pass 'Roaring Meg' power station, and cross the river on the Victoria bridge. The road then winds round the Nevis Bluff high above the river. Then cross back over the river on the Kawarau bridge, and leave the gorge.

Observe the Crown Range road (Route 89), which zigzags down the hill on the right, and then pass the junction for **Arrowtown**. It is possible to take a detour via Arrowtown and Arthur's Point (an

additional 7 km) but Route 6 continues straight on, past Lake Hayes* and across the Lower Shotover River bridge. At Frankton* junction, Route 6 turns across the river to the south. However, this itinerary continues straight ahead, round the side of the Frankton Arm of Lake Wakatipu*. Follow the road round in to **Queenstown**. (Note that the main street of Queenstown is a pedestrian mall.)

### 19A HAAST – JACKSON BAY
*49 km*

This is a no-exit road deep in to south Westland. 40 km of the road is sealed. The remaining 9 km are, however, in fair order.

### 19B WANAKA – QUEENSTOWN
*Route 89, 51 km*

This 'Crown Range' road is New Zealand's highest through road, rising to 1120 m. From **Wanaka** it rises steadily up the Cardrona* valley, but at the southern end emerges high on the hillside and has a steep zigzag down to Route 8. It is then a further 19 km to **Queenstown**. The road is unsealed, and is usually snowbound in winter. Caravans and trailers are prohibited.

### 19C QUEENSTOWN – GLENORCHY
*50 km*

This is an unsealed road hugging the lakeside slopes from **Queenstown** to Glenorchy* and Kinloch*, at the head of Lake Wakatipu*. It provides access to both the Routeburn* and Greenstone tracks.

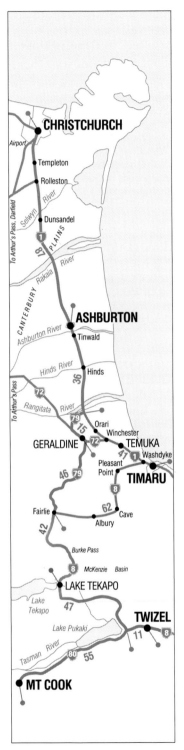

# 20

# CHRISTCHURCH – TWIZEL/MT COOK

**via Geraldine and Fairlie**
**optional route via Timaru**

*Christchurch – Twizel 284 km (4¼ hr)*
*Twizel – Mt Cook 66 km (¾ hr)*

Across the Canterbury Plains to the Mackenzie high country, and New Zealand's highest mountain.

Downtown **Christchurch** has a one-way street system, and north/south traffic on Route 1 is carried on separate streets to the east of Cathedral Square. Over Moorhouse Avenue these separate ways link up to join an arterial route heading west. Then Route 1 turns along Blenheim Road, which leads in to Great South Road (Great South Road leads off Riccarton Road and that may be a more direct route for those familiar with the city).

Route 1 continues south through Templeton where a signposted city by-pass from the north, via Christchurch Airport, also joins in. Proceed through Rolleston, and note side roads to Darfield, linking with Arthur's Pass Route 73. Route 1 crosses the Selwyn River, passes Dunsandel, and soon crosses the 1¾ km bridge (the longest bridge in New Zealand) over the Rakaia River.

The flat road allows fast comfortable travelling across the Canterbury Plains, with a view of the Southern Alps and its foothills in the distance. In due course enter the main street of **Ashburton** (87 km from Christchurch). South of the town, cross the Ashburton River, and pass Tinwald*. Then pass Hinds (and its river) and cross the two branches of the Rangitata River. Leave Route 1 (which continues south to Timaru) by following signs for Route 79 to **Geraldine**. Route 79 entering the town

Travellers who prefer to go via Timaru should stay on Route 1 after crossing the Rangitata River and travel through Orari and Winchester (where Route 72, the link road from the Arthur's Pass route, joins in).

Between **Temuka** and Washdyke note the side roads to Pleasant Point and Route 8. The main junction of Routes 1 and 8, however, is at Washdyke. From here it is 5 km in to **Timaru**, passing Caroline Bay* on the way.

To continue to Twizel or Mt Cook, return to the Washdyke junction, and pick up Route 8. Pass Pleasant Point* and rise up the pleasant valley through Cave* and Albury. In due course enter **Fairlie**.

*Cathedral Square in Christchurch.*

coincides with Route 72 (a link road from the Arthur's Pass route), but take Route 79 again to leave the town.

We now leave the plains behind and pass over undulating country, through pleasant scenery. The route is well defined, and levels out again before reaching **Fairlie**, where we join Route 8.

From Fairlie, continue on Route 8, which in time commences a steady climb to the summit of Burke Pass* (829 m). Continue over the high country, tussock-covered sheeplands of the MacKenzie Country*. Distant views of Mt Cook may be available as you approach **Lake Tekapo**.

Continue over more of this high country plateau. Cross over a canal carrying water for hydro-electric generation. (Although it is a private road connected with the power scheme, you may take the canal road to the right around and down to the powerhouse, before

looping back on to Route 8.) Now Lake **Pukaki** comes into view, and the road skirts a pebble beach at the end of the lake, with views of Mt Cook and the Southern Alps.

Note the junction of Route 80 to **Mt Cook** (see below), and proceed 11 km further to the town of **Twizel**, which is situated just off the main road.

Travellers for **Mt Cook** should turn off on to Route 80. The road skirts the shores of Lake Pukaki for 24 km, and then proceeds up the mountain-flanked Tasman valley. There should be splendid views of Mt Cook (New Zealand's highest mountain at 3764 m). The main hotel in the Mt Cook village is The Hermitage* and sometimes this name is loosely applied to the whole resort. The return journey is via the same route.

# 21

# MT COOK/TWIZEL – QUEENSTOWN

**via Omarama and Cromwell
optional route via Wanaka**

*Mt Cook – Twizel 66 km (¾ hr)
Twizel – Cromwell 138 km (2 hr)
Cromwell – Queenstown 62 km (1 hr)*

A scenic and uncrowded route from the Waitaki basin, via the Lindis Pass, to the Southern Lakes district.

From **Mt Cook** follow Route 80 down the length of Lake **Pukaki** to intersect Route 8, 11 km north of **Twizel**. The town is situated off the main road.

From Twizel, head south. Pass Lake Ruataniwha and continue across the Waitaki Basin. Pass a side road to Lake Ohau*. Route 8 proceeds across barren landscape to **Omarama**. Route 82 to and from Oamaru via the Waitaki River valley joins here.

From Omarama continue south on Route 8 and steadily ascend the gradually narrowing Ahuriri River valley to the summit of the Lindis Pass (970 m). Descend through gorge and tussock-covered hills, following the Lindis River. The route remains scenic, but the countryside gradually becomes more fertile down the Lindis valley.

In due course note the Tarras turn-off, Route 8A, for travellers to Wanaka and the Haast Pass. Otherwise, follow down the Clutha River valley. Use link road Route 8B to cross in to **Cromwell** (Route 8 carries on to Alexandra and Roxburgh).

After Cromwell, Route 6 turns in to the Kawarau Gorge and follows the Kawarau River. It passes 'Roaring Meg' power station, and crosses the river on the Victoria bridge. The road then

If you prefer to travel via **Wanaka**, take Route 8A at the Tarras junction. This crosses the Clutha River near Luggate and joins Route 6. Turn right. Soon Route 6 itself turns right for Lake Hawea and Haast Pass: however, continue straight ahead, joining Route 89, which leads in to Lake Wanaka.

Although Route 89 via 'the Crown Range' offers an alternative route to Queenstown, the suggested routing via main roads, leads back to Route 6, stays on it past the Route 8A junction, and follows down the Clutha valley to **Cromwell**. The detour via Wanaka adds an additional 41 km.

winds around the Nevis Bluff high above the river. Cross back over the river on the Kawarau bridge, and leave the gorge.

Observe the Crown Range road (Route 89) zigzagging down the hill at right, and then pass the junction for **Arrowtown**. It is possible to take a detour via Arrowtown and Arthur's Point (an additional 7 km), but Route 6 continues straight on, past Lake Hayes* and across the Lower Shotover River bridge. At the Frankton* junction, Route 6 turns across the river to the south. Continue straight ahead, however, around the side of the Frankton Arm of Lake Wakatipu* and follow in to **Queenstown**. (Note that the main street of Queenstown is a pedestrian mall.)

*The S.S.* Earnslaw *at Queenstown.*

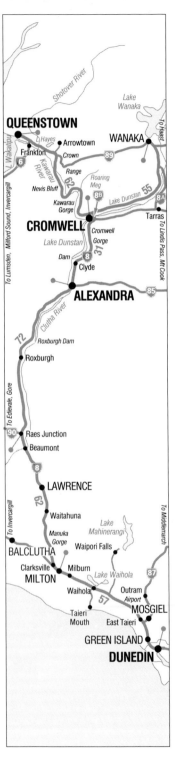

# 22

# QUEENSTOWN/ WANAKA – DUNEDIN
### via Cromwell and Milton

*Queenstown – Cromwell 62 km (1 hr)*
*Wanaka – Cromwell 55 km (¾ hr)*
*Cromwell – Milton 165 km (2¾ hr)*
*Milton – Dunedin 57 km (¾ hr)*

This route connects the Southern Lakes district with the 'Edinburgh of the South' via the barren lands and gorges of central Otago.

From **Queenstown** rise up around the Frankton Arm of Lake Wakatipu* for 7 km to the junction with Route 6 at Frankton. (To the right, Route 6 crosses the Kawarau River, and leads towards Lumsden, Milford Sound and Invercargill.) Continue straight ahead, crossing the Shotover River*, passing Lake Hayes* and noting side roads to Arrowtown. Also pass the junction of Route 89 where it zigzags down the Crown Range.

Route 6 continues through the rugged Kawarau Gorge, around the Nevis Bluffs, and past 'Roaring Meg' power station. In due course the road enters **Cromwell**, where you leave Route 6 (it carries on towards Wanaka and the Haast Pass), and connect around via the newer part of the town on link Route 8B, to intersect Route 8.

If travelling from **Wanaka**, drive to the Route 6 junction 2 km out of town. Ignore the road to Lake Hawea and Haast Pass, and follow down the upper Clutha valley. Stay on Route 6 past the Route 8A junction, and proceed to the Route 8B link at **Cromwell**. Take this short section to intersect Route 8. (The Route 8A link connecting to Route 8 at Tarras is an alternative route, but it is slightly longer.)

*The tranquil waters of Lake Wanaka.*

Turn right on to Route 8 (the road to the left leads to Lindis Pass and Mt Cook) and follow around a new section of road above the Clutha River, passing the Clyde dam in the Cromwell Gorge. Pass the town of **Clyde** (on side road) and in due course enter **Alexandra**. (Note the junction of Route 85 leading towards North Otago.)

Leaving Alexandra, cross the Clutha River, and pass through fruit growing areas before rising through rocky ground to cross a section of high country. In due course pass a side road to Roxburgh Dam*, and drop down into fruit country again, before entering **Roxburgh**. Continue down the Clutha valley, then rise over a hill to Raes Junction, where Route 90 branches off to Edievale and Gore.

Route 8 winds through rather hilly country, re-crossing the Clutha River at Beaumont and passing through **Lawrence**. Travel by the locality of Waitahuna* and through the Manuka Gorge. Route 8 ends at the Clarksville junction, where it intersects Route 1. Turn left for Milton and Dunedin (turn right for Balclutha and Invercargill).

Follow Route 1 north 3 km to **Milton**. Then continue north through the localities of Milburn and Waihola, through flat farming country, and passing Lake Waihola*. Note the side road to Taieri Mouth*, and later, the side road to Lake Mahinerangi* and Waipori Falls*. Side roads also lead to Dunedin Airport.

The main road passes East Taieri and skirts Mosgiel* (Route 87 to Outram and Middlemarch branches off here). There is a section of motorway to and through the borough of Green Island, for the climb over and then the drop down to **Dunedin**.

There is another stretch of motorway before Route 1 divides in to separate north and south streets through the central city's one-way system. Princes and George streets, the main shopping areas, are two blocks to the west.

## 22A **RAES JUNCTION – GORE**
*Route 90, 64 km*

Raes Junction is on Route 8, 32 km east of **Roxburgh**. From the arid Central Otago area, this route rises over 'Devils Elbow' and then crosses pleasant farmland through west Otago and northern Southland. It passes Edievale and **Tapanui**. The road joins Route 1 at McNab for the final 4½ km to **Gore**.

69

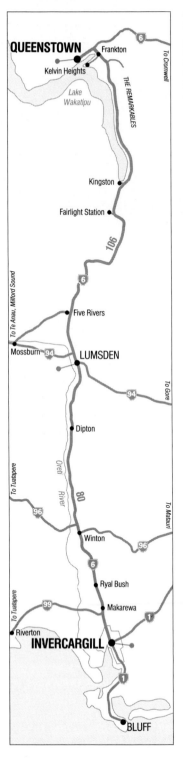

# 23

# QUEENSTOWN – INVERCARGILL
## via **Kingston and Lumsden**
*Queenstown – Lumsden 106 km (1¾ hr)*
*Lumsden – Invercargill 80 km (1¼ hr)*

This final section of Route 6 links the Southern Lakes district with New Zealand's southernmost city.

From **Queenstown** follow around the Frankton Arm of Lake Wakatipu* to Frankton* junction to intercept Route 6 and turn right over the Kawarau River (the road ahead leads to Cromwell). Note the side road to Kelvin Heights*, and another side road to the Remarkables* ski-field. Route 6 skirts around a rocky hill then emerges to follow around lakeside bluffs for 29 km. At the southern end of the lake, note the side road to Kingston*.

The road then ascends from the lake through tussock terraces, and in turn crosses the undulating grass lands of Southland. Note the side road to Fairlight* railway station, and later the Five Rivers to Mossburn short cut for travellers proceeding on Route 94 to Te Anau and Milford Sound (refer to itinerary 24).

Route 6 continues southbound in to **Lumsden**. Route 94 westbound branches off before entering the town, while Route 94, eastbound for Gore, branches off in the town. Route 6, however, proceeds straight through the town. Carry on a long, flat road, then climb over a hill to Dipton. Follow on down the valley of the Oreti River, and cross Route 96 (Mataura to Tuatapere) before entering **Winton**.

Route 6 continues over flat to undulating sheep farming country, through the small communities of Ryall Bush and Makarewa. (Note Route 99 to Riverton and Tuatapere branching off to the right.) It is

*Rolling hills and farmland near Queenstown.*

then an easy run in to the main streets of **Invercargill**. At the monument on the corner of Tay and Dee streets, note Route 1, the main road from the north, and straight ahead, the continuation of Route 1, 27 km to Bluff*.

## 23A MATAURA – WINTON
*Route 96, 50 km*

This road branches off Route 1, 1½ km south of **Mataura**, and crosses fertile farmlands, via Hedgehope, to intersect Route 6 at **Winton**.

## 23B WINTON – TUATAPERE
*Route 96, 66 km*

This continuation of Route 96 branches off Route 6, 2 km north of **Winton**. The route gives easy travelling crossing the Oreti, Aparima and Waiau rivers, via Nightcaps, Ohai and Clifden, to reach **Tuatapere**. An alternative route via Otautau also offers easy travelling.

## 23C INVERCARGILL – TUATAPERE
*Route 99*

Route 99 branches off Route 6, 7½ km out of **Invercargill**. It is easy travelling to Riverton, passing side roads to Thornbury and Otautau. Cross the Aparima River, and skirt around between the Longwood Range and the coast via Colac Bay* to **Tuatapere**.

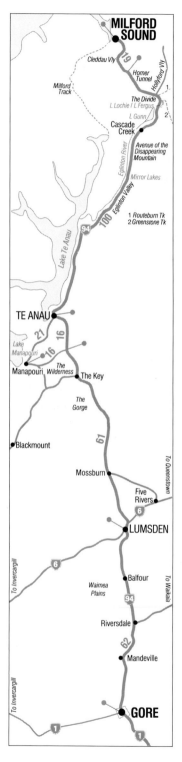

# 24

# GORE/LUMSDEN – MILFORD SOUND

## via Manapouri and Te Anau

*Gore – Lumsden 62 km (1 hr)*
*Lumsden – Te Anau 77 km (1¼ hr)*
*Te Anau – Milford Sound 119 km (2½ hr)*

The road to Milford Sound is probably New Zealand's most scenic route, but note the restrictions and our comments.

Route 94 commences at **Gore** (which in turn is on Route 1, 67 km north of Invercargill and 151 km south of Dunedin). This route across the Waimea Plains to Lumsden is frequently used as a connection between the east coast and the Fiordland area. It is flat to undulating, well defined and signposted, but some corners can be misleading, so do read the signs. The road is via Mandeville and Riversdale (junction for Waikaia*), and passes Balfour to enter **Lumsden**.

Lumsden is situated on Route 6 between **Invercargill** and **Queenstown**. Route 94 coincides with Route 6 for 2 km before it branches off again to Mossburn, where it is joined by the Five Rivers short cut from Queenstown.

Departing from Queenstown via Route 6 is described in itinerary 23. When approaching Lumsden, you may continue to the junction of Route 6 and Route 94, however, you will save 10 km by taking the signposted Five Rivers short cut.

From Mossburn the road ascends Gorge Hill, and then descends to resume flat travelling to 'The Key' junction (a direct route to south-western Southland via Blackmount intersects here). The undulating tussock country becomes quite desolate for a section aptly known as 'the Wilderness'. You will then come to a junction for **Manapouri**.

From the Manapouri junction, Te Anau and Manapouri are an equi-distant 16 km. There is a 21 km road directly between the two. Due to the beauty of Lake Manapouri, this route is recommended. On the way in, pass another link to the Blackmount road.

At the junction for Manapouri, Route 94 descends a little, with views of Lake Te Anau, to enter **Te Anau**. The direct road from Manapouri branches in just before the town.

Follow through the main street of Te Anau. When the road comes in sight of the lake again, it runs parallel to the lake for 29 km. In due course the road leaves the lake, and follows the Eglinton River up the Eglinton Valley. Enter beech forest, and note a short walking track to the small Mirror Lakes (56 km from Te Anau). Next, pass through 'the avenue of the disappearing mountain', watching the peak at the head of the road. Continue up easy grades to Cascade Creek* (which is 76 km from Te Anau).

The road then passes Lakes Gunn, Fergus and Lochie, and rises to cross 'The Divide' (533 m). Near here, the Routeburn* and Greenstone hiking tracks branch off for Lake Wakatipu. The road now drops steeply in to the Hollyford Valley*. Note the side road to the Lower Hollyford. Route 94 now has steep grades winding up to the Homer Tunnel (914 m altitude; 102 km from Te Anau).

After passing through the 1.2 km long tunnel, emerge to the spectacular Cleddau Valley, and commence a steep winding descent to **Milford Sound**. The road terminates here so the return journey is via the same route. The walking track from Lake Te Anau to Milford Sound is described under the Milford Sound listing.

## 24A MANAPOURI – CLIFDEN
*87 km*

This route runs beside the Takitimu Mountains, starting from either 'The Key' junction on Route 94, or alternatively from **Manapouri**. It passes several sheep stations such as Redcliff and Blackmount. The road gives access to Lake Monowai*, and eventually meets Route 96 near Clifden*. The route is flat to undulating, with a gentle climb over the Blackmount saddle.

## 24B CENTRE HILL – WALTER PEAK
*85 km*

Branching off from Route 94 between **Mossburn** and 'The Key' junction, this road provides access to the Mavora Lakes* and Walter Peak* on Lake Wakatipu. Return is via the same route. The road is unsealed, with several fords, and can be very dusty in dry weather.

Route 94 from Te Anau to Milford Sound is a scenic alpine road. Partially unsealed it can be subject to snow or avalanches. Caravans and trailers are prohibited beyond Cascade Creek and motorists are urged to pay strict attention to all signs erected for their safety.

The Homer Tunnel, which is 1.2 km long, is just wide enough for two-way traffic, but is usually restricted to one way only. It is open for 25 minutes past the hour for traffic to Milford, and for 25 minutes past the half-hour for return traffic. Sometimes tour buses ignore these times. Do not rush to try to coincide with these times, as the scenery at each end of the tunnel will compensate for any wait.

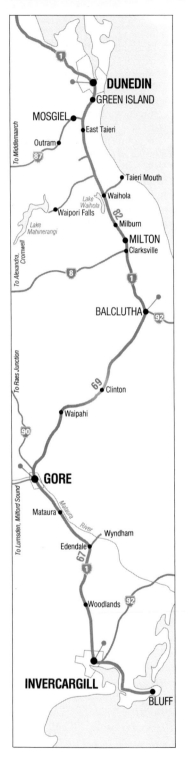

# 25

# INVERCARGILL – DUNEDIN

**via Gore**

*Invercargill – Gore 67 km (¾ hr)*
*Gore – Dunedin 151 km (2¼ hr)*

This southern end of Route 1 crosses the rolling farmlands of Southland and south Otago.

Route 1 commences at Bluff*, enters **Invercargill** on Clyde Street, and leaves it on Tay Street. Having left the city, proceed over flat farming country through Woodlands, and over a gentle hill to Edendale. Note the side road to Wyndham. Continue to **Mataura** and soon enter the main street of **Gore**. Observe the intersection with Route 94 to and from Lumsden and Milford Sound (refer to itinerary 24), cross over the Mataura River, and shortly pass the junction of Route 90 towards Raes Junction and Central Otago.

Route 1 now continues over rolling country, and the road undulates accordingly through to Waipahi, Clinton and **Balclutha**. At Balclutha, Route 92, a coastal road from Invercargill, joins Route 1.

Continue north to Clarksville junction (road on the left is Route 8, described in itinerary 22), and enter **Milton**. Then continue north through the localities of Milburn and Waihola, through flat farming country, passing Lake Waihola*. Note the side road to Taieri Mouth*, as well as side roads to Lake Mahinerangi* and Waipori Falls*. Soon also note side roads to Dunedin Airport.

The main road passes East Taieri and skirts Mosgiel* (Route 87 to Outram and Middlemarch branches off here). There is a section of motorway to and through the borough of Green Island, as you climb over a hill and drop down to **Dunedin**.

There is another stretch of motorway before Route 1 splits in

*Port Chalmers, near Dunedin.*

to separate north and south streets through the central city's one-way system. The main shopping areas of Princes and George streets are two blocks to the west.

## 25A INVERCARGILL – BALCLUTHA
*Route 92, 169 km*

From **Invercargill** this route passes Gorge Road and Fortrose*, and in due course a side road to Curio Bay*. Route 92 winds through bush past Chaslands* and then has steep winding grades over Gibbs Hill to Owaka. It has a gentler rise over Tunnel Hill, then has good conditions to **Balclutha**. This is a pleasantly picturesque alternative to Route 1, which passes the southernmost part of the South Island. Much of the road is narrow and winding, and the central third remains unsealed.

## 25B MOSGIEL – RANFURLY
*Route 87, 116 km*

This road branches off Route 1 at Mosgiel*, 14 km south of **Dunedin**. It passes Outram and then rises over high undulating sheep country, with fairly steep grades. Avoid the Old Dunstan Road and continue to Middlemarch. The road has hilly conditions flanking the Rock and Pillar Range to Hyde. It meets Route 85 on the Maniototo Plains at Kyeburn near **Ranfurly** (refer to itinerary 26A).

## 25C BALCLUTHA – KAITANGATA
*Route 91, 12 km*

This short side road from **Balclutha** to Stirling and Kaitangata is sealed and in good order.

# 26

# DUNEDIN – CHRISTCHURCH

**via Oamaru and Timaru**

*Dunedin – Oamaru 114 km (1¾ hr)*
*Oamaru – Timaru 84 km (1 hr)*
*Timaru – Christchurch 163 km (2 hr)*

This main road is initially quite hilly, but becomes flatter as it moves north.

**Dunedin** has a one-way street system in its central business district, so the north and south parts of Route 1 are separated, and are one or two blocks east of the main shopping streets, Princes and George. Follow signs northbound, past the Botanic Gardens, and pick up an arterial motorway route for the steady climb up and out of the city.

An alternative route branches off before the motorway, and follows North Road up and over Mt Cargill* (388 m). Both routes meet at Waitati*.

The road climbs up over the Kilmog hill (244 m) and down again in to Waikouaiti*. It is steady travelling through to the town of **Palmerston**, where Route 85 for Ranfurly and Alexandra branches off.

Route 1 leads north along Katikati Beach, and passes Moeraki*, famous for its spherical boulders. Undulating conditions continue, and in due course, the road leads in, past the Oamaru Gardens*, to the main street of **Oamaru**. Continuing north, re-enter open country, and soon pass the junction of Route 83 up the Waitaki valley to Kurow and Omarama. Watch for the plaque indicating the 45th parallel of latitude (halfway between the equator and the South Pole), and then cross a long bridge over the Waitaki River. Note the several side roads to **Waimate** (including Route 82). The road remains well defined across undulating

The map on the left shows the route from Christchurch to Dunedin, with the following labelled locations:

CHRISTCHURCH, Airport, Templeton, To Arthur's Pass, Springfield, Darfield, Rolleston, Selwyn River, Dunsandel, To Mt Hutt, Arthur's Pass, CANTERBURY, Rakaia River, PLAINS, ASHBURTON, Tinwald, Ashburton River, Hinds, Rangitata River, GERALDINE, Winchester, To Fairlie, Twizel, Mt Cook, TEMUKA, Washdyke, Caroline Bay, TIMARU, To Kurow, Omarama, Waimate, Waitaki River, To Ranfurly, Alexandra, OAMARU, To Kurow, Omarama, Moeraki, Katikati Beach, PALMERSTON, Waikouaiti, Kilmog Hill, Waitati, Mt Cargill, DUNEDIN

Route numbers shown: 73, 87, 1, 72, 76, 79, 72, 79, 8, 84, 82, 1, 83, 114, 85 countryside, and in due course leads in to the main street of **Timaru**.

Northbound from Timaru, Route 1 skirts Caroline Bay*. At Washdyke, Route 8 branches off for Fairlie, Twizel, and Mt Cook. Pass **Temuka**, and at Winchester, note Route 72 branching off to the north-west and providing an inland route to **Geraldine**, Mt Hutt and Arthur's Pass. Shortly Route 79 intersects from the south-west (Geraldine, Fairlie).

Cross the two branches of the Rangitata River and proceed over the Canterbury Plains to Hinds and Tinwald*. Cross the Ashburton River and enter **Ashburton**. The flat road allows fast comfortable travelling, with a view of the Southern Alps and its foothills in the distance. In due course cross the 1¾ km bridge (New Zealand's longest bridge) over the Rakaia River.

Proceed through Dunsandel, cross the Selwyn River, and note the side roads connecting to Darfield, Springfield and Arthur's Pass. Continue through Rolleston, and soon enter the southern suburbs of **Christchurch**. At Templeton note signs for Christchurch Airport, and also for the city by-pass to the north, for those preferring not to travel through the downtown area. Otherwise Route 1 leads in through the Great South Road, and Blenheim Road, and then swings on to an arterial route.

Downtown Christchurch has a one-way street system, with north and south traffic carried on separate streets to the east of Cathedral Square. Follow the signs from the arterial route to these separate streets. Those travellers more familiar with Christchurch may prefer to remain in Blenheim Road and follow Hagley Park* around to the centre of the city.

## 26A PALMERSTON – ALEXANDRA
*Route 85, 164 km*

This road, over the 'Pigroot', winds through undulating country and then passes over a high plateau. From the South Island town of **Palmerston**, the route moves inland to Dunback, and then crests four peaks (the highest being 640 m) before reaching the Maniototo Plains. At 62 km note the intersection, near Kyeburn, of Route 87 from Mosgiel via Middlemarch. Almost immediately note the side road over the Dansey Pass to the Waitaki valley. Route 85 passes **Ranfurly** and the side road to **Naseby**, and later side roads to **St Bathans**. Pass Omakau* and follow down the valley to **Alexandra**. The road can be subject to snow and ice in winter.

## 26B OAMARU – OMARAMA
*Route 83, 118 km*

This route branches off Route 1 at Pukeuri, 8 km north of **Oamaru**, and follows the Waitaki River valley through **Duntroon** (note the side road over Dansey Pass), and **Kurow** (here joins Route 82 from Waimate, and also the side road up the Hakataramea* valley). Pass the hydro-electric stations at Waitaki, Aviemore and Benmore, and then rise to **Omarama**, where Route 6 is intersected. A pleasant, easy travelling connection.

## 26C WAIMATE – KUROW
*Route 82, 68 km*

Route 82 branches off Route 1 midway between Timaru and Oamaru, and leads 9 km to **Waimate**. From there it follows undulating conditions to the Waitaki River valley. It follows the north bank of the river to Hakataramea* where it crosses over to **Kurow** and joins Route 83.

## 26D DUNTROON – RANFURLY
*79 km*

This route over the Dansey Pass links the Waitaki valley with the Maniototo Plains of north Otago. The road is unsealed, narrow, and winding, with some steep grades, but is also picturesque. It is not recommended for caravans or trailers. From **Duntroon** on Route 83, the road has a steep, winding ascent to 934 m, then an equally steep winding descent to the Kyeburn* Diggings. At the southern end you can choose road links to Kyeburn junction, **Naseby**, or **Ranfurly** — all on or adjacent to Route 85 (refer to itinerary 26A).

## 26E ASHBURTON – MT HUTT
*Route 77, 50 km*

From **Ashburton** this route slowly rises over almost flat countryside to **Methven** and on to Mt Hutt*. Here it connects with Route 72 north to the Arthur's Pass route — so providing a good connection from Timaru and points south. (Route 72 also provides a connection via Geraldine but this route is slower — see itinerary 17A).

## CHRISTCHURCH – AKAROA
*Route 75, 83 km*

From downtown **Christchurch**, Route 75 leads out via Lincoln Road over flat country, via Birdlings Flat, then inland to Little River. From here the road climbs steeply up to Hill Top for views over the Akaroa Harbour. Then drop steeply down to Barrys Bay and follow around the harbour over undulating conditions to **Akaroa**. An alternative return route is to take the high Summit Road out of Akaroa and follow the ridge around back to Hill Top.

Then again take the Summit Road from Ahuri to Dyers Pass, returning via the Dyers Pass Road leading into Colombo Street, Christchurch, or alternatively returning via Lyttelton.

*The imposing slopes of the Mt Hutt Range.*

## CHRISTCHURCH – LYTTELTON
*Route 74, 13 km*

From the **Christchurch** railway station Route 74 leads towards Heathcote, then rises slightly to enter a 2 km road tunnel, emerging suddenly into the port town of **Lyttelton**. For an alternative return, consider one of the roads over the hill — either via Dyers Pass or Sumner.

*Arrowtown, near Queenstown*

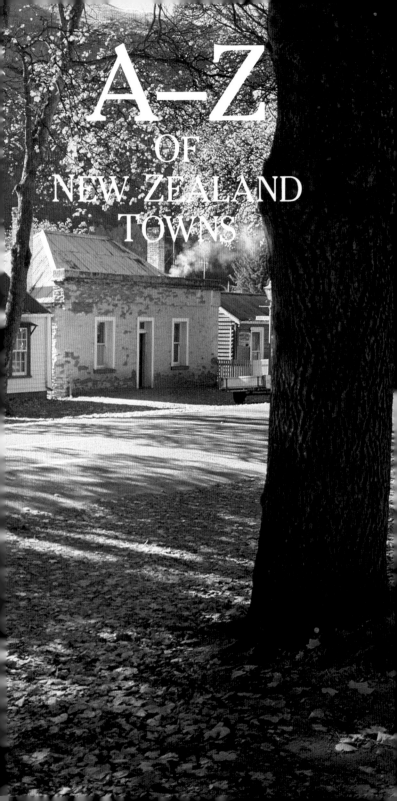

# A–Z
## OF
## NEW ZEALAND
## TOWNS

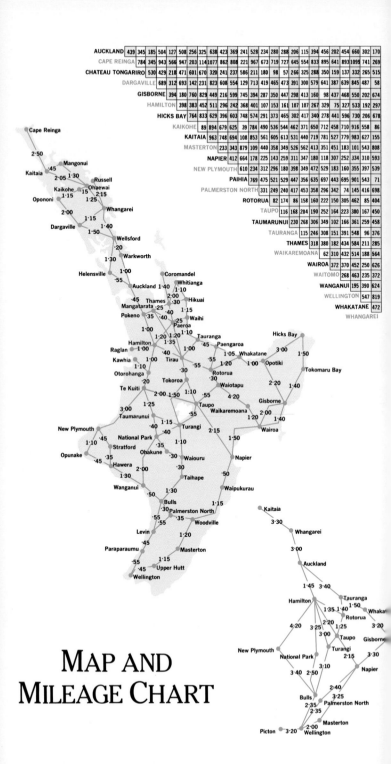

| | | | | | | | | | | | | | | | | | | | | | | | | | |
|---|---|---|---|---|---|---|---|---|---|---|---|---|---|---|---|---|---|---|---|---|---|---|---|---|---|
| **AUCKLAND** | 439 | 345 | 185 | 504 | 127 | 508 | 256 | 325 | 638 | 423 | 369 | 241 | 528 | 234 | 280 | 288 | 206 | 115 | 394 | 456 | 202 | 454 | 660 | 302 | 170 |
| CAPE REINGA | 784 | 345 | 943 | 566 | 947 | 203 | 114 | 1077 | 862 | 808 | 221 | 967 | 673 | 719 | 727 | 645 | 554 | 833 | 895 | 641 | 893 | 1099 | 741 | 269 | |
| **CHATEAU TONGARIRO** | 530 | 429 | 218 | 471 | 601 | 670 | 320 | 241 | 237 | 586 | 211 | 180 | 98 | 57 | 266 | 325 | 288 | 350 | 159 | 137 | 332 | 265 | 515 | | |
| DARGAVILLE | 689 | 312 | 693 | 142 | 231 | 823 | 608 | 554 | 129 | 713 | 419 | 465 | 473 | 391 | 300 | 579 | 641 | 387 | 639 | 845 | 487 | 58 | | | |
| **GISBORNE** | 394 | 180 | 760 | 829 | 449 | 216 | 599 | 745 | 394 | 287 | 350 | 447 | 298 | 413 | 160 | 98 | 437 | 468 | 550 | 202 | 674 | | | | |
| HAMILTON | 398 | 383 | 452 | 511 | 296 | 242 | 368 | 401 | 107 | 153 | 161 | 107 | 107 | 267 | 329 | 75 | 327 | 533 | 192 | 297 | | | | | |
| **HICKS BAY** | 764 | 833 | 629 | 396 | 603 | 748 | 574 | 291 | 373 | 465 | 302 | 417 | 340 | 278 | 441 | 596 | 730 | 206 | 678 | | | | | | |
| KAIKOHE | 89 | 894 | 679 | 625 | 39 | 784 | 490 | 536 | 544 | 462 | 371 | 650 | 712 | 458 | 710 | 916 | 558 | 86 | | | | | | | |
| **KAITAIA** | 963 | 748 | 694 | 108 | 853 | 561 | 605 | 613 | 531 | 440 | 719 | 781 | 527 | 779 | 983 | 627 | 155 | | | | | | | | |
| MASTERTON | 233 | 343 | 879 | 109 | 440 | 358 | 349 | 526 | 562 | 413 | 351 | 451 | 183 | 101 | 543 | 808 | | | | | | | | | |
| **NAPIER** | 412 | 664 | 178 | 225 | 143 | 259 | 311 | 347 | 180 | 118 | 307 | 252 | 334 | 310 | 593 | | | | | | | | | | |
| NEW PLYMOUTH | 610 | 234 | 312 | 296 | 180 | 398 | 349 | 472 | 529 | 183 | 160 | 355 | 397 | 533 | | | | | | | | | | | |
| **PAIHIA** | 769 | 475 | 521 | 529 | 447 | 356 | 635 | 697 | 443 | 695 | 901 | 543 | 71 | | | | | | | | | | | | |
| PALMERSTON NORTH | 331 | 249 | 240 | 417 | 453 | 318 | 296 | 342 | 74 | 145 | 416 | 698 | | | | | | | | | | | | | |
| **ROTORUA** | 82 | 174 | 86 | 158 | 160 | 222 | 150 | 305 | 462 | 85 | 404 | | | | | | | | | | | | | | |
| TAUPO | 116 | 168 | 204 | 190 | 252 | 164 | 223 | 380 | 167 | 450 | | | | | | | | | | | | | | | |
| **TAUMARUNUI** | 230 | 268 | 306 | 349 | 102 | 166 | 361 | 259 | 458 | | | | | | | | | | | | | | | | |
| TAURANGA | 115 | 246 | 308 | 151 | 391 | 548 | 96 | 376 | | | | | | | | | | | | | | | | | |
| **THAMES** | 318 | 380 | 182 | 434 | 584 | 211 | 285 | | | | | | | | | | | | | | | | | | |
| WAIKAREMOANA | 62 | 310 | 432 | 514 | 188 | 564 | | | | | | | | | | | | | | | | | | | |
| **WAIROA** | 372 | 370 | 452 | 250 | 626 | | | | | | | | | | | | | | | | | | | | |
| WAITOMO | 268 | 463 | 235 | 372 | | | | | | | | | | | | | | | | | | | | | |
| **WANGANUI** | 195 | 390 | 624 | | | | | | | | | | | | | | | | | | | | | | |
| WELLINGTON | 547 | 819 | | | | | | | | | | | | | | | | | | | | | | | |
| **WHAKATANE** | 472 | | | | | | | | | | | | | | | | | | | | | | | | |
| WHANGAREI | | | | | | | | | | | | | | | | | | | | | | | | | |

# MAP AND MILEAGE CHART

| 653 | 86 | 307 | 249 | 808 | 93 | 795 | 223 | 876 | 242 | 370 | 638 | 202 | 512 | 590 | 231 | 552 | 136 | 373 | 190 | 964 | 455 | 232 | 767 | 544 | **ALEXANDRA** |
| 199 | 528 | 252 | 801 | 320 | 645 | 468 | 336 | 388 | 412 | 922 | 311 | 668 | 102 | 263 | 383 | 98 | 602 | 241 | 451 | 476 | 150 | 698 | 440 | ARTHUR'S PASS | |
| 260 | 736 | 475 | 964 | 102 | 798 | 28 | 559 | 116 | 643 | 1085 | 129 | 891 | 364 | 262 | 645 | 324 | 825 | 503 | 674 | 251 | 312 | 921 | **BLENHEIM** | | |
| 885 | 318 | 446 | 187 | 962 | 217 | 949 | 362 | 1037 | 474 | 308 | 792 | 30 | 744 | 744 | 463 | 784 | 96 | 605 | 247 | 1118 | 609 | BLUFF | | | |
| 333 | 424 | 163 | 652 | 353 | 486 | 340 | 247 | 428 | 331 | 773 | 183 | 579 | 288 | 135 | 738 | 248 | 513 | 427 | 362 | 509 | **CHRISTCHURCH** | | | | |
| 314 | 844 | 672 | 1117 | 206 | 961 | 245 | 756 | 135 | 840 | 1238 | 380 | 1088 | 418 | 394 | 699 | 384 | 1022 | 582 | 871 | COLLINGWOOD | | | | | |
| 695 | 276 | 199 | 290 | 715 | 283 | 702 | 115 | 790 | 331 | 411 | 545 | 217 | 702 | 497 | 421 | 742 | 151 | 563 | **DUNEDIN** | | | | | | |
| 280 | 287 | 493 | 560 | 401 | 404 | 579 | 596 | 469 | 498 | 769 | 508 | 575 | 139 | 395 | 142 | 179 | 509 | FRANZ JOSEF | | | | | | | |
| 789 | 222 | 350 | 139 | 866 | 169 | 853 | 266 | 941 | 350 | 696 | 66 | 648 | 648 | 367 | 688 | **GORE** | | | | | | | | |
| 101 | 466 | 350 | 739 | 222 | 583 | 352 | 434 | 290 | 510 | 860 | 329 | 754 | 40 | 216 | 321 | GREYMOUTH | | | | | | | | | |
| 422 | 145 | 418 | 543 | 262 | 673 | 376 | 611 | 356 | 539 | 650 | 433 | 281 | 537 | **HAAST** | | | | | | | | | | | |
| 218 | 559 | 298 | 787 | 238 | 621 | 290 | 382 | 306 | 466 | 908 | 133 | 714 | 256 | HANMER SPRINGS | | | | | | | | | | | |
| 141 | 426 | 354 | 699 | 262 | 543 | 392 | 438 | 330 | 514 | 820 | 369 | 714 | **HOKITIKA** | | | | | | | | | | | | |
| 855 | 278 | 416 | 157 | 932 | 187 | 919 | 332 | 1007 | 444 | 278 | 762 | INVERCARGILL | | | | | | | | | | | | | |
| 331 | 607 | 346 | 835 | 231 | 669 | 157 | 430 | 245 | 514 | 956 | **KAIKOURA** | | | | | | | | | | | | | | |
| 961 | 394 | 610 | 121 | 1126 | 291 | 1113 | 526 | 1150 | 550 | MILFORD SOUND | | | | | | | | | | | | | | | |
| 664 | 211 | 211 | 484 | 684 | 328 | 671 | 216 | 759 | **MT COOK** | | | | | | | | | | | | | | | | |
| 226 | 756 | 591 | 1029 | 118 | 873 | 110 | 675 | NELSON | | | | | | | | | | | | | | | | | |
| 580 | 231 | 84 | 472 | 600 | 316 | 587 | **OAMARU** | | | | | | | | | | | | | | | | | | |
| 288 | 764 | 503 | 992 | 130 | 826 | PICTON | | | | | | | | | | | | | | | | | | | |
| 684 | 117 | 335 | 170 | 839 | **QUEENSTOWN** | | | | | | | | | | | | | | | | | | | | |
| 158 | 777 | 516 | 1005 | ST ARNAUD | | | | | | | | | | | | | | | | | | | | | |
| 840 | 273 | 489 | **TE ANAU** | | | | | | | | | | | | | | | | | | | | | | |
| 497 | 273 | TIMARU | | | | | | | | | | | | | | | | | | | | | | | |
| 567 | **WANAKA** | | | | | | | | | | | | | | | | | | | | | | | | |
| WESTPORT | | | | | | | | | | | | | | | | | | | | | | | | | |

*Mt Cook and Lake Pukaki can be seen along Braemar Road.*

# A

## AKAROA SI
**Population** 722
**Location** On Banks Peninsula, 82 km east of Christchurch on Route 75.

Banks Peninsula was formed many years ago following violent eruptions by two volcanoes, which created the harbours of Lyttelton and Akaroa. First sighted by Captain Cook (who thought it was an island) in 1770, Banks Peninsula was named after the naturalist who accompanied Cook, Sir Joseph Banks. The Peninsula was inhabited by Maoris of the Ngai Tahu tribe, whose numbers were severely depleted in 1831 when Te Rauparaha and his warriors attacked the fortified pa at Onawe.

A whaling station was established nearby in 1836. In 1838 a Frenchman, Captain Langlois, identified Akaroa Harbour as being suitable for settlement. He made a down payment with the Maoris and returned to France believing that he was the owner of Banks Peninsula. He organised settlers to return. When they did return, via the Bay of Islands in August 1840, they found that the Treaty of Waitangi had been signed and the British now had sovereignty over the country. HMS *Britomart* was hastily dispatched to Akaroa to raise the British flag and arrived there five days before the French settlers. However, the French settlers remained and were joined by a group of British colonists in 1850.

Akaroa remains unique as the site of the only attempted settlement by the French in New Zealand. Timber milling developed and as the land was cleared, dairy farming took over. A number of butter and cheese factories were established — one of which is still operational. Sheep farming, however, now predominates.

Akaroa and Lyttelton Harbours are old volcanic craters and road access entails climbing up the outside and down the inside. Appropriate care is required on all roads on the Banks Peninsula.

## ENVIRONS & ATTRACTIONS
**Langlois — Eteveneaux House and Museum** Probably the oldest house in Canterbury; now furnished as the home of an early French colonist; a modern museum is housed at the rear. Open daily 1.30–4 pm, cnr Rue Lavaud and Balgueri.
**Churches** St Peter's Anglican Church was built in 1863 with transepts being added in 1877. St Patrick's Catholic Church was the site of the first Mass held in the South Island (by Bishop Pompallier). The first Presbyterian service in the district was held in 1857 on the site of Trinity Church.
**The Gallery** Formerly a power-house and now a venue for arts and crafts. Open daily.
**Early Customhouse** Built of pit-sawn timber and sod lined, this dates from the early 1850s. Open daily 1.30–4.00 pm, cnr Rue Jolie and Balgueri.
**L'-Aube Hill** Offers fine views of the township and harbour after a short walk to the reservoir.
**Old French Cemetery** The first consecrated burial ground in Canterbury.
**French Settlers' Memorial** This granite memorial marks the approximate landing place of the French.
**Britomart Memorial** Erected at Greens Point, this memorial commemorates the raising of the

British flag by HMS *Britomart* to claim British sovereignty over Banks Peninsula.

**Akaroa Head Lighthouse** After standing for 100 years near the harbour entrance, this lighthouse was moved to Akaroa in 1980.

**The Herb Farm** Admission free; open daily to view a collection of herbs up Rue Grehan.

**Garden of Tane** Contains specimens of exotic trees, mainly those planted more than 100 years ago. A picnic area and playground are near the waterfront.

## LOCAL TOURING

**Onawe Peninsula** This peninsula is clearly visible from the main road going in or coming out of Akaroa. This was the site of the pa where Te Rauparaha defeated local Maoris in 1831.

**Settlers Cheese Factory** 12 km from Akaroa at Barrys Bay, this traditional cheese-making factory has a viewing gallery and a shop.

**Wainui** Good swimming beach with views, 20 km on the other side of Akaroa Harbour, opposite the town.

**Summit Drive** Rising above Akaroa this road semicircles the crater and its views alternate between the Akaroa harbour and the outer bays of the peninsula. It is high, narrow, but quite spectacular and joins the main road, Route 75, at Hilltop.

**Outer Bays** From the Summit Road, connecting roads link some of the smaller and more remote outer bays of the peninsula. These include Pigeon Bay (which has several attractive homesteads of historic and architectural interest), Little Akaloa (with beautiful St Luke's Church nestled in trees on a knoll above the cove), Okains Bay (sandy beach, with museum containing Maori artifacts and colonial exhibits, which is open daily between 10 am and 5 pm), and Le Bons Bay (complete with a swimming cove).

**See Also** Christchurch

# ALEXANDRA SI

**Population** 4842

**Location** On Route 8, 33 km south-east of Cromwell, 10 km south-east of Clyde, 40 km north-west of Roxburgh. Also terminus of Route 85 from Palmerston and Ranfurly.

Alexandra is built on flats where the Manuherikia River joins the Clutha, and is also on the Central Otago railway line from Dunedin. The town is associated with early gold discoveries in 1862 and some years later was also a centre for alluvial and dredging activities. As a miners' settlement, it was first known as Lower Dunstan. It was renamed as a borough in 1867. Today the town is a centre for stone fruit crops.

## ENVIRONS & ATTRACTIONS

**Old Bridge** The piers of the old town bridge (1882–1958) still stand beside the new bridge, at the southern entrance to the town. At the end of Kerry Street a suspension foot bridge built in 1879 and known as 'Shaky Bridge', is still standing.

**Knobbies Range Clock** This giant illuminated clock stands on the hillside overlooking the town.

**Sir William Bodkin Museum** This museum in Thomsom Street houses a goldmining collection. Open Mon–Fri, 2–4 pm. Also open daily in January but closed in winter.

**Vallance Cottage** This cottage in Samsom Street was built of mud bricks nearly a century ago.

**Alexandra Courthouse** Built in 1876 of schist stone, it is now recognised as a historic building by the Otago Goldfields Park. Tarbert Street.

**Tucker Hill Lookout** Take the road over the Manuherikia River and go up Little Valley Road to a viewpoint over the town, valleys and hills (1.5 km).

**Lower Manorburn Dam** Winter centre for ice skating and curling.

## LOCAL TOURING

**Omakau** Small locality, which was originally called Blacks, on railway and Route 85, 28 km north of Alexandra.

**Ophir** Just east of Omakau, this locality was a busy goldfield in 1863, and still has the remains of some early buildings, including an 1886 Post Office, now protected by the Historic Places Trust.

**Matakanui** 11 km north-west from Omakau there is little left of the old gold area.

**Ida Valley** A north–south alternative to Route 85 between Omakau, Ophir and Idaburn, which bypasses St Bathans, unless you want to make a return loop tour out and back to Alexandra. Note Idaburn Dam for skating and curling.

**Lye Bow Gardens** Drive 6 km south on Route 8 to this riverside picnic spot and alpine flower nursery.

**Mitchell's Cottage** 1 km along Symes Road from Fruitlands (12 km south on Route 8) you will find this stone cottage built in 1876 — open daily in summer.

**See Also** Clyde, Ranfurly and Roxburgh

---

# ARROWTOWN SI
Refer to Queenstown

---

# ARTHUR'S PASS SI
**Population** 138
**Location** The township is on Route 73, 95 km east of Greymouth, 146 km west of Christchurch.

*Punchbowl Falls, Arthur's Pass.*

The township is named after the Pass and there is now a National Park named after the township. The Pass itself crosses the main divide of the Southern

Alps at an altitude of 920 m. The scenery over this section of road is quite magnificent, but the nature of the road combined with possible windy conditions, prohibits it to caravans, trailers, and vehicles over 13 m long.

Otira is on the western side of the Pass section, while the

Arthur's Pass township is at the eastern end. The Pass was named after Arthur Dobson who discovered this road route from Canterbury to the west coast goldfields in 1864. This was perhaps the last road in New Zealand over which the horse drawn coaches of Cobb and Co were used regularly. An 8.5 km railway tunnel runs under the Alps between Arthur's Pass town and Otira. The railway line was commenced privately by the Midland Railway Company in 1908, and was finally completed by the Public Works Department in association with the government railways in 1923.

The township has a visitors centre for the surrounding National Park. The Park covers 98 000 ha on both sides of the Main Divide. The western side receives much more rainfall and rainforest covers its slopes and valleys; the eastern side is dryer and is largely beech forest.

## ENVIRONS & ATTRACTIONS
**Visitors Centre** This is open daily and provides information on the park, its tracks, and the area's road and railway history. Some of the many tracks in the park are listed below.
**Daisy Flat Walk** A five-minute walk from the township to the riverside flats for views and a picnic site.
**Bridal Veil Walk** A self-guided nature walk past flora and falls, from the Bealey footbridge at the north-western end of town. Allow 1–1½ hr for the round trip.
**Punchbowl Falls and Track** From the Bealey footbridge this is a 1½ hr roundtrip on a zigzagging track to falls and lookout.
**Dobson Memorial and Walk** At the top of the Pass, 5 km from the town, note a roadside memorial to Arthur Dobson. Opposite the memorial is the start

of two Dobson Nature Walks — either 30 minutes for a short loop, or 90 minutes for a longer loop past alpine tussocks and tarns. 3 km further along the road is a lookout with spectacular alpine scenery.

**See Also** Springfield and Otira

---

# ASHBURTON SI
**Population** 14 030
**Location** On Route 1, 87 km south-west of Christchurch, and 77 km north of Timaru.

---

The Rakaia River between Christchurch and Ashburton acted as a formidable obstacle during the early years of settlement on the Canterbury Plains, especially because the stretch south of the Rakaia was a veritable desert. With the eventual bridging of the Rakaia River, Ashburton was able to develop. The surrounding lands — which were either too swampy or too dry — were drained or irrigated and the foundations laid for the granary and pastoral areas of today. Pioneer John Grigg did much for agriculture in the district, and is remembered by his homestead (still occupied), his church, and a statue in Ashburton.

## ENVIRONS & ATTRACTIONS
**Baring Square** A garden square in the middle of town.
**Ashburton Domain** Trees, garden and an artificial lake on West Street (over the railway from East Street — the main road).
**Plains Village** At Tinwald, 4 km south (over the Ashburton River) this is a re-created early village, which also has a Vintage Car Club Museum.
**Plains Railway** On part of the old Mt Somers branchline,

adjacent to Plains Village, a group of enthusiasts have restored vintage engines and rolling stock — in particular an 1878 Rogers K class locomotive. Trains operate on the second Sunday of every month (all Sundays, December–February).

## LOCAL TOURING
**Rakaia** This township is 32 km north, on the south bank of the Rakaia River. The bridge over the Rakaia River is 1.75 km, the longest bridge in New Zealand.

**Ashburton Walkway** A 5½ hr (19 km) walk from the Ashburton Bridge along the riverbank of the Ashburton River to the sea.

**Sea Also** Christchurch, Methven, Geraldine and Timaru

# ATIAMURI NI
**Population** 170
**Location** On Route 1, 113 km south of Hamilton.

While Atiamuri is possibly little more than a crossroads in the centre of the world's largest artificial forest, there are several items of interest in the area. Atiamuri is centred at the junction of Route 30 (from Te Kuiti and Mangakino) with Route 1 near the Atiamuri hydro-electric dam on the Waikato River. The locality of Upper Atiamuri is centred on Route 1, 5 km further north where Route 30 branches off again to Rotorua.

## ENVIRONS & ATTRACTIONS
**Atiamuri Power Station** This is situated adjacent to the intersection of Route 30 and Route 1 on the Waikato River. There are roads to view the dam and a picnic area by the lake.

**Ohakuri Power Station** This is another hydro-electric dam on a side road leading off from Route 1 a little to the south of Atiamuri, also on the Waikato River. A road gives access to the viewing area of the dam.

## LOCAL TOURING
**Whakamaru Power Station** Located 21 km from Atiamuri on Route 30, it is a pleasant drive to this large power station on the Waikato River. Nearby is the centre that controls the output of all nine dams on the river and also controls much of the North Island's electrical power. The road traverses the dam.

**Mangakino** This town was built as a construction town and remains a servicing centre for the several hydro-electric power stations in the area. The town is on the banks of the Waikato River on a side road off Route 30, 7 km from Whakamaru.

**Maraetai Power Stations** A loop road beyond Mangakino gives access to Maraetai One and Maraetai Two dams and power stations on the Waikato River. Take the short walk to a lookout, for a view over both dams.

**Waipapa Power Station** 18 km beyond Mangakino the river goes through a gorge and has now been dammed by this power station.

**Orakei Korako** This hidden thermal valley is on a side road between Route 1 and Route 5, south of Atiamuri. It can be reached by jetboat across the Waikato River. Part of the thermal area was flooded when the Ohakuri Dam was built and the lake built up behind it. However, there is a walking track around geysers, terraces, boiling mud and thermal springs in the remaining area. The reserve is open daily and probably takes at least 1½ hr to see, including the river crossing.

**See Also** Tokoroa, Rotorua, Taupo and Te Kuiti

# AUCKLAND NI

**Population** 887 448
**Location** Latitude 36.51 south
and longitude 176.45 east. On
Route 1, 660 km north of
Wellington.

Auckland is the name given to the
area administered by the local
body Auckland City Council
(ACC). However, it also usually
applies to the greater metropolitan
area including the areas of other
local bodies surrounding the ACC
area. This greater area is the one
used by this publication.

Auckland is New Zealand's
largest metropolitan centre, by
both area and population. It is
New Zealand's greatest
commercial and industrial centre
and is the major entry point for
visitors from overseas. It is
situated on the shores of
Waitemata Harbour, which is an
inlet of the Hauraki Gulf. The
central part of the city, and all of
the ACC area, is on an isthmus
between the Waitemata Harbour
and the adjacent Manukau
Harbour — the former being an
inlet from the east coast and the
latter from the west coast. The
isthmus is broadly 11 km wide,
but can be narrower in places.
The extremities of the isthmus,
marked by Portage Road,
Otahuhu, and Portage Road, New
Lynn, are very narrow points
between river accesses and were
used by Maoris to take their
canoes overland. The Hauraki
Gulf has a number of inhabited
islands.

There are 14 extinct volcanoes
on the isthmus from which
extensive views are currently
available. The remains of terraces
on many of these peaks indicate
their earlier use as Maori pas.
There were 63 eruption points in
the greater Auckland area. All are
now dormant — the most recent

*A marina on Auckland Harbour.*

volcanic activity possibly being
the formation of the island of
Rangitoto approximately 750
years ago. The triple-peaked
Rangitoto joins with the 1020 m
long arched bridge (open 1959)
across the Waitemata Harbour in
being symbols of Auckland.

Auckland was originally settled
by descendants of the Maori
canoe *Tainui* — possibly about
1350 — but the greatest
concentration of population in
Maori times was probably during
the mid-18th century when the
Maori Chief Kiwi Tamaki ruled
the area from his Maungakiekie

(One Tree Hill) pa. By the time Europeans settled in the area in 1840, the Maori population was markedly diminished.

Auckland was named after Lord Auckland, Viceroy of India (whose family name was Eden) by Captain W. Hobson. He was the first governor of New Zealand and selected the area as the seat of government after a short spell when it was in the Bay of Islands. The original purchase price for downtown Auckland as far inland as Mt Eden was 55 pounds plus an assortment of blankets, trousers, axes and similar items.

In 1841 the population had swollen to 1500 people but the first true migrant ships — the *Duchess of Argyle* and *Jane Gifford* from Scotland — did not arrive until 1842. Parliament was opened in 1854 but the capital was transferred to Wellington in 1865. Auckland later became a city in 1871.

In 1847 the then Governor, Sir George Grey, raised a military corps in England called the Royal New Zealand Fencibles. They were retired British troops who accepted free travel and accommodation here on the basis

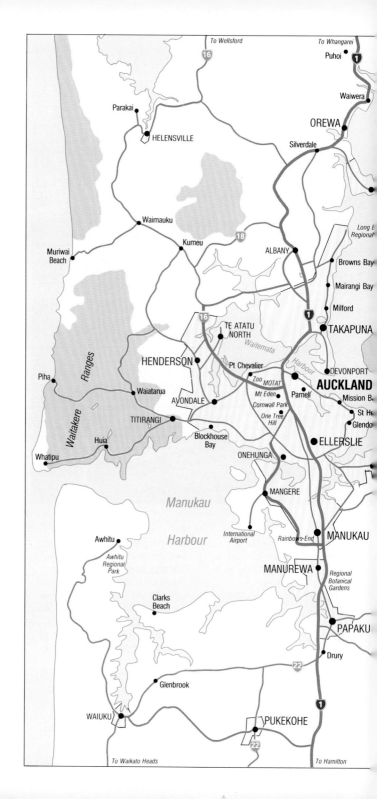

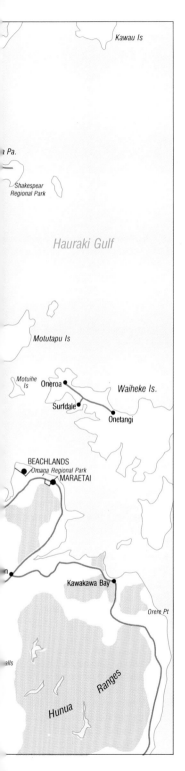

Kawau Is

a Pa.

Shakespear
Regional Park

Hauraki Gulf

Motutapu Is

Motuihe
Is      Oneroa

Surfdale      Waiheke Is.

Onetangi

BEACHLANDS
Omana Regional Park
MARAETAI

Kawakawa Bay

Orere Pt

alls

Ranges

Hunua

of doing seven years 'guard duty' to defend Auckland against possible Maori uprisings. Fencible settlements were founded in Onehunga, Otahuhu, Panmure and Howick.

However, when the Maori land wars did eventuate, British troops and local recruits were called in. After the Waikato Wars, Auckland's population declined because the British troops were recalled, settlers moved on to confiscated Waikato lands, government workers were transferred to Wellington and settlers were lured by the call of gold from the South Island. The decline, however, was only temporary and when gold was found in the Coromandel area, the city flourished once more.

A noted benefactor and public figure (and briefly mayor) in Auckland's early history was Sir John Campbell, who became involved with the founding of the Auckland Savings Bank, Bank of New Zealand, New Zealand Insurance, New Zealand Shipping, as well as newspaper and brewery interests. He gave the city his One Tree Hill estate 'Cornwall Park', which remains a public area.

Auckland's first railway line went to suburban Onehunga (on the Manukau Harbour) in 1873. Railway connected Auckland with Wellington in 1908.

Auckland is a major sea port, centred mainly on the Waitemata Harbour. There are ferry boat services to the North Shore and Gulf islands. There is also an International Airport in the suburb of Mangere (Manukau City). Mechanics Bay on the Waitemata Harbour is used by amphibian aircraft for local flights and services to Gulf islands. There is a suburban motorway system to northern, western and southern suburbs. The city now has a large Pacific Island population in addition to 'Pakehas' (Europeans) and Maoris.

The city has many sporting venues including beaches, pools, racecourses and sporting arenas. The world's largest one-day yachting regatta is held at the end of January each year.

The central business district surrounds the main shopping thoroughfare Queen Street. Karangahape Road and Newmarket are also important central shopping areas. There are many other suburban and satellite shopping centres. Parnell and Victoria Markets have been redeveloped as tourist centres. Downtown views may be obtained from the top floors of the ACC Administration building and the Bank of New Zealand Tower in Queen Street. Notable buildings in the downtown area include the Ferry buildings (1912); the old Customhouse Building (1889); and the High Court (1868), which is built like a castle with the figures of Queen Victoria, Socrates and Hone Heke carved on it. The Auckland Town Hall was built in 1911 and a statue of Lord Auckland (a gift from Calcutta) stands nearby. The Auckland Art Gallery and Auckland Public Library have extensive collections including rare books and early collections, which can be viewed by arrangement.

Albert Park near the downtown area was the site of Colonial Barracks, where more than 900 troops used to camp. It was adjacent to Fort Britomart — the walls of which still run through the University grounds nearby. St Paul's Anglican Church — Auckland's first church — was built in 1841. St Andrew's Presbyterian Church was built in 1849; St Patrick's Catholic Cathedral in 1846. The 1888 Cathedral Church of St Mary now adjoins and contrasts with the newer Holy Trinity Cathedral on the corner of St Stephen's Avenue, Parnell. Selwyn Court and Bishop Court, which were built as residences for the Bishop, are adjacent. Selwyn came to New Zealand in 1842 as a missionary and was responsible for many distinctively styled churches in the Auckland area. Another church of interest is St Matthew's in Hobson Street.

## ENVIRONS & ATTRACTIONS

**Mount Eden** Known as Maungawhau, this is Auckland's highest peak (195 m). Take the road to the top for views.

**One Tree Hill** Known as Maungakiekie, this 183 m peak now has three trees and the grave of Sir John Campbell on its summit. Adjacent is Cornwall Park, which was given to the city by Campbell and which contains his 1841 'Acacia Cottage'.

**Auckland Domain and Museum** These extensive parklands contain a museum, gardens and tropical winter houses. The large museum (open daily 10 am–5 pm in the summer, closes at 4.15 pm in winter) features New Zealand's largest collection of Maori carvings and artifacts, as well as South Pacific artifacts, a centennial street and war relics. The museum is a War Memorial.

**Kelly Tarlton's Underwater World** On Tamaki Drive at Okahu Bay and open daily 9 am–9 pm, this complex features a pedestrian conveyor, which carries visitors through a large aquarium tank that is filled with New Zealand marine life.

**Museum of Transport and Technology** Known as MOTAT for short, this complex includes cars, a railway, trams, aircraft, printing machinery and a colonial village. Situated on Great North Road, Grey Lynn, it is open daily

*Auckland Museum and the Cenotaph on Anzac Day.*

9 am–5 pm. Western Springs park is adjacent.

**Auckland Zoological Park** Situated in Motions Road Westmere (near MOTAT and Western Springs park) this facility is open daily. It houses a general selection of animals, including many New Zealand species.

**Judges Bay** This area in Parnell has a park and salt water baths. Note St Stephen's Chapel, which was built in 1856.

**Rose Gardens** Located in Gladstone Road, Parnell, these gardens are open daily but best seen from November to March. They feature displays of more than 4000 roses, native trees and shrubs.

**Waterfront Drive** From downtown Auckland, Tamaki Drive leads along the Waitemata Harbour to the Bays of Hobson, Okahu, Mission, Kohimarama and St Heliers. A Melanesian mission building, built in 1860, is near the fountain at Mission Bay. Archilles Point lookout is at the end of the road. The Lilliput amusement park is situated at Hobson Bay.

**Orakei Marae** This unique multicultural Marae is in Kitemoana Street, Okahu Bay. Open Mon–Fri 9 am–4 pm.

**Savage Memorial Park** The monument on Bastion Point (Hapimana Street off Tamaki Drive) is a memorial to the first Labour Prime Minister Michael Joseph Savage (1872–1940). The park is also a good area for views of the harbour.

*The Winter Gardens in Auckland.*

**Tahuna–Torea Nature Reserve** This 28 ha sandspit at Glendowie leads into the Tamaki River and features up to 600 bird species.

**Ewelme Cottage** At 14 Ayr Street, Parnell, this house was built by Reverend Lush in 1864; it still houses original furniture and effects. Open daily 10.30 am–noon, 1–4.30 pm.

**Kinder House** At 2 Ayr Street, Parnell, this house was built in 1857 by artist and photographer Reverend John Kinder.

**Highwic** 40 Gilles Avenue, Epsom. This house, which was built in 1862, belonged to gentleman landowner Alfred Buckland. Open daily.

**Alberton** 100 Mt Albert Road, Mount Albert. This 1862 establishment of the Kerr-Taylor family reflects their wealth (founded on gold) and high society background.

**New Zealand Heritage Park** Located at Mt Wellington on the Ellerslie–Panmure Highway, open daily 10.30 am–noon, 1–4.30 pm. Features Maori culture, agriculture and native plants and birds.

**Renall Street** Preserved Ponsonby Street of 19th century artisan houses, which are not open to the public.

**Ellerslie Racecourse** Leading racecourse in Greenlane, Remuera. Gardens open daily. Auckland also has a racecourse at Avondale and a trotting course (harness racing) at Epsom.

**Onehunga Fencibles Cottage** This fencible cottage and blockhouse are in Jellicoe Park and date back to 1847.

**Eden Garden** An old quarry that has been transformed into a landscape garden. Omana Road, Epsom.

**Other Parks** There are many other parks in the Auckland isthmus area, including Pt Chevalier and Blockhouse Bay. Most of the volcanic peaks also have park or open land on them.

## LOCAL TOURING

### NORTHERN SUBURBS

**Devonport** Marine suburb, situated across Auckland Harbour (short ferry ride). Also location of Navy base and Naval Museum (in Spring Street, open 10 am–3.30 pm).

**North Head** This reserve, which is situated on a volcanic peak, was once a military fort. Provides good views of the harbour.

**North Shore Scenic Reserves** Includes Kauri Park Reserve, Kauri Glen Reserve, Lee Roys Bush and Eskdale Reserve. There are bush walks through these native forest reserves, which are surrounded by suburban housing.

**North Shore Beaches** These beaches front onto the Hauraki Gulf. North from Devonport they are Cheltenham, Takapuna (possibly the most popular), Milford, Castor Bay, Campbells Bay, Muirangi Bay, Browns Bay, Torbay and Long Bay (also a regional park).

**Silverdale Pioneer Village** Victorian buildings including a craft gallery, with early church and school.

**Whangaparoa Peninsula** Jutting out into the Hauraki Gulf, this peninsula offers several

*The ferry boat* Toroa *on the run from Devonport to the city.*

beaches (including Stanmore Bay and Manly) and the Shakespeare regional park. 37 km from downtown Auckland.

**Orewa** Known as the 'Hibiscus Coast', 40 km from downtown Auckland. Features 3 km of splendid beach and a Leisureland amusement park.

**Waiwera** 48 km from downtown Auckland. Beach with nearby hot springs, pools and play area.

**Wenderholme** Beach reserve on side road north of Waiwera, on the site of an early homestead.

**Puhoi** Small bohemian

settlement established in 1863, on side road north of Waiwera. Note the churches of St Peter and St Paul, built in 1881, and the local tavern featuring early memorabilia.

**WESTERN SUBURBS**
**Waitakere Scenic Drive** The Waitakere Ranges feature the Auckland Centennial Park (6400 ha), established in 1940. There are 132 named tracks in the bush-clad ranges and the native trees include kauri. The park area is now administered by the

Auckland Regional Authority. A large water catchment restricted area is adjacent. The scenic drive from Henderson via Titirangi leads around to Ranui and Swanson. Waitakere peaks include Mt Atkinson (at Titirangi) and Pukematekeo — both accessible by road for views. Note the Arataki information centre and nature trail on the scenic drive 6 km past Titirangi.

**Piha** West coast surfing beach 40 km via Waitakere Centennial Park. Includes beaches and walking tracks. Other west coast beaches are Kare Kare, Bethels and Whatipu. Also note the Lake Wainamu scenic reserve at Bethels and the Cascades reserve off the Bethels road.

**Waitakere Walks** Of the many walking tracks, popular ones include Cascade tracks, Upper and Lower Kauri tracks, Ferry Falls track, Waitakere Dam Access track and Tramline track. Refer to the Arataki information centre for details.

**Huia Road** Several beaches on the Manukau Harbour, including

Cornwallis and Huia, branch off the scenic drive via Titirangi. The road continues to Whatipu at the northern Manukau Head. An old logging railway once connected Whatipu with Kare Kare and remains are still visible. From Titirangi, side roads lead down to the small beaches of Titirangi, Wood and French Bays. A track up Mt Donald McLean gives extensive views of the surrounding ranges and Manukau Harbour.

**Something Different: (formerly) Footrot Flats** A leisure and amusement park at Te Atatu, which is open daily 10 am–6 pm. A lion park is currently planned adjacent to the park.

**Fire Mountain** Pioneer farm, open weekends and school holidays 10 am–5 pm.

**Vineyards** About a dozen wineries are located at Henderson, 18 km from downtown Auckland. A further eight wineries can be found at Kumeu, 25 km from downtown Auckland. Many are open for sampling and some have restaurants.

### EASTERN SUBURBS
**Musick Point** This headland offers a good view of Hauraki Gulf. A marine radio station commemorates Captain Musick, who died in 1939 during an American survey flight from the United States.

**Howick** 23 km from downtown Auckland. This early fencible settlement is now a built-up suburb. Features All-Saints Church, which was built by Selwyn in 1847.

**Howick Colonial Village** This re-created fencible settlement, which includes houses, courthouse and church, is in Bells Road, Pakuranga. Open daily 10 am–4 pm.

**Beaches** Beaches of note include the Eastern beach on the Hauraki Gulf and Bucklands Beach on the Tamaki River. Further out are Maraetai and the Omana regional reserve.

**Clevedon** A rural, satellite township 15 km east of Papakura. It was also the site of a military redoubt during the Maori wars. It used to be possible to navigate the Wairoa River to Clevedon.

**Kawakawa Bay and Orere Point** Small coastal beach communities fronting the Firth of Thames around from Clevedon. Orere Point is on a short side road.

**Waharau** Regional reserve on the coastal road down the western side of the Firth of Thames, between Clevedon and Waitakaruru. Picnic sites and bush walks.

**Miranda** Hot springs on the coastal road along the Firth of Thames. Open daylight hours every day except Tuesday.

### SOUTHERN SUBURBS
**Manukau City** This is the most populous New Zealand local body area. The largest-covered shopping mall in New Zealand is at the Manukau City Centre. Auckland (Mangere) International Airport is also in the Manukau City area.

**Rainbows End** Adventure and amusement park on Great South Road, adjacent to Manukau City Centre. Open daily.

**Auckland Regional Botanical Gardens** These 64 ha gardens on Hill Road, Manurewa, are open 9 am–5 pm daily. There are horticultural displays, walks and information.

**Papakura** This southern suburb 20 km from Auckland has a Selwyn Chapel built in 1862 on Coles Crescent. Also note the first Presbyterian church (now a hall) built here in 1863 and fortified during the Waikato unrests.

Nearby is the site of Pukekiwiriki pa and a 200 m bush walk.

**Murphy's Bush** A reserve of mature New Zealand bush with picnic sites and walks.

**Nathan Park** A community and craft centre in Hill Road, Manurewa.

**Hunua Falls** Picnic area in the Hunua Ranges. There are also five water supply dams in these ranges but not all are readily accessible.

**See Also** Helensville, Pukekohe, Waiuku and Warkworth.

## HAURAKI GULF

This area covers the body of water between the Coromandel Peninsula and the mainland, including a number of islands, some of which are under the control of the Hauraki Gulf Maritime Park. Access to many of the islands is by scheduled ferry or sightseeing launch/catarmaran trips from near the Ferry buildings at the bottom of Queen Street. Some islands are also accessible by amphibian aircraft from Mechanics Bay.

**Great Barrier** This rugged, remote, 28 000 ha island is 90 km from Auckland. Notable settlements are Port Fitzroy and Tryphena.

**Little Barrier** This island is 80 km from Auckland and has restricted access as a wild life sanctuary.

**Goat Island** A reserve near Leigh, north of Auckland. It is also the site of Auckland University's Marine Biology laboratory. The area is noted for its variety of fish.

**Kawau** Retired homestead of Governor Grey at Mansion House, built in 1862. This island (60 km from Auckland) has old copper mine remains and is a haven for yachts. Regular daily launch access is from Sandspit, near Warkworth.

**Tiri Tiri** This small island off the Whangaparaoa Peninsula has restricted access. It is crowned by a large lighthouse.

**Rangitoto** This unique, 2300 ha volcanic island with a scoria surface is only 750 years old. There is a 4 km walk to the summit.

**Motutapu** Farm land, which is adjacent to Rangitoto.

**Motuahie** This 179 ha island was once a quarantine station, a prisoner-of-war camp, and a children's health camp. It has two beaches and is now largely farmed.

**Waiheke** Large (9900 ha) and most populous island with farms and also commuter settlements, at Onetangi, Surfdale and Oneroa. A frequent passenger service leaves from Auckland Ferry Buildings; there is also vehicular ferry service from Pakuranga. Buses meet passenger ferries.

**Pakatoa** Private holiday resort island at the far end of Waiheke.

**Moturoa** Private island, which includes a Salvation Army camp.

**Browns Island** Off Musick Point; restricted access.

# AWAKINO NI
**Population** 131
**Location** On Route 3, 76 km south of Te Kuiti and 5 km north of Mokau.

This small settlement is on the west coast of the North Island, at the mouth of the Awakino River — a seemingly remote area. The road from Te Kuiti follows the pretty Awakino River for part of its route. There is a rugged and exposed beach. The settlement has a craft shop and a museum; nearby is an aquarium. The Maniaroa Marae, which has been recently restored, is 2.5 km south. Also refer to our listing for Mokau.

**See Also** Te Kuiti, Waitomo Caves and Mokau

# B

## BALCLUTHA SI
**Population** 4227
**Location** On Route 1, 24 km south of Milton, 71 km north-east of Gore.

Situated on the main road and railway between Dunedin and Invercargill, and astride the important, fast-flowing Clutha River, Balclutha is the principal distribution and servicing centre for the farming districts of South Otago.

The Clutha River is almost as long as the North Island's Waikato River, but it has twice the water volume. The river was an active waterway during the gold rushes with boats going upstream as far as Tuapeka Mouth. Between Balclutha and the sea, the river is divided by an island called Inchclutha. Port Molyneux near the southern branch was an active port for 30 years. The distinctive concrete bridge at Balclutha was erected in 1935 and is the third on the site which was originally the location of the punt crossing.

*Grain fields around Gore, Southland.*

## LOCAL TOURING

**Kaitangata** This coal town is situated 12 km east of Balclutha by Route 91. Its coal mines were active from 1869 through to 1970; an underground explosion in 1879 killed 34 men.

**Wangaloa Domain** This picnic area and beach is 6 km past Kaitangata.

**Lake Tuakitoto** A shallow lake and wildlife sanctuary 6 km north-west of Kaitangata.

**Port Molyneux** There is little left here except the cemetery from which there is a magnificent coastal view over Molyneux Bay and the Lower Clutha. 19 km from Balclutha.

**Kaka Point** Beach locality 21 km south-east of Balclutha.

**Nugget Point** Features rocks, a lighthouse and seal colony. 29 km from Balclutha.

**Tuapeka Mouth** The Tuapeka River meets the Clutha at this point, which was also the upriver limit for steamers. Historically it was a favoured place for a ferry crossing in early days. Road access is along the northern bank of the Clutha River.

**Clinton** Farming and fishing centre 31 km west on Route 1.

**See also** Milton, Gore and Owaka

# BANKS PENINSULA SI

Refer Akaroa

---

# BAY OF ISLANDS NI

Including Paihia, Waitangi and Russell

**Population** 4615

**Location** Paihia is 241 km north of Auckland.

---

'Bay of Islands' is an all-embracing term that includes the waters and islands of the bay, and three of the communities around it. Some definitions of the area would include Kawakawa, Kerikeri, and even Kaikohe; these three, however, are covered separately in this publication.

The Bay of Islands Maritime and Historic Park is an internationally acclaimed area of coastal beauty, which contains more than 800 km of indented coastline, 150 islands and numerous mainland reserves. Apart from the renowned sailing and big-game fishing, the park has much to offer the visitor on the mainland in and around the main resorts of Russell and Paihia. The area is of great historical importance, centred around the Treaty House at Waitangi, where the Treaty of Waitangi was signed in 1840.

The Bay of Islands is known as the cradle of New Zealand, because of the important place it holds in this country's history. When the white men came to New Zealand, an extensive Maori population already inhabited the far north and these Maoris had the most contact with the Europeans. Navigators and explorers came first, then whalers and sealers, followed by the timber seekers. In their search for goods, including fresh water and food, the crews of some of these ships were lawless troublemakers.

The Bay of Islands became 'the hell hole of the South Pacific' between 1830 and 1840, when there were more than 200 Europeans in the Bay and at times 20 ships at anchor. It was a period of disreputable lawlessness, because there was no responsible authority to make and administer laws or to punish offenders. Eventually in 1832 the New South Wales authorities persuaded a reluctant British Government to appoint a 'British Resident', James Busby, whose house still stands at Waitangi. He had no executive power and could only report to Sydney or London and persuade troublemakers against lawlessness by his presence.

Against this background a chain of missionary stations was established, beginning with Samuel Marsden's mission in 1814. The missionaries taught English, religion, European agriculture, industry and art to the Maoris.

Although New Zealand had been claimed by Britain and was overseen, but not really administered, by the New South Wales government, there was still a fear that the French would take over. This fear may have contributed to the reluctant decision made by the British Government to annex New Zealand. Captain Hobson was appointed Lieutenant Governor, and arrived in the Bay of Islands at the end of January 1840. On 6 February, Maori chiefs assembled at Busby's residency at Waitangi and signed a Treaty in which they seeded sovereignty over the country to the Queen, in return for a guarantee of their possession of the land. On 8 February, the Colony of New Zealand was proclaimed and Hobson chose Okiato as the site of

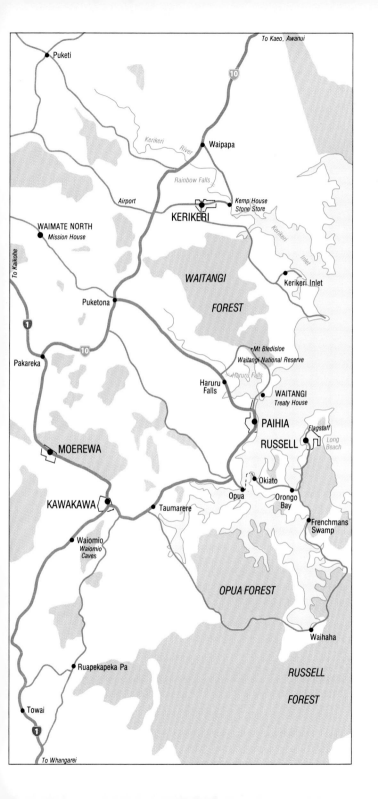

*Opua, Bay of Islands.*

his capital, which today is just above the landing of the vehicular ferry from Opua to Russell. Later that year he abandoned Okiato for a new settlement in Auckland.

Some of the chiefs who had signed the Treaty of Waitangi, notably Hone Heke, Kawiti and Pomare, were dissatisfied with the government control of land sales and openly challenged government authority by acts of war. In March 1845, Heke cut down the flagstaff carrying the Union Jack on the hill behind Russell, and Kawiti burned and sacked the town sparing only churches and missionary property. The following year Heke destroyed three more replacement flagstaffs. In the ensuing war the rebel strongholds were captured, not without difficulty, by the

British troops. The war ended in 1846 when the new Governor, Sir George Grey, captured Kawiti's pa at Ruapekapeka.

Paihia is the leading resort and tourist centre in the Bay Of Islands. It has a shopping area and a good supply of accommodation. It spreads out over three bays, but the central bay is the centre of the settlement. All three bays are suitable for swimming.

Paihia wharf is the departure point for regular ferry passenger services to Russell (vehicle service operates from Opua), and is also a departure point for launch trips around the Bay of Islands. Amphibious aircraft operate from here to Auckland; regular land-based aircraft fly from Kerikeri. Scheduled coach services

depart here for other parts of Northland and Auckland, and there are daily coach tours to Cape Reinga.

Waitangi is 2 km around the bay from Paihia. It consists of a hotel and the Waitangi National Reserve, which includes the Treaty House and a Maori memorial meeting house.

Across the harbour from Paihia is Russell (previously called Kororareka), which was an early lawless frontier town. Now it is a quiet resort — almost a backwater because its road access remains poor. Use the vehicular ferry from Opua if you require your vehicle on the other side. There are frequent passenger ferries from Paihia. Russell is the centre for big-game fishing in the area.

## ENVIRONS & ATTRACTIONS

**Church of St Paul** The present church, on the main foreshore road, is a memorial to the missionary Williams brothers, and is the fourth church on this site. New Zealand's first church (1823) once stood here. Colenso's early printing press (1834) on which the New Testament was printed in the Maori language, stood adjacent to the church.

**Shipwreck Museum** This is a renovated barque on which marine relics and treasures are displayed. Open 9 am–5.30 pm daily.

**Opua** Once the port for the Bay of Islands, and now the berth for the vehicular ferry to Russell. It is also the terminus for the original government railway, which is now operated as a tourist train to Kawakawa.

## WAITANGI BLEDISLOE

It is a 3 km drive past the Reserve to a hilltop lookout for a view over the Bay of Islands.

**Maori Centennial Memorial meeting house**  This contains carvings from many different North Island Maori tribes and was erected in 1940. A 36 m carved canoe is adjacent. Plaques to Captain Hobson and Captain Nias (Captain of the ship that brought Hobson to New Zealand) are in the grounds of the reserve.

**Treaty House**  Built in 1833 for the British Resident James Busby. In front the flagpole marks the spot where the Treaty was signed 6 February 1840. This day remains an annual public holiday in New Zealand. The Treaty House is now surrounded by the Waitangi National Reserve, and functions as a museum, containing memorabilia of the times, which includes a copy of the treaty. Open daily 9 am–5 pm.

**Waitangi National Marae**  This meeting area for all Maoris is on the Paihia side of the river.

## RUSSELL

**Captain Cook Memorial Museum and Russell Centennial Museum**

This houses a model of Cook's ship *Endeavour* and also other historical items from the Russell area.

**Christ Church**  Built in 1836, this is New Zealand's oldest surviving church. In its early days it served as a public hall and courthouse and still bears the scars of an armed conflict between Hone Heke's 'rebels' and crew from HMS *Hazard* in 1845. Graves in the churchyard include those of the sailors killed, one of the first European girls born in New Zealand, and Tamatiwakanene, a chief who favoured the Waitangi treaty.

**Flagstaff Hill**  Otherwise known as Maiki Hill, this is the location of the celebrated flagpole that Hone Heke chopped down four times. There is a good view from the hilltop. A short steep road leads up from Russell, and is a 10–15 minute walk.

**Long Beach**  This sandy beach is 1 km over the hill behind Russell.

**Pompallier House**  The ground floor of this house was built in 1842 to accommodate the printing press for Bishop Pompallier's Roman Catholic mission. It was later sold to James Greenaway who added the second storey and also the ornate features that are now evident. Although the Bishop did not actually live here, the building is now a museum depicting exhibits from the life and times of the mission.

## LOCAL TOURING

**Cream Trip**  This launch trip, which operates daily, takes its name from the days when its service handled mail and supplies. It now gives a 64 km tourist trip around the Bay of Islands, which takes at least 4½ hr (including stops). Other trips available include a half-day trip to Cape Brett, and various lunch and dinner cruises. These trips operate from both Paihia and Russell.

**Haruru Falls**  These falls on the Waitangi River are situated 3 km from Paihia on the road out to the Puketona Corner. There is road access and short walks.

**Cape Reinga**  Day trips by bus are available, including trips to Ninety Mile Beach. If you are driving yourself, refer to separate information under Kaitaia and Cape Reinga.

**Waimate North Mission House**  Refer to Kaikohe.

**Day Trip Ideas**  Kaitaia, Cape Reinga and Waipoua Forest.

**See Also**  Kawakawa, Kerikeri and Kaikohe

# BLENHEIM SI

**Population** 18 308
**Location** Near the top of the
South Island, on Route 1, 28 km
south of Picton, and 312 km north
of Christchurch.

This town, which regularly holds
the sunshine record for the
country, is situated on the Wairau
Plains at the junction of two rivers
— the Taylor and the Opawa. The
latter used to provide limited port
facilities, however, the area's
main port is now Picton.

Blenheim was originally called
Beaver Town, but changed to its
present name in 1859. The first
Europeans settled here around
1852. With the discovery of a
small goldfield inland near
Canvastown, Blenheim rapidly
increased in population.

The Wairau Plains area,
however, achieved notoriety in
1831 when a Captain Blenkinsopp
made a fraudulent land deal with
Te Rauparaha. In 1839 the
questionable land deed was sold
to Colonel William Wakefield of
the New Zealand Company. The
Company had established a
settlement at Nelson, but the
settlers looked with envy at the
Wairau Plains. When they came
to take up their land, however,
they ran into Maori resistance.

In June 1843 a group of settlers
set out to have discussions with
Te Rauparaha, but when one of
the settlers fired a rifle, the Maoris
launched into battle, killing
22 Europeans and losing 6 of their
own people. This incident, known
as the Wairau Massacre, occurred
at Tuamarina, which is 9 km
north of Blenheim. The location
of the skirmish is marked.

Eventually, Governor Grey
negotiated a new land purchase
and settlement took place.
Blenheim and Picton vied with
each other to be capital of the
recently formed (and temporary)
Marlborough province. The
province was named after the
Duke of Marlborough who led
British troops to victory over the
French at Blenheim in Germany.
Picton was one of the Duke's
Generals, who later died at
Waterloo.

Blenheim is linked by railway
with Picton and Christchurch.
There are scheduled air services
through Woodebburne Airfield.

The Wairau and the Awatere
are the two biggest rivers in the
area. The Wairau River descends
into a scenic valley, but empties
into marshes and lagoons near
the coast.

The Picton area and the
Marlborough Sounds provide
unlimited tourist possibilities.
Note also the Picton routes via
Port Underwood or via Havelock
and the Grove Road, both of
which can form an interesting
round trip journey from
Blenheim.

## ENVIRONS & ATTRACTIONS

**Market Place** Commercial
centre of the town, with main
shopping streets adjacent.
**Seymour Square** Gardens and
memorial clock tower, one block
from Market Place.
**Pollard Park** Waterlea Gardens,
rose gardens and rockery, in
Parker Street.
**Brayshaw Museum Park** How
Blenheim may have looked 100
years ago, with re-created
buildings, farm implements, also
model boats and miniature
railway. Near Renwick Road.
**Riverlands Cob Cottage**
Restored cottage with period
furnishings, built in 1860. It is
located 5 km south on Route 1.

## LOCAL TOURING

**Tuamarina** Roadside cairn and
hilltop cemetery for victims of the
Wairau massacre. 9 km north on
Route 1.

**Onamalutu Domain** 29 km out of Blenheim on Route 6, take the North Bank Road after crossing the Wairau River, for picnic area, bush walks and longer tramps to Mt Boldy. 20 km further is Pine Valley Road, which leads to Fishtail Flat bush and picnic area.

**Withers Hills Walkway** 2½ hr round trip walk with a lookout over the plains (and to the North Island). Start and finish at Taylors Pass Road, 4 km out of Blenheim.

**Wairau Lagoon Walk** From Harding Street, 7 km south, this 3-hr family walk is through 2000 ha of Wairau delta wetlands.

**Vineyards and Wineries** The Wairau Plains is an important grape growing and wine

*Hawkdun Range, Canterbury.*

producing area with at least five vineyards. Enquire locally for addresses and details of which vineyards allow sampling (and buying!).

**Argyle Hydro Lake** Part of the Branch River power project up the Wairau Valley on Route 63.

**Lake Grassmere** Salt works where salt is obtained by evaporating sea water in large ponds — for both industrial and table use. 32 km south on Route 1.

**Molesworth** New Zealand's largest sheep station is 93 km along a no-exit road up the Awatere Valley. Occasionally, there are organised tours to the Station and sometimes access is permitted on the restricted road through to Hanmer Springs.

**See Also** Picton, Havelock, St Arnaud and Kaikoura

# BULLS NI

**Population** 1799

**Location** Intersection of Routes 1 and 3, 40 km south-east of Wanganui, and 30 km north-west of Palmerston North.

The town of Bulls is a Manawatu crossroads, founded by James Bull (a hotelier and woodcarver) in 1859. A major airforce base is nearby at Ohakea. 6 km south at Sanson, where Routes 1 and 3 separate again, is the site of the old northern terminus of a bush tramway from Foxton and Himatangi, in use between 1885 and 1945.

## LOCAL TOURING

**Dudding Lake** A reserve and picnic spot 14 km north-east on Route 3.

**Ratana** A township off Route 3, 26 km north-west of Bulls. Headquarters of the Ratana Church. This movement was founded by Wiremu Ratana in 1818 as a Maori form of Christianity. There is a conference centre (Te Manuao) and a Ratana Temple (open to the public). There are other Ratana churches throughout New Zealand, which are distinguished by their twin towers.

**See Also** Marton, Wanganui, Feilding and Foxton

*The Church of the Good Shepherd at Lake Tekapo, South Canterbury.*

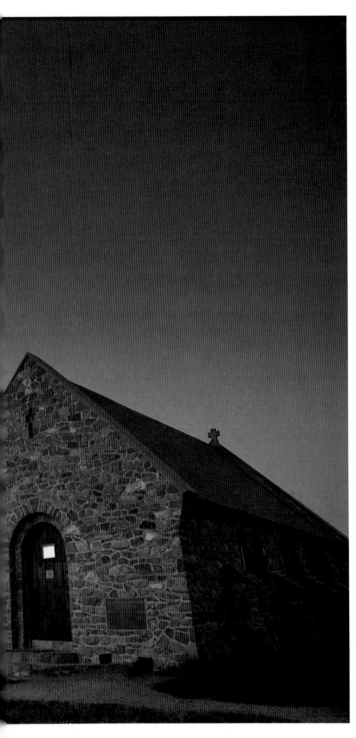

# C

## CAMBRIDGE NI
**Population** 10 145
**Location** On the Waikato River, 24 km south of Hamilton via Route 1.

Cambridge was established as a settlement for military recruits after the Waikato Land Wars in 1864. It has since developed as an English-like rural town, complete with English trees, antique shops and craft centres. There is a 'freight only' branch railway from Hamilton. This town is an important farming centre, especially for horse-racing stables and studs.

### ENVIRONS & ATTRACTIONS
**Cambridge Cultural Centre** A market in the main street for art and craft workers to display their goods, open daily in summer.
**Craft New Zealand** This restored Gothic-style church is now a leading arts and crafts centre. Most goods are available for purchase.
**Te Koutu Domain** This park and lake in the centre of Cambridge is a natural bird sanctuary.

### LOCAL TOURING
**Karapiro** 8 km south of Cambridge on Route 1, there is a short side road to this large hydro-electric power station. There are picnic facilities available. On the other side of the river (road across the dam) is a complex for rowing championships held on the large Karapiro lake, which has formed behind the dam. Back on the main road there is a lookout from Route 1 over the lake area.
**Maungakawa Scenic Reserve** This reserve and Gudex Memorial Park is 8 km north-east on Maungakawa Road up Sanatorium Hill (Pukemako) 384 m. There are picnic grounds, bush walks and walking tracks through the reserve, and extensive views of the Waikato and Hauraki Plains from the summit.
**See Also** Hamilton, Te Awamutu and Putaruru

## CAPE REINGA NI
**Population** 14
**Location** At the top of New Zealand, 114 km from Kaitaia.

Technically the North Cape and its Surville Cliffs are the northernmost parts of the North Island, but Cape Reinga, with its lighthouse, and road access, popularly serves as the top of the north. The surging waters of the Pacific and Tasman Sea meet off-shore, and the Three King Islands are visible on the horizon.

The lighthouse at Cape Reinga is now automatic. Below it lies the little point with its lone pohutakawa tree, from which, Maori legend has it, the spirits of the dead depart for their Pacific homeland of 'Hawaiki'.

Cape Reinga — and New Zealand — was discovered by the Dutchman Abel Tasman in 1642–43, though surprisingly he did not land on New Zealand soil, and later in 1769 by the English navigator Cook, and French explorer de Surville. Cook and de Surville actually passed at Cape Reinga but did not see each other, nor indeed knew of each other's existence.

The National Walkway system commences at Cape Reinga, and several options are available, including walking to Spirits Bay (10 hr), or to the Te Paki stream and Ninety Mile Beach (7 hr).

*Cape Reinga looking back to Motuopao Island.*

Cape Reinga has no commercial facilities.

## ENVIRONS & ATTRACTIONS

**Spirits Bay** This is a fine, almost deserted ocean beach with a camp ground, at the end of an unsealed road from Waitiki Landing.

**Tapotupoto Bay** A short, steep side road branches off near Cape Reinga to lead down to this sheltered bay.

**Te Paki** Now managed as a farm park, Te Paki was New Zealand's northernmost farm, or ranch.

**Waitiki Landing** This is the site of the only shop and restaurant in the Cape Reinga area.

## LOCAL TOURING

**The road to the Cape** At the time of compiling this guide, the last 16 km remains unsealed. The trip out and back from Kaitaia,

Mangonui or Paihia, however, is a popular route. Motorists must take the same road in both directions, while the tour buses on the route use the restricted Te Paki stream access, and return to Kaitaia along Ninety Mile Beach — not recommended for private vehicles.

From Kaitaia the route passes through Awanui, and by the old World War II base at Waipapakauri. Houhora Heads and its Wagener Museum are accessible on a side road. New Zealand's northernmost pub is at Houhora. The white sand in the eastern distance approaching Waitiki Landing is used in glass-making. Godwits assemble here in March to fly to Siberia. Allow up to 2¼ hr each way for this trip.

**See Also** Kaitaia

117

# CHEVIOT SI
**Population** 532
**Location** On Route 1, 74 km south of Kaikoura, 58 km north of Waipara.

This small rural community is set amid the rolling hills and river flats of North Canterbury.

## ENVIRONS & ATTRACTIONS
**Cheviot Hills Domain** A scenic reserve set in the grounds of the former homestead of pioneer landowner William Robinson (1814–89).

## LOCAL TOURING
**Gore Bay** This beach features Robinson's two-storey beach house, and an old cemetery. 8 km south-east.
**Port Robinson** A short walk at the road's end leads to the cove that served Cheviot and the Robinson estate before there were adequate roads. 3 km south of Gore Bay.
**Port Robinson Walkway** A 7 km walk from the Gore Bay Road around Mt Gibson to the mouth of the Hurunui River. There is road access at both ends.

**See Also** Kaikoura, Hanmer Springs and Waipara

# CHRISTCHURCH SI
**Population** 299 373
**Location** On Route 1, 340 km south of Picton, 362 km north of Dunedin.

Christchurch, the 'Garden City', is the largest city in the South Island. It is also considered to be New Zealand's most 'English' city. It is mainly flat, and services the Canterbury region, much of which is also flat. The port is based at Lyttelton, over the Port Hills (or through the tunnel) from

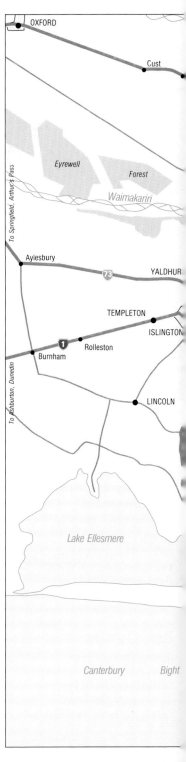

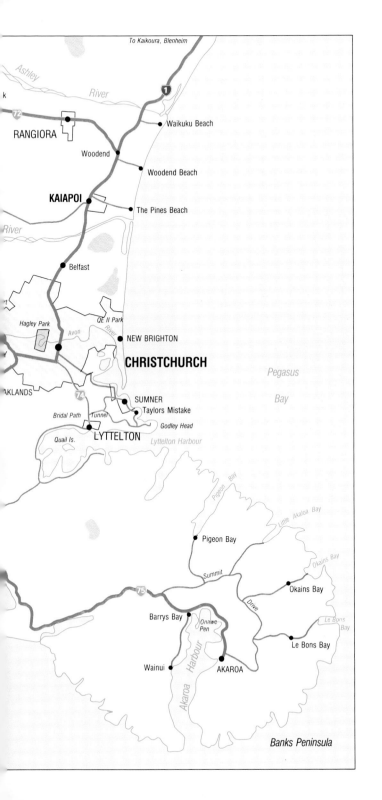

Christchurch. There is an International Airport in the suburb of Harewood. Railway services include scheduled passenger trains north to Blenheim and Picton, south to Dunedin and Invercargill, and west to Greymouth via the Waimakariri Gorge and Arthur's Pass. The short line to Ferrymead on the Heathcote River, established in 1863, was New Zealand's first true railway. For a while that river served as a port for barges from Lyttelton. However, the railway reached Lyttelton by tunnel in 1867.

The Square is the centre of Christchurch. A popular attraction is the Wizard of Christchurch, who provides stimulating and provocative discussion most lunchtimes in the Square.

The first settlers of Christchurch were the Dean brothers who came to the area in 1843. Organised settlement began with the first four ships of the Canterbury Association, which arrived in 1850. The objective was to develop a Church of England colony similar to the Church of Scotland settlement already established in Dunedin. John Robert Godley was the founding father, and the city is named after a college at Oxford, England, where Godley was educated.

Canterbury University is in the suburb of Ilam. Lincoln College is an agricultural university 21 km to the south-west.

Parts of Cashel and High streets are downtown mall streets closed to traffic. Columbo Street is reputedly one of New Zealand's longest straight streets.

To the south-east is the hilly Banks Peninsula with its town of Akaroa — described separately in this guide. The distant foothills of the Southern Alps can also be seen to the west from some parts of the city.

*Sign of the Takahe, Christchurch.*

Day trips by car or bus to Akaroa, or by train to Arthur's Pass or Greymouth, can be considered among Christchurch's touring attractions. Rangiora and Oxford are satellite towns featured separately in this guide, which may have areas of interest for Christchurch travellers.

## ENVIRONS & ATTRACTIONS
**The Square** Central pedestrian area, including a cathedral and a Soldiers War Memorial.
**Christchurch Cathedral** A Gothic-type church, with a 64 m spire. A spiral staircase leads up to a viewpoint (open 9 am–4 pm).

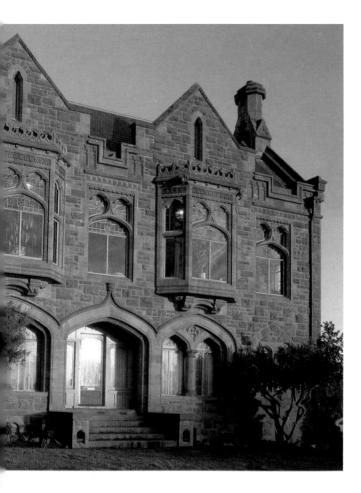

Built between 1864 and 1904, its windows and panels depict early Canterbury events and characters.

**Victoria Square** Originally Market Square, now has a Cook's statue and Bowker fountain, and is one block north of the Square.

**Town Hall** This splendid facility in Kilmore Street has two auditoriums, a restaurant and a fountain, and is next to the Avon River. It was built in 1972.

**Avon River** An attractive stream meandering through the city. Note the Bridge of Remembrance on Cashel Street.

**Riverside Walk** Begins at the west end of Oxford Terrace and follows the Avon to Kilmore Street.

**Hagley Park** 180 ha of gardens, trees and sportsfields, which is bordered by the Avon River on either side of Riccarton Road.

**Millbrook Reserve** A reserve with azaleas, rhododendrons, and gardens, which adjoins Hagley Park.

**Botanic Gardens** Next to Hagley Park. Guided tours 11 am–4 pm daily. Features a conservatory, a tropical plants rose garden, and fern and alpine plant displays.

**Canterbury Museum** Includes special displays of greenstone, a pioneer street, moa bones, and a hall of Antarctic discovery (concentrating especially on Scott). Geologist and explorer Julius Von Haast was the museum's first director. Open daily 10 am–4.30 pm, Rolleston Avenue.

**McDougall Art Gallery** Permanent display and exhibition of art and sculptures. Open daily 10 am–4.30 pm, Rolleston Avenue.

**Brooke-Gifford Gallery** Contemporary New Zealand painting and sculpture. Manchester Street. Open daily 10.30 am–5 pm.

**Canterbury Society of Arts** Works from contemporary New Zealand artists. Open Mon–Sat 10 am–4.30 pm, Sun 2–4.30 pm, Gloucester Street.

**Arts Centre** A centre for various arts, craft, and cultural groups in former university buildings. Worcester Street. Open Mon–Sat 10 am–4 pm.

**Ferrymead Historic Park** A working transport museum including trams, trains and fire engines, and re-created village. Open daily 10 am–4.30 pm. 269 Bridal Path Road, Heathcote.

**Yaldhurst Transport Museum** Includes cars, motorcycles, and horse-drawn vehicles. Main West Road. Open daily 10 am–5 pm.

**Canterbury Provincial Building** A wooden building built in 1859 with stone additions made in 1865; includes a Victorian Gothic council chamber. Durham Street.

**St Michael and All Angels Church** Built in 1872 on the site of an earlier church.

**Statues** Statues of Godley, Cook, Scott, Moorhouse (railway engineer), Fitzgerald and Rolleston (both Canterbury Superintendents) are dotted around the city.

**Mona Vale** This homestead dates from 1905, and is now used for receptions. Its gardens have exotic trees and flowers and are open daily. Fendalton Road.

**Christs College** An English-style Grammar School, Rolleston Avenue.

**Christchurch National Marae** A new multicultural marae on Pages Road, Aranui.

**Deans Bush** This bush in Riccarton is a remnant of the native forests that were once common in these parts. A cottage belonging to the Dean family has been restored as a museum.

**New Brighton** This eastern suburb with an ocean beach, once had trams and a pier, but now has shops and recreation amenities. 9 km north-east.

**Queen Elizabeth II Park** Stadium and training centre for athletes, which was built for the 1974 Commonwealth Games. Also houses a leisure centre with mini golf, bumper boats, and hydroslide. New Brighton.

**Orana Wildlife Park** An open style zoo, with special displays for the kiwi and tuatara. McLeans Island Road; open 10 am–4.30 pm daily.

**McLeans Island Railway** Steam railway preservation group. Operates some weekends.

**Willowbank Wildlife Reserve** Zoo and farmyard animals, as well as the kiwi. Hussey Road. Open 10 am– 11 pm.

**Aquarium and Zoo** Fish, crocodile, birds and animals. Beach Road, North Beach. Open 10 am–5 pm daily.

**Sign of the Takahe** On Dyers Pass Road towards Summit Road, Cashmere. A historic building with a view and restaurant, originally built as a roadhouse. The Sign of the Kiwi and Sign of the Bellbird further up the road were also built as roadhouses but now the latter is only a picnic shelter.

**Blessed Sacrament Basilica** A classic Renaissance-style Roman Catholic Cathedral. Barbadoes Street.

## LOCAL TOURING

**Bridle Path** The early colonists used this route from and to Lyttelton over the port hills. The walk commences off Bridal Path Road near the Heathcote entrance to the Lyttelton road tunnel (2 hr).

**Sumner** Beach suburb fronting onto Pegasus Bay. 5 km to nearby Cave Rock. There is also road access to Taylors Mistake beach. On the way to Sumner, see the Cobb cottage just over the Ferrymead Bridge.

**Evans Pass** A road climbing from Sumner over the Port hills via the Summit Road to Lyttelton. Views along the way.

**Lyttelton** The port for Christchurch, now accessible via a road tunnel (Route 74) and also by roads over Dyers Pass or Evans Pass. Lyttelton has three old churches. The museum features partly maritime displays, and is open weekends (also Tuesday and Thursday in summer) 2–4 pm. The Timeball Station, which was built in 1876, used to signal 'one o'clock' each day so ships could set their chronometers. Lyttelton is a volcanic crater and the Crater Rim walkway, along the Summit Road, gives views over the harbour and Canterbury. A walk from the Sign of the Takahe to the Sign of the Kiwi takes 55 minutes; from there along the Summit to the Bridal Path is 3 hr. Quail Island, situated in the harbour, has beaches and a circle island walkway.

**Barnett Park** A recreational reserve at Moncks Bay on the road to Sumner. A 4 km (1¼ hr) walkway largely through tussock, with views of World War II defences is available.

**Godley Head** Summit Road leads to this northern head and lighthouse for Lyttelton Harbour. Two sections of walkway link the road with Taylors Mistake (surfing beach) and with former defence area and cliffs.

**Northern Suburbs** Belfast (11 km north) has a winery, the Groynes picnic area, and Spencer Park. Kaiapoi (20 km north) offers river trips on MV *Tuhoe* and beaches from here to the north. See separate listings for Rangiora and Oxford.

**Pegasus Bay Walkway** A 15 km (5 hr) coastal walk from and to Kaiapoi Post Office, via Woodend beach to Waikuku surf club. It passes the berth for MV *Tuhoe* and the Waimakariri bar, sand dunes, pine trees and swamp. Road access is at both ends.

**Waimairi Walkway** An easy 5 km return walk situated within the Groynes recreation area and adjacent farmland. 7 km north.

**Airforce Museum** At the military airport of Wigram (also sometimes used as a motor racing circuit), 9 km south on Route 1. Aircraft displays and airforce memorabilia are featured.

**Lake Ellesmere** A large shallow lagoon (but with no permanent sea outlet). There are several accesses, including entry from the Kaitorete Spit, 24 km off Route 75.

**See Also** Rangiora, Oxford, Akaroa and Ashburton

# CLYDE SI

**Population** 960
**Location** On Route 8, 10 km west of Alexandra, 23 km east of Cromwell.

Clyde was the Dunstan of the gold days, and more than 4000 miners once lived in the area. When the gold ran out the survivors turned to fruit farming, and water races previously used for sluicing were now used for irrigation. It is now the site of New Zealand's largest concrete dam, and is the terminus for the Central Otago branch railway from Dunedin.

## ENVIRONS & ATTRACTIONS
**Vincent County and Dunstan's Goldfields Museum** The 1864 stone courthouse now features relics from the gold days. Newcastle Street. Open Tue–Sun, 2–4 pm. An extension to the museum in Fraser Street houses farming displays; open Tue–Sun, 3.30–5 pm.

**Other Town Buildings** A number of old buildings still remain in the town, including the Athenaeum, the former Town Hall, a former Hartleys Arms Hotel, Naylors Victoria Store and several churches.

## LOCAL TOURING
**Lookout** Across the town bridge, wind steeply for 3 km to a viewpoint overlooking the town and the Cromwell Gorge.

**Cromwell Gorge** Route 8 follows the Clutha River and leads to Cromwell. The reconstructed road overlooks the Clutha and Lake Dunstan.

**Clyde Dam** A giant dam nearing completion, 1 km north-west of Clyde on Route 8. Behind the dam, Lake Dunstan will back up the Cromwell Gorge beyond Cromwell itself.

**See Also** Cromwell, Wanaka and Alexandra

# COLLINGWOOD SI
**Population** 220
**Location** At the end of Route 60, 28 km north-west of Takaka, 136 km north-west of Nelson.

Named after Admiral Collingwood, an associate of Lord Nelson, European settlers arrived here in 1842. The town experienced a goldrush in 1857, and in 1907 was destroyed by fire. Collingwood is situated on the shores of Golden Bay, and is popular in summer particularly with trampers on the Heaphy Track.

## ENVIRONS & ATTRACTIONS
**St Cuthbert's Church** Designed and built in 1877 by explorer Thomas Brunner.

**Collingwood Museum** Local museum with goldmining relics; open most days.

## LOCAL TOURING
**Rockville** 8 km south at Rockville are the Te Anaroa Caves, with impressive stalactite and stalagmite formations (open most days in summer). Nearby is a rock formation known as 'the Devil's Boots'. About 1 km beyond, it is possible to walk around the old Aorere Goldfields (but beware of shafts and tunnels). The old Rockville Dairy Factory houses a Machinery and Settlers Museum, which features mining machinery and farming equipment.

**Cape Farewell** The Cape and Pillar Light is 26 km north of Collingwood at the end of the road. There is a 1 hr walk to a viewpoint and also a walk to Wharaiki Beach on the west coast.

**Farewell Spit** A 35 km long sandbar, which curves out and protects Golden Bay. Most of the spit is a restricted wildlife reserve, especially for birds. Each autumn it sees the beginning of a 12 000 km journey to Siberia for up to 20 000 Godwits. There is road access to the base of the spit. Safari Tours operate from Collingwood.

**Whanganui Inlet** Also called Westhaven, it is 19 km north then west to this inlet and the Kaihoka lakes on the west coast. As recommended by the Mobil Guide, try and coincide your journey with high tide.

**Kaituna Track** Choose between a 2–3 hr walk to the old Kaituna and Golden Blocks goldfields, or a 5–7 hr tramp that continues over the range to Whanganui Inlet. Commence at Aorere Valley, 15 km south of Collingwood.

**Heaphy Track** Popular 4–5 day tramp over 77 km between Bainham (30 km south from Collingwood) and Karamea. There are huts en route. There is also the option of guided walks with escort. The track passes rugged mountain and coast scenery and is subject to all weathers, and even high tides.

**See Also** Motueka, Takaka and Karamea

# COROMANDEL NI
**Population** 940
**Location** Near the top of the Coromandel Peninsula, 54 km north of Thames on Route 25.

From a vigorous history of timber felling and gold rushes, the town of Coromandel is quieter these days, though it still retains its colonial character. Coromandel has a strong conservation lobby and the area has attracted crafts people and those seeking alternative lifestyles. Originally called Waiau, the area takes its present name from HMS *Coromandel*, an old naval vessel that regularly called for spars. There is a big harbour with a number of local islands. From Coromandel there are roads to the tip of the peninsula on both coasts, however, they do not meet. South from Coromandel, Route 25 climbs over the Kirita Hill, then follows a scenic coastal

drive down the Firth of Thames to Thames. From Coromandel, Route 25 crosses the peninsula on a scenic route to Whitianga. There is an alternative road, called the 309, which offers the opportunity of a round trip.

## ENVIRONS & ATTRACTIONS
**Coromandel School of Mines Museum** Display of rock samples and old photographs. Open summer holidays 10 am–noon and 2–4 pm.

**Long Bay** A beach and bush reserve on a side road. 3 km from Coromandel.

**Northern Beaches** Oamaru Bay, Papaaroha, and Amodeo Bay north of Coromandel provide swimming beaches, camping and picnic areas.

**Colville** 26 km north, this is the most northerly town on the peninsula.

**Port Jackson** A good holiday area, but no longer a port. 56 km from Coromandel. En route the road skirts coast and cliff and the Paritu quarry, which provided stone for Auckland's Post Office, Railway Station, Museum, and also Wellington's Parliament Buildings. The road continues on 6 km to Fletchers Bay.

**North Eastern Beaches** A narrow, winding road leads to Kennedys Bay (21 km) and on to Waikawau Bay.

**Port Charles** (45 km). Small settlement and holiday resort with adjacent Sandy Bay and Stoney Bay.

**Coromandel Walkway** This is a 7 km (3–3½ hr one way) link between the Port Charles Road (from Stoney Bay) and the Port Jackson Road (from Fletcher Bay). The walkway has scenic coastal views, with bush and scrub — and one steep part, which has a chain-handhold. Unless you can position a car at either end (and the roads are almost as bad as the track!) you must do a round trip

— which makes the scenery twice as good.

**Mount Moehau** The highest point (892 m) on the Coromandel Peninsula, this can be reached (by more experienced trampers) from Te Hope on the Colville–Port Jackson Road. The climb takes 3 hr to the summit. There is a less defined route from Stoney Bay on the East Coast. The peak is sacred to the Maoris and has fine views.

**See Also** Thames and Whitianga

# CROMWELL SI
**Population** 3536
**Location** The point at which Routes 6 and 8 almost intersect, and are joined by link road 8B, 57 km south of Wanaka; 63 km east of Queenstown.

A servicing and distribution centre for an extensive but sparsely populated sheep farming and fruit growing area. The town is centred on the flat terraces above the junction of the Clutha and Kawarau rivers. Cromwell is the administrative centre for the Upper Clutha hydro-development scheme.

Cromwell was originally located at the junction of the Clutha (from Wanaka and Hawea) and Kawarau (from Wakatipu). The building of a new dam at Clyde and the consequent formation of Lake Dunstan, however, flooded the junction and indeed the lower part of the old town. A new shopping area has since been built on higher ground.

## ENVIRONS & ATTRACTIONS
**Clutha Valley Development Information Centre** Situated in the new mall shopping centre. This provides information that explains the power and development scheme and is open daily.

*Limestone, north Hahei, Coromandel.*

**Cromwell Borough Museum** Houses relics from the goldrush days, including photographs and newspaper clippings.

## LOCAL TOURING
**Bendigo and Logan Town** Old gold towns still identifiable by a few stone buildings and accessible on side roads from Route 8, 25 km north. Watch for holes and mineshafts if walking about the area.

**Bannockburn and Carrick Town** Two more old mining areas, immediately south-west of Cromwell. A few stone buildings (timber was scarce around these parts) and sluiced hillsides remain. Enquire locally if continuing beyond here on Nevis Road.

**Cromwell Gorge** The building of the Clyde dam and the proposed Lake Dunstan (still unfinished at the time of compiling this guide) have caused roading alterations, but the rugged, barren landscape is still clearly visible. The railway to Cromwell closed in 1958. Route 8 goes to Clyde and Alexandra.

**Kawarau Gorge** This main road into Queenstown by Route 6 was a wild, difficult route in the old days and is still impressive today. Note the Kawarau Gorge tourist mine (try your luck) and the 'Roaring Meg' power station.

**See Also** Wanaka, Alexandra and Queenstown

127

# D

## DANNEVIRKE NI
**Population** 5873
**Location** On Route 2, 27 km
north of Woodville, 56 km south-
east of Waipukurau.

Dannevirke is the local servicing
centre for a rich rural area
stretching from the Ruahine
Range to the East Coast; much of
the town reflects its agricultural
and pastoral activities.

About 1870 the government
invited immigrants from
Scandinavia to settle in this
southern Hawke's Bay area, and
also in the Wairarapa. The area
was part of the Seventy Mile Bush
— a dense totara forest. Most of
the bush is cleared and is now
sheep country. The rugged
Ruahine Range, however, is still a
forest park to the west. The town's
name means 'the Danes' Work'.
Dannevirke is on the main road
and rail route between
Palmerston North/Woodville and
Napier/Hastings. North of the
town, around Matamau and
Ormondville (on side road), the
railway crosses six viaducts.

### ENVIRONS & ATTRACTIONS
**Dannevirke Domain** Picnic
ground, with deer park and
aviary. Christian Street.

### LOCAL TOURING
**Norsewood** 20 km north, a
Scandinavian settlement, which
still displays its heritage in its
church and a Norwegian fishing
boat. The town has a woollen
clothing factory and a shop. The
main road bisects and virtually
bypasses the town.

**See also** Waipukurau, Woodville
and Palmerston North

## DARGAVILLE NI
**Population** 4859
**Location** 185 km north of
Auckland, 58 km west of
Whangarei, on Route 12.

Situated up the Wairoa River at
the northern end of the giant
Kaipara Harbour, the town was
founded in 1872 by a timber
merchant called Joseph McMullen
Dargaville. For many years access
for passengers and freight was by
steamer from Helensville, at the
southern end of the harbour. The
town grew as a timber centre,
using especially kauri trees and
kauri gum. Around 1883 the
Kaihu Valley Railway started a
timber train in the area, but
Dargaville was not linked to the
rest of the rail network until 1940.
Roading remained poor for many
years. Today farming has
generally taken over from timber.

### ENVIRONS & ATTRACTIONS
**Northern Wairoa Maori,
Maritime and Pioneer
Museum** Divided into three
main sections, as indicated by its
name, the museum also includes
a kauri gum collection. The
nautical section provides
information about the hundreds
of ships that were built and
worked on the Kaipara Harbour.
Open daily (9.30–11.30 am and
2–4 pm) in summer; otherwise
open on Saturday afternoons.

### LOCAL TOURING
**Baylys Beach** A popular black
sand beach about 13 km north-
west of Dargaville. Baylys is one
of the few access points to an
85 km long stretch of beach
fronting the Tasman Sea.
**Kaiiwi Lakes** The Taharoa
Domain, containing these lakes, is
35 km north of Dargaville via
Route 12. This large reserve, with
picnic and camping facilities,
allows various water-based

recreational activities and is set among sand-dunes and pine trees. The lakes are geological oddities, with no known natural inlets and outlets. There are extensive walks throughout the area with a 2.5 km walkway to the west coast beach.
**Ruawai** Small farming community 28 km south on Route 12, at the head of the Kaipara Harbour. It is a favoured place for growing kumara (sweet potato).

**See Also** Whangarei, Waipoua Kauri Forest and Maungatupoto

# DUNEDIN si
**Population** 106 864
**Location** On Route 1, 362 km south-west of Christchurch, 217 km north-east of Invercargill.

Known as the 'Edinburgh of the South', Dunedin is the chief commercial and administrative centre for the Otago region. It is situated at the head of Otago Harbour, with suburbs spreading over its surrounding hills. Although Dunedin has some city wharves, its main port is located at nearby Port Chalmers. Dunedin has air and railway networks with the rest of the country. Its railway station is a fine historic building.

The foundation of Dunedin dates from the arrival of the first ships (in 1848) of the Otago (Free Church of Scotland) Association, which resulted in a mainly Presbyterian settlement — at least initially. Dun Edin was the ancient name for Edinburgh.

In the 1860s, the Otago gold rushes brought population and prosperity to Dunedin; but the city also built its economic structure on the products of the land and industry. The first shipment of frozen meat was dispatched to England in 1883 from Port Chalmers. Burnside near the city

was the site of the first freezing works in New Zealand, and the oldest in the world.

New Zealand's first university was established in this city in 1869. The original 1878 building is preserved by the Historic Places Trust. A school of medicine is included at the University. Knox College and Holy Cross College are theological training centres.

Cablecars, similar to those in San Francisco, were a feature of the city for 75 years until 1957.

Dunedin was the first city in New Zealand to undertake municipal trading; gas was first lighted in 1863 and water was laid on in 1867. An electric tramway service began in 1903 when the Waipori power station was opened. Dunedin's successful development of these hydro-electric works prompted the Government to undertake a supply of hydro-electricity as a national enterprise.

Reclamation of much of today's valuable land from the harbour began in 1863. Dunedin became a borough in 1865 and obtained city status in 1868.

## ENVIRONS & ATTRACTIONS
**Octagon** Central eight-sided reserve — with the Star Fountain — in the downtown area, separating Princes Street and George Street. Also the site of the Town Hall and a statue of Robbie Burns.
**Queens Gardens** A grassed square near the city's commercial heart. High Street.
**Town Belt** A belt of parkland surrounding the central area of the city; includes Jubilee Park and also Unity Park, which has the Byrd Memorial and a lookout.
**Botanical Gardens** A rose walk, the Ellen Terry Garden, Rhododendron Dell, azalia beds and winter gardens all form parts of this area. Great King Street.

*Larnach's Castle, Dunedin.*

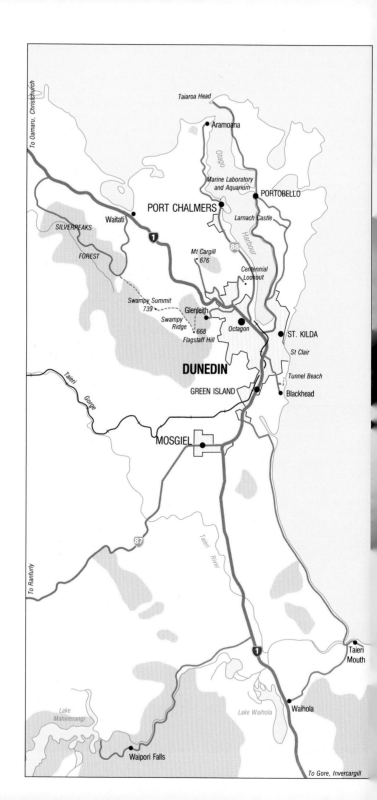

**First Church** Impressive Norman-Gothic building of Oamaru stone, erected 1868–73; adjacent to the Octagon.

**St Paul's Cathedral** A 1915 Anglican mock-Gothic church with a 20 m high vaulted ceiling; adjacent to the Octagon.

**Otago Museum** In addition to local items, includes a Maori collection and a section on Greece, Rome and Egypt. Great King Street. Open 9 am–4.30 pm weekdays; open Saturday 10.30 am and Sunday 1.30 pm.

**Hocken Library** A collection of historic books, maps and manuscripts. Albany Street. Open 9 am–5 pm; Saturday 9 am–12 noon.

**Early Settlers Museum** Pioneer relics, photos of settlers and goldmining days, and an early locomotive. Cumberland Street. Open 9 am–4.30 pm; Saturday from 10.30 am, Sunday from 1.30 pm.

**Dunedin Art Gallery** Includes English watercolours, and works by Frances Hodgkins. Logan Park, Anzac Avenue.

**Olveston** A unique Jacobean-style homestead. Furnished in keeping with the original wealthy taste of its first owner (1906). Royal Terrace. 1 hr tours are at set times daily.

**Araireeru Marae** Multicultural Marae, Kaikorai Valley.

**St Kilda and St Clair** Adjacent ocean beach suburbs to the south of the city centre.

**Ocean Beach Railway** At Kettle Park, St Kilda, a working steam railway operating weekends.

**Signal Hill** 392 m up Signal Hill Road, Opoho, to a Centennial lookout over the city.

## LOCAL TOURING

### PORT AND NORTH

**Mt Cargill** This television-topped viewpoint (676 m) is 8 km north and is accessible via the end of George Street.

**Mt Cargill Walkways** The Mt Cargill walk of 4 km (2 hr) starts in Bethunes Gully and climbs to connect with the A. H. Reed Track to the summit. Also the Organ Pipes Track leads past its striking rock formation to the Mt Cargill Road; Grahams Bush Walk continues on to Hall Road at Sawyer Bay. You can either walk all the tracks, or just parts of them.

**Flagstaff Walkway** A 5 km (2 hr) walk through the Flagstaff Scenic Reserve to its 666 m peak. You can see the city from most parts of the track. There is road access to both ends, near Glenleith, 5 km north.

**Silver Peaks Walkways** West of Waitati, 25 km north, is a series of walkways ranging from 3 to 8 hr on exposed mountain ridges. There is a connecting walkway to the Flagstaff walkway, called Swampy Ridge. There are also several other tracks in the Silver Peaks Forest.

**Port Chalmers** Major port for Dunedin and the South Island. 12 km north of Dunedin on Route 88 (from Dunedin railway station). The first settlers alighted here. Viewpoints at Flagstaff Lookout on Aurora Terrace, and at Scott Memorial, 2 km on the road from Port Chalmers to Waitati.

**Aramoana** Beach settlement at the western head to Otago Harbour, 22 km from Dunedin.

### PENINSULA AND SOUTH

**Otago Peninsula** A unique peninsula guarding Dunedin and its harbour. The Otago Peninsula Trust promotes and preserves its character, which includes wildlife, Larnach Castle and Glenfalloch Gardens.

**Larnach's Castle** Built in 1871, complete with ballroom and

*The grounds and buildings of Dunedin University.*

battlements, by W. Larnach, bank manager and parliamentarian. Floors and ceiling are special examples of skilled workmanship. Open daily 9 am–5 pm.

**Glenfalloch Woodland Gardens** These were once private gardens that created an 'English country garden' impression around a homestead.

Open daily 10 am–4 pm. 10 km from Dunedin. Best visited in September or October.

**Portobello Marine Laboratory and Aquarium** This shows saltwater specimens and is run by the Otago University. Open daily 9 am–5 pm.

**Taiaroa Head** At the tip of the

Otago Peninsula, 30 km from Dunedin, this was once the site of a Maori pa, and later a signal station and lighthouse. In 1885 coastal defences were started because of the 'Russian Scare', and one of the six-inch Armstrong disappearing guns (so called because it retracted into the ground between shots) remains as

an attraction. Open daily.

**Royal Albatross Colony** A restricted reserve on Taiaroa Head, where approximately 20 pairs of this largest seabird nest. This petrel has a wingspan of up to 3 m, a weight of up to 8 kg, and can fly perhaps 190 000 km each year at speeds of up to 120 kph. Each bird nests here during alternate years, but young birds fly away for eight years before returning to breed. A strictly controlled viewing area open daily (closed September–November) — but sometimes you might not see anything!

**Penguin Place** A vantage point to see seals and penguins — best late afternoon, especially June–August.

**Tunnel Beach** A 1½ km round trip (1 hr) walkway off Blackhead Road (beyond St Clair). Best in the mornings.

**Taieri River** The Taieri River Scenic Reserve near Taieri Mouth has a riverside track through regenerating bush. (4.5 km, 2 hr one-way). The Taieri Mouth can be reached by a side road from Waihola, or else down the coast from Dunedin via Brighton.

**Lake Waihola** A low-lying lake favoured for aquatic sports, 39 km south of Dunedin on Route 1.

**Lake Mahinerangi** An artificial lake storing river for the Waipori hydro-electric Power Station. The best and most impressive access is via Berwick off the Taieri Plains. Relics of goldmining days remain. The Waipori Gorge walking track is an 8 km (3 hr one way) track to Waipori Falls — road access both ends. The surrounding Berwick Forest has many other tracks and walks.

**Otago Excursion Train** This runs most afternoons in the summer from Dunedin up the Taieri Gorge.

**See Also** Palmerston, Middlemarch and Milton

# E

## ELTHAM NI
**Population** 525
**Location** On Route 3, 53 km south of New Plymouth, 18 km north of Hawera.

Eltham was established in 1884 when the area was bush-clad, and early settlers risked the old Maori trail to New Plymouth because it was safer than the coastal track. The town was originally dependent on local timber but then became a dairying district, particularly noted for its cheese. It also became the centre of the co-operative dairying scheme when well-known Chinese merchant

*Hoar frost at Bendrose Station, Twizel.*

Chow Chong opened a factory here in 1887. Connecting roads give access to Egmont National Park (refer to entry on Stratford).

## ENVIRONS & ATTRACTIONS
**Galaxy Cheese** Factory viewing and cheese tasting — and, of course, cheese buying.
**Taumata Park** An area of native bush, which also has a swimming pool and playground.

## LOCAL TOURING
**Lake Rotokare** 11 km east of Eltham, this 18 ha lake is surrounded by native bush. A walkway goes around the lake (allow up to 1½ hr, or longer if wet). The road to Rotokare also provides alternative access to the upper reaches of Lake Rotorangi.

**See Also** Hawera, Stratford and Patea

F

## FAIRLIE SI
**Population** 788
**Location** On Route 8, 62 km west of Timaru, also 46 km south-west of Geraldine.

Previously called Fairlie Creek and also Hamilton, the name of the town was changed to Fairlie in 1892. It is the administrative centre for the 'MacKenzie Country'. It was also the terminus for a branch railway from Timaru, until its closure in 1968.

The designation of MacKenzie country is a tribute to the legendary James McKenzie, who supposedly rustled sheep from Canterbury to sell to the miners in Otago via these back country passes and basins — aided by his trusty dog Friday. In actual fact he may only have been the caught accomplice of a runholder stealing sheep for his own run.

### ENVIRONS & ATTRACTIONS
**Fairlie Domain** On the banks of the Opihi River near the town centre.
**MacKenzie Society Transport Museum** A collection of veteran farm implements, wagons and coaches, and the old Fairlie Station. Open daily. Nearby is the Mabel Binney Cottage Museum, a blacksmith's furnished cottage.

### LOCAL TOURING
**Mount Dobson** This private road branches off 11 km south on Route 8, to a ski-field with lifts to 2107 m; open July to October.
**Burke Pass** Gateway to the MacKenzie, at 671 m altitude on Route 8, 25 km south-west of Fairlie. It marks a transition from the Canterbury Plains to the

tussock uplands of the MacKenzie Country.

**See Also** Timaru, Geraldine and Lake Tekapo

## FEATHERSTON NI
**Population** 2516
**Location** On Route 2, 64 km north-east of Wellington; 34 km south-west of Masterton.

Featherston was originally known as Burlings after the pioneer settler Mr Henry Burlings, who took up land here in the 1840s. It was renamed in 1854 after Dr Isaac Featherston, superintendent of the Wellington province.

Featherston is a centre for farming and pastoral activities. Some people commute from here to Wellington and the Hutt Valley for work. Despite the obstacle of the Rimutaka Range, a road link with Wellington was established by 1859, and a railway was built by 1878.

The railway was known as the Rimutaka Incline, and it used the Fell system, namely when small steam locomotives had a mechanism that grabbed a centre rail to assist the climb. In 1880 one train was blown off the track by wind. The incline closed in 1955 when an 8.8 km tunnel was opened.

A military training camp was opened at nearby Tauherenikau in 1916. It had a peak population of 8000 men. In 1942 the training camp was recommissioned to house Japanese prisoners of war. On the morning of 25 February 1943 the prisoners rioted; 48 Japanese and a New Zealand guard were killed.

Tauherenikau racecourse is surrounded by large trees, which make it an attractive area; picnic

*Paterson's Accommodation House, Canterbury.*

race days are held here during the summer.

## ENVIRONS & ATTRACTIONS

**Fell Engine Museum**  Found on the main road in town, the museum features a restored 1878 Fell Steam Locomotive and photographic displays. Open Saturday 10 am–4 pm, Sunday 1 pm–4 pm.

## LOCAL TOURING

**Martinborough**  19 km south-east of Featherston, this town has a population of 1379. Its streets are laid out in a Union Jack pattern.

**Lake Wairarapa**  This large shallow lake is 18 km by 6 km, and can be found 8 km south of the town. There is a distant lookout from Route 2 west of the town. Floodgates at the southern end direct the Ruamahanga River further south to Lake Omoke, right on the south coast, thereby preventing flooding in the Lake Wairarapa area.

**Lake Ferry**  A small community on Palliser Bay, 44 km south of Featherston.

**Putungirua Pinnacles**  A scenic reserve located on a 3 km walk off the Cape Palliser Road, 17 km from Lake Ferry. The Pinnacles are an eroded rock formation. There are two alternative tracks; allow 3 hr for the round trip.

**Cape Palliser**  38 km from Lake Ferry (82 km from Featherston), this is the most southerly part of the North Island. The road is unsealed past Lake Ferry, and it has some open water courses that can be hazardous after heavy rain. A lighthouse stands on the Cape.

**See Also**  Wellington, Greytown and Masterton

# FEILDING NI

**Population** 12 116
**Location** 6 km off Route 3
between Bulls and Palmerston
North; on Route 54, 30 km north-
west of Palmerston North.

A rural centre that continues to
thrive despite the proximity of
Palmerston North. The town was
laid out in 1874 by Colonel
Feilding for a Colonial
Corporation set up in England,
which was headed by the Duke of
Manchester. The land was known
as the Manchester block and the
street system was modelled on
that in Manchester, England.

## ENVIRONS & ATTRACTIONS
**Kowhai Park** In South Street, a
garden area with aviaries and lake.

## LOCAL TOURING
**Mt Stewart Memorial** 8 km
south-west on Route 3, a
viewpoint over surrounding
countryside.
**Mt Lees Reserve** Gardens with
trees and flowers, for walks and
picnics. Ngaio Road, 11 km west
of town.

**See Also** Bulls, Palmerston
North, Taihape and Marton

*The peaks of Mt Cook and Mt Tasman.*

# FORTROSE SI

**Population** 102
**Location** On Route 92, 45 km
east of Invercargill, 124 km south-
west of Balclutha.

This locality on the south coast of
the South Island was once a
whaling station and is now a rural
outpost. The Mataura River forms
a lagoon here before entering the
sea at Toetoes Bay.

## ENVIRONS & ATTRACTIONS
**Waipapa Point** Recognised as
the eastern entrance to Foveaux
Strait, this was the scene of an
1881 shipwreck, which killed 131
people. It now has a lighthouse,
with a great coastal view, on a
4 km side road from Otara, east of
Fortrose. Due to the skew of the
South Island, this road and
lighthouse are the southernmost
points on the mainland.

## LOCAL TOURING
**Curio Bay** Remains of a
fossilised forest 160 million years
old, on the coastal rocks. Follow
track at low tide onto beach. Look
carefully at the formations of low
stumps and logs embedded in the
rock shelf. It is 43 km east via
Route 92 and the rural settlement
of Waikawa.

**Cathedral Caves**  48 km east on Route 92, past Chaslands, take a short side road to Waipati Beach. A 20-minute steep track leads to a series of steep caves. Only accessible 1 hr either side of low tide; take a torch.

**See Also**  Invercargill, Owaka and Gore

---

# FOX GLACIER SI
**Population**  433
**Location**  On Route 6, 23 km south of Franz Josef, 118 km north of Haast.

---

The Fox Glacier, like its northern neighbour Franz Josef Glacier, descends the western side of the Southern Alps to a terminal face at about 300 m altitude — which is low for a temperate zone. It is named after Sir William Fox, a former premier of New Zealand.

This river of ice is about 13.5 km long and commences at 2600 m altitude. It probably creeps forward at approximately 1.5 m per day; however, the length of the glacier has receded in recent years.

## ENVIRONS & ATTRACTIONS
**Visitor Centre**  Local headquarters for the Westland National Park. Enquire here about glacier trips and local walks.
**Road to Glacier**  The glacier is

7 km up a side road, and can be seen from the road. You can walk over the river shingles to 'touch' the glacier, though at times this can be more than a half-hour walk. Walks on the glacier itself should not be undertaken without a guide. Details of guided tours and hire of boots, are available from the visitor centre.

**Chalet Lookout**  An easy forest walk to an impressive viewpoint. Access is 3 km up Glacier Road. The walk is 30 minutes each way.

**Minehaha Forest Walk**  A pleasant 20 minutes easy walk, just south of the township.

## LOCAL TOURING

**Lake Matheson**  Follow the signpost 5.5 km west on the road to Gillespies Beach, then take a 20-minute bush walk to this lake renowned for its reflections of the alps. Walk a further half-hour around the lake for the best view — preferably before breakfast for clear air and best reflections.

**Gillespies Beach**  This rugged west coast beach is 20 km to the south-west. Traces of early goldmining activity are still visible and there are local walks. Views back to the alps across the Clearwater flats are picturesque.

**Mount Fox Track**  A rough steep climb to a 1022 m viewpoint, then on to 1341 m, giving views of alps, glacier and coast. 3 hr one way.

**Copland Valley**  The first part of the Copland Pass track (3–4 days over the Main Divide) consists of a 6-hr tramp to Welcome Flat Hut — site of hot springs in a forest and alpine setting. Signposted 26 km south.

**Bruce Bay**  Timber and cattle locality, 52 km south.

**Lake Paringa**  Scenic lake and small settlement 71 km south on Route 6. The Jamie Creek Track is a 15-minute walk through native bush. The Paringa to Haast cattle

142

track, used by nearly 50 000 cattle between 1875 and 1959, has been reopened as a 2–3 day tramp for average trampers.

**Knights Point**  View of rocky coast from lookout. A plaque records the opening of the road through to Haast in 1965.

**Scenic Flights**  Sightseeing by light aircraft is popular; some flights include both the Franz Josef and Fox glaciers and also go over the alps to include the Mount Cook region. A ski landing is also possible on the Tasman Glacier over the Divide.

**See Also**  Franz Josef Glacier and Haast

---

# FOXTON  NI
**Population**  2729
**Location**  On Route 1, 30 km south of Bulls, 19 km north of Levin.

---

Situated near the mouth of the Manawatu River, Foxton was named after Sir William Fox. The town developed because the river was a satisfactory port and it became an important outlet for timber and flax from the Manawatu region.

The area used to be timber-covered and the first railway from Foxton inland to Palmerston North guaranteed the importance of the town. In 1873 a horse tramway to Palmerston North was built and then improved to railway standard in 1870, but the link to Foxton was closed in 1959. The Sanson tramway operated from Himatangi to Sanson from 1885 until 1945. Himatangi is the site of a radio transmitting station for international communication.

## ENVIRONS & ATTRACTIONS
**Foxton Beach**  Holiday area 6 km west of town.

## LOCAL TOURING

**Moutoa Flood Gates** The Manawatu River's banks near its mouth were altered to prevent flooding by installation of floodways and gates, near Moutoa, on the direct road to Shannon.

**Shannon** 16 km east of Foxton, this town developed because of the railway. Previously it was an important flax centre.

**See Also** Bulls, Palmerston North and Levin

# FRANZ JOSEF GLACIER SI

**Population** 587
**Location** On Route 6, 139 km south of Hokitika, 23 km north of Fox Glacier.

The township of Franz Josef takes its name from the nearby glacier that descends 12 km from the main divide of the Southern Alps towards the lowland forest. Julius Von Haast discovered the glacier and he named it after the Emperor of Austria. The settlement has also been called Waiho, after the river that flows from the glacier.

Franz Josef Glacier and its near neighbour Fox Glacier are unique in descending to such low altitudes of 300 m in temperate climates. The glacier has lengthened occasionally, but generally it has been receding since its discovery.

## ENVIRONS & ATTRACTIONS

**Visitor Centre** On the main road, Route 6, there is a park headquarters. Call here for information on the Westland National Park and glacier trips.

**St James Church** When the church was built, the glacier was surrounded by bush and could be seen framed in a window behind the altar. Unfortunately the glacier has now receded from view.

**Road to Glacier** A 6 km side road leads up the southern side of the river valley towards the glacier. Views of the glacier are available from the approach road. Access to the glacier face involves a tramp over river stones and shingles of probably up to 1 hr each way. If you wish to venture on to the ice, join a guided party — do not do it alone. The visitor centre can provide details of such groups, and also hires boots and other equipment if needed.

## LOCAL TOURING

**Lake Mapourika** This picturesque bush-fringed lake is 9 km north on Route 6.

**Alex Knob Track** This offers a steady climb on a well-graded track to 1295 m for impressive views of glacier and coast. 4 hr up, 3 hr down; take the Glacier Road for 2 km.

**Lake Wombat Track** A moderate forest walk to this mountain lake, about 1 hr along the Alex Knob Track up Glacier Road.

**The Forks** A road junction 13 km north on Route 6. Lake Wahapo and the timber town of Whataroa are ahead. Out to the coast 11 km west is Okarito, an old goldmining locality. A half-hour walk up to the Okarito Trig is suggested for views of the Southern Alps. The breeding area for the White Heron bird is on nearby Okarito Lagoon, though this area is restricted.

**Scenic Flights** Sightseeing by light aircraft is popular. Some flights include both glaciers, and go over the alps to include the Mount Cook region, as well as a ski-landing on the Tasman Glacier over the Divide.

**See Also** Hokitika and Fox Glacier

*Franz Josef Glacier.*

# G

## GERALDINE SI

**Population** 2143

**Location** Near the intersection of Route 72 and Routes 72 and 79, 51 km south-west of Ashburton, 36 km north of Timaru.

Geraldine is a farming community situated at the western edge of the Canterbury plains. It has New Zealand's only linen flax mill. Beyond Geraldine are the hills of the Mt Peel Ranges; beyond them are the foothills of the Southern Alps, which are intersected by some of the great rivers of Canterbury. Up these river valleys are some of the historically famous sheep runs such as Orari Gorge, Mt Peel, Erewhon and Mesopotamia.

### ENVIRONS & ATTRACTIONS

**Domain Gardens** A reserve in the centre of town, Cox Street.

**Talbot Forest** A domain of native forest on the northern fringe of town — North Town Belt Road.

**Geraldine Museum** Items of local interest in an 1885 stone building. Cox Street.

**Vintage Car and Machinery Museum** Old cars and veteran machinery in Talbot Street.

### LOCAL TOURING

**St Anne's Church** This is the oldest church in South Canterbury. Built in 1862, it is located at Pleasant Valley, 7 km south-west of Geraldine.

**St Thomas's Church** Built in 1938 in a Norman style, this church can be found at Woodbury, 8 km north-west on the road to Waihi Gorge.

**Kakahu Lime Kiln** This 1880 kiln has been restored by the Historic Places Trust. 3 km along Halls Road, branching off Route 79, 15 km south.

**Kakahu Forest** Route 79 bisects remnants of native and exotic forest, 15 km south.

**Waihi Gorge** Picnic area with bush and river, 13 km west.

**Orari Gorge Scenic Reserve** Native bush, including a 3 hr circular walk. On the south side of the river, up Tripp Settlement Road, is Orari Gorge station, where the older buildings are being restored by the Historic Places Trust.

**Peel Forest Park** This area of native bush between the Rangitata and Orari Rivers is 21 km north of Geraldine. There is a park headquarters at the Peel Forest settlement. There are a number of short (1–3 hr) tracks including an Interpretation walk from Clarke flat, Dennistoun Bush Track from Blandswood Road, and Allans Track from Te Wanahu Flat, which gives access to Fern Walk and Acland Falls Track.

**Mt Somers** This small settlement was once a quarry for building stone. From here a road leads in towards Erewhon sheep station, which was once owned by novelist Samuel Butler, and provided the inspiration for the imaginary location in his novel *Erewhon*. The road leads in over tussock downs, with views of the Ashburton River, the Ashburton Gorge and the Rangitata River. A side road leads to Lake Heron. The other half of Butler's run, Mesopotamia station, although only 10 km across the river, is many kilometres around by road, with separate access on the road through Peel Forest (refer to entry on Geraldine).

**See Also** Ashburton, Methven, Fairlie and Timaru

*Sea and mountain vistas in Gisborne.*

# GISBORNE NI

**Population** 30 020

**Location** On Route 2, 152 km south-east of Opotiki, 105 km north-east of Wairoa, 233 km north-east of Napier.

Originally called Turanganui-A-Kiwa by the early Maoris, the area was renamed Gisborne (after the then Colonial Secretary) in 1874. On 9 October 1769 Captain Cook was the first European to set foot in New Zealand, on Kaiti beach. However, it was the scene of a tragic confrontation between the Maoris and Europeans with four Maoris being killed. Cook sailed on without the provisions he wanted, and aptly named the area Poverty Bay. In most other places, however, Cook had amicable relations with the Maoris.

The first European settler came in 1831. In 1840 missionary (later Bishop) William Williams started a mission station and found that many of the Maoris were already Christian converts. They had been taught by Maoris who had been converted in the Bay of Islands. The government purchased land for the town in 1868. There had been some traders and farmers before this, notably the trader and developer Captain G. Read, but the Hauhau campaign threatened their survival.

The Hauhau movement was a blend of Christian philosophy and Maori values that manifested itself into the hatred of things European. The Maori prophet Kereopa and his followers came to the Gisborne area in 1865 to recruit local Maoris to his cause.

147

The local Maoris were divided over support for this cause, which finally resulted in two battles — one at Ruatoria and one at Waerengaahika, closer to Gisborne. Government troops assisted in the second, which took a week to quell, but ultimately squashed the Hauhau threat in the district.

However, at this battle Te Kooti, a leading Maori who was helping the government, was accused of aiding the enemy and without trial was deported to the Chathams. There he founded a new religion called Ringatu. He escaped with 300 followers in a stolen ship and returned to the Gisborne area. On arrival he resisted arrest and wrote to the government asking for peace but saying if they wanted war he would give it to them. As he did not receive a reply, he carried out his threat by killing 33 Europeans and 37 friendly Maoris (in what is known as the Poverty Bay massacre) at Matawhero in November 1868. A month later government forces killed 120 of Te Kooti's followers at Ngatapa. Te Kooti used the Urewera as a base for later strikes on other centres over four years before retiring to the King Country — at that time beyond European reach. In 1883 the government pardoned him and also gave him land at Whakatane, where he died in 1891.

Gisborne has a river port (on the Taruheru River), an airport with scheduled flights, and a railway that crosses the airport. Apart from the local flats the city is surrounded by hilly country and the railway south to Napier has several engineering and scenic highlights. There are two roads south to Wairoa and one inland towards Opotiki via the Waioeka Gorge. The coastal road around East Cape (Route 35) is a popular but much longer alternative.

## ENVIRONS & ATTRACTIONS

**Kaiti Beach** Over the town bridge and along the wharf is the obelisk where Cook stepped ashore. A cannon from his ship *Endeavour* stands nearby.

**Kaiti Hill** A signposted road leads from the town bridge up Kaiti Hill to a lookout over the city and Poverty Bay. There is a statue of Cook and a walk down the slope to the Cook obelisk near the beach at the bottom. There is also an observatory on the hill.

**Poho-o-rawire Meeting House** A large hall near the bottom of the hill road.

**Waikanae Beach** Down Grey Street from the city centre is a popular beach, marine drive and playground. There is also a statue of 'Young Nick', the 12-year-old boy on Cook's ship who first sighted land.

**Gisborne Museum and Art Centre** Historic displays of Cook, early settlers and a Maori collection. Open to 4.30 pm; closed Monday.

**Botanic Gardens** Riverside gardens down Roebuck Road.

**Star of Canada House** A private home built from the 1912 shipwrecked *Star of Canada*. Down Cobden Street — view from road only.

## LOCAL TOURING

**Wainui Beach** A popular surf beach, 5 km north on Route 35. Further north, just off this route, is Makarori Beach (13 km), Whangara Beach (28 km) and Waihau Beach (49 km then turn off down side road) — the latter not to be confused with Waihau Bay, which is on the Bay of Plenty side of East Cape.

**Matawhero** A church built in 1862 as a store house, then used as an Anglican and later a Presbyterian church. It was also the site of the Poverty Bay massacre, during which the church was spared.

**Manutuke** This Maori meeting house, which was built in 1913, replaces the 1842 original, now in the Dominion Museum, Wellington.

**Waihirere and Ormond** Route 2 leads out to the north-west over the Povery Bay flats and valley, passing corn fields and vineyards. Note Waihirere and Gray's Bush for picnics; take the road up behind Gray's Bush for a view.

**Eastwoodhill Arboretum** This is the largest collection of Northern Hemisphere vegetation in New Zealand — 65 ha of trees and flowers. It is located 35 km from Gisborne on the road to Ngatapa and Rere. (William Dobson, the founder of this reserve also gave New Plymouth its Puketiti rhododendron park.) Open summer weekends till May 10 am–4 pm.

**Rere Falls** Take the road through Ngatapa and Rere to these falls and picnic site, 50 km away.

**Doneraille Park** 28 ha native bush reserve and picnic spot on the Route 36 inland road to Wairoa.

**Tiniroto Lakes** Small fishing lakes on Ruakaka (Loop) Road several kilometres further on.

**Te Reinga Falls** An 18 m waterfall at the confluence of the Hangaroa and Ruakituri rivers, which becomes the Wairoa River. On Route 36, 61 km from Gisborne (37 km from Wairoa).

**Otoko Walkway** A 5 km (2½ hr) easy walk along an old railway formation. Starts at picnic site on Route 2, 50 km east, passes the junction of Whakarau Road, and finishes opposite Otoko hall.

**See Also** Opotiki, Tolaga Bay and Wairoa

# GORE SI
**Population** 8594
**Location** On Route 1, 65 km north of Invercargill, 75 km west of Balclutha; also 62 km south-east of Lumsden via Route 94.

Gore is situated on the banks of the Mataura River. Around 1855, settlers began to take up sheep runs in the Gore district, which was known then as Longford (taking its name from the old and long river crossing). The current name has been used since the town's founding in 1862, in honour of the then Governor. The town was connected from Invercargill by railway in 1875 and the first flour mill was established in 1878. Today its successor is the largest cereal producing factory in New Zealand, and Gore's largest industry.

The Hokonui Hills adjacent to Gore were renowned in early times for the illicit distilling of whisky, known as 'Hokonui'.

Today Gore is the centre of a rich farming district, with one of the country's highest retail spending patterns. It is also a popular trout fishing centre.

## LOCAL TOURING
**Dolamore Park** This bush-encircled park is 8 km west via Reaby Road on the fringe of the Hokonui Hills.

**Croydon Bush Walkway** Consists of three tracks: the Dolamore Track is a 45-minute return trip (with part alternative return); the Whisky Creek Track (recalling the 'Hokonui' days) is a 2-hour round trip; a detour to Poppelwells viewpoint adds half an hour to the Whisky Creek Track.

**Mataura** 12 km south situated on the Mataura River, on and just off Route 1, the town has a big papermill, which uses woodpulp

149

*Dansey's Pass near Naseby, Central Otago.*

brought in from the North Island.

**Edendale**  26 km south on Route 1, this is the site of New Zealand's first significant dairy factory, making butter and cheese.

**Wyndham**  32 km south, this small farming community on the Mataura River is accessible via Edendale.

**Waikaka**  Following a gold discovery in 1867, this town became a popular goldfield, especially for the Chinese. Located 25 km north of Gore, it is now a quiet farming locality.

**Waikaia**  Another farming locality, which was formerly the Switzers goldfield. Gold was obtained by sluicing and the King Solomon mine was the richest in the area. 52 km north-west of Gore.

**See Also**  Balclutha, Tapanui, Lumsden and Invercargill

There is a rail service from Christchurch, which includes the Trans-Alpine passenger train.

Route 6 along the west coast is one of New Zealand's most scenic highways. The road over the passes from Christchurch — Lewis Pass and Arthur's Pass — are also very scenic.

Greymouth was built on the site of a Maori village called Mawhera, and was initially explored in 1846 by the pioneer surveyor Thomas Brunner. It has developed and survived from its boom days of gold, coal and timber. There is also dairying in the area.

The west coast has a reputation for rain, and certainly the prevailing westerly winds do bring their share of moisture. When it rains it is generally heavy rain. Greymouth also suffers occasionally from a wind called 'The Barber' — a cutting breeze that funnels down through the gap in the surrounding hills where the Grey River flows out.

## ENVIRONS & ATTRACTIONS
**Dixon Park** Gardens and play area on the corner of Tainui and Brunner streets.
**King Domain** Offers a variety of views and bush behind the railway station.
**South Tip** A view of shore and distant mountains from the southern breakwater, which is accessible through the suburb of Blaketown.

# GREYMOUTH SI
**Population** 7624
**Location** On Route 6, 101 km south of Westport, 330 km west of Christchurch via the Lewis Pass, and 248 km via Arthur's Pass.

Greymouth is situated on the left (southern bank) of the Grey River on the West Coast. The river once served as a port for the town.

## LOCAL TOURING
**Shantytown** Re-created goldmining town with buildings brought in from other parts of Westland, and an 1897 steam locomotive. Take Route 6 south to Paroa then turn up signposted side road. 13 km from Greymouth and open daily.
**Paroa Wildlife Park** Features deer and other wild game, live and mounted. Paroa, 8 km south.

**Boddytown** Take Marsden Road 1 km to Boddytown, then 12 km to Marsden through a bush drive. This is an alternative route to Shantytown for the round trip.

**Kumara** 18 km south on Route 6, then 5 km inland on Route 73, brings you to the town of Kumara, one of the foremost goldmining centres on the coast. Local river valleys still show the tailings of gold dredges in the vicinity.

**Lake Brunner** Westland's largest lake is accessible on a round trip drive from Kumara up the Greenstone Valley to Mitchells, then round to the settlement of Moana. From here there is a road out to Stillwater in the Grey Valley. The lake offers fishing, boating and picnic sites.

**Cobden** Northern suburb of Greymouth, just over the town bridge.

**Point Elizabeth Walkway** A 5 km (2 hour) track from the northern end of the Esplanade at Cobden, via Point Elizabeth to Rapahoe. Both ends are accessible by road. Rapahoe to Point Elizabeth is a family walk, but the Cobden leg has a steep part.

**Runanga** This coal town is 7 km north on Route 6. Rapahoe (beach and northern access to Port Elizabeth walkway) and Dunollie are nearby. A railway used to climb the Rewanui Incline to a coalmine, but the track-bed is being turned into a scenic roadway to the mine site.

**Brunner Industrial Site** The Historic Places Trust is now preserving the site of this old coalmine with its coke ovens. There are signposted displays. An explosion here in 1896 killed 67 miners. Take Route 7, 11 km east and cross the river (by foot) on the Brunner suspension bridge or take the Taylorville Road off Route 6 over the Cobden Bridge.

*Shantytown on the west coast of the South Island.*

152

**Blackball** Coalmining township up the Grey River Valley (cross on the Cobden Bridge). The town remains a popular stopover for hikers. Mine workings are close to the town but the area also has a history of gold seeking. From Blackball there are tracks leading to the sites of old batteries, including Garden Gully mine and battery. The Croesus Track is a full day tramp (for the experienced) over the range to Barrytown on the coast. 7 km north on the Blackball Road, Moonlight Road (a side road), leads to Andersons Flat and to the Moonlight Track — a 3-hr tramp up the slopes of the Paparoa Range.

**Nelson Creek** Follow Route 7 north-east 25 km to just past Ngahere and turn east up Nelson Creek Road for tracks and goldmine sites. 16 km past Nelson Creek is old Hochstetter dam (built for gold sluicing) with tracks

(15 minutes and 2 hr) to water races and picnic sites.

**See Also** Reefton, Punakaiki and Hokitika

# GREYTOWN NI
**Population** 1888
**Location** On Route 2, 14 km north of Featherston, 20 km south of Masterton.

This borough is situated on the fertile alluvial plains of the Wairarapa region. It is the oldest settlement in the region, dating back to 1853, and is named after Governor Grey. The town originated from a concept to open up smaller tracts of land to settlers with limited means. The region used to be covered in dense bush.

## ENVIRONS & ATTRACTIONS
**Cobblestones** A museum in the main street on the site of stables, which were once owned by Cobb and Co coaches.
**Soldiers Memorial Park** 8 ha native bush reserve accessed from Kuratawhiti Street.
**Papawai Marae** In 1898, a Maori movement proclaimed this the Maori capital of New Zealand, as a step towards an alternative government system for Maoris. An old Whare Wananga meeting house and a 1911 memorial to Tamahau Mahupuku (a leading figure in the Maori Parliament movement) remain on the site. Can be found 3 km along Papawai Road.

## LOCAL TOURING
**Waiohine Gorge** A side road 4 km north leads to picnic area and access to tracks in the Tararua Forest Park.
**Carterton** This larger borough is 9 km north. It was known in its early days as Three Mile Bush.

**See Also** Featherston, Masterton and Wellington.

*Trout fishing in Lake Middleton, South Island.*

# H

# HAAST SI
**Population** 188
**Location** On Route 6, 290 km
south of Hokitika, 118 km south
of Fox Glacier, 146 km west of
Wanaka.

The locality of Haast is where the
Haast River meets the Tasman
Sea on the west coast. The road
from Wanaka over the Haast Pass
is the lowest of the Alpine passes
crossing the Main Divide and is a
most scenic connection. However,
it was not until 1965 that the
Haast River was bridged with its
732 m span and the road was
opened up to the west coast.

Haast is the junction for the
branch road to Jackson Bay in the
deep south of south Westland.
This junction is on the southern
side of the bridge. The settlement
of Haast has been relocated 2 km
upriver from the bridge — its
former position was near the
beginning of the Jackson's Bay
road.

## ENVIRONS & ATTRACTIONS
**Haast River Walk** This 20
minute, one-way walk with bush
and river views is at the north end
of the bridge.

## LOCAL TOURING
**Jackson Bay** This remote part
of New Zealand is 49 km south of
Haast. The road is unsealed for
9 km. A rugged but grand part of
the country.
**Thunder Creek Falls** 52 km
east on Route 6. Short walk
through beech forest to 30 m falls.
**Gates of Haast** Describes the
point where the road crosses the
Haast River in a narrow boulder-
strewn chasm. 54 km east.

**Fantail Creek** Photogenic falls,
60 km east.
**Haast Pass** This is 64 km east of
the road junction at Haast, on
Route 6, at 563 m altitude.

**See Also** Fox Glacier and
Wanaka

# HAMILTON NI
**Population** 101 814
**Location** On Route 1, 127 km
south of Auckland.

Hamilton is one of New Zealand's
largest cities. It is inland astride
the Waikato River and on the
North Island main trunk railway
line. It is surrounded by the rich
agricultural area of the Waikato
district, which contributes trade
and importance to the city.
However, it also has a
concentration of light industry
and warehousing. The city has a
university, and research stations
for soil, animals, meat,
agricultural engineering and
artificial breeding are nearby.

The city was established in two
sections, one on each river bank,
as soldiers' settlements on
confiscated land after the Waikato
land wars. In return for their
military services, recruited New
Zealanders — and Australians —
were allotted 50 acres for country
farming as well as one acre in the
town. This practice also occurred
in Tauranga, Cambridge and
Pirongia.

Early inland transport was by
riverboat. The road from
Auckland reached Hamilton in
1867, with the railway following
in 1877. This was also the year
that Hamilton was constituted as a
borough, becoming a city in 1945.

The city takes its name from
Captain Hamilton of the Royal
Navy, who was killed in 1864 at
the battle of Gate Pa in Tauranga.
Hamilton is a focal point for land

*Farmland on the west coast, near Greymouth.*

routes with roads radiating to Tauranga, Rotorua, Auckland and other centres. Hamilton railway station is in the suburb of Frankton, although there is a branch line that goes through (and under) the city, linking it to Tauranga and Rotorua. However, passenger service is only on the main Auckland–Wellington route. There are extensive railway marshalling yards at suburban Te Rapa. The airport is south of the city and there are daily jet services to Wellington (not to Auckland).

## ENVIRONS & ATTRACTIONS
**Hamilton Gardens** This 58 ha attraction is on Cobham Drive. There are extensive greenhouse displays, and the Hammond

Camellia Garden and the Roger Rose Garden are well worth a visit. The facility is open daily with free admission and parking is available.

**Hamilton Lake** Also known as Lake Rotoroa, there are gardens and picnic facilities around this shallow but pleasant lake.

**Hilldale Zoo Park** 8 km out on the Whatawhata road, this attraction features zoo animals, a special child section and picnic grounds.

**Memorial Park** This pleasant walking spot with gardens and open area is on the riverbank close to the city. The remains of the river steamer MV *Rangiriri* can be seen on the riverbank adjacent to the park.

**River Cruises** MV *Waipa Delta* offers morning, afternoon, lunch and dinner cruises on the river.

**River Walks** A system of walkways extends along both banks of the river between Whitiora and Cobham bridges, passing gardens and picnic spots.

**Waikato Art and History Museum** A new building with old exhibits, including a 140-year-old war canoe. Other Maori artifacts and an art collection are also featured. Open daily on Grantham Street.

## LOCAL TOURING

**Mystery Creek** The location of Farmworld, a Clydesdale and dairy museum with live shows between 10.30 am and 2.30 pm daily. Another feature of Mystery Creek is the National Field Days held in June. This is the Southern Hemisphere's largest showcase of agricultural and horticultural products and lasts for three days. Other displays are held spasmodically. 2 km from airport.

**Temple View** At Tuhikaramea, 8 km to the west, the Church of Latter Day Saints has a Temple and visitor centre.

**Day Trip Ideas** Raglan, Kawhia and Waitomo Caves.

**See Also** Cambridge, Raglan, Ngaruawahia and Te Awamutu

## WAIKATO RIVER

Hamilton is the largest city on the Waikato River, the longest river in New Zealand and the most important in the North Island. It flows 354 km from Lake Taupo to the sea, and gives its name to the extensive farming area surrounding Hamilton. South of Lake Taupo, the Tongariro River, which commences on Mt Tongariro, also uses the name of Waikato River for part of its length. A notable feature of the Waikato River is its use for electricity generation through a series of nine hydro-electric dams: Aratiatia, Ohakuri, Atiamuri, Whakamaru, Maraeti I, Maraeti II, Waipapa, Arapunui, and Karapiro. Its waters are also used for cooling the thermal power stations at Wairakei, Huntly and Meremere. The dams have created a series of lakes on the river, in fact the lake at Karapiro is used for championship rowing. All the dams are accessible, and Karapiro and Aratiatia are perhaps the most popular to visit.

The Tongariro power scheme at the southern end of Taupo captures water from the upper reaches of the Tongariro, Wanganui and Moawhango rivers, and uses it for electricity generation before discharging it into Lake Taupo and also subsequently down the Waikato River.

**See Also** Cambridge, Wairakei and Turangi

# HANMER SPRINGS SI

**Population** 1238
**Location** Situated on a 10 km side road off Route 7, 136 km north of Christchurch.

Hanmer Springs is a spa and health resort located in a sheltered upland basin. It has the largest outflow of thermal waters in the South Island. Its 366 m altitude contributes to the invigorating climate.

The township was developed by the government department of Tourist and Health Resorts, which was responsible for the installation of a sanitorium and hospital facilities equipped to treat nervous disorders. It is partially surrounded by the Hanmer Forest Park, and has a backdrop of mountains, with skiing in season.

## ENVIRONS & ATTRACTIONS

**Thermal Pools** The public and private thermal pools are open daily 10 am–12.45 pm, 2–5 pm, 6.30–7.45 pm (closed Sunday evenings). The temperature in the pools is approximately 38°C.
**Forest Park Information Centre** Features displays and details of flora and walks and is located on Jollies Pass Road (1 km).

## LOCAL TOURING

**Woodland Walk** From the information centre, this is a pleasant ramble through woodland forest. 45 minutes for loop track. There is also a special wheelchair track, which takes approximately 30 minutes.
**Nature Trail** 30-minute walk through native forest, mainly beech, from Mullans Road.
**Conical Hill Walk** A gentle climb 550 m to a lookout with views over exotic trees and Hanmer basin. 1 hr return trip.

**Mt Isobel Track** A tougher climb to 1319 m to see subalpine flora and fauna and panoramic views (5 hr return).
**Waterfall Track** A 3 hr return climb to Dog Stream Waterfall, which is part of the way up Mt Isobel.
**Amuri Ski-Field** A club-operated field (in winter) on the slopes of Mt St Patrick.

**See Also** Kaikoura, Waipara and Maruia Springs

# HASTINGS NI

**Population** 37 658
**Location** On Route 2, 20 km south of Napier, 236 km south of Gisborne, 314 km north of Wellington.

The twin cities of Napier and Hastings have downtown areas only 20 km apart, but they will be treated separately in this guide. If staying at one, you should also refer to the other.

Hastings is situated on the Heretaunga Plains, inland from the southern shores of Hawke's Bay. The city is served by the port and airport at Napier but has its own railway station.

Hastings is the centre of a large food cropping and processing industry and also fruit and grapes. Winemaking is a major industry. Previously called Hicksville and later Heretaunga, the town area was first settled around 1864. Fires in 1893 and 1907, and an earthquake in 1931, all had their toll; the town is mostly rebuilt since these days. It was proclaimed a city in 1936.

## ENVIRONS & ATTRACTIONS

**Windsor Park and Fantasy Land** A large park towards the eastern fringe of the city. Fantasy Land is a well planned children's play area with a castle, train, and other features.

**Cornwall Park** Gardens, aviary and display house in Tomoana Road.

**Frimley Park** Rose Gardens, trees and picnic site in Frimley Road.

**Oak Avenue** This is really Ormond Road, but is so nicknamed because of the 1 km row of oak trees, that hang over the road.

**Keirunga Gardens** Homestead and gardens with craft activities in Puffett Road.

**Hastings Cultural Centre** Modern building in Karamu Road with library and Maori artifacts.

## LOCAL TOURING

**Havelock North** 5 km south-east, this adjacent borough has a population of 9036. It is famous for its private residential gardens.

**Te Mata Peak** Beyond Havelock North a road climbs this 399 m peak for excellent views over Hastings and the plains.

**Te Mata Walkway** Beginning 200 m beyond Peak House Restaurant on the slopes, the track goes down 2.2 km to Waimarama Road (behind the Peak). There are steep drops.

**Waimarama Beach and Ocean Beach** Two ocean beaches 31 km and 24 km east, on branch roads, behind Te Mata Peak.

**Cape Kidnappers** This is renowned for its Gannet Sanctuary, which is believed to be the only mainland gannet colony in the world. Gannets are large, mainly white seabirds, and they are resident at the cape from August to March. Best viewing times are November–February. Road access is via Te Awanga and Clifton, 21 km east of Hastings (21 km south-east of Napier). At the end of the road it is a 2 hr walk along 8 km of beach — avoid high tide. Tours are operated over Summer Lee sheep

160

station by Gannet Safaris — also from Te Awanga on tractor and trailer by Burdens Motor Camp (it is advisable to phone the operators in advance).

**Wineries** There are a number of wineries in the Hastings district located at Meeanee, Taradale, Te Mata, and Green Meadows.

**See Also** Napier, Wairau and Waipukerau

# HAVELOCK SI

**Population** 430
**Location** Near the top of the
South Island, 41 km north-west of
Blenheim on Route 6, 35 km west
of Picton.

Havelock is situated at the end of
Mahau Sound — an inner recess
of the Marlborough Sounds. It
began as a boarding house and
timber mill, but its importance
grew in 1864 with the discovery of
gold at the Wakamarina River
area, 10 km west.

Two of Havelock's school
children who later achieved fame
were Lord Rutherford who
pioneered atomic research, and
Dr Pickering who heads part of
the United States space programme.

Today the town serves as a
tourist and supply area for the

*An aerial view of the scenic Marlborough Sounds.*

Pelorus/Kenepuru Sounds area and mussel farms.

## ENVIRONS & ATTRACTIONS
**Havelock Museum** Located in the main street, this houses displays of local gold and timber relics; also a timber locomotive that once worked in the area. Open daily.

**Town Reserve** At the top of Inglis Street, this native bush has views over the town and Marlborough Sounds.

## LOCAL TOURING
**Canvastown** This appropriately named community grew during the 1864 gold rush at the Wakamarina field. The Wakamarina River here joins the Pelorus River. The main rush was short-lived, but for a long time after, a measure of gold (and also scheelite) continued to be found up the valley. You can still fossick for gold 7 km up at Pine Valley camp.

**Pelorus Bridge Scenic Reserve** A beautiful roadside bush reserve, with some commercial facilities, and with both short (30 minutes) and longer (4½ hr) bush walks. Access is on Route 6, 18 km west of Havelock.

**Carluke Pioneer Cottage** Built in 1881 and since restored as a period museum. Up side road 2 km past Rai Valley, 27 km west of Havelock.

**Tennyson Inlet** From Rai Valley two roads go north to the Marlborough Sounds. Tennyson Inlet is 35 km over the Opouri Saddle — a steep, unsealed road not recommended for caravans — or even low-powered cars. It provides northern access to the Nydia walkway.

**French Pass** A long, winding 65 km unsealed road from Rai Valley out on a narrow finger of land to French Pass at its extremity. Not suitable for caravans. A short track leads through bush to overlook the turbulent waters of the channel between this tip and D'Urville Island. A dolphin called Pelorus Jack used to lead ships through here 1888–1912. A side road to Port Ligar and Bulwer has some gates, which should be left as found.

**Kaiuma Bay** Take the road that crosses the Pelorus River 3 km west of Canvastown. After 24 km of unsealed road this provides southern access to the Nydia walkway. Some gates to be left as found.

**Nydia Walkway** A 22 km (8 hr) track from Kaiumu Bay to Duncan Bay on Tennyson Inlet, via Nydia Bay, which was once the location of an extensive timber operation. There is road access to both ends — see above.

**Boat Trips** Some launch trips can be taken from Havelock to Kenepuru and Pelorus Sounds. In particular mail boats offer full day trips to outer reaches on Tuesday, Wednesday and Thursday; other trips are on Fridays and weekends according to season and demand. Access to the Eastern Sounds is mentioned under Picton.

**See Also** Picton, Blenheim and Nelson

---

# HAWERA NI
**Population** 8175
**Location** On route 3, 72 km south of New Plymouth, 91 km north of Wanganui.

---

Hawera is the servicing centre for the southern Taranaki area. The 51 m water tower is no longer used and is a town landmark. During the Taranaki campaigns,

General Chute marched his men through the then thick bush for six weeks up to New Plymouth via Stratford and back around the coast capturing seven pas and sacking 20 villages. However, the Hauhau followers regained control of this area. The Hawera settlers became frustrated by the apparent lack of government efforts and declared themselves a republic, which was dissolved a fortnight later when government assistance reached the district.

## ENVIRONS & ATTRACTIONS
**Hawera Water Tower**  A view of the surrounding countryside from the top of this tower in High Street.
**King Edward Park**  Park with lawns, garden and lake in Main Street.
**Tawhiti Museum**  Private museum with life-size displays of South Taranaki history.

## LOCAL TOURING
**Turuturu-Mokai Pa**  A pre-European pa, possibly 400 years old, designed for hand fighting with tunnels and satellite pas. 2 km north of Hawera on Turuturu Road. The pa's name refers to the custom of impaling heads of slain chiefs on stakes, and refers to previous battles. Next to the pa was a military redoubt, scene of a grisly Hauhau attack in 1863 when most of the garrison were killed.
**Manaia**  This town 15 km east of Hawera has two military block houses on its golf course, built by the Armed Constabulary in 1881, but never subject to attack.
**Te Ngutu-O-Te-Manu**  This area on Ahipaipa Road near Kapuni saw several ambushes between British troops and local Maoris, with varying results. One casualty was Major Von Tempsky, the celebrated but controversial leader of the Forest Rangers. The battle site is now a heavily bushed domain with a memorial to Von Tempsky.

**See Also**  Patea, Opunake and Stratford

# HELENSVILLE NI
**Population**  1347
**Location**  50 km north-west of Auckland on Route 16.

Originally known as Awaroa and Otamateanui, the area was first settled by Europeans in 1863. It became the southern port on the Kaipara Harbour, with vessels plying to Port Albert, Ruawai, and Dargaville, connecting with rail first from Riverhead and later from Auckland. The town is now a centre for dairying and other farming.

## ENVIRONS & ATTRACTIONS
**Parakai Hot Springs**  Hot mineral water springs 3 km from Helensville. These pools are popular with Aucklanders. There is also a domain and picnic ground.

## LOCAL TOURING
**Muriwai Beach**  A west coast beach resort 26 km from Helensville, with a turn-off from Route 16 at Waimauku. There is a Regional Reserve domain adjacent to the beach.

**See Also**  Warkworth and Wellsford

# HOKITIKA SI
**Population**  3427
**Location**  40 km south of Greymouth

Scenic Route 6 runs north/south along the west coast and provides road access south via the Franz Josef and Fox Glaciers through to Haast Pass and Otago. Northbound it leads to Greymouth, Westport and Nelson. Route 73 (the Arthur's Pass Road from Christchurch) intercepts Route 6, 22 km north of Hokitika, while Route 7 (the Lewis Pass road) branches off from Greymouth.

A freight-only railway connects the borough with Greymouth. Scheduled air services operate through Hokitika aerodrome. The Hokitika River once served as a port for the town, but its poor natural facilities, coupled with a drop in traffic, has resulted in its demise.

The area between Hokitika and Greymouth was favoured by the Maoris as a source of greenstone — a kind of nephrite jade used to make adzes and chisels as well as ornaments. The Arahura River was an especially important source of the stone.

The town developed as a goldmining centre from 1864, and reached its peak population of 50 000 in 1866 — a rather rapid growth! The curved river port was treacherous for sailing ships and many were wrecked. Today it is a timber centre as well as a supply town for local dairying. Greenstone is still sought for jewellery and decorative items for tourists.

The west coast has a well-deserved reputation for rain, but the weather and the backdrop of mountains have created a lush scenic landscape that travellers will admire.

## ENVIRONS & ATTRACTIONS
**West Coast Historical Museum**  Contains photographs and relics of local and regional history. Open Monday–Friday 9.30 am-4.30 pm, weekends 2-4 pm.

**Greenstone**  Two factories in the town process and sell greenstone items. Open for inspection as well as sales.

**St Mary's Catholic Church**  Built 1914 on the site of an earlier church, the present building is a Hokitika landmark.

**Gibson Quay**  This is part of the old river port.

**Lake Mahinapua**  A shallow lake partially surrounded by bush, accessible from the Ruatapu Road, 11 km south of Hokitika. The Mahinapua Walkway is a 5.5 km (2 hr one way) walk that connects the Route 6 road with the coastal Ruatapu road 14 km south of Hokitika. The walk follows an old timber tramway and has a side track to the lake. Relics of the sawmilling era are at the western end.

**Lake Kaniere**  The lake is situated 16 km east of Hokitika on Lake Kaniere Road. The Dorothy Falls Road follows the eastern side of the lake down through the Kaniere Scenic Reserve, so a loop can be driven by following round through the Kokatahi Flats. The Lake Kaniere Walkway connects down the western side of the lake for 13 km (4 hr) past bush and lake shore. The Kaniere Water Race Track starts at the northern end of the lake and follows a water race towards the Kaniere Forks power station (7.5 km, 3½ hr). There are several shorter walks in the vicinity of the lake.

**Hokitika River Gorge**  Take the road from the Kaniere turn-off to Kokatahi (or else the loop road via Lake Kaniere described above) and Kowhitirangi, and then continue for 33 km to the end of the road. A short track leads to the gorge. Beyond the gorge a track (for experienced trampers) leads over Whitcombe Pass in the alps and down into the Upper Rakaia in Canterbury.

**Goldsborough**  The Shamrock Creek Amenity Area is situated within the angle formed by the junction of Route 6 and Route 73, north of Hokitika. The Stafford–Dilmanstown road 10 km north, cuts through to Dilmanstown, and has a number of tracks off it. The area protects features of scenic, recreational and historic importance. Goldmining remains are evident. The Goldsborough track offers either a 45-minute return walk to miners' tunnels, or a 4 hr one-way walk that links Goldsborough to Callaghans.

**Ross**  Old gold and timber town 30 km south. Note its 1869 Catholic Cathedral, an opossum fur trading post, and a Walkways Commission visitors centre (located in an 1885 cottage). There are two sections of the Ross Historic Goldfields Walkway — both of 1.5 km (1½ hr each), which show old mine sites.

**Lake Ianthe**  This pretty bush-surrounded lake is 60 km south on Route 6.

**Harihari**  This 'halfway' town between Hokitika and the Franz Josef and Fox Glaciers is 79 km south on Route 6.

**See Also**  Greymouth, Otira and Franz Josef Glacier

---

# HUNTLY  NI
**Population**  6750
**Location**  On Route 1, 84 km south of Auckland, 33 km north of Hamilton.

---

The borough of Huntly is one of New Zealand s most important coalmining areas. The town was also known for its orange coloured building bricks, called 'Huntly' brick.

Coal was discovered in the area by the Austrian geologist Dr Hochstetter in 1859. The coal was used on river boats, including gunboats that were used during the Waikato wars. In 1914 an explosion in a local mine killed 43 people. In 1939, 11 men were killed in the nearby Glen Afton mine. Extensive opencast mining is still carried out and visible from road viewpoints. Huntly power station, with its 150 m chimneys, is a district landmark.

## ENVIRONS & ATTRACTIONS
**Huntly Lake**  (Lake Hakanoa) This small lake and picnic area are on the east side of the borough.

**Huntly Mining Museum**  This is a collection of coalmining equipment housed in the Historic Society's building in Harlock Place. Open 10 am–4 pm daily.

**Huntly Power Station**  This giant power station stands on the western side of the Waikato River and is clearly visible from two rest areas on Route 1. It is operated by both coal (by conveyor belt from a mine 2 km away) and natural gas (by pipe from Taranaki). Water from the river is used for cooling. The power station is not open to the public but the access road is across the Huntly (Tainui) bridge at the southern end of the borough.

**Kimihia Mine**  This coalmine is situated on the north-eastern side of Huntly; it is partly visible from the access roads to it. Admittance is not generally permitted.

**Weavers Crossing**  This is a large opencast mine on the western side of Huntly. Access across the river is via the Tainui bridge; keep ahead for 1 km for a view of the opencast mine from the road.

## LOCAL TOURING
**Rotowaro Bush Tramway**  A disused railway branch line now taken over by the Bush Tramway Club to operate old light steam trains on the first Sunday of each month in winter.

**See Also**  Mercer, Rangiriri and Ngaruawahia

# I

**See Also** Murchison, Westport and Reefton

## INANGAHUA NI
**Population** 109
**Location** On Route 6, 54 km west of Murchison, 47 km east of Westport, 33 km north of Reefton.

This is a small community amid the picturesque scenery of the Buller Gorge. The upper gorge stretches towards Murchison, and the lower gorge — perhaps even more spectacular — stretches towards Westport. The town is a junction for Route 69 south to Reefton. It is also a junction for the Inangahua River with the Buller River. It also might have been a railway junction, situated on the line to Westport, but the planned connection from Nelson never eventuated, although it was started.

At the height of the goldrush, there were around 1000 diggers in the area. An earthquake in 1968 damaged buildings and caused the town's temporary evacuation.

### LOCAL TOURING
**Lyell** A pleasant picnic site on the road 17 km east on Route 6. Display boards describe the once booming goldtown, with 3000 inhabitants. The cemetery is the only surviving part of the town.
**Lyell Walkway** A walk of 3 km (1½ hr return) from the roadside picnic spot, which was once the town of Lyell, up the Lyell Creek to the remains of the old Croesus mine. There are other shorter tracks to what was once Gibbs Town and other mines. The main walkway is an easy family walk, but beware of old shafts on other tracks.
**Hawks Crag** Where the cliff face overhangs the road on Route 6, 21 km west from Inangahua.

## INGLEWOOD NI
**Population** 695
**Location** On Route 3, 22 km south-east of New Plymouth.

Inglewood began as a milling town in dense bush. Now it is a servicing centre for the cleared dairying farmlands.

The town is set at the junction of Routes 3 and 3A — allowing travel to New Plymouth or directly to Waitara and further north bypassing New Plymouth. There is also access to Egmont National Park — refer to the entry under Stratford.

### ENVIRONS & ATTRACTIONS
**Inglewood Glass Plant** Hand-blown glass on display in Cutfield

Street. Open Tuesday, Thursday and Saturday.

**See Also** New Plymouth, Waitara and Stratford

# INVERCARGILL SI
**Population** 48 197
**Location** On Route 1, 217 km south-west of Dunedin, 30 km north of Bluff, at the southern end of Route 1.

Invercargill is the leading city and centre for the extensive fertile region of Southland. Much of the commercial base of the city revolves around agricultural, pastoral and timber activities, though the aluminium smelter near Bluff also provides a boom for the local economy. The city's port is at Bluff, though for many years the Waihopai River also handled shipping.

The city is served by railway, including passenger service to Dunedin and Christchurch; there are also scheduled air services. The city is well laid out, and the main thoroughfares are notably wide.

The site for Invercargill was purchased from the Maoris in 1853. It was named in 1857 after the first Superintendent of Otago Province. In 1861, Southland became a separate province, but suffered financially while Otago enjoyed its goldrushes, and in 1870 it reunited with Otago.

## ENVIRONS & ATTRACTIONS
**Southland Centennial Museum** This collection includes historic items such as fossilised forest, the first shipwreck, an early cannon and a Victoriana Gallery. There is also an art gallery wing. Open weekdays 10 am–4.30 pm, weekends 2–5 pm, Gala Street.

*Lower Mataura River flats near Invercargill, Southland.*

**Queens Park** Contains formal gardens, sports area, aviary and deer park; also wintergardens. The latter is open weekdays 10 am–4.30 pm, weekends 1.30–4.30 pm.

**City Art Gallery** Housed in the former Anderson homestead, in Anderson Park (7 km out of the city) the gallery contains a Lindauer and other New Zealand artists.

**First Church** Built in 1915 in Byzantine style, complete with campanile. Tay Street.

**Other Churches** St Johns (Tay Street) built in 1887; St Marys Basilica with copper dome, Tyne Street.

**Thompsons Bush** A reserve of original forest off Queens Drive.

**Waihopai Walkway** A walk along the embankment of the Waihopai River for nearly 3 km (about 1 hr) through both built-up and rural areas; from Dee Street to Racecourse Road.

**Murihiku Marae** A new complex with emphasis on the descendants of the *Takitimu* canoe. Tramway Road.

## LOCAL TOURING

**Oreti Beach** 10 km south over the Waihopai bridge and then over the Oreti River bridge to this long and exposed southern beach.

**Bluff** Port for Invercargill and Southland, 30 km south on Route 1. Formerly known as Campbelltown and Port Macquarie. Population 2537.

**Bluff Hill** A road climbs up to the viewpoint at 265 m, which overlooks Bluff Harbour across to the Tiwai Point aluminium smelter and around to Foveaux Strait.

**Stirling Point** At the end of the road there is a signpost that notes world distances. There is also a good view out to Dog and Ruapuke Islands.

**Foveaux Walkway** From

Stirling Point, or higher up from Gunpit Road, this walkway follows the coast around Bluff Hill to the main road into Bluff. 6.6 km (2½ hr).

## STEWART ISLAND
This island of 17 200 ha lies 32 km south of Bluff. Its highest point is Mt Anglem (980 m). It is well forested and has a heavy rainfall. The township of Oban (population 347) on Halfmoon

*Butterfield Beach, Halfmoon Bay, Stewart Island.*

Bay, off Paterson Inlet, is the settled area with a port and an airstrip nearby. Roading is very limited, less than 20 km, and is mostly unsealed.

Observation Rock is a 15-minute walk from Oban to a nearby summit for views. The Raroa Scenic Reserve has a pleasant track extending 1 km (20 minutes) from the western end of Traill Park to Watercress Beach. The Glory Cove to Ocean Beach track is a 2 km (1 hr) return walk from the Glory Cove wharf, and is accessible by boat from Halfmoon Bay. There are also many longer and more difficult tramps around the island, such as the north-west circuit (takes a week) or the Link Track (about 3 days). There is much birdlife on the island and it is all protected.

**See Also** Gore, Fortrose and Riverton

# K

**See Also** Mangonui, Kerikeri and Kaikohe

## KAEO NI
**Population** 376
**Location** On Route 10, 77 km south-east of Kataia, or 58 km north of Paihia.

The small farming community of Kaeo is built on the site of the first Wesleyan mission station, which was founded in 1823. The site was subject to inter-Maori conflict, which ultimately resulted in the sacking of the station.

The town is situated upriver from the spectacular Whangaroa Harbour. Surrounded by jagged hills, including the peaks of 'St Peter' and 'St Paul', the harbour is scenic and unspoiled. There is little road access, except to the wharf area on the Kaeo side and to the small community of Totara North on the other side.

The harbour received notoriety in 1809 when a party of Maoris ransacked and burnt the trading vessel *Boyd*, massacring most of its crew in the process. It was possibly motivated by revenge for the ill-treatment of a Maori crew member.

### ENVIRONS & ATTRACTIONS
**Whangaroa Wharf** The scenic wharf area is headquarters for the local fishing fleet. Harbour trips are available.

### LOCAL TOURING
**Matauri Bay** Accessible from a side road south of Kaeo, this picturesque beach looks out on to the Cavalli Islands.
**Puketi Forest** This 1 hr return nature trail walk through forest (including kauri) starts from Forest Headquarters on Waiare Road, south-west of Kaeo.

## KAIKOHE NI
**Population** 3799
**Location** On Route 12 west of the Bay of Islands, 86 km north of Whangarei.

Kaikohe was one of the largest Maori centres in north Auckland and was the scene of considerable fighting during the northern Maori wars. The area was a headquarters for the Maori leader Hone Heke who destroyed the Russell flagpole (refer to the Bay of Islands) four times between 1844 and 1845. He was consequently sought and fought by British troops, which resulted in two battles around the Kaikohe–Ohaeawai area.

The rich volcanic soil of Kaikohe was highly prized in the early days of settlement for its nurturing of bountiful food crops. In recent years it has helped in the development of a valuable dairying industry. Railway connection with Whangarei was established in 1914. When returned servicemen set up farms in the area in 1919 the town's population received a boost. The community quickly grew and in 1927 it became an independent town district.

### ENVIRONS & ATTRACTIONS
**Kaikohe Hill** About 1 km from the town this hill offers a picnic site with a view over the area. There is a Hone Heke monument to the parliamentarian and nephew of the great chief.
**The Pioneer Village** A couple of blocks from the main street, this early town is being re-created, complete with jail, courthouse, blacksmith shop and railway.

## LOCAL TOURING

**Ngawha Springs** These soda mercury springs range in colour and temperature and offer possible health cures for bathers. The springs are for soaking, not swimming. Open daily to 9 pm.

**Ohaeawai** Site of a battle in 1845 between British troops and Hone Heke's 'rebels', which resulted in defeat for the British with 41 soldiers dead. A small church marks the location. Nearby Lake Omapere was the site of an earlier battle in which the Maoris lost 30 men.

**Waimate North** In 1830 Samuel Marsden established a mission station here to teach farming, schooling and religion. It had a chequered history, including three months occupation by British troops during the 'Hone Heke war'. However, the remaining Waimate Mission House is New Zealand's second oldest building, and has been restored and refurbished with furniture and items of the period. Nearby is the church of St John the Baptist, built in 1871. Both buildings are worth visiting and are open daily. Waimate North is 19 km east of Kaikohe.

**See Also** Kerikeri, Kawakawa and Bay of Islands

---

# KAIKOURA SI

**Population** 2209
**Location** On Route 1, 132 km south of Blenheim, 191 km north of Christchurch.

---

The name Kaikoura means 'to eat crayfish' — giving an indication that the town stands on a rocky coastline. It is situated on and north of a bluff peninsula under the heights of the seaward Kaikoura mountains, which rise to 2600 m. The beginnings of European settlement at Kaikoura are associated with whaling activities, and fishing remains a local industry today.

Road and rail access hug the coast both north and south of the town, and Route 70 provides an inland (unsealed) connection to Waiau, Hanmer Springs and the Lewis Pass.

## ENVIRONS & ATTRACTIONS

**Kaikoura Historical Society** A collection of local items including Maori and whaling relics. Open weekends 2–4 pm, Ludstone Road.

**Garden of Memories** Norfolk Pines and whalebones share this small garden.

**Kaikoura Aquarium** A local aquarium for public viewing. (The nearby Marine Laboratory is not open to the public.)

**Fyffe House** The Fyffe family were early whalers and this colonial cottage was built in 1860. It is now maintained by the Historic Places Trust. Avoca Street.

**Kaikoura Lookout** Along Scarborough Terrace to the Kaikoura peninsula, this lookout has views of the ocean and mountains. Nearby are the sites of Nga Niho Pa and the restored Takahanga Marae.

**Peninsula Walkway** A coastal walk around the peninsula, which is broken into three sections. The Shoreline Walk (1½–2 hr) around the tip of the peninsula gives a close-up view of a seal colony; the Clifftop Walk (1½ hr) gives a panoramic view of the coastline beneath; the South Bay Walk (20 minutes) cuts across the neck of the peninsula.

## LOCAL TOURING

**Maori Leap Cave** 3 km south on Route 1, this large limestone cave, possibly 2 million years old, has delicate stalagtite and stalagmite formations. Conducted tours available.

**Mt Fyffe Forest**  The summit is 1602 m and is accessible by two routes, both of which are 6 hr return. For the less energetic, the Hinau Walk is 40 minutes and the Forest Walk is 1½ hr. Access to the forest is via Hinau picnic area in Postmans Road, or via Mt Fyffe Road (both roads are 8 km north).

**See Also**  Blenheim, Hanmer Springs and Cheviot

---

# KAITAIA NI
**Population** 5011
**Location** 325 km north of Auckland, near the top of Route 1.

---

Although it is historically correct to say that Kaitaia was officially founded in 1833 by the Church Missionary Society, the history of the far north goes back to around 950, when Kupe, the Polynesian navigator, supposedly arrived in Taipa, and moved around the coast to the Hokianga Harbour.

The missionaries built a mission station near an existing Maori village. They taught Christianity to the Maoris living in the area, and placated the excesses of the crews of whaling and timber ships, which operated in the area. Kaitaia was just one of a number of such outposts through the far north.

The town grew when kauri gum diggers swarmed to the area in the 1880s and 1890s. It is now New Zealand's most northern borough, and is a servicing town for agricultural and tourism industries.

The community of Awanui, 7 km further north, is the top end of Route 1. It is the junction for the coastal road Route 10 and the road north to Cape Reinga.

## ENVIRONS & ATTRACTIONS
**Aqualand**  Features a display of fish and birds.

**Reservoir Hill**  A lookout point close to the town, which offers views over the town as well as 'coast to coast'.

**Far North Regional Museum**  This contains a collection of historic artifacts including polished kauri gum and shipping relics.

## LOCAL TOURING
**Ahipara**  A small community lying at the southern end of Ninety Mile Beach. Tours in special vehicles through the old gum digging sites near here are available.

**Cape Reinga**  Refer to the separate entry under Cape Reinga.

**Houhora**  A tiny settlement about 52 km north of Kaitaia on the Cape Reinga road. The Wagener Museum is on a side road to Houhora Heads. It contains a popular collection of household and other bric-a-brac from the past. New Zealand's most northern tavern is nearby.

**Mangamuka Gorge**  Access to this gorge, located 26 km south of Kaitaia, is detailed in itinerary 3.

**Ninety Mile Beach**  Nearly 90 km long, this beach sweeps up the west coast from Ahipara almost to Cape Reinga. Main access is either from Ahipara or Waipapakauri (turnoff 12 km north of Kaitaia). The beach sand is hard below high-water mark, and can be driven on; however, we suggest you use one of the tour buses instead. *If* you drive on the beach, avoid the 3 hours either side of high tide, and do not stop your car on wet sand, even though it may be firm enough to drive on. The northern access to the beach, via the Te Paki stream, is restricted.

**Omahuta Sanctuary** Refer to itinerary 3. The turn-off for this forest reserve is at Mangamuka Bridge, 38 km south of Kaitaia. The access road is 13 km further. A half-hour bush walk offers a great display of kauri, and plentiful birdlife.

**See Also** Cape Reinga, Mangonui and Kaeo

# KARAMEA SI
**Population** 296
**Location** The terminus of Route 67, 97 km north of Westport.

At the top of the west coast, Karamea is now a centre for dairying and sawmilling. The settlement was established in 1874 and was serviced by sea until the road opened in 1915. However, the 1929 earthquake in Murchison ruined the river port.

The town is popularly known as the southern entrance (or exit) for the Heaphy Track, and also nearby for the Wangapeka track. A coast road continues north for 15 km beyond the town and gives access to the Heaphy. The Fenian Range up behind the town has several known cave systems, as well as limestone arches and some traces of goldmining. The Honeycomb Hill Cave contains sub-fossil remains and bone deposits, but is usually closed to the public.

## ENVIRONS & ATTRACTIONS
**Karamea Centennial Museum** Items of local interest on display in Waverley Street. Open Sunday, Monday and Wednesday, 1.15–4 pm (in summer).

## LOCAL TOURING
**Kohaihai River** The start of the Heaphy Track is at the end of the road north (15 km). Walk over the swing bridge and try either the first 3 km to Scotts Camp, or a 40-minute bush loop walk.

**Cavern Creek Cave System** 7 km north, turn off to the Oparara Quarry. This is the start of a 3-hr return track via Cavern Creek, Maloneys Bluff and Tunnel Cave. Continue on a loop around the Oparara–Fenian track and Miners Cave.

**Little Wanganui** 9 km south of Karamea on Route 67, this is an access point to the Wangapeka Track.

**See Also** Westport, Collingwood and Motueka

# KATIKATI NI
**Population** 1921
**Location** On Route 2, 26 km south of Waihi, 36 km north of Tauranga.

Katikati was originally founded by Irish immigrants in 1875. The town is adjacent to the Katikati entrance to the ribbon of water called the Tauranga Harbour and is shielded by Matakana Island. However, that end of the harbour was not suitable for shipping and Katikati developed merely as a stopping point for the service-cars and later the railway. Now the railway is diverted through the Kaimai tunnel and it no longer touches Katikati. The area is a dairying and fruit-growing centre and kiwifruit is also an important crop. Matakana Island is owned mainly by the Maoris and it has no tourist amenities.

## ENVIRONS & ATTRACTIONS
**Katikati Bird Gardens** This is located at the end of Walkers Road, 6 km south of Katikati. The gardens have bird aviaries, a lily pond and picnic area. Open

*The Bay of Islands at sunrise.*

10 am–4 pm, October through to May.

**Sapphire Springs** Turnoff 4 km south of Katikati. The complex includes accommodation, camp ground and restaurant. There are open air and private hot mineral pools. Open daily to 10 pm.

## LOCAL TOURING

**Athenree and Bowentown** These two communities are situated at the southern end of Waihi Beach. Turnoff Route 2 just before the Athenree Gorge.

**Omokoroa** A beach resort with thermal springs on a point jutting into Tauranga Harbour. It is on a side road leaving Route 2, 19 km south of Katikati, 17 km north of Tauranga. Nearby Pahoia is a similar beach resort.

**See Also** Waihi, Tauranga and Whangamata

# KAWAKAWA NI
**Population** 1538
**Location** On Route 1, 55 km
north of Whangarei, and 16 km
away from Paihia.

Popularised by the railway that
runs through its main street, this
community is a gateway to the
Bay of Islands, though new
roading almost bypasses the town.
The town's economy was
originally based on flax and coal
and today it is a farming and
commercial community. A tourist
railway operates on the tracks
of the original government
line between Kawakawa
and the port of Opua in the Bay
of Islands.

## ENVIRONS & ATTRACTIONS
**Waiomio Caves** Situated almost
1 km off Route 1 a few minutes
south of Kawakawa, these caves

are a mixture of sandstone and limestone.

## LOCAL TOURING
**Ruapekapeka Pa** Accessible off Route 1, 16 km south of Kawakawa, this marks the site of the final battle between Hone Heke and the British troops. The battle was supervised by Governor Grey in January 1846 and was a British victory — a total of 32 were killed. The lines of the fortification can still be traced, and a cannon stands as a stark reminder of the battle.

**See Also** Kaikohe, Bay of Islands and Kerikeri

# KAWERAU NI
**Population** 8311
**Location** Situated off Route 30, 32 km from Whakatane, 54 km from Rotorua.

Kawerau was a planned town built in 1953 to service the giant Tasman pulp and paper mill established there. The main product of the mill is newsprint paper and the mill remains the principal source of employment in the town. Logs come by rail from the Kaingaroa Forest at Murupara, and exports are railed to the port at Mt Maunganui. A geothermal station provides steam and electricity for the mill.
The Caxton mill, which makes tissues and toilet papers, is also nearby.

## ENVIRONS & ATTRACTIONS
**Tasman Mill** Tours are conducted at 1.30 pm, Monday–Friday. No children under 12 years allowed.
**Mt Edgecumbe** The Putauaki hill (805 m) behind the town was used as a burial ground by the local Ngatiawa tribe. Allow a day if you are climbing to the top (for extensive views); allow 70 minutes if you are in the annual race to the top.

## LOCAL TOURING
**Edgecumbe** This small country town is off Route 2, 18 miles north of Kawerau. It is therefore some distance from, but in sight of, Mt Edgecumbe. It is a centre for dairying on the local Rangitaiki Plains.
**Tarawera Falls** The natural outlet from Lake Tarawera (near Rotorua) is via an underground stream, which emerges through a tunnel in a sheer rock wall to plunge some 60 m. The falls are on a 15-minute bush walk from Fentons Mill Road to the south of Kawerau. As the forest is privately owned by the mill, no other tracks should be used without permission.
**Matahina Dam** This is one of two power stations built on the Matahina River. The road branches off at Te Teko, 10 miles north-east of Kawerau and then follows up the Galatea road. It eventually leads through to Murupara.
The dam is the largest earth dam in the North Island — second only to Benmore in the South Island. It is 79 m high. Further upriver is the smaller Aniwhenua dam, which uses water adjacent to the Aniwhenua Falls. Lakes containing fowl and fish have built up behind both dams.
**Murupara** Situated 65 km south of Kawerau (via Te Teko) but perhaps more accessible on Route 38 from Rotorua, this town is a timber-milling area serving the Kaingaroa Forest and sending its logs by rail to Kawerau.

**See Also** Whakatane, Rotorua and Waikaremoana

# KAWHIA NI
**Population** 456
**Location** On the west coast of the North Island, 57 km west of Otorohanga on Route 31.

Kawhia's history goes back to the *Tainui* and *Aotea* canoes of the great Maori fleet about 1350. The area was popular with the Maoris, and there were apparently many tribal battles over it. In 1821, for example, a force of 5000 Waikato Maoris defeated the renegade Te Rauparaha, and forced him and his tribe to flee southwards to the Horowhenua and Kapiti Island areas.

European settlement began with missionaries and traders in 1834, but following the land wars, they were evicted from the district (and indeed from most of the King Country) for 20 years until 1881. The town was then re-surveyed and it grew slowly. Its great harbour (perhaps the best on the North Island west coast), however, was never used to its potential because of its land access. The harbour bar may have also hindered development. Today Kawhia is still a quiet community with a small rural township. The traditional resting place of the *Tainui* canoe at Karewa Beach remains a sacred spot to many Maoris.

## ENVIRONS & ATTRACTIONS
**Te Puia Ocean Beach** A black sand, west coast beach accessible through a pine plantation 4 km beyond the town. Between low and mid-tide, thermal water wells up through the sand in a certain part of the beach, and bathers may scoop out hot water hollows in which to soak.

## LOCAL TOURING
**Taharoa** The Taharoa iron sands are 47 km around the harbour and back towards the ocean side. A large plant situated here exports iron-sand concentrate to Japan. An extraction plant and offshore port facilities have also been established.

**See Also** Raglan, Otorohanga and Te Awamutu

# KERIKERI NI
**Population** 1922
**Location** Situated on an inlet of the Bay of Islands, the town is on a side road off Route 1, 23 km from Paihia, or 88 km north of Whangarei.

Kerikeri is a picturesque and flourishing citrus fruit-growing and craft centre. Many craftspeople are now making Kerikeri their home, and the local pottery and weaving is of particular interest. There is also extensive fruit and vegetable farming in the area.

About 1 km past the commercial area is the site of New Zealand's second mission station established in 1819. New Zealand's first plough was used in Kerikeri and the first grass was also sown here.

## ENVIRONS & ATTRACTIONS
**Kerikeri Mission House** Overlooking the inlet, this building was erected in 1822 and is the oldest surviving building in the country. It was known as the Kemp House, after the missionary family and their descendants who lived in it.
**Kerikeri Stone Store** The old stone store house was completed in 1835 by the mission, but became disused when the mission declined. Today the building holds a shop and museum.
**Rewa's Village** This is a reconstruction of a Maori kainga

*An old stone store at Kerikeri.*

or village in pre-European times,
down near the inlet. It is a typical
Maori village as distinct from a pa,
which the Maoris used as a
fortress.

## LOCAL TOURING

**Rainbow Falls** Also known as
the Kerikeri Falls, these are on the
Kerikeri River and are accessible
by the road 4 km from the inlet. A
walkway leads from the Ranger
Station at the inlet and follows up
the river through bush about
3 km to the falls.

**See Also** Kawakawa, Bay of
Islands and Kaikohe

## KUROW SI
**Population** 541
**Location** On Route 83, 66 km
north-west of Oamaru, 52 km east
of Omarama.

Situated in a valley on the
southern banks of the Waitaki
River, this rural township, which
is also a fishing centre, has been

**The Chapel** Church and vicarage built in 1892.

## LOCAL TOURING

**Hakataramea Valley** Drive over the town bridge to this valley following the Hakataramea River northwards. A road of sorts continues over the Hakataramea Pass to Lake Tekapo, but check conditions locally before attempting it.

**Duntroon** This farming and fishing centre on the lower Waitaki River is 23 km east. It is also the northern entrance to the Dansey Pass.

**Takiroa Rock Drawings** Maori rock drawings of an unknown date, which are readily accessible by the roadside. 21 km east of Kurow on Route 83.

**Waitaki Dam** Completed in 1934 as the first of a now extensive chain of hydro-development on the lower and upper river. Dam and powerhouse are visible from roadside viewpoint.

**Aviemore Dam** Large concrete and earth dam built in 1968. A loop road over the dam leads up the other side of Lake Aviemore to rejoin Route 83 near Benmore and Otematata.

**Otematata** Construction town for the Aviemore and Benmore Dams, which is now a holiday spot for boating and fishing.

**Benmore Dam** A giant earth dam finished in 1965, which was New Zealand's most powerful electricity station. The dam holds back New Zealand's largest artificial lake — the blue-coloured Lake Benmore. The dam can be viewed from picnic areas on the side road from Otematata and from an observation point. The road over the dam links around Lake Aviemore and back across the Aviemore dam.

**See Also** Waimate, Oamaru, Omarama and Ranfurly

boosted by hydro-electric development up the river. Kurow is the terminus for Route 82, a link road striking north-east to Waimate and the coast. It also used to be the terminus for a branch railway from Pukeuri.

## ENVIRONS & ATTRACTIONS
**Upper Kaitaki Pioneer Gallery and Museum** Photographs and displays from the early days when the valley was the route to Central Otago (via the Lindis Pass). Open daily 3–4 pm, in the main street.

# L

## LAKE PUKAKI SI
Refer to Twizel

## LAKE TEKAPO SI
**Population** 442
**Location** On Route 8, 43 km west of Fairlie, 51 km north of Twizel.

A glacial lake, which stretches nearly 20 km, gives its name to this locality, which lies at an altitude of 710 m. The lake is dammed and the main road passes over the dam. The lake's waters pass through Tekapo A power station and are diverted by a 26 km canal to Tekapo B power station. The waters then enter Lake Pukaki and the Waitaki River power schemes.

The settlement at Lake Tekapo is small and is basically a supply centre for daily requirements for the local inhabitants and tourists.

### ENVIRONS & ATTRACTIONS
**Church of the Good Shepherd** A stone chapel on the lake promontory, which contrasts with the pale blue waters of the lake. Nearby stands the statue of a bronze sheep-dog, which commemorates all the sheep-dogs of the district.
**Mt John Observatory** Observatory operated by the Canterbury University in conjunction with two United

*The glacial Lake Tekapo.*

States universities. It has also been a satellite tracking station.

## LOCAL TOURING
**Tekapo Ski-Field** Accessible up the north-east side of the lake, this ski-field generally operates July to September. 35 km.

**Lake McGregor and Alexandrina** Bird sanctuaries on the southern side of Lake Tekapo, which are accessible from the side road beyond Mt John. 10 km.

**MacKenzie Pass** Turn off Route 8, 14 km north-east of Tekapo, to meet up again with Route 8 at Albany, bypassing Fairlie and the road to Geraldine. This is the pass supposedly used by the sheep-rustler McKenzie.

**See Also** Fairlie, Twizel and Mt Cook

# LAWRENCE SI
**Population** 552
**Location** On Route 8, 33 km west of its junction with Route 1 at Clarksville (near Milton); also 26 km east of Raes Junction and 58 km east of Roxburgh.

Lawrence is an attractive township with tree-lined streets, but there is little to indicate its meteoric growth during the height of its goldrush.

The town was founded in 1857 and named after the defender of Lucknow.

In 1861 Gabriel Read discovered gold in a valley now called Gabriel's Gully. About 12 months later the gully and surrounding Tuapeka goldfield had a population of 11 000 people

(while Dunedin itself had only 5200).

From 1866 a community of 500 Chinese sought gold at nearby Waitahuna. The discovery of gold by mining, sluicing and dredging went on in and around the district for many years.

## ENVIRONS & ATTRACTIONS

**Lawrence Museum** An excellent museum in the main street, which reflects the gold and pastoral interests of the early community.

**Tuapeka Domain** A reserve with a cairn, which celebrates Gabriel Read's famous find.

## LOCAL TOURING

**Blue Spur** From Lawrence take Gabriel's Gully Road to the viewpoint (3 km) overlooking this eroded feature — the original source of the gold in the gully. The Blue Spur township was sited 4 km up the zigzag road.

**Wetherston** 3 km north in a gully adjacent to Gabriel's, is the site of a similar goldrush. Today it has the brick remains of a brewery and a track to the Phoenix dam, which supplies water to Lawrence.

**Waitahuna** 11 km east, this twin town to Lawrence was originally called Havelock, but neither the name nor much of the town has survived. The gold-bearing Waitahuna Gully was once the scene of much mining activity.

**See Also** Milton, Roxburgh and Tapanui

---

# LEVIN NI
**Population** 15 368
**Location** On Route 1, 19 km south of Foxton, 94 km north of Wellington.

---

Named after W. H. Levin, founder of a Wellington company and a

director of the Manawatu Railway, the town developed as a railway settlement on the Manawatu Railway. The Taurarura Range forms a backdrop to the town. The surrounding area, known as Horowhenua, is a town-milk and market-gardening supply centre for Wellington. Tatum Park, headquarters and training centre for the Boys Scout movement, is 10 km south.

## ENVIRONS & ATTRACTIONS

**Lake Horowhenua** A lake area for picnics and rowing, 2 km west of town. A feature of the lake is the artificial islands, which are built by bundles of vegetation topped with sand.

**Waiopehu Scenic Reserve** A dense native bush 4 km out on Queen Street East.

## LOCAL TOURING

**Hokio Beach and Waitarere Beach** Two west coast beaches, which are 10 km and 14 km respectively west of the town.

**Lake Papaitonga** 6 km south, branch off Route 1 at Ohau to this scenic and historic lake. Te Rauparaha was invited here by local Muaupoko Maoris, but he discovered it was a trap and killed 600 of them.

**See Also** Wellington, Otaki and Foxton

---

# LEWIS PASS SI
Refer to Maruia Springs.

---

# LUMSDEN SI
**Population** 569
**Location** On the intersection of Route 6 with Route 94, 110 km south of Queenstown, 80 km north of Invercargill.

---

The community of Lumsden is situated on the east bank of the Oreti River, at the northern edge

*Farming land on the outskirts of Queenstown.*

of the Waimea Plain. It is a farming district, also known as the originator of 'Chewings Fescue' a strain of grass seed. The first land was taken here by Europeans in the 1860s and was known as Elbow, because of the nearby bend in the Oreti River.

The town is a tourist crossroad between Southland, the Southern Lakes, and Fiordland. Many travellers from Queenstown to Te Anau and Milford Sound, however, take the Five Rivers Road to Mossburn, which bypasses the town.

## LOCAL TOURING

**Mossburn** A settlement 13 km west of the junction of Route 94 with Route 6, and 19 km from Lumsden. The Matuku Engine Museum displays engines and agricultural machinery.

**The Key** 34 km west of Mossburn is the junction of the road to Clifden via Redcliff and Blackmount. An area of barren landscape around here is appropriately known as 'the Wilderness'.

**Mavora Lakes** Branching off Route 94, 14 km west of Mossburn at Centre Hill, an unsealed road leads to the small south and larger north Mavora Lakes, which are set in tussock and bush at 625 m altitude.

**Mavora–Walter Peak Road** Near the Mavora Lakes, a dry weather (and sometimes dusty) road, which has a metal surface and several fords, leads a further 42 km to the Mt Nicholas and Walter Peak sheep stations on Lake Wakatipu, opposite Queenstown. There is presently no vehicle access to Queenstown, though the possibility of one has been discussed.

**Mavora–Wakatipu Walkway** From the road's end at Mavora Lakes, a four-day walkway (51 km) leads through tussock over Pass Burn into the bush-clad Greenstone Valley to Elfin Bay on Lake Wakatipu. There is a road (and bus in the summer) connection to Queenstown.

**See Also** Queenstown and Te Anau

# M

## MANAPOURI SI
Refer to Te Anau.

## MANGONUI NI
**Population** 58
**Location** 38 km south of Kaitaia on Route 10.

The small community of Mangonui nestles on the side of Mangonui Harbour and its Mill Bay. The harbour leads into the larger Doubtless Bay, along the shores of which are several pleasant beaches. Beaching, boating and fishing are the main tourist activities in the area. The community is steeped in Maori tradition with the arrival of Kupe about 950, and the arrival of one of the canoes of the 'Great Fleet' about 1350. The French explorer D'Urville had a skirmish with Maoris here in 1769.

### ENVIRONS & ATTRACTIONS
**Coopers Beach** Just 2 km north of Mangonui, this offers an impressive sweep of beach. There is a Maori pa site on the knoll at the southern end of the beach, accessible by a side road.
**Cable Bay** Another pleasant beach 2 km north of Coopers, fronting on to Doubtless Bay. The Bay was so named because it used to be the landfall for the Pacific telegraph cable.
**Taipa** 2 km north from Cable Bay, this beach also fronts on to Doubtless Bay.
**Karikari Peninsula** 15 km from Awanui, and 15 km north of Mangonui on Route 10, a side road leads to the beaches of Tokerau, Whatuwhiwhi and Matai Bay. The area is largely underdeveloped but the Department of Conservation operates a camping ground at picturesque Matai Bay.

**See Also** Kaitaia, Cape Reinga and Kaeo

## MARTON NI
**Population** 1048
**Location** 4 km on side road off Route 1, 15 km north-east of Bulls.

Marton was originally founded by stock drovers and speculators in the 1860s, but the town really developed when the railway came in 1879. It was on the line from Palmerston North to Wanganui and Taranaki, but became a junction when the main trunk line from Auckland intersected here.

The town was originally called Tutaenui, which in Maori means 'a dung heap'. The name was therefore changed in 1869 to Marton, so commemorating the birthplace of Captain Cook in England.

The town has three church-run private schools. The national headquarters and training centre for the girl guide movement is nearby.

### ENVIRONS & ATTRACTIONS
**Marton Park** Flower gardens in the town centre.
**St Stephens Church** Built in 1873 of timber (mainly totora), it has fine interior panelling.

### LOCAL TOURING
**Hunterville District Settlers Museum** A collection of local interest, open Friday and Sunday afternoons at the town of Hunterville, 28 km north-east on Route 1.
**Vinegar Hill Reserve** On the banks of the Rangitiki River, where a side road to/from

Fielding and Palmerston North branches off Route 1.

**See Also**  Taihape, Bulls and Feilding

---

# MARUIA SPRINGS SI
**Population**  17
**Location**  On the Lewis Pass Road (Route 7), 15 km east of Springs Junction.

---

This small community lies on the scenic Lewis Pass Road between North Canterbury and Westland, and is just 5 km west of the actual pass. The hot springs in this bush, set among almost alpine scenery, offer a unique stopover.

## ENVIRONS & ATTRACTIONS
**Maruia Springs Track**  A 40-minute nature walk from the hotel through beech forest.

## LOCAL TOURING
**Springs Junction**  Intersection of Route 65 from Murchison with Route 7. There is a visitor centre here for information on tracks in the area. The junction is 15 km west of the Springs.
**Lewis Pass National Reserve** This is New Zealand's first national reserve (as distinct from National Park) founded in 1985. A number of tracks explore the beech-forested mountain country. The Lewis Pass mountain track is a 45-minute return walk from the car park at the road summit and gives views over the Maruia River, Cannibal Gorge, Gloriana Peak and the Fryberg Range. Maori parties bringing greenstone over from the west coast used to dispose of their unwanted prisoners and slaves in the gorge. Other tracks, which are signposted, include the Waterfalls Walk (10 minutes each way), and the Lake Daniells Track (3 hr return) from the Marble Hill picnic

area, 4 km from Springs Junction.
**St James Walkway**  A 66 km (5 day) route from near the top of the Lewis Pass, over the St James station, passing Cannibal Gorge and the Ada Pass. There are huts along the way.
**Rahu Saddle**  The road saddle here is 8 km west of Springs Junction on Route 7. There are a number of tracks through the beech forest, including the Klondyke Track (2 hr each way from the side road at the Saddle) to several tarns and a waterfall.

**See Also**  Hanmer Springs, Murchison and Reefton

---

# MASTERTON NI
**Population**  18 511
**Location**  On Route 2, 101 km north-east of Wellington.

---

Masterton was founded by the Wairarapa Small Farms Association. It was named after Joseph Masters, one of the early settlers and a prime force behind the association. In contrast to the large tracts of land sold elsewhere, Greytown and Masterton were sold in smaller blocks to settlers with less finance. Although Greytown promised to be the larger centre, the railway chose a flood-free route 6 km from that town; Masterton, however, continued to prosper because it was on the railway line.

Masterton is the leading town and most important centre in the Wairarapa region. The 'Golden Shears' sheep-shearing competition is held in the first week of March. The hills of Wairarapa and the east coast regions are sheep-rearing areas.

## ENVIRONS & ATTRACTIONS
**Queen Elizabeth Park**  Situated on the western bank of the Waipoua River, the park has

gardens, sports fields, play areas as well as a deer park.

**Wairarapa Arts Centre** This gallery and cultural centre is open Tuesday to Friday, 10 am–5 pm.

**Nukutaimeneha Meeting House** Built in 1908 at Carterton, this now serves as the Anglican Maori mission centre. Cole Street.

**Vintage Aviation Museum** Located at Hood airfield, the museum is open on Sundays.

## LOCAL TOURING

**Mt Bruce Reserve** This national wildlife and conservation centre is on the slopes of Mt Bruce, 30 km north of Masterton. It is a popular attraction, with birds and other animals on display. Rare birds here include the Takahe (also known as Notornis) and the Black Stilt. Open daily 10 am–4 pm.

**Mt Holdsworth Reserve** 22 km west along Norfolk and Holdsworth roads is the Tararua Forest Park and Mt Holdsworth (1474 m). There are a number of forest walks and park huts. The ranges are subject to rapid weather changes, and high country tramps should only be done by experienced trampers. However, there are several easier tracks for the less experienced.

**Donnelleys Flat** An all-weather, all-age walk of 1 km each way from the lodge at the end of the Mt Holdsworth Road.

**Holdsworth Lookout** A well-graded track (1 hr each way) from Holdsworth lodge; easy in fine weather.

**Mt Holdsworth Summit** For experienced trampers only from Holdsworth Lodge, 5 hr up, 4 hr back. An overnight stop can be made at Powell Hut.

**Riversdale Beach** This beach holiday area is 56 km from Masterton. A tractor race is held on Wellington Anniversary Day.

**Castlepoint** This coastal holiday settlement was so named by Captain Cook because of its high castle-like rock. It also has a good beach and a lagoon. A tall lighthouse, which can be reached by a 15-minute walk, stands 52 m above the sea. Nearby is the place where aerial topdressing was reportedly first done in New Zealand in 1947 — this method has since brought into production thousands of hectares of previously unsuitable land, along the east coast and elsewhere. A beach horserace meeting is held at Castlepoint during the second half of March.

**Eketahuna** Smaller borough in the upper Wairarapa area, 40 km north of Masterton.

**Makakahi Gorge** Domain on the edge of the Matakahe River 1 km from the main street of Eketahuna.

**See Also** Featherston, Greytown and Woodville

---

# MATAMATA NI
**Population** 5701
**Location** In the eastern Waikato towards the southern end of Route 27.

---

Matamata is an important dairying, horse training and breeding district in the eastern Waikato. It is also a shopping and commercial centre for the district. It is served by a (freight only) railway, and several Waikato link roads serve the district.

The town followed the development of a large estate by Josiah Firth who pioneered land development and also early road and river use. He leased his land from Wiriemu Tamihana who lived in the area.

Tamihana was a supporter of the Waikato Maoris, especially the proclamation of Te Wherowhero as the first Maori King. But Tamihana was a moderate, whereas the 'Kingites' were more persuaded by the military views of Rewi Maniapoto; his battles and the consequent confiscating of Maori land is described under other headings in this book.

## ENVIRONS & ATTRACTIONS
**Centennial Drive**  This is a pleasant drive through reserve on two sides of the downtown area. There are picnic places and gardens.

## LOCAL TOURING
**Firth Tower Historical Reserve**  This three-storeyed blockhouse built by Josiah Firth (but never used) as a precaution against attack is 3 km from Matamata. The homestead nearby is a re-creation as the original was burnt. Other buildings and artifacts are also displayed. Open daily.

**Opal (Matamata) Hot Springs**  Private and public hot mineral water pools. The facility is open daily including evenings; there is a charge for admission.

**Wairere Falls**  This 150 m waterfall in the Kaimai Range is reached by a 20-minute walk to the lookout from the road's end, a 50-minute walk to the top, or a 3 hr walk for the round trip. Access to the walks is off Goodwin Road, 14 km north-east of Matamata.

**Kaimai Lookout**  A twisting climb up Tauranga Road to the lookout for extensive views over Matamata and eastern Waikato.

**See Also**  Morrinsville, Te Awamutu and Tauranga

*A horse stud farm near Cambridge.*

# MAUNGATUROTO NI

**Population** 868
**Location** On Route 12, 8 km from its junction with Route 1 at Brenderwyn, and 36 km north-west of Wellsford.

Maungaturoto is a farming community, which serves the mid-north region between Wellsford and Dargaville. The town stretches along Route 12. It is also a station on the Auckland–Whangarei freight-only railway line.

## LOCAL TOURING

**Matakohe** On a side road off Route 12, 18 km west of Maungaturoto, this farming community has two claims to fame: First, it was the birthplace and residence of Joseph Coates (1878–1943) who became New Zealand's first native born Prime Minister (excluding a fortnight when Sir F. H. D. Bell temporarily filled the role). Secondly, it is famous for its museum — one of the best in the north — which displays relics from the past.

**Coates Memorial Church** Erected in 1950 as a tribute to Joseph Coates — returned World War I soldier (decorated with M.C. and bar) and parliamentarian (Prime Minister 1925–28).

**Otamatea Kauri and Pioneer Museum** Also known as the Matakohe Kauri Museum, there are extensive displays of kauri timber and kauri gum, along with displays of the complete kauri industry and of the people involved. Open daily 9 am–5 pm.

**See Also** Whangarei, Dargaville and Wellsford

# MERCER NI

**Population** 161
**Location** On Route 1, 56 km south of Auckland.

Named after Captain Mercer of the Royal Artillery who died at the battle of Rangiriri (20 km further south) in 1863 the town originally marked the end of the Great South Road. Travel from Mercer to Hamilton was by river.

The Mangatawhiri River just north of Mercer was recognised as the boundary between European and Maori land. When General Cameron and his troops crossed this river in 1863 the Waikato war commenced. The town is now a small settlement on the banks of the Waikato River.

## ENVIRONS & ATTRACTIONS

**War Memorials** Just down a short side road, note the remains of a gun turret from the armoured gun boat *Pioneer*, which now serves as the base for the World War 1 memorial.

## LOCAL TOURING

**Meremere Power Station** 4 km further south, note the six 46 m chimneys rising from this coal-fired station. Coal is brought in from the nearby Maramarua and Huntly coalfields. Water from the Waikato River is used for condensing and cooling before being returned to the river downstream. The six turbines can generate a total of 210 000 kw, but all the generators do not usually operate together.

**Meremere Redoubt** Behind the power station in the middle of the Meremere village is the site of a Maori pa and military redoubt, which were used during the Waikato wars. Access to this historic site is by the same road that gives access to the power station (turning sharply up the hill), or by another road further south of the town. The site is marked and the trenches of the redoubt are still clearly visible. There is a short walk and an explanatory notice.

**Whangamarino**
**Walkway** This walkway leads off a pleasant riverside area, which is accessible from Oram Road between Mercer and Meremere. The walkway leads up Mount Puketutu (376 m), past the remains of a Maori pa and a military redoubt from the times of the Waikato land wars. This walk also gives views over the remaining Whangamarino Wetland, a combination of swamp and bog that covers more than 7000 ha, and is noted for its bird, fish and plant life.

**See Also** Tuakau, Rangariri and Huntly

# METHVEN SI
**Population** 923
**Location** On Route 77, 35 km north-west of Ashburton; also by various routes about 95 km south-west of Christchurch.

Methven is a farming community at the western edge of the Canterbury plains. In recent years it has benefited from the development of the nearby Mt Hutt ski-field — a popular field with a longer season than most others in New Zealand.

Of note in the district is the Rangitata Diversion Race, which carries water from the Rangitata River 66 km north to the Rakaia River. On the way the water goes under the Ashburton River. The water is used for irrigation, especially in summer, and for power generation through the Highbank hydro-power station.

The foothills of the Southern Alps rise beyond Methven. They provided the inspiration for Samuel Butler's story of Erewhon, and are also the setting for more recent books about sheep station life in the district.

ENVIRONS & ATTRACTIONS
**Church of All Saints** Built in 1879 at Sherwood (21 km away). In 1884 it was hauled by 3 traction engines to its present site in Chapman Street.
**Methven Historical Museum** Display of photographs and memorabilia in Bank Street.

LOCAL TOURING
**Mt Hutt** The Hood Alpine Highway is a private toll road of 12 km up to the 1600 m ski-field. Good views on a clear winter's day. The road starts 13 km west of Methven.
**Highbank Power Station** 10 km north on the banks of the Waimakariri River is this small power station, which is fed by the Rangitata diversion scheme (the station is 10 km west of the Highbank settlement).
**Methven Walkway** A 14 km (3 hr) walk beginning near the Homes Road corner just north of the town, then following the Diversion Race to the Ashburton River.
**Awa Awa Rata Reserve** This bush reserve is 14 km west up McLennans Bush Road (near the road up Mt Hutt). There is a 1½ hr loop track, and a 2½ hr (one way) extension track up to Scotts Saddle (1000 m) for views over mountains and plains.
**Rakaia Gorge** 17 km north on Route 72 the road bridges the Rakaia River where it spills through this gorge. Picnic sites and jet boat rides are available. There is a 10 km round trip (3–4 hr) walkway along the north bank for bush and river views and the remains of an old coalmine.
**Lake Coleridge** A glacial lake now in tussock country, with mountain backdrop. The hydro scheme here was the first power station of this type. The lake is on a side road 37 km north-west of Methven (over the Rakaia Gorge

*Westland National Park.*

Bridge, and parallel to the north bank upriver). On the southern side of Lake Coleridge, Algidus Road leads to the sheep station, popularised in Mona

Anderson's book *A River Rules My Life*.

**Lake Ida**  A tiny lake that is popular as a winter ice-skating venue. Off Harper

Road, 35 km beyond Lake Coleridge.
**Alford Forest** River picnic area on Flynns Road from Staveley, 22 km south-west. The Sharplin Falls and a 3 km bushwalk are also off Flynns Road.

**See Also** Springfield, Ashburton and Geraldine

# MILFORD SOUND SI
**Population** 184
**Location** At the end of Route 94, 119 km north of Te Anau.

Milford Sound is the most accessible of the fiords through which the Tasman Sea permeates Fiordland. The road into Milford is perhaps New Zealand's most spectacularly picturesque. The famed Milford Track walk is equally spectacular. Refer also to the Te Anau listing. The Sound itself is 15 km long, has a comparatively shallow entrance but is deep within, and is surrounded by mountain cliffs, which rise vertically 1200 m from the sea.

## ENVIRONS & ATTRACTIONS
**Bowen Falls** A 10-minute walk leads to the base of these 160 m falls.
**Lookout** A 5-minute climb behind the hotel to this raised viewpoint over the Sound.
**Milford Sound Cruises** Launch trips on the Fiord are a prime attraction for views of Mitre Peak, Bowen Falls and out to the mouth of the Sound.
**Scenic Flights** An airstrip allows scenic flights in light aircraft over the Sound, and also over Sutherland Falls (580 m), partially up the Milford Track.
**The Chasm** A short walk off the main road into the Sound (on the western side of the Homer Tunnel) leads to the place where the Cleddau River has carved its way through a rocky gorge.

**See Also** Te Anau

# MILTON SI
**Population** 2154
**Location** On Route 1, 55 km south of Dunedin.

This borough is located on the Tokomairiro Plain and has agricultural-based industries and a forest nursery. Gold and coalmining have contributed to Milton's past development.

*MV* Milford Haven *on a day trip in the Milford Sound.*

*Stirling Falls in the Milford Sound.*

Milton was once a junction for the now closed Roxburgh railway line. The road to Roxburgh (Route 8) branches off 3 km south at Clarksville.

## ENVIRONS & ATTRACTIONS
**Tokomairiro Domain** Recreation area at the north end of town.

**Tokomairiro Presbyterian Church** Splendid stone building built in 1889 on Union Street (main road). The St Johns Anglican Church (1886) and the Catholic Church of the Immaculate Conception (1892) may also be of interest.

**Tokomairiro Historical Society** Features local exhibits including pottery. Main street. Open Fri and Sun 2–4 pm.

## LOCAL TOURING
**Toko Mouth** A seaside settlement situated at the mouth of the Tokomairiro River, 15 km east.

**McNally Walkway** A 7 km (2¼ hr return) walk, starting at the end of Cemetery Road (2 km from town) and climbing to a 317 m hilltop for views of the plain and coast.

**Lovells Flat Sod Cottage** Restored single-roomed colonial home, 11 km south on Route 1.

**See Also** Dunedin, Lawrence and Balclutha

# MOKAU NI
**Population** 162
**Location** On Route 3, 88 km north-east of New Plymouth, 5 km south of Awakino.

Mokau is situated on the mouth of the Mokau River, the dramatic and historic boundary between the Waikato and Taranaki. The river saw many inter-tribal battles, and also one brief skirmish with British troops. The river is 120 km long and is pretty but remote. The Mokau coalmines were 36 km up-river. Mokau was reputedly one of the landing places of the *Tainui* canoe, and its anchorstone remains in the town. Also commanding attention is a red German mine on the roadside, which was washed ashore in 1942 — a reminder that the German navy was off the New Zealand coast during World War II.

**See Also** Awakino, Waitara and New Plymouth

# MORRINSVILLE NI
**Population** 5281
**Location** On Route 6, 32 km north-east of Hamilton.

Morrinsville is the commercial and servicing centre of the local prosperous dairying industry. There may well be more cows within a 25 km radius of Morrinsville than anywhere else in the world. The district has sheep and beef farming and horticulture, as well as a large fertiliser works.

The town was developed by Thomas Morrin in 1874. It sits on the edge of the Hauraki Plains — a once swampy and boggy area that has required extensive drainage and redevelopment. Route 27 now comes down these plains, but you must turn off on to Route 26 to reach Morrinsville.

## ENVIRONS & ATTRACTIONS
**Morrinsville Museum** A selection of local historical items, including a Maori war canoe. Lorne Street.

## LOCAL TOURING
**Mt Kuranui** Kuranui leads off Route 26 on the Hamilton side of the town, and access to viewpoints of the district are

194

available from this road.

**Rukumoana Marae**  Site of the third Maori Parliament House, which has been restored by the Historic Places Trust. 5 km south on Kiwitahi Road.

**See Also**  Matamata, Te Aroha and Paeroa

---

# MOTUEKA SI
**Population**  5052
**Location**  51 km west of Nelson on Route 60.

---

Motueka serves a rich hinterland of tobacco, hop and fruit growing. Apples are also an important fruit, and in recent years kiwifruit has helped compensate for a reduction in tobacco cropping. These agricultural activities have helped the development of the borough. The town is situated on the right bank of the Motueka River, which has a small port.

## ENVIRONS & ATTRACTIONS
**Te Ahurewa Maori Church**  This was built in 1897 by the Maori priest Frederick Bennett who later became the first Maori Bishop of New Zealand.

## LOCAL TOURING
**Moutere**  Between Nelson/ Richmond and Motueka there is an alternative route via Upper and Lower Moutere. At Lower Moutere visitors can feed and stroke tame eels (though not in winter) at Wilsons Road. Upper Moutere was originally settled by Germans and has a fine Lutheran Church.

**Kaiteriteri Beach**  A beautiful, safe and popular beach 14 km north-west, signposted off Route 60. At the northern end of the beach is Kaka Point, a lookout and once the site of a pa.

**Marahau Beach**  9 km beyond Kaiteriteri. Walks into the Abel Tasman National Park (see

subsequent entry) begin (or end, if you access the Park from Totaranui) at Marahau.

**Riwaka Valley**  From Route 60, beyond the Kaiteriteri turn-off, a side road leads inland to the source of the Riwaka River. At the end of the road (16 km from Motueka) a short bush walk leads to a limestone cavern where the river emerges from the hillside. There are picnic sites.

**Mount Arthur Tablelands**  The Graham valley and the locality of Woodstock (32 km south from Motueka) on Route 61  provide road access to an 820 m lookout in the Mount Arthur range. Across this limestone plateau there are some local tracks as well as longer tracks to the Cobb River area. The Nettlebed Cave System of metamorphosed limestone has some of the deepest shafts and most intricate cave systems of any in the world, and are still being explored by speleologists.

**Wangapeka Track**  This track requires about 4 days to cross from the Whangapeka Valley (signposted off Route 61) through the north-west Nelson Forest Park, over the Tasman mountains to Little Wanganui on Route 67 near Karamea. The track is 50 km long and there are huts at intervals. Although this track is proving more popular, and some enthusiasts combine it as a round trip with the Heaphy Track (see under Collingwood), it does pass through rugged and difficult country and is for reasonably experienced trampers.

**Ngarua Caves**  Signposted at the top of Takaka Hill, 21 km west on Route 60, these caves have conducted tours daily in summer and weekends in winter.

**Abel Tasman National Park**  This covers an area of more than 22 000 ha of widely diverse topography, ranging from coastal islands and beaches, through bush and scrubland to rocky high country. The park starts at the Maharau Inlet and extends round the coast to Separation Point, which divides Tasman Bay and Golden Bay.

The park features bush tracks and deserted beaches. Southern road access is to Maharau, where tracks lead into the park. Alternatively there is road access into Totaranui at the northern end via Takaka. A popular access, particularly for day trippers, is by launch from Kaiteriteri Beach. You can be dropped off at one beach and be picked up several hours later at another, so providing a day of both sunbathing and walking. There are park board huts along the walks, and a 4-day guided walk operates during summer.

**Marahau–Totaranui Track** This popular coastal track, through bush and beach, is suitable for families. It takes 3–4 days, and there are huts en route. But be warned, the huts are popular in summer. There is road access to both ends.

**See Also** Nelson, Takaka and Collingwood

# MT COOK SI
**Population** 589
**Location** At the end of Route 80, 55 km from its junction with Route 8, and 70 km north of Twizel.

Mt Cook is New Zealand's highest mountain (3764 m) and is adjacent to but not part of the main divide of the Southern Alps. The name also applies to the resort settlement situated among grand and impressive scenery. The leading hotel at Mt Cook is called the 'Hermitage' and sometimes this name is applied to the settlement.

*Torrent Bay in the Abel Tasman National Park.*

*Mt Sefton looms behind Mueller Hut.*

Surrounding the village is Mt Cook National Park, an area of nearly 7000 ha of majestic alpine scenery. The Maori name for Mt Cook is Aorangi, meaning 'cloud piercer'. It was first climbed in 1894.

As Mt Cook is an alpine resort, if you are staying overnight, your vehicle may require anti-freeze in its radiator cooling system.

## ENVIRONS & ATTRACTIONS
**Visitors Centre** Features displays of the flora, fauna, rocks and history of the park. Also information on the various walks in the area. Open daily.

**Bowen Track** A 10-minute walk from the Youth Hostel to a viewpoint over the Hooker Valley towards Mt Cook.

**Governors Bush** Near the park headquarters, a loop track of 1¼ hr takes you through beech forest.

**White Horse Hill Picnic Area** This picnic area is about 3 km beyond the Hermitage. A number of tracks are accessible from here. One such easy walk is to follow the path across the shingle fans to the swingbridge over the Hooker River (½ hr each way).

## LOCAL TOURING
**Tasman Glacier** The Ball Hutt Road up the Tasman Valley is a rough, restricted road. Only the rocky glacier moraine is visible, and you must climb for a view of the glacier.

**Scenic Flights** Small planes with skis attached offer flights that land on the snowfield of the Tasman Glacier. They also cross over the divide to Franz Josef and Fox Glaciers.

**Glentanner Park** A camp and tourist base being developed on the road into Mt Cook, 20 km back from the village.

**Other Walks and Tracks** The Kea Track leads to a viewpoint overlooking the Mueller Glacier (3 hr return — shorter from the Foliage Hill picnic spot). A track up the Hooker Valley leads to Hooker Hut, via a swingbridge. The route over the Copland Pass to the west coast is an alpine crossing with an ice traverse, taking 3–4 days, and is for experienced climbers and mountaineers only.

**See Also** Lake Tekapo and Twizel

# MT MAUNGANUI NI
Refer to Tauranga.

# MURCHISON SI
**Population** 641
**Location** On Route 6, 35 km south-east of Kawatiri Junction, 130 km south-west of Nelson, 102 km north-east of Westport.

River flats between surrounding hills provide a farming base for this township situated on the Buller River. The Buller flows from Lake Rotoiti and provides impressive scenery, especially further along.

The junction of Route 65 south to Mariua Springs Junction on the Lewis Pass Highway is 11 km west on Route 6. An alternative road directly from Murchison over the Maruia Saddle is not recommended for tourists.

Murchison began as a goldmining settlement that served small groups of diggers in the Buller, Matakitaki and Maruia Rivers. In 1929 the area was the epicentre for the 'Murchison Earthquake' one of New Zealand's most severe. It affected a wide area including Westport and Greymouth; 17 lives were lost.

Another earthquake of lesser intensity struck the district in 1968. These earthquakes have changed some of the contours but the upthrusts and slips are now regenerating and even with the aid of signposts it is difficult to fully appreciate the damage they caused.

## ENVIRONS & ATTRACTIONS
**Riverside Domain** A picnic site at the northern end of town.
**Murchison Museum** A collection of memorabilia from the town's early history, including goldmining and earthquake days. Situated next to the Caltex garage.
**Commercial Stables** Original working stables from the horse-drawn era under restoration.
**Local Tracks** The West Bank Track, the Kahikatea Walk, and the longer (1½ hr each way) Skyline Walk are close to the town. They offer views of bush and river.

## LOCAL TOURING
**Braeburn Track** This is really a road, but only just! It is a back-country, bush-clad alternative route to Lake Rotoroa in the Nelson Lakes National Park. Allow 1½ hr to drive up and return via the main road.
**Six Mile Walk** The beginning of this walk is 10 km down the Matakitaki Road. The Six Mile hydro power station was one of the oldest in the country. The walkway is 3 km return, and leads to a weir on the creek following the course of a water-race built by goldminers.
**Newton Livery** An authentic horse-powered farm with Clydesdale horses. 19 km west on Route 6.
**Maruia Falls** Falls that were formed as a result of the 1929 earthquake; situated 24 km out on Route 65.

**See Also** St Arnaud, Inangahua and Maruia Springs

*Stone house near the base of Coronet Peak, Queenstown.*

# N

## NAPIER NI
**Population** 49 428
**Location** On Route 2, 216 km
south of Gisborne, 334 km north
of Wellington, 143 km south-east
of Taupo along Route 5.

The twin cities of Napier and
Hastings have downtown areas
only 20 km apart, but they are
featured separately in this guide. If
staying at one, you should also
refer to the other.

Napier is situated on the
southern shore of Hawke Bay. It is
a port, has an airport with
scheduled flights, and is served by
rail. The surrounding area is
associated with market gardening,
crop growing, frozen food
processing, and wine making.
Further out are the rolling sheeplands of the Hawke's Bay region.

The first European settler, after
various transitory whalers, was
Reverend William Colenso, sent
from the Bay of Islands in 1844 to
establish a mission station.

On 3 February 1931, at
10.46 am, a violent 2½ minute
earthquake, followed by fires,
severely damaged Napier, killing
256 people. A feature of the
earthquake was the upheaval of
part of the harbour bed to form
4000 ha of new land. Suburban
housing and the airport now stand
on this new area. The rebuilding
that took place in the 1930s lent
an 'art deco' flavour to the
downtown area. Napier became a
city in 1950.

Hawke's Bay is the title of the
region occupied by the former
province, which stretches from
Wairoa to Woodville. The name
Hawke Bay, however, is applied
to the large bight of ocean
stretching from the Mahia

Peninsula to Cape Kidnappers.
The bay was named by Captain
Cook in 1769 in honour of the
First Lord of the Admiralty.

## ENVIRONS & ATTRACTIONS
**Marine Parade** Much of the city
foreshore has been put to public
use with the building of gardens,
fountains, and other amenities. A
colonnade surrounds a sunken
garden and sound shell. The
statue of Pania, symbolising a
Maori legend about a sea goddess
in love with a human, has
become a popular fixture.
**Hawke's Bay Aquarium** Local
and exotic fish on display. The
Lilliput model railway and village
is also located here. Open daily
9 am–5 pm (weekends only in
winter), on Marine Parade.
**Marineland** Dolphin and seal
show at 1.30 am and 2 pm. Open
daily 9.30 am–4.30 pm, on
Marine Parade.
**Nocturnal Wildlife
Centre** The kiwi, morepork,
hedgehog, and other nocturnal
creatures are on display. Open
9 am–4.30 pm daily, on Marine
Parade.
**Bluff Hill** From the top of this
suburban hill you can see the bay,
port, and part of the city. Take
Coote Road off Marine Parade
Road, then follow signs.
**Botanical Gardens** These
formal gardens and natural
amphitheatre are on the slopes of
Hospital Hill. In the adjacent
cemetery you will find the graves
of several historic figures:
Reverend William Colenso, three
Bishops of the Williams family, Sir
Donald McLean, and General
Whitmore.
**Hawke's Bay Art Gallery and
Museum** This includes displays
about the Napier earthquake,
Maori artifacts, and the art of the
Maori. Open Mon–Fri
10.30 am–4.30 pm; weekends
2–4.30 pm, Herschell Street.
**The Stables Earthquake**

**Museum and Waxworks** This features a simulated earthquake and historic film. Open daily.

**St Johns Cathedral Church** This was rebuilt after the earthquake. It houses memorabilia, and a Maori Chapel. Tennyson Street.

**Kennedy Park Rose Gardens** In Storkey Street, off Kennedy Road, this garden has more than 3000 bushes.

## LOCAL TOURING

**Eskdale Valley** A grape-growing area and pleasant valley. It is also a popular riverside park, 19 km out on the Taupo Road (Route 5).

**Whirinaki** 9 km north, near the junction of Route 5, is a timber pulp mill, and a diesel fuel power station.

**Otatara Pa** A historic reserve on the site of a pa, which is about 400 years old. Springfield Road, Taradale.

**Lake Tutira** 40 km north on Route 2, this lake and bird sanctuary have been made famous by farmer-turned-author Guthrie-Smith. His book *Tutira — The Story of a New Zealand Sheep Station* documents the area. There are picnic sites and three walking tracks.

**Balls Clearing** This scenic reserve of 135 ha contains original bush including rimu and kahikatea up to 35 m high. There is a picnic area and bush tracks. 70 km north-east of Napier on Puketiri Road.

**Kaweka Forest Park** Comprises 61 000 ha of the Kaweka Range in western Hawke's Bay. Access is 70 km north-west of Napier along the Puketiri Road, and also from Route 5 at Kuripapango. There are walking tracks through the park, ranging from 2 hr to 2 days.

**See Also** Hastings, Wairoa and Waipukurau

# NATIONAL PARK NI
**Population** 217
**Location** The township of National Park is on Route 4, 43 km south of Tauramanui.

The title National Park refers to the adjacent Tongariro National Park surrounding the central North Island peaks of Mts Ruapehu (2796 m), Ngauruhoe (2290 m) and Tongariro (1968 m). The small township and its railway station are outside the park area.

The area was formerly known as Waimarino, and the 'volcanic plateau' is still sometimes known as the Waimarino Plateau, though more commonly this name refers to the plains just to the south around Ohakune and Raetihi.

The Tongariro National Park was given to the government by the Tuwharetoa Tribe in 1887, and it became New Zealand's first national park. Further land has been added since, and it now totals more than 75 000 ha. The area is popular for skiing in winter and tramping in summer.

Mts Ruapehu and Ngauruhoe are still active volcanoes — the former with a warm crater lake surrounded by snow and ice. The water is strongly acidic, and is subject to minor eruption. The lake's outlet is through a tunnel in the ice to the Whangaehu River. A sudden torrent of lake water down this river in December 1953 washed away the nearby Tangiwai railway bridge, which caused New Zealand's worst railway disaster.

Mt Ngauruhoe frequently emits steam, and occasionally it erupts. Mt Tongariro is mostly dormant, but has thermal activity on its slopes at Ketetahi Springs. It is possible to climb to the top of all three peaks. Although the large park has a wide variety of vegetation, the predominant impression is of brown tussock grass. When the mountain slopes are not covered with snow, they are very rocky from all the erupted lava.

## ENVIRONS & ATTRACTIONS

**Tongariro National Park** Park headquarters is at Whakapapa village, 16 km from National Park settlement. Displays provide information on the geology and biology of the park, and information on walks, tramps and outdoor activities. There are guided walks in summer. Access to the park is also available via the Turoa ski-field (refer to the entry under Ohakune), and from the 'Desert Road'.

**Chateau Tongariro** This hotel is commonly called 'the Chateau', and this name is often loosely applied to the whole area. More correctly this immediate vicinity is called Whakapapa village, and it gives access to the Whakapapa ski-field. Ski accommodation is available at club huts both at Whakapapa and at the Twikau village, situated at the Top o' the Bruce mountain road.

**Top o' the Bruce** This road winds up Mt Ruapehu from the Chateau and Whakapapa village (at 1127 m above sea level) to the Twikau village at 1622 m. Rough and steep in summer it is subject to snow and ice in winter. Mountain transport is available through the ski season (June to October). A number of ski-lifts and tows are available from the Top o' the Bruce.

## LOCAL TOURING

**Park Walks** Touring on foot gives many options, but it is usually best in summer when the ground is snow free and the weather less severe, though still changeable. Information on the tracks is available from the park

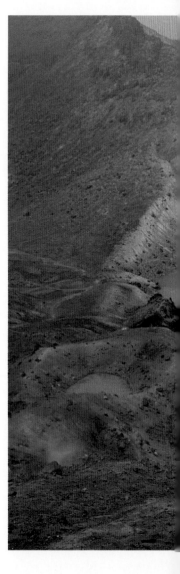

headquarters. Walks to consider include: Botanical Garden Track from park headquarters, about 1.5 km; Taranaki Falls Track, a circular 6.5 km walk over tussock and beach forest; Whakapapanui Track, which parallels access road Route 48 for 3 km, and is via bush and river from motor camp; Waihohonu Track, a full day's walk from the Chateau between Ruapehu and Ngauruhoe, to the

*Trampers in the Mt Tongariro National Park.*

Desert Road (organise transport, and take weather precautions); the Tongariro Crossing, a full day's walk from Mangatepopo to Ketetahi. There are also routes taking several days right around the mountain.

**Raurimu Spiral** A viewing area 6 km to the north of National Park on Route 4 gives views of the way railway engineers have tackled the rise of 213 m to ascend the volcanic plateau. The Raurimu Spiral incorporates a complete circle of track with three horseshoe curves and two tunnels to increase the distance and lessen the gradient. However, be aware that most trains move at night and daylight waits can be quite long.

**See Also** Taumarunui, Taupo, Raetihi and Ohakune.

*Nelson Haven and Tasman Bay.*

# NELSON SI
**Population** 34 274
**Location** On Route 6, 116 km west of Blenheim, 226 km north-east of Westport.

The city of Nelson is the commercial centre and seaport for a highly productive hinterland growing fruit, hops, tobacco and timber, as well as general farming. In particular the port is a leading exporter of apples and is situated on a stretch of water called Nelson Haven, which is protected by a natural breakwater from Tasman Bay. The city centre is surrounded and sheltered by hills, and it vies with Blenheim for sunshine records

The Tasman Bay is named after the Dutch navigator Abel Tasman who visited the area, but did not land, in 1642. European settlement began with the New Zealand company in 1841. Gold was discovered at Collingwood in 1857 and the later finds on the west coast stimulated Nelson's development. The city is named after Lord Nelson and the main shopping street is Trafalgar Street.

The city has an airport with scheduled flights. From 1912 to 1955, a railway operated 96 km from Nelson to Glenhope — part of a never finished link to Ingangahua and the west coast. New Zealand's first railway was a horse drawn tramway operating up Dun Mountain 1862–1901.

Nelson has a reputation for its local arts and crafts. Side trips to Motueka, Collingwood and the Abel Tasman National Park may be done in one day, but it would be preferable to take longer.

## ENVIRONS & ATTRACTIONS

**Christ Church Cathedral** This church (the third on the site, which was previously the site of a Maori village and later a settlers' fort) stands on raised ground at the end of the main street with steps leading up to it. Built between 1925 and 1967, it is open daily 8 am–4 pm. The cathedral is surrounded by park.

**Suter Art Gallery** A popular gallery for paintings and other displays. Also restaurant and craft shop. In Queens Gardens, Bridge Street, open daily.

**Queens Gardens** Between Bridge Street and Hardy Street, this is an attractive reserve of rare trees, ferns and ponds. The Suter Art Gallery is adjacent.

**Botanical Reserve** Walking tracks gradually climb to a summit viewpoint. This is reputed to be the centre of New Zealand. Milton Street.

**Nelson Provincial Museum** Historical photographs and Maori collection. Open Tues–Fri 10 am–4 pm; weekends 2–5 pm. Isel Park, Stoke (a southern suburb).

**Isel Park** A plantation of century-old trees from all parts of the world; also rhododendrons and azaleas. Main Road, Stoke.

**Tahunanui Beach** Called Tahuna for short, this is a popular beach with foreshore sports and play area. Enter off Rocks Road on Route 6.

**Nelson Haven** The stretch of water between the mainland and a boulder bank 13 km long, which protects the port and foreshore.

**Doris Lookout** At the end of Princes Drive, this lookout provides a view over Tasman Bay.

**Founders Park** A working museum of re-created buildings and early transport. Open daily.

**Historic buildings** Bishops School, which was instigated in 1844, has been recently restored and reopened as an educational museum (Nile Street). Fairfield House and Melrose (both in Trafalgar Street) are two stately houses built about 1876 — the former now a community centre, the latter used for receptions. South Street in Nelson contains a number of old cottages that are still in use. Broadgreen House (Nayland Road, Stoke) is a restored historic house in mid-Victorian Style.

**Dun Mountain Walkway** Walk up the route of the old horse-drawn tramway towards the disused chrome ore mine, with views en route. The walk takes 3 hr return, though there are alternatives. Commence up Brooke Valley at Tantragee Road, 5 km south of Nelson.

**Cable Bay Walkway** A 2½ hr walking track with some steep parts from The Glen (14 km north) to Cable Bay (21 km north). There is road access to both ends, which have popular picnic areas reached by car or walking.

**Maitai Valley** A picturesque recreational area. Take Nile Street and Maitai Valley Road to Branford Park, on the banks of the Maitai River. Follow the road to Maitai Dam and the beginning of the old Maungatapu Bridle Track to Havelock.

**Richmond and Hope** Smaller communities 9 km and 15 km south respectively on Route 6. Richmond has a church (Holy Trinity) that dates from 1872. Hope was originally settled by Germans and given the name Ranzau. Brightwater (19 km) is

*Historic Broadgreen House in Stoke, Nelson.*

the birthplace of Lord Rutherford, the first to split the atom. Nearby at Spring Grove the Newman brothers began their transport business. Merryland is a family park at Richmond, which has a miniature village, mini-golf and other activities. It is open weekends 10 am–6 pm, also weekdays in summer.

**Rabbit Island** Take Route 60 (between Richmond and Hope) and turn off at Appleby for road access to this island with sand dunes and pine trees. 25 km from Nelson. Beyond Appleby there are a number of other beaches, for example, Mapua, Ruby Bay and Kina.

**Spooners Range Lookout** 41 km south on Route 6 the road rises to this lookout over the Golden Downs Forest and out to Tasman Bay.

**See Also** Picton, St Arnaud and Motueka

# NEW PLYMOUTH NI

**Population** 36 860
**Location** On the west coast of the North Island; by Route 3, 369 km from Auckland, 355 km from Wellington.

The Taranaki region is dominated by the dormant volcano Mt Egmont 2518 m (also called Taranaki) and its perfectly symmetrical profile. The mountain is visible from parts of New Plymouth. The surrounding lands form one of the country's most productive dairying districts, and the port of New Plymouth was reputedly once the world's largest exporter of cheese.

New Plymouth used to be the site of several Maori pas including Paritutu, the prominent peak next to the port. The first Europeans who arrived in 1828 were whalers. In 1841 the first migrant settlers arrived to establish a town. They immediately ran into land trouble that continued with skirmishes between Maoris and settlers, and indeed a full scale war at nearby Waitara, until 1881. For a time New Plymouth was virtually a military settlement under constant siege, and many settlers left the district. The town recovered, however, after the 1881 peace agreement.

A railway from Wellington reached New Plymouth in 1886; passengers then went by sea to Auckland (Onehunga) until the completion of the main trunk railway system. The port, protected by a breakwater, grew with agricultural exports and in more recent times increased in importance during the building of the petro-chemical industry.

Today the city is an important provincial centre, boosted in recent years by the growth of the oil, gas and petro-chemical industries in the region. The city has scheduled air services to Auckland and Wellington; but the railway is freight only. There are regular bus links to all parts of the country. One feature of New Plymouth is its impressive parks, which attract the attention of many tourists.

## ENVIRONS & ATTRACTIONS

**Pukekura Park** A fine park covering 21 ha, with gardens, fernery, begonia house, and two lakes. On summer evenings the waterfall and fountains are flood lit. Mt Egmont is visible from the upper lake. There is a sportsground at the entrance. 10 minutes walk from the city centre on Liardet Street.

**Brooklands Park** This joins Pukekura Park, and has lawns, garden and bush. The Bowl of Brooklands is a natural amphitheatre that has a lake in front of the stage. Performances are given regularly throughout January and February. The park also features 'The Gables', a colonial hospital building which dates from 1848. Within the grounds is a massive puriri tree, which is 213 m high and 2000 years old.

**Taranaki Museum** Housed in the War Memorial Building, Kings Street, the museum displays a fine collection of Maori artifacts belonging to early European settlers. Open daily (afternoons Saturday/Sunday). Nearby is Richmond Cottage, built in 1853, complete with period furniture.

**St Mary's Church** Built of stone in 1845 (though since extended) by Bishop Selwyn, it has its original bell and organ. It houses the regimental colours of those British troops involved in the Taranaki campaigns (when the church was used as a military post and an ammunition dump).

**Marsland Hill** Behind St Marys church, this domain was once a

*Pukekura Park, New Plymouth.*

Maori pa, then a military barracks. It is a good vantage point for views of the city and the observatory is open Tuesday evenings.

**Mt Moturoa**  A lookout provides panoramic views over city, port, bight as well as inland.

**Paritutu**  Prominent peak next to the port and Mt Moturoa. A thermal power station using oil and gas (with New Zealand's highest chimney at 198 m) and a reserve are at its base. It is a steep winding track to the top. Rangimarie Arts and Crafts centre is nearby.

**Petroleum Museum**
Photographic displays of the local oil and gas industry. Open daily 10 am–3 pm at the base of Paritutu.

**Duncan & Davies Nursery**
New Zealand's largest plant nursery. Open daily, Tukapa Street.

**Govett–Brewster Art Gallery**
Opened 1970, includes a display of contemporary art, including Len Lye kinetic sculptures. Open daily (afternoon Saturday/Sunday), Queen Street.

## LOCAL TOURING

**Lake Mangamahoe Domain**
Picnic spot and photographic vantage point for Mt Egmont. 10 km south on Route 3.

**Hurworth**  10 km out on Carrington Road, this cottage was established in 1853 by Harry Atkinson, who became Prime Minister and was later knighted. House and contents have been restored to his times. Closed Monday and Tuesday.

**Pouakai Wildlife Reserve**
Deer, birds, sheep and goats, 12 km out on Carrington Road. Open daily.

**Pukeiti Rhododendron Trust**
A private park (360 ha) featuring rhododendrons and azaleas in native bush setting. Open daily, but is best September–November. 29 km out on Carrington Road.

*Mt Egmont rises behind the farmlands of Waverley.*

**Omata** 6 km west of New Plymouth on Route 45. This town features a picturesque church and the Omata stockade, which was a defence during the Taranaki campaign. Nearby this country's first Victoria Cross was won by W. Odgers from HMS *Niger* for bravery at Kaipopa pa.

**Oakura** This holiday beach is 14 km west on Route 45. The remains of Koru pa (perhaps dates back almost a thousand years) can be found up Wairau and Surrey Hill Road (4 km), after a short (500 m) walk at the road's end.

**Okato** 26 km west on Route 25, this town is famous for its cheese. Alternative inland roads to/from the Pukeiti Rhododendron Trust help make a circle tour.

**Cape Egmont** On a side road at Pungareahu (40 km) at this most eastern point of Taranaki stands a

lighthouse. Inland from
Pungareahu is Parihaka pa, scene
of an 1881 confrontation between
government groups and local
Maoris. Parihaka was the village
where Chief Whiti encouraged the
philosophy of passive resistance
to the European occupation of
tribal lands. British troops levelled
the village and Te Whiti's grave is
still a centre for Maori pilgrimage.
**Stony River Walkway**  A 4 km
walk from Okato Domain, down the
Kaihihi Stream, crossing farmland
to go back up the Stony River.
**Round The Mountain**  It is both
possible and pleasant to drive
around Mt Egmont in one day, via
Route 45, visiting some of the
above mentioned places. You can
move inland to visit the Pukeiti
Rhododendron Trust, and/or
Kapuni; then return to New
Plymouth via Route 3.

*The rugged Taranaki coastline.*

## TARANAKI GAS AND OIL

Oil was discovered in New Plymouth in 1865 and for many years the city had its own unique brand of petrol. However, in the last 20 years or so there has been much commercial development of other finds in the region.

The McKee and Pouri oilfields are located up Otaraoa Road inland from Waitara. Only one wellhead is visible from the road (and it is not very impressive!), but there is a visitor viewpoint at the Oilfield Production Station, further down that road. This station receives the oil from the several wells, and pipes it to New Plymouth for shipping to a refinery near Whangarei.

Motunui, east of Waitara, is the site of the world's first commercial synthetic fuel plant. It makes methanol from gas piped from the Maui and Kapuni gas fields, and

214

then turns that methanol into gasoline. The plant is on the main road, Route 3, and there is a visitors centre.

Near Waitara (up the Waitara River valley) there is another big plant, which uses natural gas and makes methanol (mainly for export). The port at New Plymouth receives Motunui gasoline by pipe to be shipped to the Whangarei (Marsden Point) oil refinery for blending. Adjacent are the Omata storage tanks for Synfuel and Mckee oil, and a de-ballasting treatment plant that cleans seawater used by tankers as ballast when they come in empty. The thermal power station at the port uses gas.

The Kapuni gas field south of Mt Egmont was discovered in 1962. The natural gas from here is piped around the North Island, and to the New Plymouth and

Stratford power stations. Kapuni also has an ammonia–urea plant, which produces urea fertiliser.

The larger Maui gas field is 34 km off the Taranaki coast. The giant rig Maui A platform is the offshore wellhead. The onshore production station that receives the Maui gas piped in from the Maui field and treats if for piping north is at Oaonui, near Opunake. Oaonui has a visitor centre.

Many of these petro-chemical industries were developed under the 'Think Big' political strategy of the National Party who were then in government, and some have been surrounded in controversial economics. Most of the installations have visitor lookouts or information centres; but the plants themselves are usually off-limits.

**See Also** Waitara, Opunake and Stratford

---

# NGARUAWAHIA NI
**Population** 4639
**Location** On Route 1, 108 km south from Auckland, 19 km north of Hamilton.

---

Ngaruawahia is situated where the Waipa River flows into the Waikato River. It is the headquarters of the Waikato Maoris and the Turangawaewae Marae is the residence of the Maori Queen. A regatta is held annually on the Waikato River on the Saturday closest to 17 March. The use of traditional Maori canoes has always been a feature of this regatta.

Due to its situation at the junction of the two rivers, Ngaruawahia was an important Maori settlement for many years. It was settled by Europeans in 1864 after the Waikato land wars. The Maori King at the time, Te Wherowhero (otherwise known as 'Potatau the first') fled south and established a new 'King Country' south of Te Awamutu. Following a reconciliation with the government in 1883 an area was set aside for the re-establishment of the Maori headquarters in Ngaruawahia.

## ENVIRONS & ATTRACTIONS
**The 'Point' Park** A large open picnic area known as The Point marks the area where the two rivers meet. It is visible from the main road and is accessed from a side road, which crosses the railway line. The area is a focal point on the regatta day each March. Also note the remains of a gun turret from the riverboat *Pioneer*, which helped take Ngaruawahia in 1863.
**Turangawaewae Marae** Situated on the banks of the Waikato River and visible from the nearby Waikato River bridge and river road, this complex is a focal point for the Maori people and residence of the Maori Queen. This land was confiscated during the land wars but was eventually bought back from the settlers in 1921. The buildings contain some of the finest examples of Maori carving and decoration in New Zealand. The marae is generally only open to non-Maori people once a year, usually on regatta day.

## LOCAL TOURING
**Taupiri Mountain** Situated 6 km north of Ngaruawahia. On the slopes of this mountain is the most sacred burial ground for the Waikato Maori tribes. There is pedestrian access from Route 1 across the railway line.
**Waingaro Springs** These thermal soda springs are situated in the grounds of a hotel and picnic area, 23 km west of Ngaruawahia on a signposted side road. They are open daily.

**See Also** Mercer, Rangiriri and Huntly

# O

## OAMARU SI

**Population** 12 652
**Location** On Route 1, 84 km
south of Timaru, 115 km north of
Dunedin.

Situated on the main road and
railway between Christchurch and
Dunedin, Oamaru also has a port
and an airfield. It is a leading
pastoral, commercial and
distribution centre for northern
Otago. It began as a grazing run
acquired by Hugh Robinson in
1853. A town board was set up in
1862.

In the early days the Port area
was exposed and it suffered
setbacks and disasters until a long
breakwater was built. South of the
town is the estate from which
New Zealand's first load of frozen
export meat originated. There is
also a monument to Thomas
Brydone who pioneered the
scheme, which was the
forerunner of a large frozen meat
industry operating today.

Oamaru stone, which is
quarried nearby, can be cut with
handsaws when freshly quarried,
but hardens with exposure. The
white stone has been used for
many buildings in the borough
and elsewhere (including
Auckland's Post Office and
St Matthew's Church, Wellington's
Customhouse, and Dunedin's first
church). In Oamaru itself the
stone buildings add to the
attraction of the town.

On Route 1, 10 km north of
Oamaru, a roadside plaque
records its midway location
between the equator and the
South Pole.

## ENVIRONS & ATTRACTIONS

**Oamaru Gardens** A beautiful
park with garden displays including
an oriental section and a
Wonderland statuary. Severn Street.

**North Otago Museum** The
Athenaeum (1882) houses a small
district museum that features
geology and settlers memorabilia.
Thames Street.

**Forrester Art Gallery** Located
in the old classical Bank of New
South Wales building (1884),
Thames Street. Open Mon–Thur
10 am–4.30 pm, Fri until 8.30 pm,
Sun 1–4.30 pm.

**St Pauls Church** Built in 1876,
this is the leading Presbyterian
church in the district. Coquet
Street.

**St Patricks Basilica** Built in
1893 of Oamaru stone, and
complete with portico and doors.
Usk Street.

**Other Buildings** Other fine
examples of Oamaru stone
include the former County
Council and Borough Council
Chambers, the Courthouse (1883)
the old (1864) and new (1884)
Post Offices.

**Cape Wanbrow** A lookout
behind the port gives a view over
the town.

**Graves Walk** A one-hr walk
from the end of Waterfront Road
(behind the port) around a coastal
reserve to Bushy beach. The last
part is covered with water at
high tide.

**Fenwick Park** A reserve of
native flora beyond the public
gardens in Chelmer Street.

**South Hill Walkway** A 5 km
(2¼ hr one way) walk from King
George Park via Lookout Point to
connect with Graves Walk. It then
passes through the town and its
gardens to Fenwick Park.

**Skyline Walkway** A 4.6 km
(2 hr one-way) walk from Fenwick
Park to Orana Park in Orwell
Street, via undeveloped recreation
reserves west of the borough.

*The old Post Office and War Memorial in Oamaru.*

## LOCAL TOURING

**Waitaki** 22 km north the large Waitaki River forms a boundary between South Canterbury and North Otago. The bridge is more than 1000 m long. There is fishing here. Between Waitaki and Oamaru note the roadside plaque indicating its midway location between the equator and the South Pole.

**Herbert Forest** This mainly pine forest is located 25 km south. Rimu and totara are evident on the 3-hr Podocarp Track. The forest is reached by a 10-minute drive from Herbert Forest Headquarters on Queens Road, or a 15-minute drive from Forest Headquarters in Diamond Hill Road.

**See Also** Waimate, Kurow and Palmerston

# OHAKUNE NI

**Population** 1496
**Location** On Route 49 (and the intersection of Route 49A) between Raetihi and Waiouru, and 35 km south of National Park.

The town centre lies on Route 49 and the town spreads between there and the railway station 2 km to the east. The station is on the main trunk line and used to be a junction for a line to Raetihi.

Ohakune was originally built as a railway town and owed its continued existence to the railway, particularly in the days of steam. The railway transported timber and when that was cleared, the district became a market gardening area. In recent years the town has developed as a ski resort due to the completion of the Ohakune mountain road and the Turoa ski-field on the southern slopes of Mt Ruapehu. For information on Tongariro National Park refer to our National Park listing.

## ENVIRONS & ATTRACTIONS

**Ohakune Mountain Road** A sealed 17 km road through bush then rocky hillside from Ohakune Station to 1600 m above sea level. Views are available from the top. The road is subject to snow and ice in winter.

**Turoa Ski-Fields** Chairlifts and ski support facilities are available at the top of the Ohakune Mountain Road. The ski season lasts from June to October.

## LOCAL TOURING

**Mangawhero Forest Walk** From the Ranger station on the Mountain Road this is a short track (1–1½ hr return) through mature forest. It also passes an old volcanic crater.

**Mangawhero Falls Track** It is just a 5–10 minute round-trip walk from near the top of the Mountain Road to view these 23 m falls.

**Tangiwai Bridge** The scene of a 1953 railway disaster when 151 people were killed by a torrent of ice, mud and water from Ruapehu Crater Lake, which rushed down the Whangaehu River and destroyed the bridge shortly before a night express train was due to cross. A new bridge is visible across the paddocks from the road, 19 km along Route 49 towards Waiouru.

**Lake Rotokuru** An ecological reserve controlled by the New Zealand Forest Service. Take Karioi Station Road, then ½ km walk; 11 km east on Route 49.

**See Also** National Park, Ruetihi and Waiouru

# OMARAMA SI

**Population** 436
**Location** On Route 8, 29 km south of Twizel, 116 km north-east of Cromwell; also at the junction of Route 83, 52 km west of Kurow.

Situated in the Ahuriri Valley at the junction of the Omarama Stream with the Ahuriri River, Omarama is an important tourist and stopover point in the 'middle of nowhere'. Its Maori name means 'the place of the moon'. The settlement, however, is an overflow for accommodation in the Mt Cook region and a stopover for travellers on the inland route linking that region with the Southern Lakes. It is also a centre for fishing and gliding enthusiasts.

The large dams of the Waitaki — Benmore, Aviemore, and Waitaki — (described under our Kurow heading) are downriver from Omarama. To the south is the Lindis Pass route, which winds over towards the Wanaka and Cromwell districts.

**See Also** Twizel, Kurow, Wanaka and Cromwell

# OPOTIKI NI
**Population** 3719
**Location** On Route 2, 58 km east of Whakatane.

Opotiki is situated at the eastern end of the Bay of Plenty at the mouth of the Waioeka River, and is where the East Cape Road (Route 35) branches off Route 2. Though now overshadowed in commercial importance by Whakatane, Opotiki remains a servicing town for the local area and also for the East Cape district.

In 1865 German missionary Reverend Carl Volkner was captured by Kereopa and his fanatical Hauhau followers. He was hung, his eyes were gouged out and eaten, his severed head was placed on the church altar, and his blood was passed around in a communion chalice. The church was re-dedicated and renamed in 1875; Kereopa was caught and hanged.

Most Maoris respected Christian churches and sites, even while they were fighting the Pakeha. The Hauhau movement, however, was a blending of Christian and Maori beliefs and detested everything European.

## ENVIRONS & ATTRACTIONS
**Church of St Stephen the Martyr** This is situated in Church Street, at the centre of the town, and is also the site of Reverend Carl Volkner's death at the hands of the Hauhau.
**Waitohi Beach** 9 km of beach across the Waioeka River to the west of the town.

## LOCAL TOURING
**Hukutaia Domain** Turn off Hukutaia Road just over the Waioeka bridge to the west of the town to reach this block of bush reserve with bush walks.
**Waioeka Gorge** Route 2 to the south-east of Opotiki, follows through and rises up the Waioeka Gorge for 58 km. There is pretty gorge and mountain scenery.
**East Cape** Route 35 branching off from Opotiki, follows the curve of the Bay of Plenty round up towards Cape Runaway. The road is in view of the coast most of the way, passing beaches and communities including Te Kaha and Waihau Bay. The one-way distance to Waihau Bay is 106 km. The complete distance round the East Cape to Gisborne is 330 km.

**See Also** Whakatane, Te Kaha and Waihau Bay

# OPUNAKE NI
**Population** 1616
**Location** On Route 45, 61 km south-west of New Plymouth, 44 km north-west of Hawera.

This country town standing between the sea and the slopes of Mt Egmont, developed from a military settlement that was established when British troops landed in 1865 during the Taranaki campaign. The fortification here was one of a series that extended along the coast to the north of New Plymouth. The road between New Plymouth and Wanganui was impassable (except for troops) for five years because of hostility with the Maoris. The British troops, however, endeavoured and temporarily succeeded in re-opening the road. The Hauhau

Maori cult was reportedly founded here by Te Ua Haumene.

## ENVIRONS & ATTRACTIONS
**Opunake Beach** A black iron-sand beach, with picnic facilities. It is crescent-shaped and backed by tall cliffs.

## LOCAL TOURING
**Oaonui** 8 km north of Opunake is the landfall for the Maui offshore natural gas field. The onshore production station features a visitors centre with a giant model of the 34 km offshore Maui platform — usually invisible out to sea.
**Kapuni** A natural gas field was discovered here in 1962. The large wellhead installation pipes gas and condensate to New Plymouth and Waitara. Kapuni is also the site of a large ammonia–urea plant that uses Kapuni gas. Kapuni is 25 km from Opunake but can be easily fitted into a round Mt Egmont itinerary.

**See Also** New Plymouth, Stratford and Hawera

---

# OTAKI NI
**Population** 4407
**Location** On Route 1, 20 km south of Levin. 74 km north of Wellington.

---

Otaki is situated where the Tararua Range closes in towards the west coast. It is an important market gardening district, which supplies produce to Wellington. Many of the Maori settlements were originally established by Ngati-Raukawa tribes people, when they travelled south from the Waikato in 1820, led by renegade Te Rauparaha. From Kapiti Island and the Otaki area, Te Rauparaha embarked on Napolean-style domination of the south-western part of the North Island and the northern parts of the South Island. He negotiated land sales to settlers in the Wellington area and also in Marlborough.

Kapiti Island, offshore, is now a restricted bird reserve. The mainland coast from Otaki south through Waikanae to Pukerua Bay is now known as the Kapiti Coast.

## ENVIRONS & ATTRACTIONS
**Rangiatea Maori Church** Built in 1849 mainly of totora, this church has a massive ridge pole and Maori interior decoration of great intricacy. Opposite the church is a monument to and possible grave of Te Rauparaha.
**Otaki Maori Mission** Just beyond the Rangiatea is the site of this Roman Catholic Mission established in 1844.
**Otaki Beach** A holiday area 2 km west of the main road.
**Hyde Museum** Local historical items are housed in a former dairy factory 5 km south at Te Horo.

## LOCAL TOURING
**Otaki Gorge** The Otaki Gorge road leads 9 km into the Tararua Range and forest park. The Range offers a wide variety of tramping trips, from easy to difficult.

**See Also** Wellington, Levin and Foxton

---

# OTAUTAU SI
**Population** 841
**Location** 25 km north of Riverton.

---

This community lies on the Wairio branch railway line from Thornbury. Formerly a timber town it is now a dairying and sheep farming centre.

## LOCAL TOURING
**Longwood Forest** Several tracks run through the Longwood Range, following old water-races and bush tramways. Also note the

*The nocturnal kiwi.*

northern entrance to the Pourakino Walkway (refer to the entry under Riverton).

**Nightcaps** This small community 21 km north of Otautau, was originally built to house coalminers.

**Ohai** Another small coalmining community, which is 29 km north of Otautau. The mine and town developed when the Nightcaps mine ran out. The Ohau Railway Board still runs a private railway connecting with the government line at Wairio to carry Ohau coal.

**See Also** Invercargill, Riverton and Tuatapere

# OTIRA SI
**Population** 128
**Location** On Route 73, 14 km west of Arthur's Pass, 81 km east of Greymouth.

Otira is a railway town on the line between Christchurch and Greymouth near the 8.5 km Otira Tunnel. The tunnel is electrified

and Otira is the place where diesel-hauled trains change to an electric engine or vice versa. At the time of compiling this guide the railways were considering removing the electrification, which would probably severely reduce the Otira community.

Between Otira and Arthur's Pass, Route 73 climbs over the Pass through the Arthur's Pass National Park. The countryside is very scenic but the road zigzags up and over the main divide of the Southern Alps. Vehicles over 13 m long as well as caravans and trailers are prohibited due to road conditions and possible high winds.

**See Also** Arthur's Pass, Greymouth and Hokitika

# OTOROHANGA NI
**Population** 2747
**Location** On Route 3, 59 km south of Hamilton.

The town started as a construction point for railway workers on the main trunk line in the 1880s, and developed as a tourist centre after the discovery of the Waitomo Caves. The area is rich in Maori history and before the European settlers arrived there were about 4000 Maoris resident on the fertile river flats. The Maoris allowed the main trunk railway line to be built through their King Country on the condition that no liquor was brought into the area. Following on from this the district remained 'dry' until 1955 when the first liquor licences were granted. Today it is a farming and servicing centre for the southern Waikato and northern King Country area.

## ENVIRONS & ATTRACTIONS
**Kiwi House and Bird Park**
Situated 1 km off the main road, the Kiwi house at the Otorohanga zoological gardens is a popular attraction. There is also a closed-off breeding area for the kiwis. The park is open daily.

**See Also** Te Awamutu, Kawhia and Waitomo Caves

# OWAKA SI
**Population** 376
**Location** On Route 92, 31 km south-east of Balclutha.

A rural community in the Catlins district, on the east coast south-west of Balclutha. The area was heavily forested and sawmills operated for many years in the district. Catlins Lake is the name given to the tidal estuary of the Catlins River. It was an active port for timber loaded ships — at least until the coming of the branch railway in 1896. The Catlin State Forest Park lies to the south and is the largest concentrated area of native bush on the east coast of the South Island.

## ENVIRONS & ATTRACTIONS
**Catlins Historical Society Museum** Small collection of relics of local interest, Waikawa Road.
**Tunnel Hill Historic Reserve** A 200 m tunnel off the old railway branch 5 km north on Route 92. Allow 45 minutes and take a torch.
**Pounawea** Tidal estuary with 15-minute round trip nature walk. Also a 2½ hr one-way beach walk to Cannibal Bay.

## LOCAL TOURING
**Jacks Bay** A beach with a blowhole in open farmland vented by a subterranean tunnel; 11 km by bridge over Catlins Lake.
**Wilkes Falls** A 5 km, 2 hr return track through the Hina Hina forest to these 30 m falls. Accessible from Lower Lanshaw Road, across Catlins Lake.
**Purakaunui** Bay, river and falls, 15 km south towards the coast.
**Tahakopa Bay Scenic Reserve** A 2 km (40 minutes return) track follows an old coach road. Access is from the Tahakopa River bridge 27 km south.
**Tautuku Bay** A bush-backed beach 31 km south on Route 92.
**Catlins Forest Park** The Catlins River valley walk through the forest starts at the Tawanui picnic area 13 km from Owaka or up Chloris Pass Road. The walk is a series of three tracks stretching 15 km; allow 5 hr one way.

**See Also** Balclutha, Fortrose and Invercargill

# OXFORD SI
**Population** 1088
**Location** On Route 72, 33 km west of Rangiora, 21 km north-east of Sheffield.

*Lindis Pass, Otago*

A farming and sheep raising district in North Canterbury, which started as a sawmilling camp about 1852.

## LOCAL TOURING
**Waimakariri River** Route 72 leads south across the Waimakariri River bridge, but other roads lead west to where the river leaves its gorge. Views and picnic sites 14 km west.

**Ashley Gorge** Where the Ashley River leaves its gorge. Picnic sites are 8 km north. 1 km north of the bridge, a waterfall track leads through bush to 12 m waterfall (45 minutes each way).

**Mt Thomas Forest** A forest reserve north of the Ashley River with several walks including Loop Track (2 hr return) and Waterfall Track (30 minutes return), from Glentui picnic area 23 km north.

**Oxford Forest** A forest reserve 11 km north-west with access at View Hill and Coopers Creek. From the latter, a 2½ hr one-way track leads through beech forest to Ryde Falls.

**See Also** Christchurch, Rangiora and Springfield

# P

## PAEROA NI
**Population** 3661
**Location** On the eastern
Hauraki Plains on Route 2 at its
intersection with Route 26; 32 km
south of Thames, 21 km north of
Te Aroha.

Paeroa is the centre for farming
and commercial activity in the
Thames Valley district. It is
situated at the foot of the
Coromandel/Kaimai Ranges and
at the junction of the Waihou and
Ohinemuri Rivers. In the late 19th
and early 20th centuries the river
was used by vehicles to and from
Thames and Auckland — in fact
even Captain Cook explored it in
1769. The area was known by the
Maoris as Ohinemuri.

Boom times followed the
discovery of gold at nearby
Mackaytown, Karangahake, and
Waihi in 1874. Paeroa became a
gateway to this area. The swampy
Hauraki Plains prevented direct
land access from Auckland and
the railway from Hamilton
reached Paeroa in 1895. In 1905 a
spectacular branch extended to
Waihi.

A nationally marketed soft
drink 'Lemon & Paeroa' once used
mineral water drawn from a deep
well in the borough.

## ENVIRONS & ATTRACTIONS
**Paeroa Museum** Features
displays and photographs of the
town and river. Open three days a
week and school holidays.
**Historical Maritime Park**
4 km north of Paeroa on the
Auckland road. This museum has
developed beside a loop in the
Waihou River. The museum is
restoring a number of old river
vessels including the
paddlesteamer *Kopu*. Open
weekends and holidays.
**Primrose Hill** This local hill
offers a vantage point over the
town and plains.

## LOCAL TOURING
**Karangahake Gorge** Route 2
follows a spectacular chasm
through the Coromandel Range.
Note rest area and signs at
Karangahake and further on
access to the Karangahake
walkway. This walkway follows
the old railway route through a
1 km tunnel at the end of which
you can either return on a
walkway following the other
bank, or carry on to a road
junction a further 3 km east.
Ruins of old goldmining batteries
are clearly visible and are also
signposted. The road leads
through the narrow gorge towards
the Waitawheta Falls and Lily
gardens, Waikino and Waihi. The
walkway through the tunnel and
back on the riverbank is
interesting and probably requires
about 1½ hr for the round trip
from and to the carpark. The
tunnel is partially lit but take a
torch if possible.

**See Also** Te Aroha, Thames and
Waihi

## PAIHIA NI
Refer to the Bay of Islands.

## PALMERSTON SI
**Population** 846
**Location** On Route 1, 59 km
south of Oamaru, 56 km north of
Dunedin.

In goldmining days Palmerston
was a main entry point to the
central Otago diggings over the
Pigroot Road. The road, now
Route 85, developed as an

alternative to the Old Dunstan Road (south of Dunedin). Palmerston grew with it. Route 85 now climbs steadily up to Ranfurly and the Maniototo Plains. Route 1 south to Dunedin goes over two hills — the Kilmog and Mt Cargill.

## LOCAL TOURING

**Shag Point** A holiday area with traces of an old port, an old railway, an old coalmine and a seal colony. Turn off Route 1, 7 km north.

**Moeraki** 21 km north off Route 1 on a side road, the village of Moeraki is situated on a small peninsula. However, Moeraki's main attraction is its spherical boulders (measuring up to 4 m in circumference), which are just off the main road. There is a visitors centre and a short walk to the site of the boulders.

**Trotters Gorge** A picnic spot amid native bush and limestone cliffs, accessible via Horserange Road, north of Palmerston.

**Waikouaiti** 14 km south, it has an Early Settlers Museum (main road, open daily, except Sunday 2–4 pm). Two churches (Wakouaiti Presbyterian, 1863, and St Johns Anglican, 1858) may be of interest.

**Karitane** The home of the Plunket Society, founded by Truby King, for baby care. A Maori Foreshore Reserve near the wharf has a short track up to a memorial lookout. 21 km south of Palmerston.

**Seacliff** On a coastal road, 27 km south of Palmerston, are the remains of Cherry Farm asylum, now being changed to a museum of Transport and Technology.

**Warrington** St Barnabas's Church was built in 1873 and is located in Warrington, which is 10 km south of Karitane on the coast road.

**See Also** Oamaru, Ranfurly and Dunedin

# PALMERSTON NORTH NI
**Population** 60 503
**Location** 145 km north of Wellington, 74 km south-east of Wanganui.

The city of Palmerston North is situated on the right bank of the Manawatu River, and is the centre of a rich farming area. It receives scheduled air services through its airport at Milson, and is the junction for the east coast railway line (Woodville, Napier, Gisborne) with the main trunk Auckland–Wellington railway line. It is served by good road connections, but it is off the most direct Auckland–Wellington road routes.

Route 3 from Bulls and Sanson provides a connection from Route 1; alternatively from the north, Route 54 leaves Route 1 at Mangaweka, or (perhaps better) a road from Vinegar Hill; from the south there are connections via Route 57 from Levin and Route 56 from Himatangi.

The east-west direction of Route 3 from Palmerston North through the Manawatu Gorge to Woodville is an important and scenic connection to the Wairarapa and Hawke's Bay areas of the east coast.

The central district of the city is noted for its 'Square' containing 7 ha of gardens (which used to be the railway station until it was shifted to the outskirts in 1963).

Massey University is noted for its agricultural studies, and nearby are research facilities for grasslands, seed testing, artificial breeding and dairying.

Palmerston North became a city in 1930. Its first settlers arrived about 1870. The direct railway from Wellington, built by the private Wellington and Manawatu railway company, was completed in 1886. An earlier bush tramway ran to Foxton from 1873, and was converted to railway in 1876. Then the government built a roundabout connection from Wellington via the Rimutakas and the Wairarapa. However, it was the direct line that opened up the Manawatu and provided access to the heavily timbered land, which enabled it to be cleared into the farmland of today. In 1908 the government took over the private railway.

Foxton had been the port for the Manawatu, but the direct railway connection from Wellington bypassed Foxton, and initiated its decline as a port. Palmerston North, however, never looked back.

## ENVIRONS & ATTRACTIONS
**The Square** Spacious park and gardens area in the central business district; it contains a clock tower, a statue of Rangitane chief Te Awe Awe, and the Civic Centre.
**The Esplanade** By the Manawatu River Bridge, this large park area includes rose gardens, sports grounds and miniature railway. There is also a 10 km walk by the riverside.
**Manawatu Museum** Provides historic displays of early settlers and is open every afternoon, except Monday. Church Street.
**Anzac Park** Just across the Fitzherbert Bridge, a side road leads to viewpoint and observatory.

## LOCAL TOURING
**Manawatu Gorge** The gorge starts 16 km east of Palmerston North; follow through 13 km to Lake Wairarapa lookout and Woodville.

**Tokomaru Steam Engine Museum** This collection of working steam engines, including traction engine, fire engine, road roller and locomotives is in Tokomaru, 19 km south on Route 57. Live operating days are held at regular intervals. Open daily 9 am–noon, 1–3.30 pm.

**See Also** Woodville, Feilding and Taihape

# PATEA NI
**Population** 15 681
**Location** On Route 3, 63 km north of Wanganui, 28 km south-east of Hawera.

Patea is situated on the Patea river — a waterway navigable by launches for nearly 30 km. It serves a rich dairying and pastoral district. The beach nearby contains substantial deposits of ironsand. The town was established by British troops when General Cameron built two redoubts, which accommodated 200 men in 1865 — later extended to accommodate up to 600 — but they were never attacked.

## ENVIRONS & ATTRACTIONS
**Aotea Canoe Replica** A concrete model of the famous canoe, one of the Great Fleet that arrived in 1350. It was erected in 1933 by Maoris claiming descent from this early tribe.

## LOCAL TOURING
**Lake Rotorangi** New Zealand's newest artificial lake set amid virgin bush, accessible by Ball Road 35 km north of Patea. Launch trips are available on the lake. From the Patea dam, a walkway of 1.5 km provides fine views of bush, lake and dam. The upper reaches of this dam can be

reached from Eltham and Stratford.

**Waverley** 17 km south of Patea on Route 3, this town has the remains of a military redoubt by the Post Office. 6 km away the Kohe Maori rock drawings can be found on a private property. Interested tourists should enquire for directions and permission at Waverley.

**See Also** Hawera, Stratford and Wanganui

---

# PICTON SI

**Population** 4129
**Location** At the top end of the South Island, and the beginning of the South Island section of Route 1, 28 km north of Blenheim.

---

Picton is situated in the recesses of Queen Charlotte Sound, one of several picturesque waterways forming the Marlborough Sounds. It is a port and South Island terminus for the inter-island ferry service. There is a rail service from Picton to Blenheim and Christchurch. There are also scheduled coach services from Picton to many parts of the South Island connecting with at least one ferry sailing each day.

The Picton settlement was laid out on the site of Waitohi pa in 1848. It vied with Blenheim for some years to be the capital of Marlborough province.

The Marlborough Sounds is a drowned valley system with unlimited boating opportunities. Queen Charlotte Sound and Tory Channel (an eastern short cut) allow access to Picton; while Pelorus Sounds and its many recesses — including Kenepuru Sound and Mahau Sound — are accessible by boat from Havelock. Road access around the Sounds is limited, but the two main ones are the Kenepuru Road, described subsequently, and the French Pass Road, described under the Havelock heading. Queen Charlotte is the route followed by shipping into Picton and is a more popular Sound, but the Pelorus and Kenepuru waterways are possibly the more scenic, by boat or by car.

## ENVIRONS & ATTRACTIONS
**Smiths Picton Museum**
Includes relics from whaling days. Open daily 10 am–3 pm, London Quay.
**The New Zealand Experience**
Shows every 30 minutes of this dramatic multi-screen presentation. Also displays of halographs and a film on the tuatara lizard. Corner London Quay and Auckland Street.
*Edwin Fox* The hulk of a clipper ship built in 1853 for the East India Company. It carried tea, troops, convicts, refrigerated meat and coal and is currently being restored on the Picton waterfront.
**Victoria Domain** From the foreshore a bridge and a track leads to Shelly Beach. Walk 1 km further to reach Bobs Bay. There is also a branch road off Waikawa Bay Road that leads 2 km to a Picton and Sounds lookout.
**Grove Road Lookout** Drive 1.5 km on Queen Charlotte Drive for a view back over Picton.

## LOCAL TOURING
**Waikawa Bay** Sheltered bay and yacht haven 5 km north on Waikawa Bay Road.
**Boat Trips** There are popular boat trips (seasonal and subject to numbers) to Mamorangi Bay (also accessible by Grove Road), Mistletoe Bay and Onahau Bay, also to Torea Bay and by connecting minibus to the Portage Hotel. Longer trips to Furneaux

*The inter-island ferry berthed at Picton.*

Lodge and Ship Cove (visited by Captain Cook three times) are also available depending upon demand.

**Grove Road** Officially Queen Charlotte Drive, this road reaches 34 km around the Grove Arm of Queen Charlotte Sound and the inner recesses of Pelorus Sound to Havelock. It is scenic, but not suitable for caravans. En route, you will pass the side road to

Anakiwa Outward Bound training school.

**Kenepuru Road** Branches off the Grove Road at Linklater (22 km) and proceeds out along the finger of land separating Queen Charlotte Sound and the Pelorus/Kenepuru Sounds. 36 km to Portage, 45 km to head of Kenepuru Sound, 50 km to start of Endeavour walkway and 70 km to Titirangi Bay near Port Gore. It

has a metal surface and road conditions are subject to weather; unsuitable for caravans. The 22 000 tonne liner *Mikhail Lermontov* sank in 33 m of water off Port Gore in February 1986.

**Queen Charlotte Walkway** Divided into three sections: Anakiwa (9 km, 4 hr, road access both ends), Kenepuru (22 km, 13 hr, a new middle section), and Endeavour (11 km, 9 hr, no road access to the far end, but launch return can be arranged from Furneaux Lodge).

**Port Underwood** A winding but scenic coastal route from Picton to Blenheim (110 km) — not recommended for caravans. Start out on Waikawa Bay Road, then rise to scenic overlook, passing locality where Major Bunbury proclaimed sovereignty of the South Island on behalf of

Governor Hobson and the Queen. The route also passes Kakapo Bay, which was once the site of a big whaling station and where up to 30 whaling ships could anchor. Their crews introduced measles and other European illnesses, which caused innumerable deaths among the local Maoris, and weakened the local tribe so that they easily fell prey to Te Rauparaha. Allow 3 hr for this road journey.

**See Also** Blenheim and Havelock

# PUKEKOHE NI
**Population** 9398
**Location** 52 km south of downtown Auckland on Route 22.

Pukekohe is the centre of a fertile farming and market gardening area. Much of the town commerce relates to this farming industry. Although located a little off the main South Road, it is on the main trunk railway line. The area was settled in 1864 mainly by immigrants from Ireland and Cornwall. The Pukekohe Racecourse is the venue for the New Zealand International Grand Prix motor racing circuit.

## LOCAL TOURING
**Mt William Walkway** Mt William in the Bombay Hills offers extensive views over the Auckland area. The one-way walk of 6.5 km takes 3 hr. The start and finish is signposted off Puketutu Road Bombay, or the McMillan Road off Route 2 just after it commences at Pokeno. The walk is closed in the lambing season, August to September.

**See Also** Waiuku, Tuakau and Auckland

# PUNAKAIKI SI
**Population** 144
**Location** On Route 6, 56 km south of Westport, 47 km north of Greymouth.

Squeezed between the mountains and the sea, Punakaiki is best known for its Pancake Rocks and blowholes. Behind the town the Paparoa Range now encompasses the new Paparoa National Park. The community is a convenient stopping point between Westport and Greymouth but the attractions of bush and beach can entice longer stopovers.

## ENVIRONS & ATTRACTIONS
**Pancake Rocks and Blowholes** An easy 10-minute walk from the road leads to views over the stratified limestone rocks, and the large blowholes where the ocean surges in. This area is known as Dolomite Point.
**Cavern Track** A short track down a wooden stairway gives access to one of a number of caves in the area. Take a torch.
**Truman Track** An easy 15-minute walk through forest and coastal scenery, starting 3 km north from the Punakaiki information centre.

## LOCAL TOURING
**Paparoa National Park** This new park stretches up the western slopes of the Paparoa Range. There are a number of tracks including the Punakaiki–Pororari Track (3 hr return), which offers a round trip walk. There are also tracks up to Bullock Creek, Cave Creek and Fox River Caves. Because these tracks and cave systems can be flooded after heavy rain, enquire at the Punakaiki visitors centre before entering the park.

**See Also** Westport and Greymouth

*A black sand beach near Punakaiki.*

# PUTARURU NI
**Population** 4197
**Location** On Route 1, 64 km south of Hamilton.

The town owes its existence to the forestry and timber industries; and particularly now to the exotic pine trees that grow so readily in the pumice soils of the volcanic plateau and surrounding area. The town is on a branch railway. Putaruru is also regarded as the camellia town of New Zealand.

## ENVIRONS & ATTRACTIONS
**Timber Museum** Features displays on the history of local forestry in the area. Open daily except Saturday.

## LOCAL TOURING
16 km west of Putaruru is the Arapunui hydro-electric power station — the oldest of the present nine on the Waikato River. It was built in 1929. There is access by road and pedestrian swingbridge to the dam and powerhouse.
**Okoroire Hot Springs** These private pools of mineral waters, which contain sodium chloride and sodium silicate, are 15 km north of Putaruru via Tirau. There is a hotel, golf course and picnic area. Open daily except Thursday.

**See Also** Cambridge, Rotorua and Tokoroa

*An aerial view of Queenstown.*

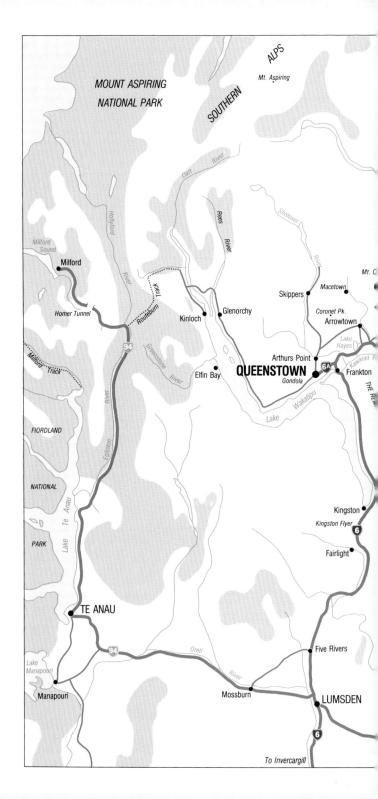

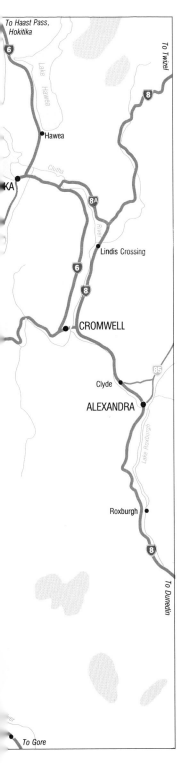

# QUEENSTOWN SI

**Population** 3659
**Location** Adjacent to Route 6,
187 km north of Invercargill, also
283 km north-west of Dunedin,
and 486 km south-west of
Christchurch. Route 6 passes
5 km from the town centre, which
is linked by Route 6A.

Probably the premier holiday
resort of the South Island,
Queenstown is very much a
tourist town with an international
flavour, offering year round
holidays. It is located on the
eastern shore of Lake Wakatipu,
with the business section of the
town occupying gently rising
ground that slopes up from a bay.
Connected to the bay is a
peninsula that has a park reserve.
Most of the rest of the lake has
mountainous sides.

Queenstown receives
scheduled air services through its
airport at Frankton. Many bus
services and coach tours operate
to and through the town; there are
also lake tours and excursions.

Europeans David McKellar and
George Gunn were probably the
first white men to explore the
lake, in 1857. Donald Hay
followed in 1859. William Rees
settled in the area now called
Queenstown, but had to move on
when it was declared a goldfield.
The Otago goldrush from 1862
was the country's largest, and
there seemed to be traces of gold
throughout the whole region with
big nuggets discovered in many
parts of the Queenstown district.

Nearby Arrowtown (population
953) developed as a mining town,
and was the scene of feverish

activity. Arrowtown is now very much a tourist centre. It is listed under Queenstown, because a tourist to Queenstown would probably also see Arrowtown.

Lake Wakatipu is the South Island's second largest lake (after Te Anau). It is z-shaped, and measures approximately 85 km × 5 km.

## ENVIRONS & ATTRACTIONS

**Queenstown Mall**  Lower Ballarat Street is a shopping precinct, closed to vehicular traffic.

**Library**  Built in 1877, this historic stone building is in Ballarat Street.

**St Peter's Anglican Church** 1932 stone church in Camp Street.

**Queenstown Gardens**  On the peninsula adjacent to Queensland Bay, these gardens have lawns, flowers, trees and recreation area. To reach the gardens it is a pleasant walk along the beach from the town.

**St Omer Park**  This reserve is along the Esplanade by the shore of the lake.

**Queenstown Gondola**  Take the cableway up Bobs Peak for dramatic views over the town, lake and mountains. Brecon Street.

**Queenstown Motor Museum** An auto show near the base of the Gondola in Brecon Street.

**Goldfields Town Museum Park**  A re-created goldmining town; 3 km out towards Frankton.

**Queenstown Water World** Underwater viewing gallery of lake fish.

**ISS *Earnslaw***  Lake Steamer that offers daily lake excursions. The ship was built in 1912 in Dunedin and re-assembled at Kingston.

## LOCAL TOURING

### QUEENSTOWN & FRANKTON

**Queenstown Walkways** Queenstown Hill walkway is an easy climb up to 902 m behind

*Jetboat rides on the Shotover River.*

the town for views. Start from the top of Edgar Street; allow 2½–3 hr return. The Frankton Arm walkway is a lake shore stroll that follows around most, but not all, of the Frankton Arm of the lake, from Queenstown to the Kelvin Heights (10 km, 3 hr return). One Mile Creek offers a 1¼ km each way walk from the end of Thompson Street, past an old pumphouse and waterworks to a dam. It is no longer used for electricity generation; but it is advisable to keep away from the dammed creek. The Ben Lomond Walkway rises to 1747 m and requires 5–6 hr for return. This is a climb through bush and tussock for a panoramic summit view. Commence off Skyline Access Road, or from the end of the One Mile Creek Track.

**Cecil Peak, Walter Peak, Mt Nicholas** These high country sheep stations are across the lake from Queenstown. They are generally accessible via tourist half-day launch trips.

**Frankton** A suburb of Queenstown, where Route 6A intersects Route 6. The airport is located here and the Kawarau River flows out of the lake. Route 6 crosses the river over the old Kawarau dam — a largely unsuccessful effort to drain the river in order to pick up gold from the bottom.

**Deer Park Heights** Deer and goats in a natural setting with panoramic views over lakes and mountains, near Kelvin Heights, beyond Frankton.

**The Remarkables Road and Ski-Field** The Remarkables form a dominant backdrop to Queenstown. There is a spectacular 14 km toll road and then cableway to the crest of the mountain. It offers panoramas in summer and skiing in winter (June to October). Your rental vehicle may not be insured on this road.

**Kingston** Lake port and settlement at the southern end of Lake Wakatipu, 46 km from Queenstown.

**Kingston Flyer** A steam-hauled tourist train now operating from Kingston to Fairlight, twice daily, November through to May.

**Milford Sound** There are full day sightseeing tours that operate via Te Anau, the Eglinton Valley and Hollyford Valley to Milford Sound.

**Scenic Flights** Can be taken · around Queenstown and over the lake, or over the mountains to Lake Te Anau, Southerland Falls and Milford Sound (landing on the airstrip there). These popular flightseeing options leave from the Queenstown airport at Frankton.

## ARROWTOWN AND DISTRICT

**Arrowtown** Stroll along its main street, Buckingham Street, to savour old pubs and tourist shops.

**Lakes District Centennial Museum** This popular collection of Wakatipu region memorabilia includes relics from the goldmining days. Open daily 9 am–5 pm.

**Queenstown–Arrowtown Road** Arthurs Point Hotel (5 km) and Packers Arms restaurant (7 km) are historic buildings on the way to Arrowtown. From the Edith Cavell Bridge over the Shotover River, watch jetboats ride the river, then go down for a ride yourself. Jetboat tours on the Shotover and the Kawarau are also packaged with transport from downtown Queenstown.

Immediately before the Shotover bridge is a vehicle track of 1 km leading to a picnic spot and the site of the Oxenbridge Tunnel — a 1907 attempt to divert the river water so that the riverbed could be worked for gold. The scheme was unsuccessful but much of the river water continues to flow through it. Also on the way to Arrowtown see the Cattledrome, a cattle and dairying display (7 km). There are two shows most days.

**Coronet Peak**  This is a leading ski resort from June to September, but is equally attractive at other times when the road and chairlift (operates all year to the peak at 1650 m) offer panoramic views. There is an observation gallery at the road's end (15 km).

**Skippers**  From the Coronet Peak Road, branch off at an observation point for this precipitous road. It is for experienced drivers only — if in doubt take a tour! It is the thrill of the road through the Skippers Canyon that is now the major attraction; in the past it used to be the lure of gold. Your rental vehicle contract may prevent you from driving on this road.

**Macetown**  An old gold town 15 km up the Arrow River, accessible by four-wheel drive tours, including river crossings. Also accessible via horseback tour or the Big Hill walkway. Macetown is one of the scattered locations of the Otago Goldfields Park.

**Arrowtown Walkways**  The Big Hill Track is an old 12 km bridle track (4–5 hr each way) that climbs steeply to Eichardts Terrace, then has easier grades over a saddle to intercept the Macetown four-wheel drive track about 20 minutes from its destination. The Sawpit Gully Track provides an opportunity for a loop walk with the first part of the Big Hill Track (7 km, 3 hr return). Hayes Creek Track (3 km, 1¼ hr) starts and finishes at different parts on the Macetown Road, and passes old goldmining relics.

**Lake Hayes**  A small but much

*Lake Wakatipu in Queenstown.*

painted lake between Arrowtown and Route 6, especially favoured with autumn colours.

**Crown Terrace**  The southern end of Route 89 as it zigzags up the Crown Range is an interesting climb in the summer, but avoid the snow and ice of winter.

## TOP OF THE LAKE

**Glenorchy and Kinlock**  The road to the head of the lake hugs the shore or the cliffside for 44 km to Glenorchy, and then crosses the Rees and Dart Rivers to Kinloch (80 km). Beyond Glenorchy side roads lead to

Paradise, Route Burn, and Elfin
Bay — connecting to various
walking tracks. 22 km up the Rees
Valley from Glenorchy is the
40-minute bush walk to the
remains of the Invincible
abandoned goldmine, one of the
scattered locations of the Otago
goldfields park.

**Routeburn Track** A 3–4 day
climb from the Routeburn Valley
at the head of Lake Wakatipu over
the Harris Saddle to the Milford
Sound Road near 'the Divide'.
Road access at both ends. Options
of freedom walking, or guided
walk with comfortable overnight
huts. 39 km.

**Greenstone Valley** From Elfin
Bay on the west side of Lake
Wakatipu, there is a 40 km tramp
of 11 hr (two days) to Lake
Howden and The Divide.

**Caples Track** Similar and
parallel to the Greenstone Valley
tramp. It is possible to walk a
round trip in 3–4 days.

**Rees-Dart Track** At the head of
Lake Wakatipu, this tramp leads
up the Rees Valley and down the
Dart over the 1447 m
Cunningham Saddle (four days).
Experienced trampers only
should attempt this track.

**See Also** Wanaka, Cromwell
and Lumsden

# R

## RAETIHI NI
**Population** 1323
**Location** On Route 4, 34 km south of National Park and 90 km north of Wanganui.

The town owes its development to timber, though now market gardening and general farming has taken prominence. However, an area of pine forest has been planted between the town and Pipiriki. The town was on a branch railway from Ohakune but this has now closed. In early days the Wanganui River was a transport artery and a rough mountain road was built for the 28 km between Raetihi and Pipiriki on the river. Some would say that the road still has not improved!

## LOCAL TOURING
**Pipiriki** In the days of riverboats, Pipiriki and its hotel were important staging points for river traffic, but little remains now. However, a restored riverboat, the *Ongarue* is on display and Pipiriki may also receive new prominence with the recent creation of a Wanganui National Park. A restored colonial house is the present ranger house and museum. Jetboat rides on the river to the Drop Scene, a beautiful part of the river not accessible by road, are popular with tourists. Jetboats also provide access to the 'bridge to nowhere', the track that follows the remains of a road built to service now-abandoned farms, and to the river end of the Matemateaonga walkway.
**Wanganui River Road** This is a rugged road winding around bluffs above the historic Wanganui River. The route via Pipiriki adds 17 km to the direct Raetihi–Wanganui journey and a lot more time. There are many points of interest, both historic and scenic. Some leading places are described as follows.
**Jerusalem** 12 km from Pipiriki, 40 km from Raetihi. A small community (population 54) in a picturesque setting, dominated by a church built in 1892 and a Catholic convent. The settlement received publicity in the early 1970s with the establishment of a commune for up to 200 people run by the poet James Baxter. The Maori name for the town is Hiruharema. Pause for a view of the village from the southern roadway.
**Kawana** 51 km from Raetihi. An old flour mill here has been restored by the Historic Places Trust. It was the longest operating and most successful of the many mills that were on the river. It was established in 1854 and is accessible down a short track from the roadside sign.
**Koriniti (Corinth)** 59 km on a side road is a marae with three historic buildings. 300 people lived here in about 1848, when the whole river valley carried a much larger Maori population. The Reverend Richard Taylor built missions on the river in 1848 and gave them New Testament place names: Corinth (called Koriniti by the Maoris), Hiruharama (Jerusalem), Atene (Athens), and also Ranana (London).
**Atene** 71 km. The Wanganui River used to curve around here in a near circle, but it broke through the narrow neck and left the circular meander. The Skyline walkway follows the ridge around the old riverbed, starting and ending on the road 2 km apart. It is a 6–8 hr walk with views of both river and forest.

**Aramoana (Gentle Annie)**
90 km. This summit 230 m above
sea level offers a picturesque view
of the river. On fine days distant
Ruapehu is visible. From here the
road winds over to join the main
Route 4.

Additional information about
the Wanganui River is given
under the Wanganui listing.

**See Also** Wanganui, Ohakune
and Taumaranui

# RAGLAN NI
**Population** 1815
**Location** Situated 47 km west of
Hamilton on Route 23, on the
shores of Raglan Harbour.

This peaceful harbourside town,
with black sand ocean beaches
nearby on the coast, is a popular
beach and fishing area for the
people of Hamilton.

First settled in 1854 by
Europeans, the area was largely
isolated from the Waikato land
wars and was slow to develop
afterwards. The name Raglan
commemorates a British General
at the Crimean War of 1853–55.
The harbour is 13 km in length
and 2–3 km across. It used to be
a port and today is still a fishing
centre. The original Maori name
for the town was Whaingaroa.

## ENVIRONS & ATTRACTIONS
**Raglan Pioneer District
Museum** Includes items
of local interest. Located in the
municipal buildings, open
Saturday.
**Whale Bay** A 10 km road
around the southern head of the
harbour gives views of the rugged
coastline sweeping north towards
the Waikato Heads. On the way,
pass Ocean Beach, which is
accessed from a side road. Also
Manu Bay for left break surf.

## LOCAL TOURING
**Bridal Veil Falls** A spectacular
waterfall down a 60 m
escarpment. Accessible by a
10-minute walk through the bush;
there is also a steep track to the
bottom of the falls. These falls are
situated 21 km south of Raglan on
a road linking across to Kawhia.

**See Also** Ngaruawahia,
Hamilton and Kawhia

# RANFURLY SI
**Population** 961
**Location** On Route 85, 80 km
north-west of Palmerston, 90 km
north-east of Alexandra.

Ranfurly is a country town on the
Maniototo Plains — an inland
plateau in north Otago. The
locality was first settled by farmers
in the 1880s, and the township
developed when the railway from
Dunedin to Alexandra was
completed in 1898.

## LOCAL TOURING
**Patearoa** Small goldfield from
1863. A hydraulic sluicing nozzle
is on display. The old Sowburn
diggings were near the bridge.
17 km south of Ranfurly.
**Paerau** Earlier called Styx, this
town was an overnight stop for
coaches and wagons from
Dunedin to the goldfields via the
Old Dunstan Road. 39 km south.
**Old Dunstan Road** This was
formerly the main road to the
goldfields before the Pigroot Road
opened. Still accessible in
summer, preferably by four-wheel
drive vehicles over the Rock and
Pillar Range, between Paerau and
Clarks Junction on Route 87.
**Middlemarch** Small township
on Route 87, 66 km south of
Ranfurly, situated in the Taieri
Valley (in the lee of the Rock and
Pillar Range).

**Kyeburn Diggings** At the southern entrance to Dansey Pass, note the sluiced banks and tailings by the Kyeburn River; also the historic Dansey Pass Hotel.

**Naseby** An old goldtown and holiday retreat set in a little basin off Route 85, 13 km north of Ranfurly. Of interest still is the old (1865) Athenaeum building on the road in, and also the Maniototo Early Settlers Museum, open weekends 2–4 pm. Ice-skating and curling are done on a local dam in winter.

**Naseby Forest** This is the highest exotic forest in the South Island and lies on the foothills of the Mt Ida Range. The Hogburn Gully and One Tree Hill Historical Track offer a walk of 1½–2 hr from near the post office building. The Welcome Inn walking track leads from the bottom of Leven Street to a viewpoint over the town.

**St Bathans** Situated on a loop road off Route 85, 36 km west of Ranfurly, this town, like Naseby, is a small holiday retreat that was once a goldtown. Among the old or ruined buildings still visible is the Vulcan Hotel (1869), which dominates the bottom of the main street. The nearby Blue Lake, which is sometimes green, fills the sluiced excavations of the goldmining days.

**See Also** Palmerston, Kurow, Alexandra and Dunedin

# RANGIORA SI
**Population** 6674
**Location** On Route 72, 7 km west of its beginning at Woodend, 33 km east of Oxford.

Situated on the right bank of the Ashley River, the borough serves a rich agricultural and pastoral district, and is also a satellite town for Christchurch.

ENVIRONS & ATTRACTIONS
**Rangiora District Historical Museum** Includes an 1869 Cobb cottage, and other colonial items. Good Street, open Sunday 2–4.30 pm.

**Victoria Park** Picnic park with fine selection of trees, Percival Street.

**St John the Baptist Church** Built in 1860, it is possibly one of Canterbury's most beautiful churches. High Street.

LOCAL TOURING
**Satellite Station** 5 km north, this is the television and telephone communications station for the South Island.

**Amberley** Via the main road on Route 1, 30 km north of Rangiora. Amberley has two historic churches: Holy Passion (1866) and Holy Innocents (1876).

**Ashley Forest** Lies 11 km north of Rangiora on downland and the foothills of Mt Grey. There are some roads and several tracks through the forest including Cramptons Bush Road inland from Amberley.

**See Also** Christchurch, Waipara and Oxford

# RANGIRIRI NI
**Population** 277
**Location** On Route 1, 20 km south of Mercer, 15 km north of Huntly.

The main road here virtually bisects the battleground where in 1863 British troops attacked the Maoris; 49 Europeans and 50 Maoris were killed. This was an important battle in the Waikato land wars. After a day's fierce fighting the Maori defenders slipped away during the night and the pa was taken by the British troops the following day.

## ENVIRONS & ATTRACTIONS

**Rangiriri Battle Site** Reached by a small path from the parking area on the west side of Route 1. Trenches are still clearly visible and there is an explanatory sign. 400 m to the south-east is Te Wheoro's redoubt. This is accessible after a short walk from the side road that is opposite the parking area.

**Rangiriri Maori War and Early Settlers Cemetery** On a short eastern side road from Route 1, this cemetery with its memorial gates contains the bodies of 46 British troops who were killed during the battle of Rangiriri.

## LOCAL TOURING

**Te Kauwhata** This community of 900 people is just off Route 1 to the north of Rangiriri. A side road serves several shops visible from the main road, but the town of Te Kauwhata itself is 2 km away. It is known for the government viticultural station that researches grape growing and wine making. The research station is closed to the public but some roadside vineyards are open for wine sales.

**Lake Waikare** A popular yachting and picnic spot for locals from Te Kauwhata; part of the lake is a bird sanctuary.

**See Also** Tuakau, Mercer and Huntly

---

# RAWENE NI

**Population** 408
**Location** 6 km down side road off Route 12, 43 km west of Kaikohe.

---

The Hokianga Harbour used to provide access for both passenger and timber carrying ships, despite the dangerous bar at its mouth. Now it is mainly a resort area. Rawene is the area's commercial centre, quaintly situated on the harbour side. There is a car and passenger ferry service across the harbour to Kohukohu, which operates hourly.

## ENVIRONS & ATTRACTIONS

**Clendon House** Home of James Clendon (trader and first United States Consul) built in 1860. Open Sat–Wed 10 am–noon and 2–4 pm.

## LOCAL TOURING

**Kohukohu** Located 3 km from the Narrows ferry landing on the opposite side of the harbour. It has a number of old buildings, a library/museum with historical photographs, and perhaps New Zealand's oldest bridge. The Lance Andrewes Memorial Park 1 km up behind the town offers wide views over parts of the Hokianga Harbour. The remote Mitimiti beach (via Motukaraka and Panguru) is 39 km west.

**Horeke** Former timber and shipping centre. Nearby is the Mangungu Mission House, first built in 1838, now restored with replicas of original furnishings. Open Sat–Wed 10 am–noon and 2–4 pm. Horeke is 16 km along a side road from Taheke — which itself is 18 km east of the Rawene junction on Route 12.

**Opononi** On the Hokianga Harbour, 17 km west along Route 12 from the Rawene junction. This summer beach resort near the harbour entrance is remembered for 'Opo', the friendly dolphin that played with children during the summer of 1955–56. Omapere, 3 km further west, is a similar seaside resort.

**See Also** Kaikohe and Waipoua Kauri Forest

*An old goldmining hut at Skippers, near Queenstown.*

# REEFTON SI
**Population** 1224
**Location** On Route 7 at its junction with Route 9, 33 km south of Inangahua, 78 km northeast of Greymouth.

Reefton is situated on the Inangahua River at the western end of the Lewis Pass route from Canterbury. It is a centre for farming, coalmining, forestry and sawmilling. It was a centre for gold (alluvial gold being discovered in 1866) and quartz mining, which began in 1870.

Reefton (also at times called Reeftown and Quartzopolis) was a boom town of the period. Quartz

reef mining requires capital for the plant and equipment, and as news of the gold finds went out, money flowed in. Reefton had its own stock exchange, and the shares of mining companies rose astronomically — until the inevitable crash. Nevertheless, much gold was extracted from the region.

When the gold ran out some of the equipment was used for coalmining, but this too has declined in recent years. The town also claims to have been the first in the Southern Hemisphere with an electric light in 1886, followed two years later by its own hydro power scheme. Watch out for hidden shafts and tunnels

when exploring mine sites in the Reefton area.

## ENVIRONS & ATTRACTIONS
**School of Mines** Started in 1886, this houses one of the finest collections of minerals in the country, including samples from local mines. Admission is via the adjacent State Coal Mines district office. Shiel Street.

**Blacks Point Museum** Photographs and displays of equipment used in Reefton's goldmines. Housed in an 1876 church 2 km east on Route 7. Open Wednesdays and weekends 1.30–3.30 pm. There are walks from here to the Murray Creek gold and coal sites, which range from 15 minutes to a full day.

**Bottled Lightning Powerhouse** A 45-minute round trip walk from the town centre to view the foundations of this early powerhouse.

## LOCAL TOURING
**Local Mine Sites** The 'Crushington' Wealth of Nations gold battery — or at least its remains — are visible on the roadside, 4 km east of Route 7. 5 km across the river are the remains of the old Globe battery. The turn-off to Garvey Creek, site of a state coal mine is 9 km out. 10 km east a bush track offers a half-day walk to the old Progress water-race and to the Golden

Head battery. Also 9 km up Soldiers Road, just south of Reefton, is a 90-minute loop track taking in the Alborns Coalmine.

**Larrys Creek** 16 km north on Route 69 this 2-hr (3 km return) easy walk leads past Potters Flat and the still impressive Caledonian battery, to Larrys Creek goldmine. Do not cross the creek if it is in flood.

**Waiuta** This was once a town at the top of the South Island's richest goldmine, and the one with New Zealand's deepest shaft (879 m). It was in use until 1951. The site is now a ghost town. The 17 km side road to Blackwater and Waiuta branches off Route 7, 21 km south of Reefton. There are several walks, including an old town walk, a 30-minute (each way) walk to the Snowy battery, a 5 hr walk to the Big River town site and then another 5 hr onto the Inangahua River, on Route 7, 27 km east of Reefton. A hut is at Big River. There is also a four-wheel drive track into Big River from Reefton.

**See Also** Inangahua, Maruia Springs and Greymouth

---

# RIVERTON SI
**Population** 1465
**Location** On Route 99, 38 km west of Invercargill.

---

This farming and fishing community in western Southland also has a history of flax milling and sawmilling. The town is regarded as the oldest settlement in Southland.

From the end of the 18th century sealers from New South Wales, after working in and around the Sounds area and the western coast, would visit Riverton to replenish their provisions. In 1836 the site of Riverton was known as Jacobs and a whaling station was established here.

The town is adjacent to a large lagoon known as the Jacobs River Estuary, but it also receives the waters of the Aparima River. A network of timber tramways used to run across the estuary. Riverton was on the railway line from Thornbury junction to Tuatapere, but that line is now closed.

## ENVIRONS & ATTRACTIONS
**Riverton Domain** Recreation ground on the north bank of the river, which is accessed from Leader Street or via a track from the town end of the bridge.

**Riverton Museum** Relics from early days, including portraits of Captain Howell, founder of the whaling station and town. Palmerston Street. Open daily 2–4 pm.

**Howell Memorial** A stone monument commemorating Captain Howell. On the southern riverbank in Towack Street (over the bridge).

**Observation Point** A view over the town estuary and coast. Richard Street, up past Camp Longwood (over the bridge).

## LOCAL TOURING
**Riverton Rocks** Coastal community and beach holiday area with picnic spots amid rocky outcrops. 9 km at the end of the road at Howells Point.

**Colac Bay** 11 km west of Riverton via Route 99, this bay has a broad, south-facing beach.

**Pourakino Walkway** This walk follows the Pourakino River through the edge of the Longwood Forest to the north-west of Riverton. Access is via Ermedale Road; northern end is via Redfern Jubilee Hill Road, south-west of Otautau. The walk is 8.5 km (3 hr).

**See Also** Invercargill, Otautau and Tuatapere

# ROTORUA NI
**Population** 51 602
**Location** On Route 5, 107 km south-east of Hamilton, 82 km north of Taupo.

Situated on the so-called volcanic plateau of the North Island, Rotorua is an important tourist and cultural centre. Your arrival in the area will be heralded by whiffs of a hydrogen sulphide smell, which has given the city the nickname of 'Sulphur City'. You get used to the smell quickly.

Rotorua is built at an altitude of 279 m and in addition to the thermal activity of hot springs, geysers, and boiling mud, it has a number of attractive lakes, as well as both indigenous and exotic forests.

The Rotorua Maoris are mainly of Arawa descent, their ancestors being those who came on the *Arawa* canoe (part of the Great Fleet) that landed in Maketu possibly around 1350. Their more recent history includes an attack in 1823 by Hongi Hika and his northern Ngapuhi followers, who, armed with purchased muskets, attacked the traditionally armed Arawa in revenge for an earlier incident. Hongi dragged his canoes overland, between lakes and rivers, from the coast to Rotorua, and part of the track (possibly?) used on the outskirts of Rotorua still bears the name Hongi's Track. The Arawa tribe sheltered on Mokoia Island but were defeated.

In 1864 the Arawa sided with the government in the Waikato campaigns, and battled East Coast Maoris at both Rotorua and Maketu, to prevent them crossing Arawa land to aid the Waikato tribes. In 1870 Te Kooti and his followers attacked the Arawa because they were such strong supporters of the government.

Lieutenant Mair and his troops, representing the government, came to their aid and helped them defeat Te Kooti.

The first European to enter the district in about 1830 was the Danish trader Tapsell. The Arawas traded flax for guns so that they could defend themselves against the northern Ngaphui (who were among the first to be armed with guns). In 1835 a missionary called Chapman established a mission station at Rotorua.

Pakeha history in the area really begins with the lease in 1881, and the purchase in 1890 of the land for a town to be built adjacent to the village of Ohinemutu. The curative waters of the thermal springs were quickly recognised and the government erected a large bathhouse, spa and hospital. Until 1922 the town was administered by the government department of Tourist and Health Resorts. Today, the Queen Elizabeth hospital still continues that therapeutic tradition.

The early tourist growth of the district was hindered by the 1886 eruption of Mt Tarawera, which devastated three Maori villages, killed 153 people and destroyed the pink and white silica terraces that had been a leading attraction. A coach road from Auckland was built in 1884. A railway reached Rotorua in 1894.

In 1895 trout were released in the lakes to give birth to the present big fishing activity; and in 1897 the first tree nursery was established, the forerunner of a primary industry for the area. Today the Forestry Research Institute is based there.

The thermal activity that is such a feature of Rotorua is part of a band of volcanic activity that stretches from White Island in the Bay of Plenty, through the

*Waiotapu thermal area, Rotorua.*

Rotorua and Taupo areas, to the Tongariro National Park. This area is publicised as the Tourist Diamond. There are also many other places in the North Island that have hot springs.

Although we list many attractions, our list is by no means complete. You can go jetboating or flightseeing (including options of floatplanes and vintage aircraft), get lost in mazes, visit the Waipa sawmill, as well as

attend Maori hangis and concert parties.

## ENVIRONS & ATTRACTIONS
**Lake Rotorua**  This is the North Island's second largest lake and the largest in the Rotorua area. It covers 83 square km and measures 10 km × 12 km at its extremities. Boating and fishing are popular attractions. The lake front at Rotorua is the centre for tourist trips and hiring equipment.

**Mokoia Island** This historic and sacred island of the Arawa people is situated on Lake Rotorua. There are 4 km of walks on the island. Usually there are two launch trips daily.

**Ohinemutu** This Maori village was the first settlement in the area. Of interest is the church of St Faith (built in 1910) with Maori decorations within, and with a recent sandblasted window of Christ draped in a chief's cloak walking on the lake's waters seen through the window. There is also the Tamatekapua Meeting House and the grave of Lieutenant Mair who headed the colonial troops at the time of the Te Kooti emergency.

**Rotorua (Government) Gardens** This pleasant park area at the end of Arawa Street and on the banks of the lake contains flower beds and bowling greens; there is also a sports centre and Tudor Towers.

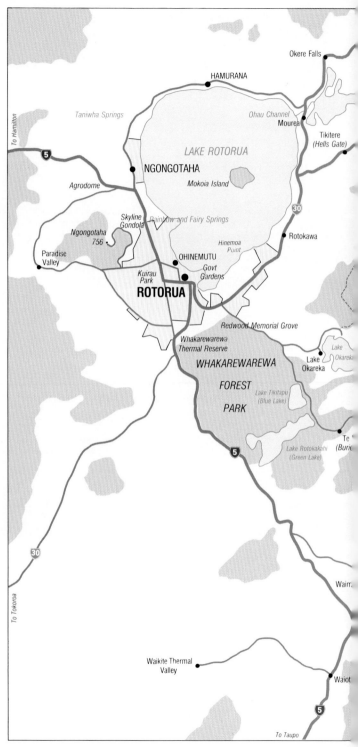

**Tudor Towers** This 1908 bath house was built by the government and stands in the Government Gardens. It now houses an art and history museum.

**Polynesian Pools** These are hot thermal pools, both public and private, in the grounds of the Government Gardens; they are open until 10 pm daily. They offer massage and sauna and were previously called the Ward Baths.

**Orchid Gardens** Open daily until 8.30 pm, this is an indoor showcase of hundreds of orchids, plus a microworld display. Hinemaru Street.

**Kuirau Park** This park has a children's play area and thermal hot foot pools. It extends over 20 ha and is situated on Ranolf Street.

**Whakarewarewa Thermal Reserve** Commonly known as 'Whaka', this is probably the most famous of Rotorua's thermal areas. It features the Pohutu Geyser, which usually plays every 20–30 minutes. There is a replica of a Maori village, and examples of how the Maoris used the hot pools for bathing and cooking. The little Village Craft Centre is at the entrance to Whaka. Nearby is the New Zealand Maori Arts and Crafts Institute, which helps preserve Maori traditions. This is also open to the public.

**Redwood Memorial Grove** The Whakarewarewa State Forest Park includes an extensive grove of California Redwoods with their cathedral-like arches. A forest information centre is open daily 11 am–4 pm.

**Leisure World** An entertainment complex in Marguerita Street, which features car rides, bumper boats, hydroslides and a children's playground.

## WESTERN AREA

**Mt Ngongotaha** This 778 m peak dominates the Rotorua area. There is a 12 km road to the top for extensive views.

**Skyline Gondola** 4 km out on the slopes of Mt Ngongataha, this cableway system takes travellers up for views over the Rotorua area. At the top there is also a luge (toboggan) gravity slide.

**Rainbow and Fairy Springs, Rainbow Farm, Hillside Herbs** This complex of several tourist attractions is adjacent to the Skyline gondola. The Springs offer trout viewing and other wildlife. The farm shows New Zealand farming activities. The herb garden includes a souvenir and gift shop.

**Paradise Valley** A wildlife and trout sanctuary (now with lions) in a bush and park setting 11 km out behind Mt Ngongataha. A trout hatchery is nearby.

**Agrodome** A popular display at 9.15 am, 11 am, and 2.30 pm daily, of 19 sheep breeds, sheep dogs and shearing. It is situated 8 km out near the community of Ngongataha and is adjacent to the Route 5 road.

**Taniwha Springs and Hamurana Springs** These are two trout sanctuaries around Lake Rotorua. The first, 10 km from Rotorua, also has a walk to a pa site. The second has a park with ducks and swans, and also a Redwood Grove. Hamurana Springs gush up to 5 million litres of water per hour. It is situated 17 km around the lake. Both springs are open daily and can easily form part of a round the lake drive from Rotorua via Ngongataha and returning via some of the Eastern area attractions.

## EASTERN AREA

**Hinemoa Point** At Holdens Bay 7 km from Rotorua, Hinemoa is supposed to have made her

*A Maori meeting house at Te Kuiti.*

legendary swim. It is also the location of the Te Amorangi Trust Museum, which houses Arawa exhibits. Open regularly but check hours.

**Ohau Channel**  The small waterway that feeds the waters of Lake Rotorua into Lake Rotoiti. The outlet is a popular fishing area.

**Lake Rotoiti**  The 36 sq km lake receives the waters of Lake Rotorua through the Ohau Channel. Its local communities are Okawa Bay and Okere Falls. Much of the shoreline is scenic reserve and both Routes 30 (to Whakatane) and 33 (to Te Puke) run alongside it.

**Okere Falls**  21 km from Rotorua, these falls are the outlet for Lake Rotoiti via the Kaituna River. There is a 10-minute bush walk to the falls, with a steep

# HINEMOA AND TUTANEKAI

New Zealand's favourite love story concerns the legend of Hinemoa, daughter of an Arawa chief who fell in love with Tutanekai, a foster son of another chief living on Mokoia Island in Lake Rotorua. Hinemoa's father forbade the courtship because he considered Tutanekai to be beneath his daughter. To prevent them eloping he made sure the tribe's canoes were drawn up securely on the beach. One night, however, Hinemoa swam to the island, drawn by the flute playing of Tutanekai. Tutanekai was delighted to see Hinemoa and they were married with the blessing of both chiefs when they saw the strength of their children's love. Tourists to Rotorua will come across many references to this story in the district.

*The Rotorua Art Gallery.*

descent via Hinemoa Steps down to caves near the bottom of the falls.

**Tikitere** Commercially known as Hells Gate, this is a very active thermal area with bubbling pools and boiling mud; also sulphur bath and thermal pools. Situated 16 km from Rotorua shortly after the junction of Route 30 and 33 at Te Ngae.

**Lake Okataina** This scenic lake 31 km from Rotorua is accessible by a bush-clad side road branching off Route 30 at Ruato on the shores of Lake Rotoiti. The road ends at the lake. There are walks through the bush (which has much birdlife) and fishing in the lake waters.

**Okataina Walkways** The Western walkway (22 km, 7–8 hr) commences from Route 30 near Ruato, parallels the road towards Okataina, then follows a westerly

route above the lake to terminate near Lake Okareka. There is alternative road access here. The eastern walkway commences at the end of the Lake Okataina road on the lake shore, parallels the eastern shore and crosses over to Lake Tarawera. Currently the walkway terminates there; you must return the same way or organise boat transport to pick you up (8 km, 2½–3 hr).

**Hongi's Track** This is a section of road on Route 30 through thick bush between Lakes Rotoiti and Rotoehu. It is supposedly named after part of the route where Hongi Hika, a Maori war chief, dragged his canoes overland between the lakes.

**Lakes Rotoehu and Rotoma** These lakes are situated along Route 30 towards the eastern limits of the Rotorua lakes system. Rotoma is 35 km from Rotorua;

*A Maori dancer in Rotorua.*

Rotoehu a further 5 km. Both are holiday lakes with fishing, boating and picnic sites.

## SOUTHERN AREA
### Blue and Green Lakes
Properly called Lake Tikitapu and Lake Rotokakahi, these lakes are separated by a narrow isthmus, which provides an excellent vantage point from which to compare the colours of the two — most marked on a fine day. They are situated 11 km south-east of Rotorua on Tarawera Road.

**Lake Okareka** Another small lake, with a residential community; access off Tarawera Road. Also provides exit/entrance to the western Okataina walkway.

**Te Wairoa Buried Village** As a result of the 1886 eruption of Mt Tarawera, this Maori village was buried under 2.5 m of mud and debris. Excavations and photographs show parts of the old village. There is an optional steep side track to Te Wairoa Falls. The site is 16 km out on the Tarawera Road.

**Lake Tarawera** At 39 square km this is one of the largest Rotorua Lakes. It is situated adjacent to the volcano Mt Tarawera. Road access to one side of the Lake is via Tarawera Road,

*The brooding volcano Mt Tarawera.*

the Blue and Green Lakes and the Te Wairoa buried village. There are launch cruises operating on the lake most days and the lake shore has a picnic area.

**Mt Tarawera** This big, brooding volcano, 1111 m high, now has a 5 km long crater due to the violent eruption on 10 June 1886, which killed 153 people. The mountain is visible from Lakes Tarawera and Rotomahana. There is some road access to its lower slopes on the southern side via Lake Rerewhakaaitu; then either walk to the top or continue by four-wheel drive. There are organised tours to the top to view the crater. The volcano is currently dormant.

**Waimangu** This thermal valley is located 26 km south of Rotorua on Route 5. It features a 4 ha lake of boiling water known as Waimangu Cauldron, plus walks, other springs and boiling mud in a bush setting. Open 8 am–5 pm daily. Allow 1¼ hr for round trip walk, or 2¼ hr if you combine a walk with a launch trip on Lake Rotomahana.

**Lake Rotomahana** This lake, which is accessible via the Waimangu thermal valley, has an area of 8 sq km and depths of up to 246 m. It is a crater lake associated with the adjacent Mt Tarawera. When that mountain erupted, the lake itself also exploded. The resulting devastation drowned the famous pink and white terraces, which were a leading tourist attraction. The lake still features steaming

cliffs and hot springs, and is also a wildlife refuge.

**Waimungu Round Trip** This one day tour from Rotorua combines Waimungu thermal valley, a cruise on Lake Rotomahana, a short walk across the isthmus to Lake Tarawera for another launch trip through to the Te Wairoa buried village, and returns to Rotorua past the Green and Blue Lakes. The trip offers insight into some of the attractions of the Rotorua area, which are not accessible by car.

**Lake Rerewhakaatu** A smaller lake surrounded by green fields. Tours to the top of Mt Tarawera normally pass this. It is accessible from side roads off Route 5.

**Waiotapu** 27 km south on Route 5, this thermal area, which is situated in the remains of a collapsed valley, features geysers and other thermal activity. The Lake Knox Geyser is made to perform at 10.15 am each day by adding soap to its blowhole. The area also offers silica terraces and coloured waterfalls. Open daily.

**Waikite Thermal Valley** On a side road off Route 5 (behind Waiotapu), this area has hot mineral outdoor swimming pools and a picnic and barbecue area. Open daily 10 am–10 pm.

**Golden Springs** Warm mineral springs, baths, and a stream that has coloured fish living in the warm water. 47 km south.

**See Also** Kawerau, Atiamuri and Taupo

257

# ROXBURGH SI
**Population** 721
**Location** On Route 8, 40 km south-east of Alexandra, 58 km west of Lawrence.

Roxburgh is an important fruit-growing area for berry stone and pip fruits, centred on the river flats. The borough is situated on the right bank of the Clutha River and was the scene of goldmining activities in earlier times. The dredges followed later.

The surrounding country consists of barren and stoney hills, though autumn tints on the trees can be beautiful. The nearby Roxburgh Dam was commenced in 1949 and commissioned between 1956 and 1962. The town had a separate railway branch line from Milton between 1928 and 1968.

## ENVIRONS & ATTRACTIONS
**St James Church** Built in 1872 of stone. Scotland Street (main road).
**Teviot Union Church** A stone Presbyterian church built in 1880. Scotland Street.
**Roxburgh Museum** In the 1872 Methodist Church. Abbotsford Street.

## LOCAL TOURING
**Roxburgh Dam** 10 km north-west along Route 8 a short side road leads to an observation point. The area was known as Coal Creek because lignite mines used to be here.
**Pinders Pond** A former sluicing claim is now a tiny lake and picnic spot. Cross the Clutha at Roxburgh and continue 5 km through Roxburgh East.
**Lake Onslow** A fishing and picnic spot in the Lammerlaw Range, and headwaters for the Teviot River. 30 km.
**Gorge Creek Goldminers Monument** A roadside

memorial 21 km north-west of Roxburgh on Route 8, commemorating miners who died in the great snowstorm of 1863.

**See Also** Alexandra, Lawrence and Tapanui

# RUATORIA NI
**Population** 815
**Location** 1 km up a side road off Route 35, 130 km from Gisborne.

Ruatoria was the hometown for Sir A. Ngata, the first Maori

258

*The posts of the old town bridge in Alexandra, central Otago.*

graduate from a New Zealand university (1897); and also for Te Ngarimu, the first Maori to win the Victoria Cross in Tunisia. Because of its height, nearby Mt Hikurangi (1839 m) is supposedly the first part of New Zealand to receive the morning sun's rays. There is natural gas in the area, but it is not used commercially.

## ENVIRONS & ATTRACTIONS

**Mangahanea Marae** Maori meeting house with ornate carvings. Permission is required to enter.

## LOCAL TOURING

**Tikitiki** The ornate Maori memorial church of St Mary is located on the roadside at Tikitiki, 20 km north of Ruatoria. Well worth a visit.

**See Also** Gisborne, Tokomaru Bay and Te Araroa

## RUSSELL NI

Refer to the Bay of Islands.

# S

## ST ARNAUD SI
**Population** 213
**Location** On Route 63, 103 km south-west of Blenheim, 25 km east of Kawatiri Junction.

The township of St Arnaud is the headquarters for the Nelson Lakes National Park, a 96 000 ha area of mountains and lakes. St Arnaud is situated on the shores of Lake Rotoiti. Lake Rotoroa is the other lake in the park, but it has not been developed commercially. The glacial lakes are surrounded by sheer mountains, covered with snow in winter. The surrounding bush is mostly beech, though some rata and kowhai add summer colour. Rotoiti is the headwaters for the Buller River; Lake Rotoroa flows out of the Gowan River, which joins the Buller.

The small town and the National Park are tourist orientated. There is camping, swimming and boating in summer, and skiing in winter. Fishing and hunting permits are available from the visitors centre. Sandflies at the lakes, and wasps down at Kawatiri Junction can be distracting!

## ENVIRONS & ATTRACTIONS
**Lake Rotoiti** Has a visitors centre for the National Park.
**Peninsula Walk** A 2-hr walk around the peninsula at the town end of the lake.
**Mt Robert Lookout** The lookout is 8 km from St Arnaud. Take the West Bay Road and climb to 884 m for a view over the lake and town. The road gives access to a private ski-field.

## LOCAL TOURING
**Rotoiti Tracks** The visitors centre can give information on other walks in the area, such as the Pinchgut track and the track to the head of the lake.
**Tophouse** An old hotel and tavern built in 1887, which for nearly 100 years was a stopover point but is now a private farmhouse, 9 km from St Arnaud. It is situated near the junction of a connecting link from Golden Downs (Route 6), which links to Route 63 for travellers to/from Nelson. A memorial to explorer John Cotterell is at the corner.
**Lake Rotoroa** Road access from St Arnaud is down the Buller River to Kawatiri Junction, along Route 6 to the Gowan Bridge and then up a separate side road — a total of 43 km. There are a number of tracks, including Lake Lookout (1½ hr return from car park) and a lakeside track to the head of the lake, which is 6 hr each way.
**Kawatiri Junction** This is 25 km west of St Arnaud where Route 63 meets Route 6; and is also the point where the Hope River meets the Buller River. The remains of a railway that was started in 1930 but never finished are visible.
**Rainbow Valley Ski-Field** From July to October the Rainbow is Marlborough's favourite ski-field, accessible on a 26 km side road (chains in winter) off Route 63. It offers skiing with views.

**See Also** Blenheim, Nelson and Murchison

## SPRINGFIELD SI
**Population** 225
**Location** On Route 73, 68 km west of Christchurch, 83 km east of Arthur's Pass.

Situated where the Canterbury Plains meet the foothills of the

Southern Alps, Springfield began as a staging point for the Cobb & Co coaching service. Although the plains appear flat, Springfield is actually at an altitude of 380 m.

From here to Arthur's Pass the road and railway separate, with the former climbing over Porters Pass, and the railway winding around the Waimakariri Gorge. Both are scenic routes.

## LOCAL TOURING

**Sheffield** This small farming community is 9 km east of Springfield on Route 73. Near Sheffield, Route 72 makes a 'dog leg' crossing of Route 73. Turn north for Oxford, Rangiora and the Kaikoura Coast; turn south for Methven, Geraldine and Timaru.

**Darfield** This is a farming and administrative centre for the Midland–Canterbury area. 23 km east.

**Porters Pass** From Springfield, Route 73 climbs 19 km west to the 944 m summit over this pass in the Torlesse Range. This pass is a little higher than the road over Arthur's Pass.

**Lake Lyndon** This small alpine lake is 21 km west over Porters Pass. A side road here connects south to Lakes Ida and Coleridge and to the Cave Stream Scenic Reserve where the stream has created a 362 m tunnel, which may be entered.

**Castle Hill** A small holiday and ski resort 34 km west on Route 73. Nearby are the winter ski areas of Broken Hill and Porter Heights.

**Cass** This is a railway station ½ km north of Route 73, 57 km west. The turn-off for Craigieburn ski-field is here. Nearby are Lakes Pearson and Grassmere. 2 km west of Cass is a side road to the Waimakariri River and picnic site. There are a number of tracks in the Craigieburn forest park.

**See Also** Christchurch, Arthur's Pass, Oxford and Methven

# STRATFORD NI
**Population** 5528
**Location** On Route 3, 41 km south of New Plymouth, 29 km north of Hawera.

The town was laid out in 1877. In 1879 a railway line from New Plymouth was opened, and in 1885 it was opened through to Wellington. A later railway line striking inland through rugged country to Ohura and Taumarunui was opened in 1932.

The town was originally known as Stratford on Patea, and its street names are Shakespearean characters. The Patea River runs through the town. An old Maori trail connecting southern and northern Taranaki used to go through the dense bush in the area. Now the area is cleared farmland.

There is still much bush further inland surrounding Route 33 towards Ohura and Tauramanui. Stratford is an important gateway to the Egmont National Park, and the dormant volcanic cone of Mount Egmont (2517 m) dominates the town.

## ENVIRONS & ATTRACTIONS

**King Edward Park** A 20 ha bush reserve on the banks of the Patea River one block off the main street.

**Taranaki Pioneer Village** A growing pioneer village and information centre with more than 36 buildings including a gaol and a railway station, which is under restoration. Open daily, 2 km south of town.

**Stratford Power Station** Using natural gas from Kapuni, this was finished in 1976.

## LOCAL TOURING

**Egmont National Park** The 2518 m symmetrical cone of Mt Egmont (Taranaki to the Maoris) is visible from most parts of the region now called Taranaki. Its

*The Craigeburn Range, near Springfield.*

most recent thermal activity was about 1620.

Maori mythology originally places the mountain in the central North Island, until an argument with neighbouring Tongariro caused Taranaki to flee westwards. In its flight it carved out the Wanganui River. Egmont was named by Captain Cook in 1770 in honour of the First Lord of the Admiralty.

It is possible to trek to the summit and back in a day — preferably in groups and in summer. Weather can be changeable at all times. There are many walking tracks on and around the mountain. Sealed roads give access to three places on the eastern slopes.

**East Egmont** The Stratford Mountain House (845 m altitude) is 14 km west of Stratford up Pembroke Road. The road continues another 3 km to a lookout and provides access to the Manganui ski-field. There are walking tracks from the Mountain House north to Curtis Falls (3 hr return); and also to Dawson Falls (3½ hr return). Experienced trampers can go around the mountain in two or three days staying in park board huts.

**Dawson Falls** The Dawson Falls Tourist Lodge (924 m altitude) is on the south-east slopes, with road access along Manaia Road. It is a short walk to the 18 m falls. There are also walks to Mountain House (3½ hr return) and to Lake Dive (5 hr return and dangerous in winter).

**North Egmont** Road access from Inglewood (or New Plymouth, 26 km) along Egmont Road. There is a visitors centre with displays and walks to Holly Hut and Bells Falls (6½ hr return), and also over to Dawson Falls (4 hr one way).

**See Also** New Plymouth, Inglewood and Eltham

# T

and 30 minutes along the second); the tree is one of the largest known kauri in New Zealand.

**See Also** Whitianga, Whangamata and Thames

## TAIRUA NI
**Population** 1109
**Location** On Route 25, 42 km south of Whitianga, 49 km north of Whangamata.

Tairua is a developing holiday settlement on the eastern side of the Coromandel Peninsula. It is popular with divers because of its proximity to the Shoe and Slipper Islands — popular diving areas. The town is mainly situated on the river estuary known as Tairua Harbour, however, it also has an ocean beach.

### ENVIRONS & ATTRACTIONS
**Paku** Twin peaks dominate this town. Take the road up their slopes for views over Tairua, its harbour and Pauanui.

### LOCAL TOURING
**Pauanui** Although just across the harbour, it is 26 km by road to this prestigious beach settlement.
**Hikuai** The district upriver from Tairua where the newer Kopu–Hikuai (Route 25A) meets the roundabout Route 25.
**Broken Hill** An old gold and timber area on a side road near Hikuai. There is also access from Route 25A, but the two roads do not link. There are several roads linking the walking tracks with the sites of the old Broken Hills and Golden Hills mines. You can walk through the Golden Hills mine (once you locate it) for 500 m, but you will need a good torch and boots.
**Devicich Kauri** Near the crest of the Route 25A Kopu–Hikuai Road, a northbound track along the ridge, called the Kaitarakaiha Track, has a branching walk (nearly 1 hr along the first track

## TAIHAPE NI
**Population** 2472
**Location** On Route 1, 28 km south of Waiouru, 85 km north-east of Bulls.

Situated in the district of the Upper Rangitikei, where road and rail, having descended from the central volcanic plateau of the North Island, face the hills and terraces of the broad Rangitikei Valley.

Originally called Hautapu, then Otaihape, the town developed as a sawmilling and railway location. In common with most of the North Island, this area was densely bush-clad. The Hautapu River still has a reserve of native bush on its banks.

The town has a festive Gumboot Day on the Tuesday after Easter.

### ENVIRONS & ATTRACTIONS
**Taihape Museum** Open Sunday afternoons and school holidays, it features displays of local settlers.
**Taihape Domain** Reserve with native bush along the banks of the Hautapu River. The Mt Stewart Bush Reserve is north of the town. Both reserves offer walks and picnic spots.

### LOCAL TOURING
**Mangaweka** 23 km south on Route 1. There are some notable railway viaducts in the vicinity, but since the 1981 deviation of the line, only two remain visible from Route 1. Note the DC3 restaurant in the town.

**See Also** Waiouru, Marton and Feilding

# TAKAKA SI
**Population** 1194
**Location** On Route 60, 57 km north-west of Motueka, 108 km north-west of Nelson.

---

Takaka is situated a little inland from the shores of Golden Bay. When Abel Tasman discovered New Zealand in 1642, his only contact with the Maoris was here where four of his crew were killed. He sailed away without landing and called the place Murderers Bay.

Timber seekers were the first Europeans to settle in the area, and a lot of timber was exported from local river ports. The area now has a dairying base. The mountainous country between Takaka and Motueka prevented early land access, but in 1878 a road over the Takaka Hill was opened. The hill is still quite formidable today, but the road is good, and there are excellent views from it.

Takaka provides access to the northern end of the Abel Tasman National Park, through Wainui Inlet and Totaranui. Further details about the park are mentioned under Motueka.

## ENVIRONS & ATTRACTIONS
**Takaka Museum** Collection of local items, including samples from the old Onekaka ironworks. Main Street.

**Pupu Springs** New Zealand's most prolific springs with a daily outflow of 2000 million litres — probably from the Takaka River. 5 km from Takaka (down side road 2 km west).

**Pupu Walkway** A 3 km return (1½ hr) walk at the end of Pupu Valley Road, 8 km west. The walkway visits a water-race built for goldmining and restored for a small hydro power station.

**Anatuki River** Hand-fed tame eels, 5 km south.

## LOCAL TOURING
**Pohara Beach** A popular beach 9 km north-east of Takaka.

**Tasman Memorial** This memorial for Abel Tasman is in a commanding position past the site of the Golden Bay Cement Works at Tarakohe, 11 km north-east.

**Wainui Inlet** A bay on the road to Totaranui. There are tracks from here around separation point to Totaranui as well as a shorter walk to Wainui waterfall.

**Totaranui** At the northern end of Abel Tasman National Park, 38 km by road from Takaka. A number of park tracks connect to other areas in the park. Limited facilities only.

**Harwoods Hole** This is a remarkable sinkhole formed by underground water dissolving the limestone until the ground eventually sank. This hole is 370 m deep. Take Canaan Road at the top of the Takaka Hill, followed by a 45-minute walk from the road's end. Care is required near the hole.

**Rameka Track** Drive 5 km up Rameka Road from Central Takaka. Then it is a 2-hr walk to the Canaan Plateau on Takaka Hill. Other tracks connect to roads at Canaan Road (on top of Takaka Hill) and to Wainui Inlet (on the Totaranui Road). Canaan is a barren plateau of marble rocks with sinkholes, including Harwoods Hole, and tracks are for more experienced trampers.

**Cobb River Hydro** A dam and power station in rugged country south of Takaka. The turn-off is at Upper Takaka (bottom of Takaka Hill). The powerhouse is 18 km from turn-off and the dam is 13 km further. The road requires careful driving and takes longer than the distances imply. There are several walking tracks in the area.

**See Also** Nelson, Motueka and Collingwood

# TAPANUI SI
**Population** 924
**Location** On Route 90, 29 km
south of Raes Junction, 35 km
north of Gore.

A settlement in a broad pastoral
valley beyond the Blue
Mountains, Tapanui is a sheep-
farming centre and a timber
centre. Some wheat is grown. The
town was laid out in 1868.

## ENVIRONS & ATTRACTIONS
**West Otago Vintage Museum**
District relics and veteran farm
machinery. Upper
Northumberland Street.
**Blue Mountain Nursery** A
commercial nursery producing
container trees and shrubs, also
cut flowers. Bushy Hill Street,
open daily except Sundays.

## LOCAL TOURING
**Black Gully** A pleasant domain
on the western slopes of the Blue
Mountains. Take Black Gully
Road off Route 90, 8 km north.
**State Forests** The Dusky Forest
features a picturesque picnic area
on the upper reaches of the
Pomahaka River, 17 km west via
Kelso. The Conical Hill Forest
features the South Island's largest
and most modern sawmill. 11 km
south-east.
**Todd Cottage** In Dee Street,
Heriot, 14 km north-west, this is
the early home of industrialist
Charles Todd (motor vehicles and
oil), which has been restored.
**Edievale** Tiny locality named
after John Edie (1835–1918), an
early runholder who settled in the
district with the rewards from
goldmining. 24 km north on
Route 90. It was once the
terminus of a branch railway from
Waipahi.

**See Also** Roxburgh, Lawrence
and Gore

# TAUMARUNUI NI
**Population** 6387
**Location** On Route 4, 83 km
south of Te Kuiti, 43 km north of
National Park. At the confluence
of the Ongarue and Wanganui
Rivers.

The first European here was a
trader in 1874, but the King
Country was risky for Pakehas
until a peace agreement allowed
the building of the main trunk
railway. For a while Taumarunui
was the railhead from the north,
with passengers continuing on a
3-day journey down the
Wanganui River to rejoin the
railway at Wanganui. The town
was also the limit of navigation for
river vessels.

Today tourists may canoe or
jetboat downriver from here;
there is also a 5-day boat and
camping trip that departs weekly
in summer. The timber industry
was once predominant, and is still
important, but general farming
now exists on the cleared land.

## ENVIRONS & ATTRACTIONS
**Crocker Stationary Engine
Collection** A privately-owned
collection, available for viewing,
of stationary farm engines.
**Cherry Grove** Launching site
for canoes and jetboat trips at the
confluence of the Ongarue and
Wanganui Rivers.

## LOCAL TOURING
**Te Maire** The 'River Road' from
Taumarunui leads to Te Maire
Bluff. A bridge here leads to a
narrow road high above the river
with views down but no access to
the confluence of the Ohura River
with the Wanganui River and the
site of Maraekowhai. Alternatively
the Te Maire Valley Road leads to
a scenic reserve, with a 2-hr
round trip bush walk. There is

also a river flat and picnic area just over the bridge.

**Maraekowhai** The Maori Hauhau movement was a blending of Maori and Christian beliefs, and between 1862 and 1866 its followers displayed fervent zeal against European settlers and soldiers. Maraekowhai was a Hauhau stronghold and the remains of two Nui celebrant poles are still visible. Access along Tokirima Road (35 km down the River Road) then follow to its end. A 10-minute walk and a swing bridge across the Ohura River (in sight of the Ohura Falls) leads to this site. Nearby on the Wanganui River there was once a moored houseboat used as an overnight stop by river steamers, but there is no trace left of that.

**Whakahoro** Back roads in from Owhango and Raurimu (both south of Taumarunui) lead to a landing on the Wanganui River from where jetboat rides of the central stretch of the river can be done (but book in advance at Taumarunui). There is no road access beyond here. The Kaiwhakauka Valley Track leads from here up a disused road through regenerated bush, and past abandoned farms to the Mangapurua trig (8 hr each way). From here you can either tramp 5 hr out to Ruatiti Road, or wind down the Mangapurua Valley Track (12 hr), past abandoned farms to the Mangapurua landing on the Waikato River. Jetboat connection has to be prearranged. The concrete 'bridge to nowhere', 3 km from the landing, is part of the remains of a road that was built too late to save abandoned farms originally settled by returned servicemen after World War I.

**Ohura** Route 33 from Taumarunui leads 43 km to Ohura, via the Wanganui and Ohura Rivers. The Ohura museum features displays on the history and development of the district. A circular road trip can be done by linking back to Route 1 on Route 40. Alternatively the road to Stratford passes through the rugged Tangarakau Gorge.

**See Also** National Park, Raetihi and Wanganui

# TAUPO NI
**Population** 15 873; 1094 at Wairakei.
**Location** In the centre of the North Island near the intersection of Routes 1 and 5; 280 km south of Auckland, 82 km south of Rotorua, 380 km north of Wellington.

Taupo was established as an Armed Constabulary Redoubt in 1869. It is situated where the Waikato River emerges from Lake Taupo.

The lake is New Zealand's largest, with an area of more than 600 sq km at an altitude of 369 m. While the lake has a vast drainage area, perhaps its most notable inflows are the famous fishing waters of the Tongariro River (also known as the Upper Waikato, near Turangi) and the Waitahanui River. The lake's outflow is the Waikato River, New Zealand's longest river. The natural discharge rate of about 140 cubic metres of water per second has now increased a further 10 per cent by the addition of water diverted by the Tongariro Power scheme.

With its lake and surrounding rivers, Taupo is a popular centre for fishing and holidaying. There are pockets of thermal activity around the lake, especially at Wairakei 9 km north of Taupo. The area is an accommodation overflow for the ski-fields of the

*The marina at Lake Taupo.*

Tongariro National Park. The nearby pine plantations form the basis of a timber industry.

Trout were introduced into the lake in 1868, and some 400 tonnes a year are caught at an average weight of 1.5 kg. From the hatchery at Turangi, rainbow ova are regularly exported, even to California, which is the home of the species.

One highlight of Taupo is the approach from Wairakei along a pleasant parkway that drops down to the town, with spectacular views over the lake and distant mountains. The lakeside area at the bottom of the main street is also pleasant.

The attractions of Wairakei are included under this heading. Although it has few commercial amenities, it does have several important attractions that should be seen by travellers to Taupo.

## ENVIRONS & ATTRACTIONS
**Taupo Domain** A park area between the main street and the Waikato River outlet. Gates under the river bridge control the river outflow. The remains of the

Armed Constabulary Redoubt and an old courthouse are in the grounds.

**Armed Constabulary Baths** Built a century ago, but since modernised, these hot thermal pools offer open or private bathing and a sauna and spa. Open daily to 9 pm.

**De Brett Thermal Pools** Situated ½ km down the Taupo–Napier Road, these hot pools offer open air and private baths. Open daily to 10 pm.

**Cherry Island** This island in the Waikato River features a tourist park that is accessible by footbridge from the end of Waikato Street.

**Waikato River Lookout** Along Spa Road, a view of the river over steaming cliffs.

**Waipahihi Botanical Reserve** Gardens including azaleas, rhododendrons and a view. Shepherd Road.

LOCAL TOURING
WAIRAKEI
**Taupo Lookout** From the approach road into Taupo by the radio station, a lookout offers

extensive views over the town, lake and distant mountains.

**Huka Falls** On a loop road off Route 1, north of Taupo, the Waikato River boils through a narrow chasm and falls over an 11 m ledge to form these spectacular falls. A pedestrian bridge crosses the falls to a number of viewpoints on the other side. The Taupo walkway also passes these falls. Nearby is the re-created historic Huka Village. Open daily.

**Wairakei Geothermal Power Field** At Wairakei, near the intersection of Routes 1 and 5, the many pipes and belching steam indicate the location of this active geothermal area. Wells are sunk to tap the geothermal activity, and the steam is separated into hot water and dry steam. Pipes with U-bend expansion/contraction loops take the steam to the nearby power station. You may drive through the field in daylight hours keeping to the road and climbing the hill at the end for a view. Call at the information and display centre on the main road. Open daily except 12–1 pm.

**Wairakei Geothermal Power Stations** The electricity generating station that uses the geothermal steam is down by the river. The operation is noisy and there is a public viewing gallery.

**Aratiatia Dam and Rapids** Situated on a side road off Route 5, 5 km north of Wairakei, this road leads across the small Aratiatia Dam. A tunnel carries water through to a powerhouse. However, twice daily at 10–11.30 am and 2.30–4 pm, water is diverted over the old river bed and the many huge boulders that form the Aratiatia rapids. Here the river drops 28 m in 800 m, and the spectacle of the dry river bed changing into a torrent is dramatic. The road leads around to several vantage points.

**Wairakei Thermal Valley** A bush-clad valley containing several thermal activities, including a small geyser that creates a hot waterfall. 1.5 km north of Wairakei.

**Craters of the Moon** Set amid pine trees, this is an active thermal area with steaming craters. Keep to paths and watch children. On signposted side road 2 km south of Wairakei.

**Taupo Walkway** This is a 3-hr walk (one way), which leads from County Avenue in Taupo along the banks of the Waikato River, to Huka Falls (4 km) and on to the Aratiatia Rapids (10.5 km). Good views along the way. There is parking at each end and at the halfway point at Huka Falls. The track can be slippery after rain.

## OTHER AREAS

**Acacia Bay** This is almost a suburb of Taupo, with a side road leading off over the Waikato River bridge. It is a holiday bay.

**Kinloch** A holiday community at the northern end of the lake. Accessible by side road off Route 1. 27 km.

**Restpoint Park** This honey factory and craft outlet is 1.5 km on the road to Kinloch. Open daily to 5 pm.

**Waitahanui River** South along the lake shore following Route 1, the river mouth is a favourite area for anglers.

**Opepe** 17 km from Taupo on Route 5 towards Napier. The site of a Maori village, which later became an Armed Constabulary Stockade, can be accessed by a track leading off the main road. In 1869 nine soldiers were killed here in a surprise attack by the Hauhau warriors of Te Kooti.

**See Also** Rotorua, Atiamuri and Turangi

# TAURANGA NI

**Population** 41 611; 12 375 in Mt Maunganui.

**Location** By Route 2, 206 km south-east of Auckland; by Route 29, 167 km east of Hamilton; by Route 33, 86 km north of Rotorua.

The name Tauranga means 'quiet waters' or 'sheltered anchorage', and refers to the 38 km long harbour, which is protected by Matakana Island. Eventually the Mission Station and European settlement on Te Papa point at the southern end of the harbour were also referred to by this name. Matakana Island is owned largely by the Maoris and is not accessible by the public. The Mt Maunganui peninsula is a well developed boundary between the harbour and sea, and is also included under this heading.

The pleasant and fertile landscape and seascape made the area a popular dwelling place for Maoris going back about 600 years. There are traces of many pas and middens from Maori villages.

During the Waikato land wars the Tauranga tribe Ngaiterangi sided with the Waikato Maoris. Many Ngaiterangi warriors were actually in the Waikato when General Greer and his British troops landed at Tauranga in HMS *Miranda* to protect the eastern flank and to prevent military supplies from unscrupulous Europeans getting through to the Waikato Maoris. The Ngaiterangi therefore rushed back from the Waikato, built a pa near the gate to the mission station (Gate Pa) and challenged the British. On 28 April 1864 the British took up the challenge and pounded the pa with a fierce artillery barrage and then stormed it. However, they were repulsed with 31 killed and 80 wounded. During the night the Ngaiterangi slipped out to a more distant pa, Te Ranga, and a week later the British also attacked there, killing 120 Maoris and finally bringing to an end the Waikato campaign. The Ngaiterangi land was confiscated (in 1981 the government paid $250,000 to a Trust Board as compensation for this act).

Tauranga is now a solid and prosperous city, and the centre of a large citrus and kiwifruit growing area. The railway reached the town in 1928, on a roundabout routing via Paeroa and Waihi, but the opening of the 8.8 km Kaimai tunnel in 1978 improved the access. The satellite town of Mt Maunganui across a sheltered arm of the harbour is now the country's largest export port (not including oil products), having the log, pulp and paper traffic from the Kaingaroa forest area to the south-east as well as the products of the Waikato area.

Tauranga is also a base for big-game fishing. Route 2 skirts, but does not enter the central business district. There are scheduled air services through the airport near Mt Maunganui.

## ENVIRONS & ATTRACTIONS

**Gate Pa** This famous battle-ground, some 5 km from the present city centre, is now bisected by Cameron Road. St George's Church has been built on the site and there is a commemorative memorial and plaque.

**'The Elms' Mission House** Built over a period of nine years from 1838 this complex is now one of New Zealand's oldest homes. It was built by the early missionary Archdeacon Brown. Much of the house is still in its original condition, and it contains furniture and fittings from those times. The gardens are open daily and a conducted tour of the house is available at 2 pm. It is situated on Mission Street, off Cliff Road.

**Monmouth Redoubt** This redoubt at the southern end of Cliff Road was built in 1864 by the British troops. European women and children of the early settlers sheltered here during the emergency leading up to the battle of Gate Pa. Many of the redoubt's earthworks are still well preserved; you are able to walk round this park-like area.

**Otemataha Pa Military Cemetery** Also known as Mission Cemetery, this site holds the graves of many who died at the Gate Pa and Te Ranga battles. A number of the officers who had dined with the Archdeacon on the eve of the Gate Pa Battle were buried by him here a couple of days later. Captain Hamilton, after whom the Waikato city is named, is also buried here. Access is over the railway bridge at the end of Cliff Road.

**Robbins Park** Situated on the eastern side of Cliff Road, this park has rose gardens and a begonia house. It is a pleasant area situated between the Monmouth Redoubt and the Mission Cemetery. The Mission House is less than a block away.

**The Domain** This sports area at the northern end of Cameron Road was once used as a military camp for troops during the battles of 1864, and later during the Te Kooti campaign.

**The Strand** This downtown street skirts the waterfront, or more correctly the parking area that has been reclaimed from the waterfront. However, there are pleasant gardens here. At the northern end is the *Te Awanui* Maori War Canoe built with voluntary donations from Tauranga residents in 1970.

**Memorial Park** Situated adjacent to the middle section of Devonport Road, this park contains a hall, youth centre, children's playground, picnic area and miniature railway.

**Tauranga Historic Village** This is an active working outdoor museum that re-creates colonial life, complete with houses, shops, train, wharf, sawmill and military cottages. The village also serves as the headquarters of a number of local hobby groups. Situated in 17th Avenue West, the facility is open daily (except Christmas Day and Good Friday) 10 am–4 pm. At weekends many exhibits are in working mode.

## LOCAL TOURING

**Te Ranga** This battleground that brought to an end the Waikato campaign, is now just an open paddock with a sign near the fence commemorating the site. The location is 2.5 km down Pyes Pa Road.

**Mt Maunganui** Commonly known as 'The Mount', this area is an important and separate town to residents but visitors usually combine it with the greater Tauranga area. The town has its own shopping area and also has one of New Zealand's largest ports. The Mount itself is a 232 m hill situated at the end of a narrow peninsula. There are walks around the hill and to its top, which are recommended. The harbourside beach is called Pilot Bay, while the Ocean Beach on the other side of the peninsula runs many kilometres and merges with Papamoa. The beach is a popular one. The Leisure Island Pool complex is situated near the Mount end of the beach. The Domain Hot Salt Water pools at the foot of the Mount are unique, and are open daily to 10 pm. There is now a toll bridge ($1 per car) connecting Mt Maunganui across the harbour.

**Papamoa Beach** This is a

continuation of Mt Maunganui's Ocean Beach; however there are separate access roads off Route 2 about 15 km from Tauranga.

**Welcome Bay** This thermal springs and pools complex is situated on Welcome Bay Road, which goes around the most eastern corner of the harbour.

**Kaiaiate Falls** 19 km from Tauranga these falls are accessible on Waitoa Road, which branches off Welcome Bay Road. There are in fact three waterfalls and there is a short track to see them. The road to the falls also gives views over the Mt Maunganui peninsula.

**Oropi and Ohauiti** Roads in this area form a scenic drive from which spectacular views of the greater Tauranga area are obtained. Ohauiti Road leads off from the eastern end of the Welcome Bay Road and a round trip is possible by driving past Mt Misery, along McPhail Road and back down Oropi Road to Tauranga.

**Pyes Pa Road** Continuing past the Te Ranga battle site, this road through bush and mountain via the Ngawaro Gorge provides an alternative route to Rotorua (63 km). However, part of the road is unsealed, narrow and winding.

**Minden Lookout** Accessible via Minden Road from the Te Puna corner, (8 km out of Tauranga on Route 2 heading north), this lookout provides a view over the rural and harbour areas of the greater Tauranga area.

**Whakamarama Scenic Reserve** This is accessible up Whakamarama Road, 6 km past Te Puna. The reserve includes bush walks.

**Mclarens Falls** A park here offers picturesque bush walks and views of the falls, which are on the upper reaches of the Wairoa River, used for electricity

generation. They are accessible off Route 29 (Tauranga–Matamata road). The Omanawa Falls are nearby and equally attractive, though a car is needed to move between the two.

**See Also** Kati Kati, Matamata and Te Puke

# TE ANAU SI
**Population** 2818
**Location** On Route 94, 78 km west of Lumsden, 121 km south of Milford Sound.

The township and tourist centre of Te Anau is situated on the south-east edge of Lake Te Anau. It is a gateway to the Fiordland region and National Park, and a stopover on the impressive road to Milford Sound.

Lake Te Anau is the South Island's largest lake, covering 344 sq km. Although much of the eastern shoreline is developed farmland its western shores have several fiords that penetrate into the rugged mountains of Fiordland. The lake is 61 km long and at an altitude of 212 m. The lake's waters flow into the Upper Waiau River for 18 km to Lake Manapouri. Across the lake from the Te Anau township are the Murchison Mountains, a wilderness area that is restricted to protect a rare flightless bird called takahe or notornis.

Nearby Lake Manapouri has an altitude of 178 m and is New Zealand's deepest lake (to 443 m maximum depth). It is also popularly known as New Zealand's most scenic lake. It is surrounded by mountains, except on its eastern shore where the Waiau River flows in and out, and the settlement of Manapouri (population 442) is situated. The lake's natural outlet has been dammed and the waters now plummet to an underground powerhouse and a 10 km tunnel tailrace out to Doubtful Sound. It is New Zealand's only large power station and an imaginative engineering operation.

Because of the proximity of Manapouri, its attractions are included under this Te Anau section. There is an airport serving the combined Te Anau/ Manapouri district. The Mobil Guide warns that swimmers and children playing in shallow lake water may sometimes be affected by 'duck itch', and should change promptly afterwards.

## LOCAL TOURING
### TE ANAU
**Lake Trips** A number of lake excursions are available, including visits to Te Ana-au Caves or Glade House.

**Te Ana-au Caves** A launch trip over the lake will take you to this cave of rushing water, underground waterfall and glow-worms. You have to stoop to enter, but the ceiling height soon increases.

**Glade House** Situated at the head of the lake, this hostel is the starting point for the Milford Track.

**Milford Track** A 4-day walk (53 km) from Glade House at the head of Lake Te Anau through beech forest, over the McKinnon Pass, and down the Arthur River to Sandfly Point on Milford Sound. The 580 m Sutherland Falls are visited en route. Boat access is required, and is scheduled both ends — although there is a trampers route for the experienced to Glade House over the Dore Pass from the Eglinton Valley Road. This 'world's wonder walk' is usually begun from the Te Anau end and is very popular. You may choose a conducted walk staying overnight at mini-hostels, or a freedom walk,

*Clinton Valley on the Milford Track.*

staying at park board huts — bookings are essential for either. Although the track is available for all ages, some advanced training is desirable. Raincoat and sandfly repellant is essential.

**Hollyford Track** This is an 80 km, 4-5 day walk down the Hollyford Valley to Lake McKerrow and Martins Bay. The return is likewise. An alternative route is via Lake Alabaster to Big Bay. In summer there are conducted tramps that include part jetboat and air return.

**Other Tracks** The Routeburn Track, Greenstone and Caples Tracks from Lake Wakatipu exit

on the Milford Sound Road near the Divide. The Kepler is a track of 3–4 days through the mountain vastness between Lakes Te Anau and Manapouri — but it is not for the inexperienced. If you seek walks of only 1 or 2 hr, try the Ivon Wilson Park and Wildlife Centre on the Te Anau–Manapouri Road just past the motorcamp; or the walk to Dock Bay or Brod Bay from the lookout point at the control gates at the lake outlet.

## MANAPOURI

**The Outlet** This natural outlet of Lake Manapouri is now dammed downriver, but it remains a scenic boat harbour.

**Circle Track** A 3½ hr walk along shoreline then climbing to an outlook. But you must first cross the Waiau River (the Outlet) by hiring a dinghy locally. Adjacent to the Circle Track are the Hope Arm and Back Valley Tracks (both 6 hr return, with a hut en route).

**Lake Trips** Various launch trips showing off the lake's beauty, including a viewpoint at Hope Arm, and the power station at West Arm.

**West arm** Launch trip over the lake, then a bus trip down a spiral

*Lake Manapouri, Southland.*

tunnel to the giant powerhouse hewn inside the mountain.

**Doubtful Sound**  Offered as an extension to the West Arm trip, this involves a bus ride over Wilmot Pass  and another launch on the Deep Cove recesses of Doubtful Sound, one of the west coast fiords. All combined it is a great outing from Te Anau or Manapouri. There is no public road access.

## THE MILFORD SOUND ROAD

**Te Anau Downs**  A sheep station on the road to Milford, 31 km. There is also a cove on the lake where launches to Glade House may stop.

**Mirror Lakes**  A short walk from the main road, 56 km out of Te Anau.

**Avenue of the Disappearing Mountain**  Route 94 follows an avenue of beech trees, with a distant peak gradually dropping from view.

**Cascade Creek**  Picnic place and settlement 74 km from Te Anau. Caravans and trailers prohibited beyond here.

**Lake Gunn**  Bush-clad roadside lake, 78 km. There is a nature walk looping around the lake (30 minutes).

**The Divide**  This pass between the Eglinton and Hollyford valleys is 82 km. The track to Key Summit branches off, with the Routeburn track, to give a 3 hr return climb to 910 m summit and viewpoint. Also a track to Lake Howden. Tracks also connect to the Greenstone and the Caples.

**Hollyford Valley**  Hollyford camp and its museum of historical items from the district is 93 km from Te Anau via an 8 km branch road off Route 94. The road continues through the great scenery of the Lower Hollyford another 9 km to the road's end (the start of the Hollyford Track), and also a 30 minute return walk

to the Humboldt Falls. Near the start of the Lower Hollyford Road is a track to Lake Marian.

**Homer Tunnel**  A 1200 m tunnel, rock hewn and unlined, with a slope of 1 in 10 down to the Milford end. Open each way for 25 minutes of each hour (though tour buses sometimes ignore this) but the scenery is grand so do not worry if you need to wait. The eastern portal is 98 km from Te Anau, 19 km to Milford Sound.

**See Also**  Queenstown, Lumsden and Tuatapere

---

# TE ARAROA  NI
**Population**  252
**Location**  177 km north of Gisborne on Route 35, 165 km north-east of Opotiki.

---

Most of the East Cape area — particularly the coastal fringes — was populated by the Maoris prior to European times. There are many places that have been the sites of inter-tribal battlegrounds. In 1820 the Ngapuhi tribe from Northland — the first Maoris to acquire guns and muskets — raided this area and either killed or took away as prisoners 3000 of the local tribe.

Te Araroa boasts perhaps the world's most easterly hotel and New Zealand's largest pohutakawa tree, which is around 600 years old.

## LOCAL TOURING
**East Cape Lighthouse**  13 km up a side road to this most easterly point. The lighthouse is at 139 m altitude. A walking track (with 600 steps) to the lighthouse takes about 1¾ hr for the round trip.

**Hicks Bay**  12 km from Te Araroa, this is the site of an old freezing works and is a popular area for fishing, swimming and camping. The Tuwhakairoa Meeting House, which was built in 1872, is also in Hicks Bay.

**See Also** Gisborne, Ruatoria and Waihau Bay

# TE AROHA NI
**Population** 3510
**Location** On the eastern side of the Hauraki Plains on Route 26, 54 km from Hamilton, 21 km south of Paeroa.

Originally a goldmining town in the 1880s, Te Aroha is now the centre of a dairying district. It lies at the foot of 952 m high Mt Te Aroha, from the top of which extensive views are possible. The town is also situated on the bank of the Waihou River and although the town originally developed as a port, it no longer has port facilities. Gold, lead and zinc were once mined in the vicinity. The town is now a thermal health resort with a spa situated in the centre of town.

## ENVIRONS & ATTRACTIONS
**Te Aroha Domain** This domain has Victorian-like bath houses and kiosks with drinking fountains that use the three types of mineral waters that spring here. One of the waters is a thermal alkaline similar to the Vichy water of France. There are public baths and a tea kiosk. The grounds and baths are open daily; the Te Aroha and district museum contained in one of the bath houses is open during school holidays.

**St Marks Church** This church reputedly contains the oldest organ in the Southern Hemisphere, which was originally built in the Northern Hemisphere in 1769. The organ came from Shropshire in England and was given to St Marks in 1927. An unusual feature of the organ is that the black and white colouring of the keys are reversed.

## LOCAL TOURING
**Mt Te Aroha** From the domain marked tracks lead first to Bald Spur (305 m), a knob from which visitors can view the entire Thames Valley (1 hr). Alternatively carry on for the complete 3-hr walk to the summit (953 m); from the top, there is an extensive view over both sides of the Kaimais. At the summit is a television mast at the end of a private road. A tour operator from Te Aroha is able to use this private road, and provides four-wheel drive tours to the top.

**See Also** Matamata, Morrinsville and Paeroa

# TE AWAMUTU NI
**Population** 8096
**Location** On Route 3, 30 km south of Hamilton

Te Awamutu is a market and servicing centre for the southern Waikato. It developed as a frontier community during the Maori land wars of 1863–64. The Maori King movement of the Waikato Maoris had been chased out of the northern Waikato and re-formed to fight a heroic battle (300 against 1500 British troops) at the pa site of Orakau to the south-east of the town. After three days of fighting, suffering huge losses as well as shortages of food and ammunition, Rewi Maniapoto and his followers made a dash for freedom. The Puniu River nearby became the boundary between the Waikato, controlled by British troops, and the 'King Country' in which the 'King' Maoris were allowed to live. Their rich former lands in the Waikato were confiscated.

## ENVIRONS & ATTRACTIONS

**Rose Gardens** Te Awamutu is popular as a rose growing area and the Te Awamutu rose gardens are at their best from November through to April. The gardens contain over 2000 bushes and 80 different varieties. Located on Arawata and Gorst Streets.

**St John's Church** This church was built in 1864 and has magnificent coloured lead glass windows. There are also memorial tablets and the graves of both British and Maori casualties of the Waikato Wars.

**Te Awamutu and District Museum** A collection of artifacts relating to the Maori Wars and pioneer times; also containing a sacred Maori carving called Uenuku, which was supposedly brought to New Zealand in the Polynesian migration.

**Waikato Railway Museum** This is an open static display of New Zealand Railway steam locomotives. Open in the afternoon of the third Sunday of each month. The site is sign-posted off Racecourse Road.

## LOCAL TOURING

**Kihikihi and Orakau** 4 km south of Te Awamutu is the small town of Kihikihi. In its main street is a memorial to Rewi Maniapoto who was the war chief at the Battle of Orakau. The battle site is marked by a plaque about 4 km down the side road that leads towards Arapuni and Putaruru.

**Pirongia** Situated 11 km west of Te Awamutu, Pirongia is a small farming community. The area was a battleground when Northland Chief Hongi Hika and his Ngapuhi tribe invaded the Waikato in 1822 with newly purchased muskets, killing perhaps 2000 Waikato Maoris not familiar with such weapons. Behind the town is the Alexandra Redoubt (a short walk across a paddock), which was built by colonial troops in 1864. The earthworks are still clearly visible.

**Pirongia Forest Park** Mount Pirongia rises to 959 m and there are many walking tracks through the park. The area is popular for trampers and nature lovers because of the range of vegetation. A number of tracks lead to the summit. The Tirohanga Track from Corcoran Road (north-west of the town) is a 3-hr climb to the top. The track from either Te Tahi Road or Pirongia West 2 No. Road are about 3½ hr one way.

**Kakepuku** A prominent volcanic cone (449 m), 8 km south-west, has a scenic reserve and a 1½ hr track to the top. Follow Pokuru Road and Mountain Road.

**See Also** Otorohanga, Waitomo Caves and Kawhia

# TE KAHA NI
**Population** 280
**Location** On Route 35, 69 km from Opotiki, 273 km from Gisborne.

The small town of Te Kaha is set in a picturesque cove. The area was the scene of many inter-tribal battles. A whaling station was established here in 1882 and operated for 40 years. The motel at Te Kaha has a photographic display of the whaling days. Route 35 along the east coast of the Bay of Plenty passes magnificent coastal scenery.

## ENVIRONS & ATTRACTIONS

**Te Kaihi** Local Maori meeting house with fine carving.

**See Also** Waihau Bay, Opotiki and Whakatane

# TEKAPO *SI*

Refer to Lake Tekapo

# TE KUITI NI
**Population** 4787
**Location** On Route 3, 78 km
south of Hamilton, 83 km north of
Taumarunui.

The town of Te Kuiti is adjacent to
the Mangaokewa Stream tributary
of the Upper Waipa River. Sheep
and cattle farming are the chief
activities of the surrounding
district; there is also a cement and
lime works. This is the main town
of the King Country. It was the
centre for the 'Kingites' when they
fled to the 'King Country' after the
battle of Orakau in 1864. There
was little intrusion by Europeans
until development of the main
trunk railway in 1887.

## ENVIRONS & ATTRACTIONS
**Te Tokanganuianoho Meeting
House** Built in 1878 by Te Kooti,
this is one of the most impressive
original Maori buildings
remaining in the country. It is
situated by the railway crossing at
the southern end of town;
permission to enter must be
obtained.

## LOCAL TOURING
**Mangaokewa Scenic Reserve**
A pleasant reserve surrounded by
limestone cliffs. Access is under
the Waiteti railway viaduct 4 km
south of the town on Route 30.
**Pureora Forest Park** This
large forest of mainly native bush
contains tawa, rimu, matai and
totara. Forest headquarters is on a
side road off Route 30, 57 km
from Te Kuiti. Both short and long
forest walks are available.
**Wairere Falls and Totoro
Gorge** Branch off Route 3 at
Piopio 23 km south-west, on Aria
Road and Totoro Road, for these

back country sights. There is now
a dam at the falls.

**See Also** Waitomo Caves,
Awakino, Taumarunui and
Atiamuri

# TE PUKE NI
**Population** 5106
**Location** On Route 2, 31 km
east of Tauranga.

Route 2 becomes the main street
of Te Puke. European history
dates back to 1875 when it, like
Katikati, was founded by Irish
immigrants. The Maori history is
closely allied with that of Maketu
and goes back many centuries.
   Today Te Puke is the centre of
a rich fruit-growing area,
especially citrus and kiwifruit —
indeed, it is 'the kiwifruit capital
of the world'. This egg-shaped
fruit, green with furry skin, was
previously known as a Chinese
gooseberry, after its native land.
New Zealand was one of the first
countries to grow the fruit commercially and the change of name
must count as a marketing
success. Te Puke also has a dairy
factory, abattoir freezing works,
and timber milling activities.

## LOCAL TOURING
**Maketu** The historic town of
Maketu is situated 6 km off Route
2, 6 km east of Te Puke. The
*Arawa* canoe arrived here with
the Great Fleet in 1350. Maketu
remained the coastal centre for
the Arawa tribe, many of whom
lived and still live in the Rotorua
area. In 1769 Captain Cook
estimated that there were 10 000
Maoris living in the Maketu area.
The Arawa tribe did not join in
the Waikato land wars, but a
notable battle took place in 1864
when they heard that some east
coast tribes planned to march

through Arawa territory to join the Waikato battles. The Arawas fought and defeated the east coast tribes.

St Thomas' Church, built in 1868, marks the site of the first mission station built in 1842. The Te Awhioterangi meeting house and Whakaue meeting house are historic Maori buildings. Bledisloe Park, 3 km from Maketu, marks the site of one of the skirmishes during the 1864 battle.

**Kiwifruit Country** 6 km east of Te Puke is this horticultural theme park with its emphasis on the kiwifruit industry. There are rides in kiwi-carts, also a restaurant and souvenir centre.

**See Also** Tauranga, Katikati and Rotorua

---

# THAMES NI
**Population** 6461
**Location** On Route 25, 30 km east of its junction with Route 2, which in turn is 31 km east of its junction with Route 1 near Pokeno; also 32 km north of Paeroa on Route 26.

---

Thames is the business, shopping and servicing centre for the surrounding area, which includes a part of the Hauraki Plains and Thames Valley district. It is the largest town on the Coromandel Peninsula and serves as a gateway to this rugged but scenic holiday area.

Thames used to consist of the two separate towns of Shortland on the Waihou River and Grahamstown further north on the Firth of Thames. They are now merged with the name Captain Cook originally applied to the Waihou River.

Poor access over the Hauraki swamps and the Waikato land wars hindered the town's early growth; the usual link with Auckland was by sea. However, much timber was extracted from the area and road and rail connections were established via Te Aroha in the late 1880s and 1890s respectively. These links were further developed following the discovery of gold in 1867. A year later it had a population of 18 000 (with 90 hotels) — much larger than Auckland, which was in decline at that time. In fact it was said that Thames saved Auckland.

Most Thames and Coromandel area gold was from quartz rock, which required batteries of big stampers to crush it. In 1871 there were reportedly 693 stampers in 40 batteries pounding the rocks, creating continual noise day and night. The decline of gold between 1910 and 1920 coincided with drainage plans for the swamps of the Hauraki Plains and in due course a pastoral economy replaced the gold.

Note that some of the hills and river banks around Thames were honeycombed with mining, and bush walkers should be careful of uncovered shafts.

## ENVIRONS & ATTRACTIONS
**Thames Mineralogical Museum** Contains a model of a stamper and other mine equipment, with many mineral samples. Located in the former School of Mines building, corner Cochrane and Brown Streets. Open 2–4 pm (also 10 am–noon school holidays). Closed Sunday.

**Thames Museum** General collection of colonial items and photographs, corner Mackay and Sealey Streets. Open 1—4 pm Wed, Fri and Sun; daily Jan–Feb.

**Queen of Beauty Pumphouse** Goldmines required pumps to keep out water and this pump could raise 13 000 litres of water from 300 m down. Corner Bella and Campbell Streets.

**Hauraki Prospectors Association** Battery and mine open only Christmas and New Year holiday season until 31 January (10 am–4 pm, closed Sundays).

**Moana Taiari Stream Track** Just north of the Hauraki Prospectors Association, take Moana Taiari Creek Road inland for ½ km and then walk another ½ km to the remains of Lucky Shot mine. Keep to the south side of the stream as there are no tracks to other areas.

**Totora Pa** Hongi Hika and his Ngapuhi tribe from Northland attacked local Maoris here, killing many. It is now a cemetery with a view over the town and the Firth of Thames.

## LOCAL TOURING
**Kauaeranga Valley** Scenic and historic valley behind Thames and the site of an extensive timber boom with tramways and dams. Temporary dams were put across streams; when released the logs were carried downstream. Now there are picnic sites and many walks; we mention only two. Details of the many other signposted tracks are available from the forest park headquarters, 12 km from Thames. A replica kauri dam is displayed here.

**Hoffmans Pool Walk** A nature walk 2 km beyond the park headquarters. 30 minutes each way, the walk runs parallel to the road.

**Webb Creek – Hydro Camp – Billygoat** A 4½ hr walk at the road's end, passing relics of timber days; superb views.

**Northern Beaches** North of Thames the picturesque road hugs the coastline through Whakatete Bay, Ngarimu Bay, Thorntons Bay and Te Puru.

**Waioumu** 13 km north of

Thames, this is another beach resort. Up Waioumu Road is a track that leads to the ridge track along the main Coromandel divide (for more experienced trampers). The easier and lower parts of this track lead to the old Monowai mine and a kauri grove (2 hr return).

**Tapu** From this beach resort climb the rugged Tapu–Coroglen Road, which before the opening of Route 25A, was the main access to Whitianga. At Tapu the Rapaura Falls watergardens are open from October to April. 8 km inland from Tapu is a square kauri (a 10-minute walk signposted track) over 1200 years old.

**See Also** Paeroa, Coromandel and Whitianga

# TIMARU SI
**Population** 27 757
**Location** On Route 1, 163 km south of Christchurch, 199 km north of Dunedin.

The city of Timaru is situated on the eastern edge of the Canterbury Plains, on the Canterbury Bight. It is on the main road and railway line between Christchurch and Dunedin and has an airport north of the city with scheduled flights to Wellington. There is an active port.

The southern Canterbury district has climatic conditions and soil suited to crop growing, especially wheat. Caroline Bay, just north of the port, is a sandy beach, where a Christmas/New Year Carnival is held annually. Washdyke to the north, is the city's main industrial suburb.

Richard Pearse made New Zealand and possibly the world's first powered flight from Waitohi in 1903, near the present airport. Legendary racing horse Phar Lap

*The North Island township of Thames.*

came from the Timaru district in the late 1920s.

Ancient Maori tribespeople seem to have inhabited caves and rock overhangs and some of their drawings remain in inland caves. The later Maoris who migrated from the north introduced the Maori culture that is standard today.

A European whaling station was established near Timaru in 1837. The settlement of Timaru was laid out in 1857, with the first true immigrants arriving in 1859. A fire destroyed much of the town in 1868.

## ENVIRONS & ATTRACTIONS
**Caroline Bay** A popular beach with foreshore amusements.
**Pioneer Hall Museum** Collection of items including Maori artifacts and photographs of port develop-ment. Perth Street.

Open 1.30–4.30 pm (not Saturday or Monday).
**Botanical Gardens** Extensive gardens and reserve (on Queen Street and Kings Street, Route 1).
**Aigantighe Art Gallery** Local permanent and touring exhibitions. Wai-iti Road. Open daily 2–4.30 pm, except Monday and Friday.
**St Mary's Church** Built in 1886 on the site of the city's original church in an early English style. Perth Street.
**Catholic Basilica** Built in 1910 with two towers and a large dome. Craigie Avenue.
**Hadlow Game Park** Includes deer, wallaby, pig and bison. Hadlow Road, 10 km west along Waiti Road.
**Museum of Childhood** Includes dolls and toys. Open Monday–Saturday 10–4.30 pm.

## LOCAL TOURING

**Timaru City Walkway** In two sections along the coast and creek (2.7 km, 1¼ hr) and through Centennial Park (3.5 km, 1 hr).

**Pareora River Walkway** In several parts, totalling 16½ km, along the north bank of the Pareora River, 13 km south-west of Timaru.

**Otaio Beach Walkway** A 3 km return walk from Route 1 to the beach at Otaio, 19 km south of Timaru.

**Temuka** 18 km north of Timaru on Route 1. The centre is known for its ceramics and pottery. A factory shop is in King Street. There is a Courthouse Museum open Thursday and Sunday afternoons. St Peters Church, built in 1899, may also be of interest.

**Pleasant Point** 19 km north-west of Timaru on Route 8. In the town centre is the Pleasant Point railway and museum (at the site of the old station) with an Ab type locomotive, which used to operate on the former Fairlie branchline. The Station Museum is open Sunday afternoons and holiday periods. At holiday weekends steam trains operate to/from their workshop 2 km east.

**Hanging Rock** A picnic area by the Opihi River Bridge, 11 km north-west.

**Pioneer Park** Off Middle Valley Road 17 km north-west. Picnic sites and walking tracks in a 510 ha reserve. The Home Bush walk takes 1 hr; the White Pine walk takes up to 4 hr.

**Raincliff Forest** This 84 ha reserve of English oaks and Austrian pines is further along Middle Valley Road. There are several walks in the forest, for example, the Raincliff walk of 1½ hr return, and the Ponderosa walk of 30 minutes return through Ponderosa pine.

**Cave** Settlement 35 km north-west of Timaru on Route 8. See the St Davids Pioneer Memorial Church (up side road 2 km from settlement) built with glacial boulders in a Norman style.

**See Also** Geraldine, Fairlie and Waimate

# TOKOMARU BAY NI
**Population** 440
**Location** 88 km north of Gisborne on Route 35.

Tokomaru Bay is named after the Maori canoe — one of the Great Fleet arriving around 1350. Captain Cook visited here in 1769. It was also a headquarters for a whaling station, one of the many around the East Cape. There were skirmishes here during the Te Kooti campaign in 1866. The bay was a calling place for passenger ships (before the road was built) until the 1920s. There are remains of a big freezing works near the wharf.

## LOCAL TOURING

**Te Puia Springs** Natural hot pools 11 km north of Tokomaru Bay.

**Waipiro Bay** An almost abandoned settlement, which was once one of the most important towns around the East Cape area. The first 'Kerridge' theatre was established here.

**See Also** Gisborne, Tolaga Bay and Ruatoria

# TOKOROA NI
**Population** 17 628
**Location** On Route 1, 86 km south of Hamilton

Tokoroa's early history was as a rural farming and mill town, but it experienced rapid growth with the development of the timber pulp and paper mill at nearby Kinleith. Perhaps the world's largest man-made forest of pine trees is adjacent to the town.

## ENVIRONS & ATTRACTIONS
**Colson Hill** Immediately adjacent to the main road through town, a short drive leads to the top from which there are panoramic views of the town and surroundings.

## LOCAL TOURING
**Kinleith Mill** This giant industrial complex is on a side road 6 km south of Tokoroa. The mill processes radiata pine trees into woodchips, pulp and paper, much of which is exported. Guided tours for adults are available 10.30 am weekdays.

**See Also** Cambridge, Putaruru and Atiamuri

# TOLAGA BAY NI
**Population** 680
**Location** 55 km north of Gisborne on Route 35.

Captain Cook landed near here in 1769, and again on a later voyage in 1777. The Hauhau leader Te Kooti made a raid on the settlement in 1870. The bay is noted for its long wharf (655 m) at the south-east end.

## ENVIRONS & ATTRACTIONS
**Cooks Cove Walkway** Leads along the top of cliffs with views over the township, Uawa River, and the Bay, then winds down to Cooks Cove. There is a side track to the Hole in the Wall rock. Walk 2 km each way (2½ hr return).

## LOCAL TOURING
**Anaura Bay** 14 km north of Tolaga Bay, marks the site of Cook's second landing in New Zealand. There is a walkway of 3.5 km (2 hr return).

**See Also** Gisborne, Tokomaru Bay and Opotiki

# TONGARIRO NATIONAL PARK NI

Refer to National Park.

# TUAKAU NI
**Population** 2195
**Location** Adjacent to Route 22, 9 km south of Pukekohe.

The borough of Tuakau services the southern parts of Rodney County towards the lower reaches of the Waikato River. The nearby Alexandra Redoubt and Camerontown army depot were important locations in the initial stages of the Waikato land wars.

## ENVIRONS & ATTRACTIONS
**The Alexandra Redoubt** This fortification was built on a bluff 90 m above the Waikato River. Troops were able to oversee the river at this point; and they were also able to take part in the defence of the Camerontown depot when it was sacked (1863). It is interesting to view the excavations of the redoubt and gravestones.

## LOCAL TOURING
**Port Waikato** This is the beach settlement at the mouth of the Waikato River. During the Waikato land wars, a dockyard and servicing depot was built for the British Forces. There is no longer a port here but the area remains popular for holiday-makers and fishermen. Situated 42 km from Tuakau, cross the Waikato River bridge and follow out on the southern side of the river.

**See Also** Pukekohe, Waiuku and Auckland

# TUATAPERE SI

**Population** 859

**Location** Where Route 96 meets Route 99, 88 km north-west of Invercargill.

This township is situated on the lower Waiau River. Farming and sawmilling — particularly the latter — have helped the town grow over the years. It used to be a railway terminus but the line is now closed.

## ENVIRONS & ATTRACTIONS

**Tuatapere Scenic Reserve** A stand of beech forest, accessible over the Waiau River bridge.

## LOCAL TOURING

**Te Waewae Bay** Southern shoreline, accessible on Route 99 at Orepuki and Waihoaka; also along Bluecliffs Beach on the road to Port Craig (over the Waiau Bridge).

**Port Craig** A once busy but now abandoned timber town, 40 km by road and track from Tuatapere. Allow a full day for return shoreline walk from the end of the road.

**Clifden** 13 km north of Tuatapere on Route 96, this settlement is named after the area's limestone cliffs (many with caves).

**Lake Hauroko** A 31 km side road from Clifton leads to this bush and mountain lake. It is situated within the Fiordland National Park. There are several local bush walks ranging from 20 minutes to 4 hr return.

**Lake Monowai** Travel 44 km north from Clifden on the picturesque road parallel to the Takitimu Mountains, and branch off at Blackmount to reach Lake Monowai. This is a hydro-lake and was one of the first hydro power schemes. Drowned tree stumps where the lake was raised are still visible. A local track leads to Rodger Inlet (3½ hr).

**See Also** Te Anau and Riverton

286

# TURANGI NI

**Population** 3913

**Location** On Route 1, 51 km south of Taupo at the southern end of Lake Taupo.

Turangi owes its existence to two factors: fishing and electricity. The nearby Tongariro River and Lake Taupo are renowned to anglers and Turangi is a servicing and accommodation centre for that tourist industry. The town was also the headquarters and living area for the workforce employed on the Tongariro power scheme. By a series of canals and tunnels, this project captures the headwaters of the Tongariro, Wanganui and Moawhango Rivers, and diverts them through powerhouses to Lake Taupo and subsequently the Waikato River. In addition to the power that is generated directly by this scheme, the Waikato River plants were able to increase capacity. There are controls to ensure that the fishing waters, especially the Tongariro River, have an adequate supply of water.

The Tongariro National Park is nearby, with its large recreational area, and skiing facilities in winter. Turangi is used for skiers' accommodation in season.

## ENVIRONS & ATTRACTIONS

**Visitors Centre** The Turangi Information Office has a model and displays of the power scheme

**Tongariro Fish Hatchery** This is a rearing station for rainbow trout. The facility is open weekdays May to October.

**Lake Taupo** North of the town Route 1 follows the lake shore, with beaches and picnic areas.

## LOCAL TOURING

**Tokaanu** A small township 5 km west of Turangi. The Tokaanu mineral pools have public and private thermal pools, which are open daily.

**Waihi Village**  8 km west of Turangi, on a side road, this Maori village features an ornate church of Saint Werenfried, the Mausoleum of Te Heuheu and two meeting houses. The village is at the bottom of a steep thermal cliff by the lake shore. The Waihi Falls drop down the cliff. The village is private and permission should be obtained from the villagers before entering any building.

**Kuratau**  Kuratau junction is where Route 32 (west Taupo road) intersects Route 31, 22 km west of Turangi. The Kuratau hydro-electric power station, and the Kuratau Spit, a picnic area on the lake shore, can be accessed by side roads.

**Lake Rotopounamu**  Route 47A climbs up and over the Te Ponanga Saddle (also known as Pihanga Saddle) — note view of Lake Taupo from lookout — then leads to the beginning of a walking track to this lake. The small lake features bush, beach and birds, and is a 20-minute walk from the road. Allow 2 hr to circle the lake and return to the road.

**Kaimanawa Forest Park**  The ranges and park are to the south-east of Turangi with access from the Desert Road. The park has a rough and broken terrain, largely covered by beech forest. Tramping, camping and safari tours are available. There is a park headquarters at Turangi.

**See Also**  National Park, Taupo and Waiouru

---

# TWIZEL  SI

**Population**  1234

**Location**  On Route 8, 56 km south-west of Tekapo, 30 km north of Omarama, and 11 km south of the junction of Route 80 to Mt Cook.

---

Twizel developed as a construction town for the Upper Waitaki and also for power development schemes in the late 1960s. It reached a peak population of nearly 6000 in 1976. It takes less people to operate the completed scheme, but Twizel remains an important tourist town for the region. It has a harsh climate, with extremes in summer and winter.

The power scheme diverts water from Lake Tekapo via two power stations and a canal into Lake Pukaki. With water from Lake Ohau the combined volume flows through three Ohau power stations before discharging into Lake Benmore, and being used by the three hydro stations in the lower Waitaki. In this scheme Lake Tekapo is a bank, which stores spring and summer water until needed in the peak winter seasons. The level of Lake Tekapo has been raised as part of this scheme.

## ENVIRONS & ATTRACTIONS

**Lake Ruataniwha**  This hydro lake is now a rowing course, south-west of Twizel.

**Tekapo B Dam and Power House**  This power station stands on the banks of Lake Pukaki and is fed by canal waters from Tekapo. You can visit the outside of the powerhouse and a lookout at the top of the penstocks. Follow the canal road embankment to intercept the main highway.

## LOCAL TOURING

**Lake Ohau**  Lake and settlement 29 km south-west of Twizel, branching off Route 8. The settlement is on the south-west side of the lake. There is a ski-field high above the lake 6 km further on.

**See Also**  Lake Tekapo, Mt Cook and Omarama

*Ben Ohau Range in the MacKenzie Country, near Twizel.*

288

W

# WAIHAU BAY  NI
**Population** 230
**Location** On Route 35, 106 km
from Opotiki, 236 km from
Gisborne.

This is a tiny settlement with a
fine broad beach. Do not confuse
Waihau Bay with Waihau Beach,
which is between Gisborne and
Tologa Bay. Route 35 passes
magnificent scenery along the
eastern coast of the Bay of Plenty
and beaches at Oruaiti and
Whanarua also provide good
fishing, picnicking and
swimming.

## ENVIRONS & ATTRACTIONS
**Raukokore** This fine
architectural church beside the
sea is a landmark, 6 km south of
Waihau Bay.

## LOCAL TOURING
**Whangaparaoa** 7 km north
of Waihau Bay, this is thought
to be the landing place of the
*Arawa* and *Tainui* canoes,
though the former sailed on
towards Maketu in the Bay of
Plenty; the *Tainui* later left
for Kawhia. It is also the place
where kumara was first planted in
New Zealand.
**Cape Runaway** This peninsula
is the eastern boundary for the
Bay of Plenty. It is the site of an
old whaling station. Milk
tankers from Opotiki service the
road to Cape Runaway daily — it
is New Zealand's longest milk
run (293 km round trip). There
is no road access to the
cape.

**See Also** Te Aroha, Te Kaha and
Opotiki
290

# WAIHI  NI
**Population** 3679
**Location** On Route 2, 21 km
east of Paeroa, 62 km north of
Tauranga.

Now a servicing and farming
town, Waihi grew as a result of
the Martha Hill goldmine, that is,
until the miners strike of 1912.
Gold and silver were discovered
in 1878 and mined until 1952 at
Martha Hill, immediately behind
the town. The deepest shaft there
went down over 550 m and the
tunnels and drives exceeded
160 km. Much of the ore was
crushed at the giant Victoria
Battery at Waikino (the
foundation of this is still visible
across the river at nearby
Waikino). The mine was only just
profitable in its early years due to
the difficulty of extracting gold
from the ore, but when a cyanide
process was introduced in 1898
the mine and town boomed.

The mine and battery required
much power, originally provided
from coal, which was sent by boat
to Paeroa and railed to Waikino
and Waihi. In 1913, however, the
company built a hydro-station on
the Waikato River and brought
the power overland for more than
80 km. The Hora Hora power
station is built under the lake
water that was formed by
Karapiro Dam. At Martha Hill the
concrete pumphouse (built in
1901) is the only building
remaining to keep the mine clear
of water.

Gold is found either in free
form, as in the alluvial deposits of
Otago, or locked up in quartz
veins and reefs as in the Waihi
and Coromandel area. Where it
occurs in reefs it is often
associated with silver, and may
occur underground as it does at
Waihi. The ore is pulverised and
the addition of a solution of

sodium cyanide takes about three days to dissolve the gold and silver from the ore.

## ENVIRONS & ATTRACTIONS
**Martha Hill** The old pumphouse ruins remain on Martha Hill, but be aware of renewed mining activity on the hill.

**Waihi Museum and Art Gallery** Open five days a week, this collection has models and photographs showing the workings of the Martha mine and others in the area.

**Goldfields Vintage Railway** A local society is restoring a 7 km section of line from Waihi to Waikino. Operates during summer holidays.

## LOCAL TOURING
**Waikino** The settlement of Waikino is situated 7 km out of Waihi on the road to Paeroa. Across the river the foundation of the giant Victoria Battery can be seen. The road continues through the Karangahake Gorge and provides access to the Karangahake walkway (refer to Paeroa).

**Waterlily Gardens** Situated on Pukekauri Road, 8 km out of Waihi towards Paeroa, this garden contains a variety of waterlilies, which are grown commercially. There are picnic facilities. Open from October to April, 10 am–4 pm. This road also passes the Owharoa Falls. There is alternative access from Route 2 south of Waihi.

**Waihi Beach** Situated 11 km from Waihi on the east coast, this 10 km long beach is situated on the western shores of the Bay of Plenty and extends south to the entrance of Tauranga Harbour.

**See Also** Paeroa, Thames and Katikati

# WAIKANAE NI
Refer to Wellington.

# WAIKAREMOANA NI
**Population** 145
**Location** On Route 38, between Rotorua and Wairoa — 160 km and 62 km respectively.

Lake Waikaremoana is often rated as the North Island's most beautiful lake. Situated at an altitude of 614 m, this 19 km by 10 km lake is surrounded by mountainous ramparts. It is almost landlocked, and water exits by fissures at the eastern end. The outlet has now been harnessed for hydro-electric power generation using three stations (Tuai, Piripaua and Kaitawa) to capitalise on the short steep outfall.

Waikaremoana is popular for fishing, hunting and tramping. It is surrounded by the Urewera National Park — a mountainous reserve of 211 000 ha. The Tuhoe tribe ('children of the mist') eked out a secluded existence here for hundreds of years with little outside contact. After the Maori renegade Te Kooti escaped from the Chatham Island in 1869 he and his followers used the Urewera for four years as a base from which to attack Whakatane and Rotorua and generally harass Europeans. Two government and military campaigns failed to catch him; and later he fled to Te Kuiti to live in the King Country beyond the reach (then) of Pakeha influence.

The Tuhoe tribe also became involved with a Latter Day Saint called Rua Kenana who established a Maori revivalist movement and temple at Maungapohatu in the Urewa. He was hunted down by the government for defying liquor laws.

The Urewera National Park contains deer, pigs and goats. The park is heavily forested with rimu at lower levels, and mountain beech on the higher peaks.

Route 38 is the only through road that gives access to Waikaremoana and the Urewera. It is still a mountain road — mostly unsealed — and is not suitable for caravans approaching from the Rotorua side. The northern fringes of the park can be entered south of Whakatane. There used to be a hotel at Waikaremoana called Lake House, and at times this name was applied to the locality. The park headquarters is at Aniwaniwa on the lake shore.

Because of the lack of roads, movement through the park is mainly by foot tracks. There are many such tracks: some of an hour or more, others lasting several days, either around the Waikaremoana area or connecting this area with the northern fringes through towards the Bay of Plenty.

## ENVIRONS & ATTRACTIONS

**National Park Headquarters** At Aniwaniwa on the lake shore, this has a display of photographs and artifacts. Information on the park is readily available, especially regarding walking tracks and hunting permits.

**Onepoto** This is the locality at the south-east end of the lake where the road from Wairoa meets the lake.

**Mokau Falls** A waterfall where the Mokau River falls into the lake. It can be seen 500 m past the bridge due to the curvature in the road.

**Hoporuahine Landing** This landing is at the western end where the road from Rotorua meets the lake.

## LOCAL TOURING

**Aniwaniwa Falls** A 30-minute round trip walk from the park
headquarters to visit Bridal Veil Falls and Aniwaniwa Falls.

**Lake Waikareiti** A 1 hr each way track from near the park headquarters to this smaller lake, which is 275 m higher up. The lake has small islands, one of which also has a tiny lake. Other tracks lead further around the lake to Sandy Bay and Kaipo Lagoon.

**Ngamoto Track** A 4 hr return track from opposite the lake house site to a summit at 1201 m for extensive views.

**Mount Whakataka Track** A one day return track from Hoporuahine Landing to this 1262 m summit for extensive views.

**Round the Lake Track** This 35 km track takes 3–5 days, but it is still a popular track. There are five huts but they are all well used in summer. Start at Hoporuahine Landing and finish at Onepoto.

**Ruatahuna** On Route 38, 28 km west of the Hoporuahine Landing, this was the regional base for the Tuhoe people and also where 200 Tuhoe Maoris died from starvation in 1870. The Mataatua Meeting House (built in 1888) is 4 km up a side road.

**See Also** Rotorua, Wairoa and Whakatane

# WAIMATE SI
**Population** 3250
**Location** On Route 82 (which branches off Route 1), 46 km south of Timaru.

The settlement of Waimate was founded when Michael Studhulme arrived in 1854 and took up land here. The neighbourhood was at one time densely wooded, and timbermilling was the basis of the town's economy. But in 1878 a fire burnt much of the town and the bush. The town had a branch railway until 1966, which branched off the South Island mainline at Studholme junction. Former Labour Prime Minister Norman Kirk (1923–74) was born and buried at Waimate.

## ENVIRONS & ATTRACTIONS
**Seddon Square** Small park in town centre. Queen Street.
**Knottingley Park** A 30 ha park, accessible on Nottingley Park Road. 3 km.
**St Augustine's Church** Built in 1872 from roughsawn timber, with a distinctive tower. John Street.
**Waimate Historical Museum** Includes a military room, a clock room, farming implements and a gaol in an 1879 courthouse building. Sherman Street. Open Mon–Fri 1–5 pm, 2–4 pm.

## LOCAL TOURING
**The Hunter Hills** A range of hills behind the town. Distant reserves include Hook Bush and Mt Nimrod Scenic Reserve. Kelseys Bush (7.5 km out on Mill Road) with picnic spots and walks, including a climb up the Divide (884 m) for views of south Canterbury is a closer reserve.
**The White Horse** This 16 by 20 m concrete replica honouring the work done by Clydesdale horses is at the Hillside lookout (416 m) in Centre Wood Park. Though perhaps better viewed from a distance, a 6 km road provides access.
**Waimate Walkway** A 3 km (2½ hr return) walk commencing 2 km out on Pt Bush Road and climbing up to the White Horse.

**See Also** Timaru, Oamaru and Kurow

# WAIOURU NI
**Population** 3318
**Location** On Route 1, 53 km south of Turangi, 104 km south of Taupo, at the southern end of the Desert Road and the intersection of Route 49 from Ohakune and Raetihi.

Waiouru is the New Zealand Army's principal training facility. Its altitude of 813 m makes it the highest town on the main trunk railway line — and indeed the highest station in New Zealand. The town commands a fine view of the southern aspect of Mt Ruapehu, and is also a staging point for traffic crossing the Desert Road.

## ENVIRONS & ATTRACTIONS
**Army Memorial Museum** Situated on the main highway, this museum houses a large display of guns, uniforms and insignia used by the New Zealand Army in its various campaigns. Open daily except Christmas Day and New Year's Day.

## LOCAL TOURING
**Rangipo Desert** From Waiouru, Route 1 leads on to Turangi via the Desert Road across the Rangipo Desert. Although not a true desert, the adjacent mountains seem to create there own climate zone and the area is subject to dry winds, which, combined with the lack of soil, makes plant life difficult. The road can be subject to closure at times due to snow and ice. Part of the desert is Army training reserve. The Waihohonu Track leads from midway along the Desert Road through to 'The Chateau'. The Kaimanawa Range and forest park skirts the eastern boundary.

**See Also** Turangi, Ohakune and Raetihi

*The Desert Road, Central North Island.*

# WAIPARA SI
**Population** 197
**Location** On Route 1, 56 km north of Christchurch, at the junction for Route 7 via the Lewis Pass to the west coast.

A farming community in North Canterbury. Moa bones were discovered in nearby swamps as early as 1867 by Julius Von Haast. In 1939 five almost complete skeletons were found and are now in the Canterbury museum in Christchurch. North at Waikari, examples of early Maori rock art have also been found.

## LOCAL TOURING
**Weka Pass Railway** A group of enthusiasts operate diesel-hauled trains over an old railway line through craggy country.
**Lake Sumner** From Waikari, the road is narrow, winding and unsealed with water courses to cross. The last 8 km beyond Lake Taylor are suitable for four-wheel drive vehicles only.
**Motunau Beach** 23 km north then 14 km east to the beach settlement at Motunau. The northern end of the beach is popular with fossil hunters.

**See Also** Cheviot, Hanmer Springs and Rangiora

**Parangahau** Small township on the estuary of the Parangahau River. 45 km south-east of Waipukurau. The Maori meeting house was built in 1912 and has interesting carvings. Nearby is a small hill with New Zealand's longest placename: Taumatawhakatangihangakauauotamateapokaiwhenuakitanatahu.

# WAIPUKURAU NI
**Population** 3862
**Location** On Route 2, 52 km south of Hastings, 54 km north of Dannevirke.

The town was founded as a farming settlement for contract farm workers in 1860. Its neighbouring town of Waipawa, only 7 km away, had a similar beginning. Both are now farming centres, but Waipawa has a smaller population.

## ENVIRONS & ATTRACTIONS
**Reservoir Hill** Once the site of a Maori pa, this hill gives a view over the town.
**Tukituki River** A picnic site is located by the bridge.
**Waipawa** Neighbouring town and farming community, 7 km north, with a population of 1849.

## LOCAL TOURING
**Pourere Beach and Kairakau Beach** Two east coast beaches, accessed on different roads, 39 km east.
**See Also** Dannevirke, Hastings and Napier

# WAIPU NI
**Population** 791
**Location** On Route 1, 130 km north of Auckland.

Waipu was settled in 1853 by Scottish migrants from Nova Scotia under the leadership of Reverend Norman McLeod. The town is now a farming centre.

## ENVIRONS & ATTRACTIONS
**Waipu House of Memories** A museum commemorating the Scottish pioneers of the district.

## LOCAL TOURING
**Waipu Cove** A beach resort 9 km out on a side road. The cove is part of almost continuous beach that leads through Urititi Beach and Ruakaka Beach. They all face on to Bream Bay, opposite the Whangarei Heads. An unsealed extension of the road leads onto Langs Beach and Maungawhai Heads. Alternative access to these heads is from Kaiwaka, 24 km south of Waipu on the southern side of the Brynderwyn Hills.

**See Also** Wellsford, Matakhoe and Whangarei

# WAIPOUA KAURI FOREST NI
**Population** 42
**Location** 64 km north of Dargaville on Route 12.

Part of the extensive Northland Forest Park, this huge reserve contains the largest remnant of the extensive kauri tree forests that once covered North Auckland and the Coromandel Peninsula. There are about 300 types of trees and plants to be found, including taraire, rata, towai, rewarewa, rimu, totara and kahikatea.

The giant kauri trees take several hundred years to grow, and can be up to 1500 years old. Fully grown trees can reach 36 m in height, and have straight trunks of up to 3 m diameter. In earlier days kauris were prized for timber, spars, and also for their gum, which was used to make

*Kauri tree bark at Waipoua.*

varnish. Route 12 winds through the forest for about 16 km.

## ENVIRONS & ATTRACTIONS
**Tane Mahuta** 'The God of the forest' is a 51 m giant kauri tree, which is more than 12 centuries old. The first branch is 12 m above the ground, and has a girth of around 12 m. It can be reached after a 3-minute walk from the main road. The tree is signposted.

## LOCAL TOURING
**Trounson Kauri Park** Situated south of Waipoua on a side road near Donnelly's Crossing, about 40 km north of Dargaville. There is a picnic area, and a suggested half-hour round trip walking track through the forest.

**See Also** Dargaville, Opononi and Rawene

# WAIROA NI
**Population** 904
**Location** On Route 2, 93 km south-west of Gisborne, 119 km north-east of Napier.

This borough is the servicing centre for the sheep farming area of the northern Hawke's Bay. There is also other mixed farming and some cropping. The Wairoa River flows through the town.

The original Maori inhabitants called the area Te Wairoa. The first Europeans to visit were flax traders in the 1820s followed by whalers in the 1830s, missionaries in the 1840s, farmers in the 1850s and soldiers in the 1860s. The soldiers set up a military base in 1865 to help prevent attack from the Maori Hauhau sect.

The hills both north and south of the area restricted land access, so Wairoa developed as a port. However, with the development of road and railway, the port fell into disuse. Wairoa is also at the eastern end of Route 38 to Waikaremoana. The Mahia peninsula, 43 km east, is the northern tip of Hawke's Bay.

## ENVIRONS & ATTRACTIONS
**Portland Island Lighthouse** Originally situated near the tip of the Mahia peninsula, it is now on Marine Parade.
**Wairoa Museum** Artifacts and photographs of Maoris and early settlers. Marine Parade. Open daily 2–4 pm.
**Takitimu Marae** Off Waihirere Road over the town bridge, this 1935 meeting house contains some fine carvings. The house commemorates Sir James Carroll (1853–1926), a Maori parliamentarian.
**Whakamahi Beach** A popular local beach, 5 km.

## LOCAL TOURING
**Whakakaki Lagoon** One of four lagoons lying between the main road and the coast, 18 km east.
**Morere** Hot Springs, picnic site and camp ground, 40 km east of Wairoa.
**Mahia Peninsula** The road branches off Route 2 at Nuhaka (32 km east), passes Opoutama Beach and leads to Mahia Beach. The rest of the peninsula is a hilly promontory. Reverend William Williams (later Bishop) baptised more than 240 Maoris in 1842 at the Whangawehi Coronation Reserve.
**Mohaka** The Mohaka railway viaduct (95 m) is on Route 2, 37 km south of Wairoa. It is New Zealand's highest viaduct.

**See Also** Gisborne, Waikaremoana and Napier

# WAITANGI NI
Refer to the Bay of Islands

# WAITARA NI
**Population** 6402
**Location** On Route 3, 15 km east of New Plymouth.

Northern Taranaki was a well populated and well contested area in pre-European times. But the arrival of European settlers coincided with the return of the Ngati-Awa tribe in 1848 from Wellington to their ancestral lands near Waitara where they resettled.

The European settlers in New Plymouth coveted this choice Maori land and set about purchasing it. One chief sold some land without the support of other chiefs, or his tribe, and they set out to block the Europeans from taking up their land. This led to Colonel Gold and 400 troops building a redoubt on the disputed land in 1860, and twelve months of hostilities followed until the Maoris surrendered.

In recent years the town of Waitara has been boosted by the development and construction of petro-chemical industries in the area, on top of a solid dairying and sheep farming base. The town is on side roads off Route 3, where the Waitara River meets the coast.

## ENVIRONS & ATTRACTIONS
**Marine Park** Beach and river reserve on the left bank where the Waitara River meets the sea.
**Manukoroihi Meeting House** On the Owai Marae, a magnificently carved meeting house and memorial (built in 1936) to Sir Maui Pomare (1876–1930), a parliamentarian who advanced Maori culture and social standing. On North Street, Waitara East. A lookout is nearby.
**Motunui** Large synthetic fuel plant, which changes natural gas to methanol and then to gasoline. The plant is closed to tourists but

there is a tourist information centre. Situated on Route 3, 5 km east of Waitara.
**Waitara Valley Methanol Plant** This large plant that processes natural gas to methanol (mainly for export) is up the river valley (visible off Route 3). The side road leads past the plant to an overlook.

## LOCAL TOURING
**Pukerangiora Pa** Beautiful but with a bloody history, this pa is on a high cliff next to the Waitara River, 7 km inland on Waitara Road. In 1861 General Pratt and his British troops took weeks to dig a 1.6 km trench to assault the pa. A short bushwalk leads to a precipice and viewpoint.
**Oilfields Production Station** 12 km up Otaraoa Road (opposite Motunui syn-fuel Plant). There is a visitors outlook, but the actual wellheads are not accessible.
**Sir Peter Buck Memorial** The prow of a canoe is a memorial to this noted authority on Polynesian anthropology (1877–1951). On Route 3, 15 km north of Waitara, past Urenui.
**Pukearuahe** This is the entrance to Taranaki on the traditional overland route for Maoris, traders and troops from the Waikato. Accessed on a side road off Route 3 (past Urenui), a historic reserve stands on the site of a former pa. In 1865 it became a military redoubt, the most northerly in the chain of Taranaki defences.
**Whitecliffs Walkway** This commences at the Pukearuahe historic reserve and follows through bush (with some low-tide beach options) 9.6 km (5 hr) north to Tongatotutu following trails along the traditional overland route towards the Waikato. The walkway is named after the striking white cliffs near Pukearuahe; part of the route

follows the Kapuni and Maui gas pipelines.

**See Also** New Plymouth, Inglewood and Mokau

# WAITOMO CAVES NI
**Population** 299
**Location** 8 km up a side road off Route 3; the junction is 8 km south of Otorohanga, 11 km north of Te Kuiti.

The locality (and county) of Waitomo takes its name from the group of three large limestone caverns called the Waitomo Caves. Although known to the Maoris, they were not discovered by Europeans until 1887.

The most popular of the three is also known individually as Waitomo Cave, and it is noted for its galleries, chambers, stalactite and stalagmite formations. However, it is especially renowned for its glow-worm grotto, where tourists in a boat on an underground river may gaze up at the glow-worm lights on the roof of the caves. A hotel, commercial facilities and visitors centre are near this cave.

2 km further on are the Aranui and Ruakuri caves. The former is possibly the most beautiful of the three, while the latter is the largest. There are many other known caves of all sizes in the King Country area and probably a number of unknown ones as well.

## ENVIRONS & ATTRACTIONS
**Waitomo Caves Visitor Centre** This museum has displays on the Waitomo Caves

*The Ruakuri Cave at Waitomo.*

*Glow-worm grotto, Waitomo Caves.*

and the insect life in them. There are also displays of birds. Tickets for inspection of the caves may be purchased here.

**Waitomo Caves** There are guided tours hourly. Tickets can be purchased at the visitors centre.

**Aranui Cave** Tours run at 11 am and 2 pm. This cave is 2 km from Waitomó Cave and adjacent to Ruakuri Cave. Check at the visitors centre for times and tickets.

## LOCAL TOURING
**Mangapohue Natural Bridge**
Also known as Te Koipu, this is a spectacular 15 m limestone arch, which bridges the Mangapohue stream. It is situated 16 km on the same road up and past the Waitomo Caves. There is a 10-minute walk across the paddocks, which is signposted. The track follows a stream into a deep gorge, which is bridged high above by natural rock.

**Marokopa Falls** The spectacular scenic reserve with waterfalls falling 36 m over rock ledges is about 30 km on the same road up and past the Waitomo Caves. The falls lookout can be reached by high standard walk tracks from the road (10 minutes), which descend to the river through thick native bush.

**Waitomo Walkway** This walkway, which is still being developed, starts at the carpark of the Waitomo Cave and passes through forest farmland and limestone formations, including the Ruakuri natural bridge. The walk takes 3–4 hr round trip. There are picnic tables and toilets at the entrance to the Ruakuri scenic reserve. Enquire at the Waitomo Caves visitors centre.

**Merrowvale** This is a model of New Zealand in miniature, complete with 'operating' Northerner train. The model is situated on the road to the caves.

**Ohaki Village and Weaving Centre** Dedicated to preserving the arts, crafts and weaving skills of the Maori people. Also on the road to the caves.

**See Also** Otorohanga, Te Kuiti and Kawhia

---

# WAIUKU NI
**Population** 4357
**Location** 64 km south from Auckland, 21 km south-west of Pukekohe.

---

The borough of Waiuku developed as a trading post in the 1840s on an ancient Maori portage route, for overland carriage of canoes between the Manukau Harbour and the Lower Waikato River. During the Waikato land wars, Waiuku became a frontier town with a blockhouse. The town suffered in the skirmishes leading up to the wars. Today the giant Glenbrook steel mill, at nearby Glenbrook, provides economic support for the area. The plant uses coal from Huntly and ironsand from the vast reserves of blacksand on the Northern heads of the Waikato River. The area remains a farming district as well.

## ENVIRONS & ATTRACTIONS
**Glenbrook Vintage Railway** This 6 km steam hauled railway route is operated by local enthusiasts on Sundays and Public Holidays (except 25 and 26 December) between Labour weekend in late October and Queens Birthday weekend in early June. Train rides and railway memorabilia are sold. The Glenbrook station is well signposted from local roads.

**Karioitahi Beach** This west coast blacksand beach is accessible by road through sandhills to the west of the borough.

**Sandspit** This pleasant picnic spot with views over part of the Manukau Harbour lies 2 km along Sandspit Road from Waiuku.

## LOCAL TOURING
**Manukau Heads** This term is loosely applied to the large peninsula north from Waiuku, which forms a boundary between the Manukau Harbour and the Tasman Sea. The roads wind over rolling countryside and there are small communities and beaches at Awhitu, Grahams Beach and Orua Bay. The South Head, 40 km from Waiuku has a trig station with a view over the entrance to the Manukau Harbour — the scene of many shipwrecks in the harbour's earlier days. There is a regional park at Awhitu.

**Clarks Beach** This holiday locality, with a long, shallow, sandy beach, lies on the southern shore of the Manukau Harbour. It is not suitable for swimming at low tides.

**See Also** Pukekohe, Tuakau and Auckland

---

# WANAKA SI
**Population** 1710
**Location** On Route 89, 2 km from its junction with Route 6, 57 km north of Cromwell.

---

Wanaka is a popular southern lakes tourist resort on the southern shores of Lake Wanaka. The lake itself is one of the South Island's largest, and is the source for the Clutha River. It measures about 48 by 6 km, at an altitude of 281 m. The head of the lake receives the Makarora River from the Haast Pass area.

Route 6 to the head of the lake skirts Lake Hawea before climbing over a narrow neck between the two lakes to hug the sides of the cliff at the head of Lake Wanaka. On the other side is a road that passes the Glendhu arm of the lake and leads up the Matukituki River valley towards Mt Aspiring (3027 m) and the Mt Aspiring National Park.

Route 89 goes up the Cardrona Valley and then over the Crown Range to zigzag down the other side towards Arrowtown. Though spectacular at its southern end, the road is unsealed, can be snowbound in winter and is prohibited to caravans.

Lake Hawea is a neighbour

*The township of Wanaka rests on the southern shores of the Lake.*

lake, which is about two-thirds the size of Lake Wanaka.

Prior to 1940 the settlement of Wanaka was called Pembroke. It has retained the flavour of a typical New Zealand holiday town, in comparison to Queenstown, which has become an international resort. The Cardrona Valley was the scene of a small goldrush from 1862. Wanaka is now mainly a tourist resort, surrounded by majestic mountain scenery, and a ski resort in winter. Wanaka junction is the intersection of Route 89 with Route 6, 2 km to the north-east of the town. Route 6 crosses the Clutha River, after it emerges from the lake, at Albert Town.

## ENVIRONS & ATTRACTIONS
**War Memorial Lookout** This

lookout over the town and lake is in Chalmers Street.

**Eely Point** A tree planted reserve on the lake shore.

**Pigeon Island** It is a local boat trip to this island with its own lake.

**Mt Iron** A 1¼ hr return walking track for a view at 527 m.

**Roys Peak** A track for extensive views from this high 1585 m viewpoint, 5 hr return. 7 km out on Glendhu Bay Road.

**Wanaka Maze** Passageways to get lost and found in; average time 40 minutes. 2 km from Wanaka.

**Glendhu Bay** A favourite part of the lake shore, 11 km around the lake. It is especially scenic with autumn colours.

**Mt Aspiring National Park Visitor Centre** On the main road, Route 89, immediately north-east of the town.

## LOCAL TOURING
**Clutha River Outlet** 12 km around the eastern side of the lake, it flows out and becomes the Clutha River.

**Dublin Bay** 18 km, via Albert Town, to this sheltered bay on the eastern side of the lake.

**Lake Hawea** This is a storage lake in conjunction with the Roxburgh/Clutha power scheme; its raised water level offers no beaches. There is a dam adjacent to the road and Hawea River outlet on Route 6.

**Timaru River** Picnic area 15 km around the eastern shoreline of Lake Hawea.

**Mt Grandview** A walking track from Back Road, Hawea, to 1398 m for extensive views.

**West Wanaka** 11 km past Glendhu Bay to this lake shore beach.

**Matukituki Valley** A pleasant drive into mountain scenery 47 km to Raspberry Creek and Cameron Flat. This road gives access to the Mt Aspiring National Park. The road beyond to Big

Creek has creeks to forward and should be avoided after rain.

**Matukituki Walk** A 9 km walk from the road's end at Raspberry Creek to the Aspiring Hut over grassy flats (2½ hr each way). Beyond Aspiring Hut to Cascade Saddle and the Dart Valley is for experienced parties only.

**Cardrona Valley** Take Route 89 up the first part of the Crown Range Road to reach old goldfields and hotel/restaurant; 25 km. Beyond is the Cardrona ski-field.

**Treble Cone** This ski-field is 29 km on the road out past Glendhu Bay. The ski-field is open approximately June to October.

**Luggate** This town is 13 km east on Route 6, at the junction of the link road with Route 8A to Tarras and the Lindis Valley. It is the site of an old flour mill used during the goldrush days. Lucerne is now grown locally and processed into stock food.

**Tarras** A locality on Route 8 immediately north of the 8A junction from Luggate. The Lindis River and other streams have been scoured for gold with limited success. The Lindis Pass was an access to central Otago before routes via the Dunstan and the Pigroot were in use.

**See Also** Omarama, Haast and Cromwell

# WANGANUI NI

**Population** 38 084

**Location** At the mouth of the Wanganui River and the junction of Routes 3 and 4; 195 km north of Wellington, 160 km south-east of New Plymouth.

The locality of Wanganui and its river made it a popular habitat for both Maoris and Pakeha, but not without several conflicts. There were a number of inter-tribal clashes, including a battle in the early 1800s. In 1830 the renegade Te Rauparaha attacked and ate many of the local Maoris.

There were also accounts of murder and massacre in the early days of European settlement. On behalf of the New Zealand Company, Colonel Wakefield purchased the town site with an assortment of blankets, mirrors and pipes. The Maoris, however, apparently thought these were gifts and only realised later it was payment for their land. After more clashes, the Maoris were finally given 1000 pounds for approximately 32 000 ha.

The town was originally named Petre. The central city bridge and the National Park upriver are spelt Whanganui. The city has a port for coastal shipping at Castlecliff, which is at the river mouth. The railway (now freight only) passes through suburban Eastown and Aromoho; downtown Wanganui and Castlecliff are branch lines.

## ENVIRONS & ATTRACTIONS

**Queen's Park** Originally a stockade to protect early settlers, this park now contains the Regional Museum, Sarjeant Art Gallery and War Memorial Hall. The museum houses one of the country's finest collection of Maori artifacts, including a war canoe and a collection of Lindauer paintings of Maori figures. There are also other relics from the days of British troops and early settlers. Open daily except Christmas Day and Good Friday. The nearby art gallery contains British and New Zealand paintings, including Hoyte and Goldie. Open every afternoon. The War Memorial Hall features a modern architectural style. Queen's Park is one block from the Main Street.

**Cook's Gardens** Also close to the main street is the 1880 Watch

Tower and the Ward Telescope Observatory. However, the main feature in the gardens is the sports centre, where New Zealander Peter Snell first broke the 4-minute mile in 1962.

**Durie Hill** Across the Whanganui City Bridge is a pedestrian tunnel leading to an elevator that rises 66 m through the hill to a lookout. A short walk to the nearby War Memorial Tower gives an even better (and windier!) view.

**Virginia Lake** The neatly laid out gardens, hot-houses, lake and floating fountain are 2 km north on Route 3. The lake is situated on St Johns hill and a lookout from the hill over the city is nearby on Parsons Street.

**Putiki Church** Near the southern end of Cobham Bridge, St Pauls Memorial Church, which was built in 1937, features Maori carvings and decoration. This is the fifth church built on this site; previous churches were destroyed by fire and earthquake.

## LOCAL TOURING

**Castlecliff** The suburban beach resort of Castlecliff lies on the coast, 9 km west of the central city. The road to it passes the river mouth and port.

**River Trips** An old river vessel *Waireka* gives local trips on

# WANGANUI RIVER

According to Maori legend, when Mt Egmont (called Taranaki) had an argument with the other three peaks of the central North Island, it fled to the west, gouging out the river course as it went. The river is 290 km long (the third longest in New Zealand) and is possibly the most beautiful. It rises on Mt Tongariro and flows through Taumaranui and some inaccessible country to Pipiriki, Wanganui and the coast. Most of the surrounding land is very hilly and forested, and a new National Park is being developed around it — probably with Pipiriki as its centre.

The river was a favoured waterway to and from the central North Island. A chain of mission stations was set up in 1843 by Reverend Richard Taylor, and a Catholic mission was established at Jerusalem by Mother Mary Aubert. In the late 19th and early 20th centuries, there was much European river traffic on the river. A three-day boat trip via the Pipiriki hotel and an en-route houseboat (moored originally near the confluence of the Ohura River and later near the confluence of the Retaruke River) was a popular trip.

There is a river road from Wanganui to Pipiriki and Raetihi (refer to Raetihi), and parts of the river around Taumaranui are also accessible. However, the central and most beautiful parts of the river, do not have road access. Jetboat trips are available, and there are walking tracks (Matemateaonga, Maungapurua and Kaiwhakauau) adjacent to these central parts.

After World War I returned servicemen were granted blocks of land to farm, but were beaten by poor soils and poor access and most farms were abandoned. Roading was brought too late, and the 'bridge to nowhere', a concrete structure now surrounded by bush, is a symbol that the roads were abandoned as well. Plans for a railway linking Wanganui and Raetihi never eventuated. Today access to the river remains poor, and the development of the new Whanganui River National Park is awaited with interest.

Sundays to Hipango Park, 32 km out of Wanganui. The Holly Lodge Winery also has boat trips most days to its wine and craft centre on the river. Longer jetboat trips to Pipiriki and beyond may be arranged. The river used to be navigable as far as Taumaranui. A five-day downriver cruise and camping trip from Taumaranui runs weekly in summer. Canoe trips are also available downriver from Taumaranui.

**See Also** Taumarunui, Raetihi, Patea, Bulls and Marton.

---

# WARKWORTH NI
**Population** 1989
**Location** On Route 1, 67 km north of Auckland.

---

In common with most of the North there seems to have been extensive Maori habitation in the area. Contact with Europeans began in the 1820s with seamen and timber traders searching for kauri spars. A timbermill was established in 1854 followed in 1865 by a cement works. The Mahurangi River once gave shipping access to the town wharf. The business area of Warkworth is 1 km off Route 1 and is worth the detour.

## ENVIRONS & ATTRACTIONS
**Kowhai Park** A small picnic area near the town centre.
**Parry Kauri Park** A readily accessible (2 km) reserve of native bush containing two large kauri trees, up to 800 years old.
**Satellite Earth Station** This New Zealand link to the world-wide satellite communications system is situated on a side road, 5 km south of Warkworth. There are three large dish antennae. The facility has a public observation and display area.

## LOCAL TOURING
**Mahurangi Peninsula** This partially developed peninsula jutting out from Warkworth includes the three fine beaches of Snells, Algies and Martins. The road leads out from the northern end of the town.
**Mahurangi Regional Reserve** This reserve, which is administered by the Regional Authority, is 8 km along a side road off Route 1, 11 km south of Warkworth. A narrow road goes to Sullivans beach and there are walking tracks to other beaches. A similar farm park is being developed at Tawharanui — another peninsula accessible via the northern junction from Warkworth.
**Sandspit and Kawau Island** This marina and wharf 8 km from the northern end of Warkworth provides launch access to nearby Kawau Island, which is about 8 km offshore. Part of this island belongs to the Hauraki Gulf Maritime Park and it offers beaches and walks. The island is remembered for Manganese mining last century, and for being the residence of Sir George Grey, Governor of New Zealand. A ferry leaves daily about 10 am, returning about 5 pm.
**Leigh** Holiday settlement 23 km north-east of Warkworth. There is a walking track (1 hr return) around Leigh Harbour (Omaha cove). Alternatively take Goat Island Road to the Marine Laboratory operated by Auckland University, to commence a 2½ hr cliff top return walk with coastal views. Goat Island is part of the Hauraki Gulf Maritime Park.

**See Also** Wellsford, Maungaturoto and Helensville

# WELLINGTON NI

**Population** 400 424

**Location** At the southern end of the North Island, 655 km south of Auckland, 145 km south of Palmerston North, 334 km south of Napier, 355 km south of New Plymouth.

This listing includes the Hutt Valley and the Kapiti Coast areas, which are separate local bodies. Wellington has been the capital city of New Zealand since 1865. It was named after the first Duke of Wellington. The harbour is called Port Nicholson, after the 1825 Harbour Master at Sydney.

The Maori history of the area starts with Kupe's visit about 950, but tradition places Whatonga and his sons (about 1150) as being the founders of Maori habitation in the area.

Edward Gibbon Wakefield and his British-based New Zealand Company established the first settlers on the Petone foreshore, though they shifted to the Thorndon foreshore (persuaded by a fire, an earthquake and a flood), where the central city is today. Much harbour area has been reclaimed since. In 1842 the government (then in Auckland) ruled that the New Zealand Company land purchases were questionable, and one transaction was ruled invalid. Local Maoris were perturbed at the speed at which they were losing land, and in 1845 there were skirmishes in the Hutt Valley and the Plimmerton area.

In 1865 Wellington became the capital of New Zealand as Auckland was deemed to be too far away by South Island settlements and today it remains the capital and the centre of government for the country. Many businesses and institutions have also chosen to have their head office here. The Wellington city area is the commercial and

*The Royal Port Nicholson Yacht Club with Mt Victoria in the background.*

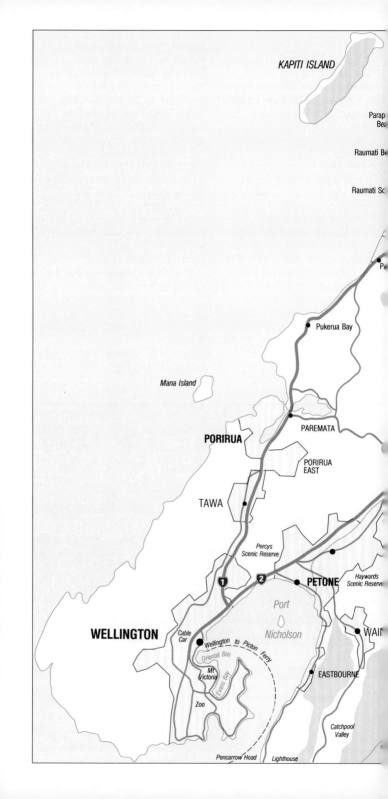

administrative centre, while the Hutt Valley is a centre for industry. The Kapiti coast area is mainly a dormitory suburb.

The port can handle overseas shipping and containers. The harbour is largely land-locked and surrounded by high hills on most sides. Suburban electric trains operate to the Hutt Valley (Petone, Lower Hutt and Upper Hutt) at the head of the harbour, to the Kapiti Coast (Porirua, Paekakariki and Paraparaumu), and on a shorter line to Johnsonville. Motor bus and some trolley buses serve other parts of the built-up areas.

There is a ferry service from Wellington to Picton (in the South Island) several times a day. The city is the southern terminus for the North Island main trunk railway north to Auckland; also to New Plymouth and up the east coast. It has an international airport at Rongotai, and has scheduled flights to Australia as well as to many parts of New Zealand.

Wellington's main shopping streets are Lambton Quay, Willis Street, Manners Street and Cuba Street (Mall). At the southern end of Lambton Quay under the Bank of New Zealand Tower there is an underground shopping area.

The Victoria University for the Wellington area is situated at Kelburn, and is visible from the cablecar ride.

A sightseeing idea for Wellington-based travellers is to take a day trip to Picton. Inter-island ferries operate several times a day out of Wellington Harbour across Cook Strait to the Marlborough Sounds. The ferry terminal is at the northern end of Aotea Quay, but there is a connecting bus service from platform 9 at the Wellington railway station.

Other places of interest in the Wellington area are a Rugby

309

*Wellington Harbour.*

Museum (Lower Hutt), a Cricket
Museum (Basin Reserve,
Newtown) and a Doll and Toy
Museum (Paraparaumu).

## ENVIRONS & ATTRACTIONS
**Parliament Buildings**  Built in
1922 from Coromandel granite
and Takaka marble, this building
contains the House of
Representatives and also an upper
house chamber that is now used
for ceremonial occasions. A small

entrance beside the main steps is
the office for visitor tours. The
adjacent round 'Beehive' building
was designed by Sir Basil Spence
and erected in 1981. It houses
ministerial offices and the cabinet
room. Also adjacent is the General
Assembly Library, built in 1897,
which serves as an extensive
library for Parliament and
contains one copy of every New
Zealand publication. Statues of
Seddon and Ballance — former

New Zealand Prime Ministers — are nearby. There is also a cenotaph erected in 1929 in honour of World War I. This complex is situated near Lambton Quay and Bowen Street.

**National Library of New Zealand**  Situated in Molesworth Street, open Mon–Fri 9 am–5 pm. It also houses the historic collections of the Alexander Turnbull Library, including manuscripts by early pacific voyagers, New Zealand visitors, a Milton collection and other historical publications. Open Mon–Wed 9 am–8 pm.

**Government Building**  This is the largest wooden building in the Southern Hemisphere. It was built in 1876 and is in Lambton Quay,  near the main railway station.

**Old St Paul's Church**  A church built in 1866 from native timbers in the Gothic revival style. This imposing and historic building is in Mulgrave Street.

**National War Memorial, Art Gallery and Museum** A complex in Buckle Street. The memorial has a hall of memories and carillon. The museum has displays on Maori, Polynesian and early settlers. The art gallery has a collection of early etchings and engravings. Open daily 10 am–4.45 pm.

**National Archives** Situated in the Air New Zealand building in Vivian Street, it includes the original Treaty of Waitangi. Open Mon–Fri 9 am–5 pm.

**Wellington Cablecar** From Lambton Quay to Kelburn, this 610 m long cableway rises 120 m in height on a 1 in 5 gradient. It operates every 10 minutes; weekdays to 10 pm, weekends to 6 pm. At the top there are views of Wellington, the Carter observatory (open Tuesday nights March–October), the meteorological office, and entrance to the Botanic Gardens.

**Botanic Gardens** An interpretive centre (with maps of the area) is at the top entrance near the cablecar (open daily till 4 pm). There are paths down the slopes to 'the Dell' and Lady Norwood Rose Gardens, which are at the bottom entrance and are also accessible through Bolton Street.

**Antrim House** Built in 1903, this is now the headquarters for the New Zealand Historic Places Trust. In Boulcott Street or up Plimmer steps from Lambton Quay, it is open weekdays 10 am–4.30 pm.

**Ascot Terrace** A small street of 1870 houses; view from road only. Also note Plimmer House (historic home and restaurant) in Boulcott Street and a colonial cottage at 68 Nairn Street (open Wed–Fri 10 am–4 pm, weekends 1–4.30 pm).

**Katherine Mansfield** Memorial Park to New Zealand's most famous short story writer in Murphy Street; her birthplace at 25 Tinakori Road is also open to the public.

**Other Downtown Buildings** The Wellington Town Hall and Michael Fowler Centre are in Wakefield Street; the City Art Gallery (open 10.45 am–6 pm) is in Victoria Street; Wellington Central Library is in Mercer Street; the Planetarium is in Harris Street; the Wellington Trade Centre is in Cuba Mall; and the Ngati Poneka Marae is at the bottom of Featherston Street. Poneke is Maori for 'Port Nick', the abbreviated name for Port Nicholson.

**Johnston Hill** Hatton Street, off Karori Road, leads to Fletchers lookout, which gives views over parts of Wellington and its harbour. Penilgton's track leads up the hill for 20–30 minutes to the summit at 360 m for even better views.

**Tinakori Hill** Behind the downtown area, this part of the city green belt offers walking tracks through the bush with views. The northern walkway commences in St Mary's Road, off the top of Bowen Street, near the Botanic Gardens. (1 hr to summit, 2 hr round trip).

**Newtown Zoo** In Daniel Street, Newton, this contains the usual zoo animals plus a nocturnal kiwi house. Open daily 8.30 am–4.30 pm.

**Otari Museum of Native Plants** In Wilton Road, Wilton, this is an open air collection of New Zealand trees and plants.

**Other Collections** An interesting Maritime Museum is in Shed 11, Jervois Quay, open weekdays 9 am–4.30 pm, weekends 1–4.30 pm. The Alex MacKay geological museum is in the Cotton building at Victoria

University; Post Office Museum and archives are at Thorndon Quay; the Film Archives museum of cinema is in Tory Street; and the Castle collection of musical instruments is in Colombo Street.

## LOCAL TOURING
### WELLINGTON'S OUTER SUBURBS

**Mt Victoria** This 196 m ridge offers excellent views over the Wellington city and harbour area. A suggested road access is via narrow Majoribanks Street (off Kent Terrace) and Hawker Street, following signs around to the top. There are several stopping places at the peak; carry on south along the ridge to exit at Alexandra Road off Constable Street.

**Oriental Bay** Kent Terrace leads into Oriental Parade around the inner Lambton Harbour opposite the downtown area. It is a residential area with views.

**Marine Drive** Follow Oriental Parade around Point Jerningham into Evans Bay, pass shipping slips along Evans Bay Parade, follow Cobham Drive to the end of the airport runway, and then Shelly Bay Road along the other side of Evans Bay. Roads lead from here up to Mt Crawford (163 m). Alternatively you can carry on at sea level around Point Halswell to see Massey Memorial (commemorating previous Prime Ministers), then continue south past the beaches of Scorching Bay and Worser Bay to Seatoun. Breaker Bay Road leads south to the harbour entrance, from where you can look out to Barretts Reef, scene of the shipwreck disasters of *Wanganella* in 1947 and *Wahine* (51 passengers drowned) in 1968. Pencarrow Head is across on the other side of the harbour entrance. The road carries on into Lyall Bay, passing the southern end of Wellington Airport and then into Helton Bay and Island Bay. You can return to the city either directly from Island Bay along the Parade into Adelaide Road, or around the Esplanade into Happy Valley Road.

**Makara Beach** 16 km west of Wellington on Ohariu Bay, this is a remote area on the rugged west coast. The Makara walkway offers 6 km of tramping (3–4 hr).

### HUTT VALLEY

**Petone and Lower Hutt** These residential areas in the Hutt Valley, bounded by high hills at the head of the harbour, also have a concentration of industrial and commercial areas. The Hutt River flows down the valley into Port Nicholson. The area is connected by motorway and electric railway with Wellington city centre.

**Petone Early Settlers Museum** Situated on the site of the original Petone settlement, the museum displays settlers relics. On the Esplanade, open weekdays noon–4 pm, weekends 11 am–4 pm.

**Dowse Art Museum** An art collection, which includes Maori Pataka displays, on Laings Road. Open weekdays 10 am–4 pm, weekends 1–5 pm.

**Percys Scenic Reserve** A 20 ha bush-clad park, with a 20-minute climb to a waterfall. Off Western Hutt Road near Petone railway station.

**Riddiford Park** Horticultural Park and gardens with bedding plants, conservatory, orchid display and fern house. Access is via Queens Drive or Myrtle Street.

**Haywards Scenic Reserve** Original bush reserve on the eastern slopes of the Hutt Valley. 30-minute bush walks for view. Off Whites Line East Road.

**Other Parks** Jubilee Park in Normandale Road has a begonia house and fernery with some small bush walks; also note Maidstone Park, Harcourt Park, Pleasure Park (with children's play area) and also the Petone Esplanade.

## UPPER HUTT

32 km north of Wellington this residential area in the northern part of the Hutt Valley is served by motorway and electric railway from Wellington.

**Wallaceville Blockhouse** Off McHardie Street, this wooden building was built during the Maori land skirmishes but was never used.

**Silverstream Railway Museum** This train museum is on Reynolds Bach Drive. Open weekends 1–5 pm. Train rides on Sundays.

**Staglands Wildlife Reserve** This reserve containing animals and birds is up the Akatarawa Valley Road. 16 km from Upper Hutt; open daily, except Tuesday, to sunset.

**Akatarawa Road** Drive through bush up and over the Akatarawa Range to Waikanae on the Kapiti Coast (37 km from Upper Hutt).

**Kaitoke Regional Reserve** This bush reserve and Pakuratahi Gorge are 13 km north of Upper Hutt. There is a nature loop walk (15 minutes) and river terrace walk (1 hr round trip).

**Rimutaka Incline Walkway** A walkway that mainly follows the route of the old Fell railway line to Wairarapa. Ascend for 3–4 hr to the 800 m summit tunnel, then descend for 90 minutes to Cross Creek on the other side.

**Wainuiomata** This suburb is hidden over the Wainui Hill 6 km from Lower Hutt. The hill road to it offers excellent views over the Hutt Valley and harbour; there is also a signposted 10-minute walk to a better vantage point. There are several other tracks in the hills around Wainuiomata into the Wainuiomata scenic reserve and the Rimutaka Forest Park.

**Catchpool Valley** This part of the 120 000 ha Rimutaka Forest Park is 9 km south of Wainuiomata (45 km from Wellington). There is a picnic ground, which is sometimes the site for outdoor concerts. Note the Catchpool walking track (45 minutes return), the Orongorongo (1½ hr each way) track, and the older and muddier Five Mile track, which offers interesting bushwalks.

**Eastbourne** This seemingly remote hillside suburb is 24 km right around to the eastern side of the harbour (there is direct ferry service).

**Butterfly Creek** This track, which is accessible via Kowhai Street and Muritai Park from Eastbourne is a popular bush outing for Wellingtonians. There is natural bush and picnic sites with four walks varying between 60 and 90 minutes.

**Pencarrow Light** A walk (3 hr round trip) or bike ride (8 km each way) along a road south from Eastbourne to the site of this old lighthouse at the entrance to Wellington Harbour.

## KAPITI COAST

**Porirua** This is a satellite town 20 km north on Route 2. It surrounds the Porirua Harbour and is connected by motorway and electric railway service to Wellington. Police and Traffic Departments have training centres here; the former also has a museum.

**Porirua Museum** On the corner of Te Hiko and Ngatitoa Streets, this has exhibits, displays and diagrams, which illustrate the history of the area. Open Wed–Sun, 10 am–4.30 pm.

**Paremata Barracks** Over the Paremata Bridge, spanning the entrance to the Pauatahanui Inlet (with an alternative route through to Lower Hutt) are the remains of the Paremata Barracks. Poorly built in 1847 as a military post to guard Wellington's northern approaches, the building started to deteriorate almost before it was finished. The barracks were not used in battle and only some fenced-off ruins remain today.

**Colonial Knob Walkway** This walk (5 hr round trip) begins off Broken Hill Road entrance to the reserve, and leads to the summit for views. It emerges at Elsdon youth camp and Raiha Street. Most of the track is gentle but there is a steep part.

**Gear Homestead** The fully restored home of the meat packing tycoon. Whitford Brown Avenue.

**Paekakariki** This northern Wellington suburb is bound between the sea and the hills. Road and rail access from Wellington is via a scenic coastal route along Route 2. Behind the town the Paekakariki Hill Road — an alternative route to Wellington — offers an outstanding lookout from the hilltop.

**Paekakariki Engine Shed** A steam train museum open Saturdays 9 am–5 pm. The station area is a historic precinct.

**Queen Elizabeth Park** This coastal strip of farmland, sand dunes, marsh flats, peat swamps and playing fields is between Paekakariki and Raumati South. At MacKays crossing, north of Paekakariki, the Memorial Gates commemorate the camp for United States Marines located here during World War II.

**Tramway Museum** At MacKays crossing, this museum offers both trams on display and those running. 2 km of track, operating weekends and holidays 11 am–5 pm (44 km from Wellington).

**Southward Car Museum** On Otaihanga Road at Waikanae. A fine and famous collection of veteran and vintage cars. Open daily 9 am–5 pm.

**Paraparaumu** Northern terminus of Wellington's electric suburban railway. The Paraparaumu and Raumati beach foreshores with play areas are 3 km west. The beach foreshore continues up to Waikanae.

**Nga Manu Bird Sanctuary** Off Route 1 at Waikanae this collection of birds includes kakas, keas and ducks. There are also bush walks through the sanctuary. Open Tues–Fri 10 am–4.30 pm; weekends 10 am–5.30 pm. Also in the area is the Waikanea River Mouth Wildlife Reserve (visit at low tide for birdlife; there are short tracks); the Waimeha Lagoon Wildlife Reserve; the Aotea Lagoon, with rose gardens, ferns, walks and play area, in Papakowhai Road; the Otaihanga Reserve and Edgewater Reserve.

**Lindale Farm Park** Daily sheep shows (11.30 am) and cattle shows (2 pm), cheese factory and farm walks. Open 9 am–5 pm, off the main road at Paraparaumu.

**Our Lady of Lourdes** Monument above Paraparaumu. Access track and views, via Tongariro Street.

**Kapiti Island** Formerly a stronghold of Te Rauparaha, then a whaling base, it is now a bird sanctuary administered by the Department of Survey and Lands. A permit is required for landing and walking on the island.

**See Also** Otaki, Featherston and Picton

---

# WELLSFORD NI
**Population** 1627
**Location** On Route 1, 88 km north of Auckland.

---

Originally called Whakapirau the name was changed to Wellsford, which is an acronym of the initials of early settlers. Wellsford originally developed as a kauri gum digging settlement, but is now well established as a farming community.

## LOCAL TOURING
**Kaipara Harbour** Route 16 provides an alternative link south to Auckland, via Helensville, and Auckland's western suburbs. This road gives views over the southern reaches of the large Kaipara Harbour — well used as a shipping artery in days gone by. Wellsford itself is not on the harbour, but was partially served through Port Albert, a now abandoned settlement established in 1860.

**See Also** Warkworth, Matakohe and Dargaville

# WESTPORT SI
**Population** 4660
**Location** On the west coast of the South Island, 6 km along Route 67 from its junction with Route 6. 104 km north of Greymouth.

Route 6 comes down the Buller Gorge and turns south down the west coast on the outskirts of the town of Westport. You must, however, take Route 67 to enter the town even though some of the listed touring sights are south of the town.

Westport has been a large coal exporter from its port on the Buller River. A lot of coal is also railed through to Christchurch and its port of Lyttelton. Timber was also a principal industry and there is a cement works.

Although it was the search for gold that started the town, it is the coal industry (black gold) that has ensured its continued existence. A British engineer Sir John Coode designed the river port for its most effective use.

The Westport coal is a shiny black bituminous type and has better heating qualities than the country's normal lignite or sub-bituminous types. The town is situated on the right (northern) bank of the Buller River.

## ENVIRONS & ATTRACTIONS
**Coaltown** Photographs, relics and displays of coalmining in the area, including a display on the Denniston Incline. Open daily 9 am–4.30 pm, Queen Street.
**Victoria Square** Gardens and sport centre in the town centre.
**Westport Domain** A wooded picnic spot at the eastern end of Palmerston Street.
**North Beach** Local town beach (usually with much driftwood on its shores) at the western end of Derby Street.
**Carters Beach** A popular beach on the coast south of the river, 5 km from Westport.

## LOCAL TOURING
**Cape Foulwind** A lighthouse stands at the top of the cliff, with a track down to the beach. 12 km (signposted) south of Westport, off Route 67 after crossing the Buller Bridge.
**Tauranga Bay** Sheltered bay and beach a little past Cape Foulwind. 15 km from Westport.
**Cape Foulwind Walkway** A 4 km (1–1½ hr) walk from Cape Foulwind to Tauranga Bay with attractive coastal views and also a seal colony.
**Charleston** The remains of this once thriving goldtown are on Route 7, 25 km south of Westport. Only one of its 90 hotels remains and it has a display of photographs of the old days. 20 km further south at Woodpecker Bay is the site of Brighton, another old goldtown.
**Mitchells Gully** This working goldmine with waterwheel and tunnels is 1 km north of

*The Buller River.*

Charleston. Open daily
9 am–4 pm.

**Denniston** The Denniston
Incline was a gravity worked
tramway where wagons of coal
were lowered 610 m down the
mountainside from the Denniston
coalfield to the railway below. The
descending wagons would haul
the empty ones back up along
with equipment, supplies and the
occasional brave miner. Although
the incline has gone, the remains
of the town on top of the hill are
still visible. As there is now road
access to the top, the miners
reside at the bottom in
Waimangaroa, 16 km north of
Westport on Route 67. The
Denniston walkway starts at the
top and winds 5 km down to
Waimangaroa (or vice versa if you
prefer!). There is a side access to
Denniston Road halfway along
the walkway.

**Granity** 29 km north on Route
67, this town serviced the
Stockton coalfield, 6 km up a side
road. At Stockton an overhead
cableway carried the coal from an
opencast mine. There is a good
coastal view from near the top of
the hill.

**Ngakawau** The present rail
terminus for coal brought by
cableway from the mine at
Stockton is 31 km north.

**Charming Creek Walkway** A
spectacular walk along the old
railway formation from
Ngakawau, up the Ngakawau
Gorge, to the Charming Creek
coal mine and the Seddonville
road. The 10.5 km walk takes
2½–3 hr. There is road access to
both ends — the other end being
the side road through
Seddonville.

**Chasm Creek Walkway** A
1 km easy walk off the road to
Seddonville, crossing the Chasm
Stream and following the
Mokihinui River. Easily combined
with the Charming Creek
Walkway. There is a road at both
ends.

**Seddonville** Small timber and coal community 47 km north of Westport. Access to both Charming Creek and Chasm Walkways.

**Britannia Track** This graded walk commences 19.5 km north of Westport and follows through the Mt Frederick Forest passing the sites of the Great Republic battery and Stoney Creek battery to the Britannia goldmine and Stamper battery. 3½ hr return.

**See Also** Karamea, Inangahua and Punakaiki

# WHAKATANE NI
**Population** 12 800
**Location** On Route 2, 96 km east of Tauranga, 202 km north-west of Gisborne.

Situated at the mouth of the Whakatane River, which forms its harbour, Whakatane is the principal centre of the Rangitaiki Plains. The town's name is associated with the arrival of the *Mataatua* canoe, part of the great fleet, but the area traces its history back to the arrival of the Polynesian navigator Toi in 1150. Long before the arrival of Europeans, Whakatane was a thickly populated Maori stronghold, and until the turn of the century the number of Pakeha residents remained small. There was a small Hauhau disturbance in 1865, and Te Kooti sacked the town in 1869.

Although Whakatane remains the chief town and servicing area in the eastern Bay of Plenty, it is now dominated by the vast board and paper mills on the fringe of the town. Whakatane lays claim to being the North Island's top sunshine town. Accordingly, particularly in summer, nearby Ohope Beach is very popular.

The railway serves Whakatane West 6 km away; lines-end for the Bay of Plenty railway is at Taneatua 12 km away. The town is served by scheduled air services but the harbour can only be used by light boats.

## ENVIRONS & ATTRACTIONS
**Pohaturoa Rock** Situated in the centre of town, this imposing rock has had a sacred Maori history. A model of the *Mataatua* canoe is beside the rock.

**Whakatane Heads** A short 2 km drive beyond the town centre to the traditional landing place of the *Mataatua* canoe.

**Puketapu Lookout** Near the corner of Seaview and Hillcrest Roads, on the hill behind the town, this vantage point offers views over the town and coastline. Nearby is Toi's Pa, possibly the oldest such site in New Zealand.

**Wairere Waterfall** The Wairere stream falls from the hills behind the town. Seen from Mataatua Street off the Strand.

**Whakatane Museum** In Boon Street, off the Strand, this museum houses Maori artifacts and New Zealand books.

**Whakatane Board Mills** This large factory mainly produces cardboard. It is situated off Route 2 on the western outskirts of the town. Visitor inspections 10.30 am Mon–Fri, February through to November.

**Guerren's Mill** Historic site, identified by a memorial, where Frenchman Jean Guerren fought and held up Te Kooti's advance on Whakatane for two days before being killed. The site is signposted 6 km out on a main road to Taneatua.

## LOCAL TOURING
**Ohope Beach** 6 km east of Whakatane, over the headland,

## WHITE ISLAND

The volcanic White Island is approximately 50 km out in the Bay of Plenty; it is visible from Whakatane. The island is so named (by Captain Cook) because of the white steam usually seen escaping from the crater. The island is quite active with thermal activity and with large sulphur deposits. These were mined until 1914 when 10 people were killed in an explosion. The island is now off limits to tourists, but you can charter aerial flights over it.

this is a long and popular beach. Although this resort has a swelling population in summer, it is virtually a suburb of Whakatane with around 2000 local residents.

**Port Ohope** This is an extension of Ohope Beach, situated on a peninsula backing onto Ohiwa Harbour. It is good for fishing and picnicking.

**Awakeri Hot Springs** These are 14 km from Whakatane on the road to Rotorua (Route 30). There are soda thermal pools with camping ground and picnic area. Open daily to 9.30 pm. Public and private pools are available.

**Waimana Valley** Off Route 2 beyond Taneatua, the Waimana Valley Road leads through river valley and picnic areas. The valley is surrounded by the Urewera National Park.

**Urewera National Park** A fuller description of this vast park is contained under the Waikaremoana heading. There is a ranger station at Taneatua serving the northern parts of the park. Access to the northern parts is either up the Whakatane River valley through Ruatoki or the Waimana River valley through Matahi.

**Matata** On Route 2, 22 km west of Whakatane, this beach area beneath the cliffs offers a long, sandy coastline. The Matata Lagoon is also a bird sanctuary for wild ducks and swans.

**See Also** Opotiki, Kawerau and Waikaremoana

# WHANGAMATA NI
**Population** 2479
**Location** On Route 25, 29 km north of Waihi, 39 km south of Tairua.

Situated on the east coast of the Coromandel Peninsula, Whangamata settlement is a developing beach holiday area. Consequently its population in summer is boosted by holiday makers. Some big game fishing is done off shore, and there are tracks into the ranges inland. In common with other Coromandel area towns, it has had a history of timber and gold, and some traces of those days are still visible in the ranges (Tairua Forest) behind the town. Road access was opened up in 1928.

## ENVIRONS & ATTRACTIONS
**Local Beaches** Whangamata has an ocean beach and a sheltered shoreline up the harbour. The Otahu River mouth at the southern end of town is a pleasant picnic spot.

## LOCAL TOURING
**Opoutere** A small beach community 19 km north on a side road with an ocean beach and a harbour area. Just past the settlement there is a steep walk to the Wharekawa lookout, which overlooks the harbour.

**Onemana** A developing resort area on a side road branching off 30 km north.

*A Maori Ratana Church in the North Island.*

*Sunrise at Whangarei Heads.*

**Whangamata Peninsula** Off the side road to Onemana (Whitipirorua Road) take Peninsula Road the length of the Whangamata Peninsula to a neatly laid out picnic area and lookout for views back over Whangamata. From here there is a short 20-minute loop track to another lookout and a beach track down to water level (on the wrong side of the harbour). Off Peninsula Road, 1½ km before its end, there is a 20-minute walk down through pine forest to Te Ananui ocean beach.

**Wharekawa Valley** Taungatara Road branches inland 3 km north off the Onemana Road junction (and forestry headquarters), and after 3.5 km provides access to several walking tracks, including

the Luck at Last goldmine — a scenic 1 hr walk to the remains of the old battery and other gold relics.

**Wentworth Valley** Inland to the ranges up the Wentworth River Road, a popular walk leads on from the road's end to Wentworth Falls, 1 hr each way. There are now trail bike tracks over the ranges near here; the old Wires Track is reportedly overgrown.

**Wharekirauponga Stream Track** It is 6.5 km south of Whangamata to Parakawai Quarry Road. From the Quarry there is a 3 hr round trip walk along the route of an old horse drawn tramway that served the Royal Standard and Royal Sovereign goldmine and battery. Although a lot of battery

Captain Cook in 1769. Shipping was the prevalent mode of communication with the rest of New Zealand. The railway from Auckland was not completed until 1925, and roading remained poor until the mid-1930s.

Whangarei was declared a city in 1964. It remains the leading commercial centre north of Auckland and a regional base for agriculture. It has an industrial base with its port and other industries include the Portland Cement Works and the Marsden Point Oil Refinery.

## ENVIRONS & ATTRACTIONS

**Clapham Clock Museum**
Unusual collection of more than 500 clocks and watches. Started by Mr Archibald Clapham, and later acquired by the city council. Situated in the Rose Gardens, Water Street.

**Coronation Scenic Reserve**
Set in the Western hills in beautiful surroundings. The main walk track, the Frank Holman Memorial Track (2 hr) is a comfortable walk. The track runs through magnificent native bush, past Maori diggings and pa sites. The Rust Track features an old gold mine. Access is via Western Hills Drive.

**Mair Park**  At the western foot of Parahiki, this park has well preserved native bush, which is bisected by the Hatea River.

**Parahaki**  A bush-clad volcanic mountain. The summit can be reached by Memorial Drive or a 30-minute (one way) walk from Mair Park, for views over Whangarei and surrounding area.

**Town Basin**  A haven for yachts and a hive of activity on sunny days when boating enthusiasts abound.

**Northland Regional Museum**
Historic house and exhibits on 25 ha of land. Open Tue–Sat 10 am–4 pm. 8 km out on Dargaville Road.

machinery was dragged up the tramway, no gold was ever dragged out.

**Whiritoa**  Small beach resort 16 km south.

**See Also** Thames, Tairua and Waihi

# WHANGAREI NI

**Population**  40 179
**Location**  170 km north of Auckland, accessible on Route 1.

Originally known as Ahipupu, Whangarei's first pakeha resident was William Carruth in 1839. Whangarei developed as a settlement in the early 1860s.

The name Whangarei originally applied to a small place near the harbour heads, visited by

**Whangarei Falls** 4.5 km out on the north-eastern boundary of the city, the falls drop 24 m into a forest-fringed pool, which can be viewed from a bridge across the stream.

## LOCAL TOURING
**Marsden Point Oil Refinery** There is a visitors centre near the main entrance. Crude oil from the Middle East and Taranaki is processed here to supply 80 per cent of the country's needs, including petroleum, diesel oils, jet fuel and asphalt. Nearby is Marsden Power Station, which is actually two stations (Marsden A and B). Residual oil from the oil refinery is piped to fuel the two 120 megawatt generators. Marsden B has been officially mothballed because of continued fluctuations in the world price of oil.
**Pukenui Forest Walkway** This loop track through both open pasture land and native bush is 5 km west of Kamo on Three Mile Bush road. Rock walls are a feature of the pastureland. Many native trees are in the forest, including some kauri. The 10 km round trip walk takes 3–4 hours.
**Ruakaka Beach** This is the nearest and perhaps most popular beach and is about 20 minutes south of the city near the Marsden Point area.
**Tutukaka and Matapouri** Tutukaka (29 km) is a sheltered harbour and picnic resort. There are deep-sea fishing facilities and permanent marina berthing. Matapouri (35 km) is a fine stretch of sandy beach in an almost circular bay. A pleasant round trip from Whangarei, heading in a north-east direction, is available by taking the direct route out through Ngunguru and returning via Hikurangi and Kamo.
**Waro Scenic Reserve** This reserve is at Hikurangi, on the main road north of Whangarei. Scattered through the reserve are numerous heavily eroded outcrops of limestone rock.
**Whangarei Heads** The heads is a craggy promontory, dominated by Mt Manaia (419 m). The road starts over the Town Basin and goes in a south-easterly direction for 35 km. Drive past Onerahi (Whangarei's airport) and continue south to Parua Bay, McLeod Bay and Urquhart Bay. A smaller road leads over to Ocean Beach. There are views across to Marsden Point and Ruakaka from the harbour-side bays.

**See Also** Waipu, Dargaville and Bay of Islands

# WHITIANGA NI
**Population** 2503
**Location** On Route 25, 114 km north of Waihi, 46 km south-east of Coromandel by Route 25.

In 1769 Captain Cook anchored in Mercury Bay, off Whitianga, and took possession of New Zealand in the name of King George III. He and his party also made observations on the transit of Mercury, hence the bay's name. One of the main reasons for Cook's voyage in the first place was to observe the transit of Venus, which he did at Tahiti.

The Coromandel Peninsula was heavily wooded and the traders who followed in Cook's wake around 1830 took away a great deal of timber, much of it through Mercury Bay. Fishing (commercial and big game) and tourism are the main activities now.

## ENVIRONS & ATTRACTIONS
**Buffalo Beach** This is the town beach and the site where HMS *Buffalo* was wrecked in 1840. Its anchor remains on the foreshore.
**Mercury Bay Museum** Timber

equipment, kauri specimens and shipwreck items are collected in the old dairy factory. Open afternoons in holiday periods.

## LOCAL TOURING
**Ferry Landing** A passenger ferry runs 7.30 am–6.30 pm across the narrow entrance from Whitianga to the other side, which is known as Ferry Landing. The original settlement was on this side. Alternatively the road around the harbour is 42 km.

**Whitianga Rock** From the Ferry Landing, there is a short 15-minute walk to this scenic and historic reserve. A pa used to be at the top. There is now a fine view over Whitianga.

**Shakespeare Cliff Lookout** From the Ferry Landing a 45-minute walk leads to another historic and scenic reserve. Alternatively, drive round to Flaxmill Bay and the walk is only 20 minutes. At the 76 m trig station, there is a good view over Mercury Bay.

**Cooks Beach** Energetic walkers can tramp the road from Ferry Landing; otherwise drive around via Coroglen to this popular beach.

**Hahei** Another popular beach resort accessible on the road via Coroglen.

**Hot Water Beach** From the road's end, take a short walk along the beach between the low and mid-tide area where you can scoop warm pools in the sand. Also accessible via Coroglen, off Hahei Road.

**Kuaotunu** It is 18 km north-bound from Whitianga up and over to this ocean beach. A side road, Black Jack Road, leads to Opito Bay.

**Whangapoua** Developing beach resort area further round past Kuaotunu (37 km).

**See Also** Thames, Coromandel and Tairua

# WOODVILLE NI
**Population** 1647
**Location** At the junction of Route 3 with Route 2; 27 km east of Palmerston North, 86 km north of Masterton.

Both a road and rail junction, Woodville's location marks the eastern entrance to the Manawatu Gorge, which is one of the main east-west arteries in the southern part of the North Island. The Gorge has a railway line on one side and a road on the other and is a scenic thoroughfare. But there are alternative roads either over the Ruahine Saddle or via the Pahiatua 'track'. The gorge makes a break between the Tararua Range to the south and the Ruahine Range to the north. The Manawatu River (and also the Ohinemuri River between Waihi and Paeroa) seems to defy logic by rising near one coast and breaking through the central mountain chain to exit on the other side.

The Woodville area was once known as Seventy Mile Bush, but there is little evidence of that now.

## LOCAL TOURING
**Whariti Peak** A minor road, which rises to a viewpoint in the Ruahine Range.

**Pahiatua** A borough 10 km south of Woodville, noted as birthplace and home of Sir Keith Holyoake, former Member of Parliament, Prime Minister and Governor General. A Polish refugee memorial 3 km south, commemorates 734 Polish children brought here during and after World War II. A direct road from Pahiatua to Palmerston North (known as the Pahiatua Track but of a better standard than the name implies) offers views over the surrounding countryside.

**See Also** Palmerston North, Masterton and Dannevirke

*The Kingston Flier.*

# New Zealand Railway System

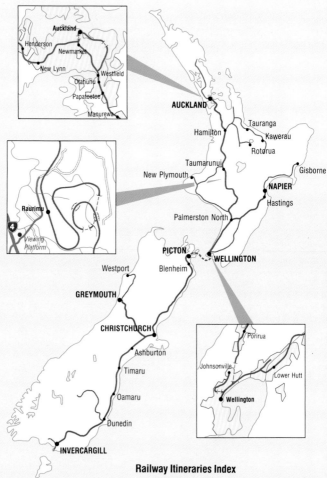

Passenger routes ——————
Freight only ——————
InterIsland Ferry - - - - - - -

**Auckland** (inset): Henderson, Newmarket, New Lynn, Westfield, Otahuhu, Papatoetoe, Manurewa

**Raurimu** (inset): 4, Viewing Platform

**Wellington** (inset): Porirua, Johnsonville, Lower Hutt, Wellington

AUCKLAND
Tauranga
Hamilton
Kawerau
Rotorua
Taumarunui
Gisborne
New Plymouth
NAPIER
Hastings
Palmerston North
PICTON
Blenheim
WELLINGTON
Westport
GREYMOUTH
CHRISTCHURCH
Ashburton
Timaru
Oamaru
Dunedin
INVERCARGILL

## Railway Itineraries Index

# New Zealand by Rail

## 1

## AUCKLAND– TAUMARUNUI NI

The city of **Auckland** has western, southern and eastern suburban railway lines. The southern line enters a tunnel shortly after leaving the main station, passes Newmarket junction, Penrose junction (where there are industrial sidings) and meets up with the eastern line near Westfield marshalling yards. The Western line branches off at Newmarket and in due course turns north towards Dargaville, Whangarei and Otiria. Passenger services, however, are not operated further than suburban Waitakere.

The eastern line is the main line leaving the city via Hobson Bay. Enter a short tunnel, meet up with the southern line at Westfield and continue through suburbs to Papakura. Then cross open country, pass **Pukekohe**, meet up with the Waikato River and pass Meremere* Power Station. Verge the Whangamarino Wetlands, pass Te Kawhata* and enter the important coal town of **Huntly**. Follow the Waikato River again to **Ngaruawahia**, shortly pass Te Rapa marshalling yards and enter **Hamilton** station in the suburb of Frankton (138 km from Auckland).

From Hamilton, other lines go to Tauranga and Rotorua, but the main line continues over flat lands then hillier country through **Te Awamutu** and **Otorohanga**. Overhead electrification commences at Hamilton.

Then leave the Waikato area and enter the 'King Country'. After **Te Kuiti** there is a steep climb through rugged hill country across the Waiteti viaduct; in due course go through the 1.3 km Porootarao tunnel. You now leave the Waikato/Waipa watershed and wind down into the Ongarue River valley, a subsidiary of the Wanganui River. At Okahukura*, a line from Stratford and New Plymouth joins from the west via a doubledecker road-rail bridge. All this mountain area was once heavily forested, and light timber railways used to operate around here. The land is now mostly cleared for sheep farming, but some plantations can still be seen. Follow the Ongarue River to enter **Taumarunui**, 283 km from Auckland. The branch lines to Tauranga and Rotorua, and to Stratford and New Plymouth, do not currently have scheduled passenger service.

## 2

## TAUMARUNUI– WELLINGTON NI

After leaving **Taumarunui** station, cross the upper reaches of the Wanganui River, and follow the river. Then leave it to climb higher in more rugged country, and in due course ascend the Raurimu Spiral*. This middle section of the line between Auckland and Wellington took a lot of survey and construction. The spiral allows the track to ascend 215 m altitude in 11 km up the volcanic plateau. At the top is **National Park**, and views of Mt Ngauruhoe (2290 m) and Ruapehu (2796 m). On fine days distant views of Mt Egmont (2517 m) can be seen in the west.

The track crosses several viaducts, especially 79 m high Makatote. Cross the new Hapuawhenua viaduct (the old viaduct can be seen on the left) and pass **Ohakune** station; the town centre is 2 km further west. Then continue past farming and tree plantations, cross the Tangiwhai Bridge (scene of a 1953 rail disaster when 160 people were killed), and rise up to **Waiouru** — the highest New Zealand Railway station (814 m above sea level).

Then gently wind down through broken hill country to **Taihape**. Shortly the line crosses three modern viaducts as part of the Mangaweka Deviation, along the terraces above the Rangitikei River. In due course arrive at **Marton** where a line from Stratford and New Plymouth joins. Descend to cross the Rangitikei River. The country through **Feilding** to **Palmerston North** (261 km from Taumarunui; 136 km to Wellington) is much flatter. Overhead electrification terminates here. Note the junction for Napier and Gisborne (described in the next itinerary).

From Palmerston North, cross the Manawatu River and traverse flat country west of the Tararua Range. Past **Levin**, the flat plain gradually gets squeezed between mountain and sea and you enter the northern fringes of the capital's suburbs and suburban rail services at Paraparaumu* and Paekakariki*. Overhead electrification recommences. The line hugs the coast through a number of tunnels, crosses the Porirua harbour and enters two long tunnels (4.3 km and 1.2 km respectively). Suddenly the city and harbour of Wellington spring into view. Note suburban tracks and motorway from the Hutt Valley on the left and the Johnsonville line on the right.

# 3

# GISBORNE– WELLINGTON NI

At the time of compiling this guide, the passenger service between Gisborne and Napier had been withdrawn.

After leaving **Gisborne** the track crosses the airport. It then winds through hilly country, passing through many tunnels, and providing some splendid coastal views.

Pass through **Wairoa** and continue through more hill country and tunnels. Cross the Mohaka River on New Zealand's highest viaduct (97 m). In due course wind down to the coast to enter **Napier**.

From Napier it is flat running to nearby **Hastings**. Then the line gradually rises up the Waipawa River Valley and keeps on through undulating country past **Waipukurau**, passing over several viaducts on to **Dannevirke**. Then arrive at **Woodville** junction, where an alternative line to Wellington branches off. The track then enters the spectacular Manawatu Gorge before entering **Palmerston North**. This track from Gisborne and Napier now connects with the North Island main trunk line. For a continuation of this track please refer to the previous itinerary.

The alternative line from Woodville travels south through the Wairarapa to **Masterton**. In due course enter the 8.8 km Rimutaka* tunnel; this replaces the former incline that used to go over the range. At Upper Hutt you meet up with the Wellington suburban electric system. Follow down through Lower Hutt, and skirt the harbour to enter **Wellington** station.

# 4

## PICTON– CHRISTCHURCH SI

From the inter-island ferry port of **Picton** the railway climbs out of the town, crosses a trestle, and then comes down on to the Wairau Plains. Cross the Wairau River, pass the freight terminal at Spring Creek and enter **Blenheim**.

In due course rise up the Dashwood Pass, then cross the Awatere River, and skirt around saltworks at Lake Grassmere. The track then follows a spectacular route down the coast between the seaward Kaikoura mountains and the Pacific Ocean to the town of **Kaikoura**. Cross the Clarence River and traverse several tunnels en route.

South of Kaikoura the line continues to hug the shore before rising inland to dry sheep-farming country. The line crosses the Conway, Waiau and Hurunui Rivers.

It then descends to the plains of North Canterbury, crossing more rivers, including the Waimakariri River, before entering **Christchurch**. This north line intersects the line from the south (and west) and enters the station from the west. (The track then continues 9 km onto Lyttleton via a 2.6 km tunnel).

# 5

## CHRISTCHURCH– GREYMOUTH SI

This Trans-Alpine line from coast to coast of the South Island branches off the south line at Rolleston, 22 km south of **Christchurch**. It then heads westward over the seemingly flat Canterbury Plains, but actually it gradually rises in altitude through Darfield and Sheffield as the Southern Alps and its foothills get closer.

After **Springfield** (70 km) the plains are left behind and the track almost immediately enters hill country, and follows around above the gorge of the Waimakariri River. This is a spectacular section of line with tunnels and bridges, including the 73 m high Staircase viaduct. Then leave the gorge, by following up Broken River, and go down the Cass bank to meet up again with the Waimakariri — this time in a much broader valley. The track crosses the river and then follows the Bealey River to **Arthur's Pass** — deep in the Southern Alps (138 km from Christchurch; 95 km to Greymouth).

From here there is a sloping 8.5 km tunnel through to the western side of the alps. The track passes Otira and follows down the Otira River to meet up with the Taramakau River. Shortly the track crosses that river and skirts through scrubby country to Moana* on Lake Brunner. In due course the line reaches Stillwater where a track north to Westport branches off. The line follows the Grey River down to the Port town of **Greymouth**. Note another branch line that crosses the river from coalfields at Runanga and Rapahoe.

Beyond Greymouth the railway line continues to Hokitika, but there is presently no passenger service; nor is there a passenger rail service to Westport.

# 6

## CHRISTCHURCH– INVERCARGILL SI

The first third of this route is flat running across the

Canterbury Plains. From **Christchurch** the line travels through Rolleston where the west coast railway branches off. It crosses the Selwyn River, and then crosses the Rakaia River on New Zealand's longest rail bridge. Observe the views of the Southern Alps and its foothills to the west.

Continuing south, it is steady going through to **Ashburton**, over its river, and later over the two arms of the Rangitata River. Skirt Caroline Bay* before arriving at **Timaru** Station (161 km from Christchurch).

The railway then crosses gently undulating countryside down to **Oamaru**. En route it crosses the Waitaki River, the provincial boundary between Canterbury and Otago, and then the 45th parallel — the halfway point between the equator and the South Pole.

The land becomes hillier south of Oamaru with coastal views north of **Palmerston**, and more spectacular coastal scenery to the south. Enter a few tunnels past Port Chalmers*, and follow around Otago Harbour into **Dunedin** (368 km from Christchurch; 223 km to Invercargill).

The line tunnels out of Dunedin via the 1.4 km Caversham tunnel and crosses the Taieri Flats. The junction for the Otago central line to Alexandra and Clyde is at Wingatui. Excursion passenger trains are operated on this line daily in summer for about 45 km through the Taieri Gorge. The south line continues to **Milton** and on to **Balclutha** (over the Clutha River). The countryside is quite hilly to **Gore** then fairly flat going across the Southland plains to **Invercargill**. The track, but not passenger service, continues to the port of Bluff* — a further 26 km.

332

*Wellington Railway Station.*

# INTER-ISLAND FERRY

Wellington and Picton are linked several times a day by a ferry service for travellers, cars and other freight (including rail freight). The total sailing time is 3 hours 20 minutes; most of the first hour is spent leaving Wellington Harbour, the second hour is spent crossing Cook Strait, while the third hour is spent travelling through the scenic Marlborough Sounds. Cook Strait has the reputation of being a windy and rough stretch of water — and sometimes it can be — but most times the sailing trip will be a scenic and interesting journey.

The ferries have large lounges with seats, catering facilities and a bar. Sleeping accommodation is

*The Picton ferry in Port Nicholson.*

not usually provided, though two of the ferries have four cabins for private use.

The Wellington terminal is on the northern end of Aotea Quay, almost under the motorway. Foot passengers may use bus transfers from platform 9 — the bus loading terminus — at the Wellington Railway Station. At Picton, scheduled buses and rental cars are available at the end of the wharf. It is a short walk to the Picton Railway Station, and not much further on to Picton's main street. At least one sailing a day has a rail connection to/from Christchurch as well as bus connections to Blenheim, Nelson and the west coast.

Travellers with cars should book ahead for space on the boats. Those with rental cars or motor-homes should check with their operator regarding a change of vehicles at Wellington and Picton rather than paying for passage on the ferry. There are off-season discounts so enquire when booking.

*The Ohau ski-field in the MacKenzie County.*

# LIFESTYLE

## THE PEOPLE

New Zealand has a long history of immigration. Large scale immigration from the United Kingdom and European countries over the last 200 years has influenced the cultural base of New Zealand, which in turn has been modified by more recent movements from the South Pacific and Pacific rim.

Between 1873 and 1876, 63 000 migrants from Europe were assisted to New Zealand. From the late 1860s significant numbers of Chinese came here to work on the goldfields. The arrival in the 1880s of immigrants from the Dalmatian coast of the Austro-Hungarian Empire added an important new dimension to the population. The inward migration between 1919 and 1945 was predominantly British with some Indian and European settlers but after World War II refugees from continental Europe, Hungary, Chile, Uganda, Iran, Vietnam, Laos and Kampuchea arrived. The numbers of Dutch immigrants rose during the 1950s. Of long-term significance is the growth of migration from the South Pacific Islands. By the mid-1960s people born in the British Isles no longer comprised more than half the permanent and long-term arrivals.

By world standards New Zealand's population is small at approximately 3.3 million but compared with some European countries its rate of natural increase is relatively high. Pacific Islanders have a growth rate of 28.4 per cent, Maoris of 7.9 per cent and Europeans of 2.3 per cent.

The North Island has 74 per cent of the total population and the greater Auckland area has 45 000 more people than the total South Island population. Almost 84 per cent of New Zealanders live in urban areas and over recent years there has been a population drift northward. This includes the Maori population who now live mainly in North Island towns and cities.

More than 68 per cent of private households are 'one-family only' with 'one-person only' being the next most common type of household occupation. The size of the average family is 3.1 and there are about eight marriages per 1000 people. The most popular age for a bride is 22, and for a bride-groom 24. Eighty-eight per cent of private households own one or more cars. There are 980 males to every 1000 females. Females tend to outnumber males in urban areas and to be outnumbered in rural areas. Almost 58 000 New Zealanders live in long-term de facto relationships. The total of the working population (15 years and over) is about 2 450 000, but only about 1 500 000 are employed. At present unemployment is a major economic and social problem in New Zealand.

*Murray Garr at Garrs Camp, Hollyford Valley.*

*Church on Nile Street, Nelson.*

# RELIGION AND CUSTOMS

New Zealand was introduced to Christianity early through its contact with Europeans. The first Christian service was preached at Rangihoua in the Bay of Islands on Christmas Day 1814 by the Reverend Samual Marsden of the Church of England's Church Missionary Society. Other major Christian denominations followed quickly — the Wesleyans in 1823 and Roman Catholics in 1838. Presbyterianism arrived in Otago along with the Scottish settlers.

Most New Zealanders (24.7 per cent) belong to the Anglican church; 18 per cent to the Presbyterian church; 15 per cent to the Roman Catholic church and 5 per cent to the Methodist church. However, there is a slow, long-term decline in the number of people identifying with these four major tradi ional religions.

Most Christian denominations are practised in New Zealand and people of any recognised religious belief are permitted to worship freely. Jewish synagogues are present in most major centres. Eastern religions such as Baha'i, Zen Buddism and Hinduism exist alongside Muslim, Christian pentecostal and peculiarly Maori faiths such as Ratana.

Many of our customs are based on the Northern Hemisphere Christian calendar and on British traditions, for example, Christmas, Easter and Guy Fawkes night. Minority ethnic groups also keep alive their own traditions, which enrich and diversify the range of traditional celebrations.

Because Christmas Day falls in mid-summer the celebration is marked by some families with cold salad foods and meats, and the traditional dessert pavlova. Other families, however, will consume the traditional English Christmas fare of turkey and plum pudding.

Waitangi Day (6 February) is a national holiday to commemorate the signing of the Treaty of Waitangi; Anzac Day (25 April) is a national day of remembrance for those who fell in the two world wars and subsequent wars. Memorial services are held on these days and most commercial activities cease as they do on other major holidays.

Shops and offices are open weekdays from 9 am to 5.30 pm. Many centres have late-night shopping on Fridays when they remain open until 9 pm. Saturday shopping is generally from 9 am until midday, though in tourist areas shops remain open longer. There is no Sunday trading and commercial transactions such as banking are confined to weekdays 9.30 am to 4.30 pm. Many government departments have an 8.30 am–4.30 pm working day.

# PUBLIC HOLIDAYS

| | |
|---|---|
| New Year's Day | 1 January |
| 2 January | 2 January |
| Southland Anniversary Day | 17 January |
| Wellington Anniversary Day | 22 January |
| Auckland Anniversary Day | 29 January |
| Nelson Anniversary Day | 1 February |
| Waitangi Day | 6 February |
| Otago Anniversary Day | 23 March |
| Taranaki Anniversary Day | 31 March |
| Good Friday | |
| Easter Monday | |
| Anzac Day | 25 April |
| Queen's Birthday | 21 April |
| Labour Day | 4th Monday in October |
| Hawke's Bay Anniversary Day | 1 November |
| Marlborough Anniversary Day | 1 November |
| Chathams Anniversary Day | 30 November |
| Westland Anniversary Day | 1 December |
| Canterbury Anniversary Day | 16 December |
| • Canterbury North and Central | |
| • Canterbury South (Timaru) | |
| Christmas Day | 25 December |
| Boxing Day | 26 December |

*Vineyards in Ormond Valley.*

# FOOD AND DRINK

There are few countries in the world that achieve the quality of New Zealand's natural food products. Because of the widely varied climatic conditions, fruits and vegetables grow in abundance and range from subtropical through to hardy winter varieties, requiring colder temperatures.

The land is fertile and the sea teems with different types of fish and seafood; both are continuing sources of fresh natural produce for home consumption and for exporting around the world. New Zealand produces sweet lean lamb, beef, pork, venison and wild game; a variety of fish including rock oyster, scallops, lobster, terakihi, snapper, orange roughy and cod; fresh-water fish such as trout and salmon; stone fruits such as cherries and apricots, berry fruits, apples and pears; an array of world standard cheeses and honeys; an assortment of breads and dairy

produce made from locally grown ingredients. Added to these are the international award winning beers and wines, a variety of fresh fruit juices and the local 'pop' — Lemon and Paeroa (a mixture of lemon juice and lemonade). New Zealand can also boast the purest water in the world. Even water from the tap is safe to drink.

Traditionally, New Zealand produced English-style foods but today it is a gourmet nation offering a wide variety of ethnic restaurants that compare favourably with those in most other countries. What was once regarded as the national dish — the roast of lamb complete with mint sauce, gravy, roast vegetables and fresh garden greens — is still widely available and enjoyed. Maori feasts (hangis) cater for overseas and local visitors, as do wine trails and festivals, fruit festivals and in

342

some parts of the country, local markets.

A feature of New Zealand is the roadside stall where produce is sold to the traveller at the farm gate or shoreline. Fruit, vegetables and fish are locally grown or caught, and are guaranteed to be fresh and cheap. The range varies greatly but can include anything from avocados, sweetcorn, grapes, flounder, pipi (small delectable shellfish), crayfish (lobster), honey, homemade jams and even pinecones for a winter fire.

Many orchards and market gardens advertise 'pick-your-own' fruit and vegetables. Once again the wide-ranging produce, which may include tomatoes, beans, strawberries and peaches through to chestnuts, are fresh and cheap.

New Zealand chefs are gaining a world-wide reputation for innovative cuisine using local produce. For those who wish to taste genuine New Zealand foods, watch for the sign 'Taste New Zealand', which is displayed in the windows of restaurants and cafes serving New Zealand cuisine.

Many restaurants are fully licensed; others are BYO (bring your own) where patrons select and buy their own wines at a hotel bottle store or wine shop to enjoy with their meal. BYO restaurants and cafes are generally cheaper than licensed eating places.

# A GUIDE TO LIQUOR LAWS

**Hotels**
Hours: Mon–Thurs 11 am–10 pm
Fri–Sat 11 am–11 pm
• operate a public bar and smaller more intimate private bars where drinks are more expensive

**Restaurants**
Hours as advertised
• licensed restaurants provide full liquor service
• BYO restaurants cannot sell liquor on the premises but patrons may take wines, spirits or ales to drink with a meal
• unlicensed restaurants are prohibited the sale or consumption of liquor on the premises

**Bottle stores**
Same as hotel hours
• are run in association with hotels
• permit the purchase of unrestricted amounts of liquor

**Wholesale liquor merchants**
Hours: Mon–Sat 9 am–7 pm
• the cheapest way to buy liquor
• an excess of 8 litres must be bought at one time

**Wine shops**
Hours: (can vary but generally) Mon–Sat 9 am–7 pm
• sale is of an unrestricted amount

*Yachting in Auckland.*

# CULTURE AND SPORT

## CULTURE

In New Zealand the government and local authorities recognise the importance of the arts in the community and provide support for this purpose. The traditional sources of assistance are: The Queen Elizabeth II Arts Council; the New Zealand Historical Places Trust; the National Art Gallery and Museum; and the New Zealand Authors' Fund. Profits from state-run lotteries are used to assist art galleries, museums and cultural organisations. The Ministry of Foreign Affairs fosters the arts through its Cultural Exchange Program, which facilitates exchanges in all branches of the arts, and through overseas programs for our cultural achievements.

The Queen Elizabeth II Arts Council includes three regional councils and a national network of community arts councils. A council for Maori and South Pacific Arts was established in 1978 and provides a range of programs including schemes to assist the arts at community level — sponsorship, travel assistance and the promotion of Maori and Pacific Islands arts and bi-cultural traditions.

The Arts Council supports six professional theatres, four regional orchestras, a modern dance company, a ballet company and a professional opera program. Individual artists and performers are assisted in their respective fields — crafts, dance, film and video, music, theatre, galleries.

The New Zealand Symphony Orchestra is widely recognised for the high standard of its public concerts. Its tour program is one of the most extensive in the world involving 20 000 kilometres of internal travel annually.

There are more than 200 public museums and art galleries. Many are small collections orientated towards the history or fabric of a particular location. The larger museums carry out research and print catalogues, and maintain education programs for visitors.

## SPORT

The successful New Zealand sportsperson represents the archetype of the 'battler' who succeeds against all odds. International sporting events in which New Zealand is involved have the power to arouse intense national fervour. New Zealanders have fared exceptionally well in the international arena despite the their distance from the world's major venues and a comparative lack of state or corporate funding. At the 1984 Los Angeles Olympics, for example, New Zealand achieved a greater medal ratio per head of population than any other nation competing.

There are many reasons put forward for this success. A small population may have helped to produce an affinity between the national hero and the weekend athlete, and while a generally temperate climate has made it possible for athletes to train all year, there is sufficient variety of terrain and climate to foster a wide range of summer and winter pursuits.

Traditionally rugby union has been regarded as the national sport and has acquired inter-national fame through the All Blacks. But New Zealand has also sustained international success in rowing, netball, squash, softball, cricket, yachting and many other disciplines.

The success at an elite level is founded on a broad base of mass participation and support. The New Zealand Assembly of Sport, which represents 50 national associations, claims a collective membership of more than 1.5 million. A survey taken in 1987 found that 19 per cent of the population had taken part in competitive activity in the previous four weeks and that 35 per cent of the adult population belonged to sport-related clubs.

The intensity of New Zealand's interest in sport is reflected in its coverage by Television New Zealand. More than 10 000 hours per year are allocated to sports broadcasting; at 7.2 per cent of total broadcasting time, this makes it one of the highest percentages in the world.

# FACTS AND FIGURES

The New Zealand dossier:

- a population of 3.3 million.
- a length of 1600 km.
- a combined area of 268 000 sq km.
- a prevailing westerly wind.
- 2000 sunshine hours per year over most of the country.
- one uniform time, which is 12 hrs ahead of co-ordinated universal time.
- one hour of daylight saving from 2 am on the second Sunday in October to 2 am on the third Sunday in March.
- Chatham Island time is 45 mins ahead of New Zealand time.
- Aotearoa, the Maori name for New Zealand, is commonly used.
- the Maori name for the South Island is Te Wai Pounamu (place of green-stone).
- the Maori name for the North Island is Te Ika a Maui (the fish of Maui).
- Auckland has the largest population; Wellington is the capital city and commercial centre.
- Auckland is built on more than 50 extinct volcanoes.
- Molesworth Station is the largest holding in the country (200 000 ha).
- there are 12 national parks (more than 2 million ha), 21 forest parks (1.7 million ha) and 4000 reserves.
- rural areas include towns of less than 1000 people.
- about 11 per cent of the world's most endangered birds are endemic to New Zealand.
- New Zealand women were given the vote in 1893 and were made eligible as members of parliament in 1919.
- New Zealand ratified the United Nations Convention on the Elimination of All Forms of Discrimination against Women in 1984.
- a Ministry of Women's Affairs was created in 1985.
- New Zealand uses the International System of Units for measurement (metric).
- New Zealand has an alternating current (AC) 230-volt, 50 hertz mains electricity supply.
- most hotels and motels provide 110-volt AC sockets (20 watts) for electric razors only.
- decimal currency was introduced in 1967.

## NEW ZEALAND MONEY

New Zealand operates a decimal currency system based on dollars and cents.

| Single notes | Single coins |
| --- | --- |
| 1 dollar | 1 cent |
| 2 dollars | 2 cents |
| 5 dollars | 5 cents |
| 10 dollars | 10 cents |
| 20 dollars | 20 cents |
| 50 dollars | 50 cents |
| 100 dollars | |

- one and two cent coins are currently being phased out.

- credit cards are widely used. The most common are: American Express, Diners Club, Visa, Master Charge and Bankcard.

- Saturday trading began in 1980. Sunday trading is being considered.

- a goods and services tax (GST) of 12.5 per cent now operates in New Zealand.

- the New Zealand dollar was floated in 1985 and authorised foreign exchange dealers now negotiate rates of currency exchange.

- the average weekly expenditure for a family of four is about $600.

- the minimum legal age for marriage is 16 years.

- there is a law against discrimination on the grounds of colour, race, ethnic or national origin.

- New Zealanders live mainly in single detached houses and are owner occupiers.

- nearly 50 per cent of workers use their own transport to and from work.

- Maori is an official language.

- more than 50 000 New Zealanders are fluent in Maori.

- education is compulsory from 6–16 years.

- the school year has three terms.

- there are 260 public libraries, with more than 7 million books in stock. In a year more than 25 million issues are made.

- resident New Zealanders are entitled to medical and related benefits.

- ACC (Accident Compensation Commission) provides 80 per cent compensation for loss of earnings through accident.

- drivers licences are valid without renewal until the age of 71.

- the wearing of seatbelts is compulsory.

- New Zealanders drive on the left-hand side of the road.

- pedestrians and cyclists are forbidden on motorways.

- cyclists may not ride on footpaths unless they are designated for that purpose.

- it is an offence to drive with a blood/alcohol level exceeding 80 micrograms of alcohol per 100 millilitres of blood.

- speed limits are: 50 km/h for towns and cities, 70 km/h for areas with speed limits, 100 km/h for highways and motorways.

- alcohol can be sold to persons 20 years and over, 18 years if accompanied by a spouse or parent over 20, or to a person 18 years or over when it is accompanying a meal.

- there are about 325 horse racing days a year; 200 trotting days and 30 greyhound racing days.

- more than 700 000 overseas persons visit New Zealand annually.

- the New Zealand emblem the silver fern was first worn by a rugby team visiting Britain. The All Blacks have worn it ever since.

- the kiwi became an infantry regimental badge in 1911.

- black and white are the national colours.

- the New Zealand ensign became the national flag in 1981.

- 'God Defend New Zealand' is the national anthem.

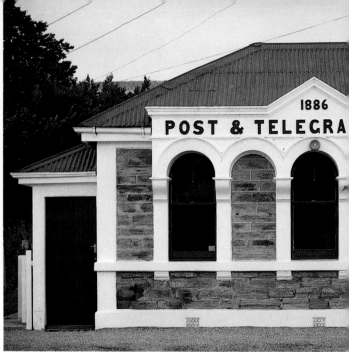

*The old Post and Telegraph Office at Ophir in Central Otago.*

# TRANSPORT AND COMMUNICATIONS

New Zealand's transport system has always been characterised by its remoteness from many of its trading partners and by the country's relatively small population. International air and telecommunication links have overcome this isolation but there is still a heavy reliance on sea transport for overseas trade. More than 90 per cent of our exports and imports by value and almost 99 per cent by volume are carried by sea.

Air New Zealand and Ansett New Zealand (an Australian owned company) are the largest domestic air service operators. The Mount Cook Group Limited provides mainly tourist-orientated passenger services, while Safe Air provides a freight service. Commuter operators provide regular services throughout the country. In addition, at most aerodromes there are light aircraft operators providing facilities for flight training and private flying.

A railway network, which extends more than 4300 kilometres, links almost all the principal centres of population. There are also a number of short private railways mainly serving collieries and other industries. Rail services are operated by the New Zealand Railways Corporation. In addition to suburban services, New Zealand Railways Corporation runs the Silver Fern Daylight Express railcar five days a week between Auckland and Wellington; the Northerner Express, which runs nightly between Auckland and Wellington; the Southerner, which runs six days a week between Christchurch and

Islands were linked by telegraph cable in 1866 and by telephone cable in 1926. From 1 April 1987 the post office was split into three separate state-owned corporations and New Zealand Post Limited commenced operations as a separate enterprise. Its principal business is the provision of postal services. Postal business generates about two-thirds of its revenue; the balance comes from acting as an agent for government and other business agencies.

New Zealand Post handles more than 800 million pieces of mail annually. The company employs more than 9000 staff in its 513 post offices and its mail processing, transportation and delivery network. Any postal item up to 20 kilograms can be sent by fast post or by standard post. Fast post offers assured overnight delivery between more than 500 centres. Standard post offers overnight delivery across town or two or three days elsewhere.

New Zealand has one of the highest telephone densities in the world with 69.7 telephones per 100 head of population. Since the first telephone exchange was installed in 1881 the telephone system has expanded to more than 800 exchanges serving 1 323 000 subscribers. The exchanges are grouped in 157 toll-free calling areas within which there is no charge for local calls. Toll fees are charged for calls between different toll-free calling areas at varying rates according to time and distance. Subscriber toll dialling is available to 96 per cent of subscribers.

Telephone communications by cable, satellite and radio are available to almost all countries of the world. International subscriber dialling is available to 94 per cent of subscribers who may dial 150 countries and territories.

Invercargill; the Trans-Alpine between Christchurch and the west coast, which runs seven days a week; and the Coastal Pacific express (daily between Picton and Christchurch).

Provincial passenger services to other districts are operated by Railways Road Services. This is one of the country's largest road operators. Its passenger services cover more than 10 000 kilometres of highways, which is more than 10 per cent of the 93 000 kilometres of formed roads and streets.

Two ferries carrying road and rail vehicles and passengers operate between Wellington and Picton. A private operator provides a passenger/freight service to and from Stewart Island.

The first post office was opened at Kororareka (Russell) in 1840. The same year overland mail routes were begun and in 1858 the post office became an independent department of state. A telegraph system began in the 1860s; the North and South

# FARMING AND INDUSTRY

Probably New Zealand's best known statistic is that it has more than 20 times as many sheep as people. The best sheep farms can carry up to 25 sheep per hectare throughout the year. The best dairy farms carry 3.5 cows per hectare throughout the year. The sheep population is around 67.5 million; beef cattle number 4.7 million.

In the North Island beef cattle are predominant in the far north. There is dairying in Waikato and Taranaki and sheep in the hills and far south of the island. In the South Island sheep farming is the main form of pastoral agriculture with some beef cattle in the high and hill country and wetter flat areas. There is some dairying on the flat land of both coasts. Livestock are rarely housed but feeding of small quantities of supplements such as hay and silage can occur in the winter. Stock are grazed in paddocks with movable electric fences. Lambing and calving are carefully managed to take full advantage of spring grass growth. Phosphatic fertilisers are used extensively on the predominantly grass/clover pastures.

Deer and goats have become important livestock and there are 3500 registered deer farms. Goats are farmed for their milk, mohair and meat production as well as for weed control. Major crops exported include kiwifruit, pipfruits, summer fruits (stonefruit) and berry fruits. Grapes are grown mainly for domestic purposes and for wine production.

New Zealand is the largest supplier of coarse wools, contributing 40 per cent to the world total. It is used for carpet, handyarn and blanket manufacture. The dairy industry is geared towards the overseas market. New Zealand is the world's largest exporter of casein and caseinate products.

The forestry industry is based on nearly 1.1 million hectares of forest plantations consisting mainly of conifers, and this resource continues to increase. Australia is the largest customer and Japan is next. There are restrictions on the export of native timbers.

Our 200 mile Exclusive Economic Zone (EEZ) with an area of about 1.2 million square nautical miles is one of the largest in the world. New Zealand has control of conservation and management, and polices the area with fishery-protection patrols. The total allowable catch set for territorial and EEZ waters was 494 000 tonnes of finfish and 121 000 tonnes of squid for the 1988 season. The tuna catch was estimated to be more than 20 000 tonnes. An annual quota system is used to manage our fisheries.

Some of our major secondary industries (apart from those associated with meat and dairy processing, timber and forest products) include: aluminium, electronics, engineering, food and beverage production, motor vehicle assembling, plastics, steel, textiles and footwear. Energy sources are many and diverse: oil is the primary fuel source but we do not produce enough for domestic consumption; natural gas is a premium energy resource, although its use is largely confined to the North Island. Natural gas sources are located in the Taranaki region. Coal represents the largest fossil fuel resource. Most is found in the

*Beef cattle grazing on Pinnacle Hill, South Auckland.*

south of the South Island. Approximately 76 per cent of all electricity comes from hydro generation and about 70 per cent of this is produced in the South Island. There are nearly 200 separate geothermal fields or hot springs in the country. It is estimated that there is potential for over 75 000 petajoules in terms of heat stored above 80°C. More than one third of our net petrol needs come from the synthetic petrol plant at Motunui. The balance is produced at the Marsden Point Refinery. The main refinery feedstocks are indigenous condensates and crude oil, as well as various imported oils.

351

# GOVERNMENT AND THE LAW

New Zealand is a monarchy with a parliamentary government. Queen Elizabeth II has the title of Queen of New Zealand. The Governor-General is the Sovereign's representative and is appointed on the Prime Minister's recommendation for a term of five years. The Governor-General's main constitutional function is to arrange for the leader of the majority party in Parliament to form a government. The Governor-General is required to follow the advice of ministers but in exceptional circumstances can reject advice if he or she believes a government is acting unconstitutionally.

Government administration is carried out by the Crown through its ministers and state servants. The Crown, however, must act according to its ministers' wishes and they in turn must retain parliamentary support. The principal function of Parliament is to enact laws, supervise Government's administration, vote supply, provide a government and redress grievances by way of petition. The Governor-General's assent is required before bills can become law.

It is the function of the opposition party with the highest number of seats to oppose government and to present itself to the people as an alternative government.

Persons 18 years and over have the right to vote. Enrolment as an elector is compulsory but voting is not. The government is elected for a three-year term. There are 97 electorates in New Zealand, four of which are Maori seats. Maoris, including people of Maori descent, may choose to enrol for either a Maori or a general electorate.

Ombudsmen (Parliamentary Commissioners for Investigation) enquire into complaints related to administrative decisions of government departments and related organisations, hospital boards, education boards and all local authorities. Complaints to an Ombudsman must be made in writing and investigations are conducted in private.

There is a separate system of local government made up of many local authorities that are mainly independent of the central executive government. They are, in the main, elected by the residents of the districts they represent and are responsible for such things as roading, water supply, sewage, libraries, parks, land use and pensioner housing.

Special-purpose boards, councils and authorities are responsible for one major function each, for example, hospital services, electricity or gas distribution.

Twenty regional councils and two regional authorities are responsible for such functions as regional planning, civil defence, urban transport and community services. District Maori councils come under the direction of the New Zealand Maori Council.

New Zealand has a tradition of an independent judiciary, which is seen as protection against unnecessary intrusion by the state into the lives of citizens. High Court judges and District Court judges are appointed by the Governor-General and have security of tenure. They can only be removed from office on grounds of misbehaviour or incapacity. No person can be

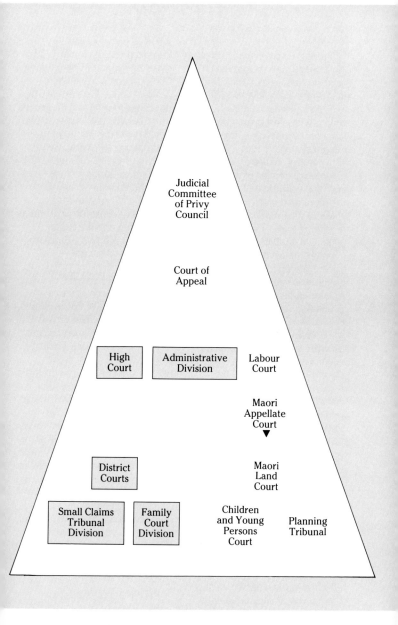

Judicial
Committee
of Privy
Council

Court of
Appeal

High
Court

Administrative
Division

Labour
Court

Maori
Appellate
Court
▼

District
Courts

Maori
Land
Court

Small Claims
Tribunal
Division

Family
Court
Division

Children
and Young
Persons
Court

Planning
Tribunal

appointed a judge unless they have held a practising certificate as a barrister or solicitor for at least seven years.

There are resources for legal aid in New Zealand for both civil and criminal proceedings as it is upheld that no one should be prevented by lack of means from having their case determined fairly by the courts.

# HISTORY

## MAORIS

The Maoris have lived in New Zealand since before the 8th century. Numerous voyages were made from Hawaiki and tradition tells of a number of famous canoes whose occupants were the founders of tribal groupings that remain distinctive today. By the 12th century, settlements were scattered over most of the country and Maori culture had adapted to the more moderate climate.

Maori society comprised groups of varying sizes — whanau (extended families of 10 to 30 people), hapu (subtribes) and iwi (tribes). Membership of these groups was based on descent from a common ancestor.

Life was communal and economic and social activities were shared. Land belonged to the tribe as a whole. Kaumatua (elders) headed families; communities were ruled by rangatira (chiefs) whose positions were hereditary but had to be reinforced by performance. Tapu (meaning sacred) protected chiefs and their possessions, safe-guarded cultivation and burial grounds and functioned as a social control. Tapu was regulated by tohunga (priests) whose high status embodied tribal history and knowledge. Lesser tohunga were specialists in such things as carving and canoe-building.

Fiercely protective of their social identities, they were deeply attached to the land, which gave them physical and spiritual life.

## EUROPEAN EXPLORERS

In 1642 Abel Tasman from the Dutch East India Company sighted a 'large, high-lying land', which he named Staten Landt, soon to be renamed 'Nieww Zeeland'. Tasman's experiences did not encourage explorers to follow in his wake and no European returned until 1769 when the explorer Captain James Cook circumnavigated New Zealand on his first voyage. His published journal and the reports from the scientists and artists on board made this country known to the rest of the world. Cook returned in 1773–74 and 1777.

Other explorers included the Frenchmen Jean de Surville, Marion de Fresne and D'Entrecasteaux; the Englishman Vancouver; and the Italian Malaspina, who led a Spanish fleet to New Zealand.

## TRADE AND RELIGION

After a penal colony was established at Port Jackson (Sydney) commercial exploitation of Aotearoa's resources became practicable. Deep-sea whaling began in 1791. Most of the whalers were American or British and bay whaling and sealing stations were established. These became the focal points for European settlement. Timber was a major resource and mills were opened around the richly forested northern coasts. The first mission station was established in the Bay of Islands under the auspices of the Church of England's Church Missionary Society in 1814. The Wesleyans opened a mission in the Hokianga area in 1823 and a Roman Catholic Marist Mission began in Northland in 1838.

## BRITISH SOVEREIGNTY

As trade and settlement increased New Zealand moved further into the British sphere of influence. British sovereignty over the country was established on 14 January 1840 and Captain William Hobson was appointed Lieutenant-Governor. At Waitangi on 6 February 1840

*Pouerua Pa.*

he obtained from local Maori chiefs the first signatures of the Treaty of Waitangi. The Maori version was couched in considerably vaguer terms than the English and as a result, the significance of this document has been debated ever since. In 1841 New Zealand became a colony and the capital shifted from Russell in the Bay of Islands to Auckland.

## LAND

As more colonists arrived questions of land ownership became pressing. The Crown began extensive land purchases. Thirteen million hectares had been obtained by 1853 but much of the North Island was still beyond government control and the wars that broke out had much to do with the contest for this land. Fighting began in Taranaki in March 1860. In 1861 the focus shifted to the Waikato. A military road was constructed to the Waikato River and the invasion began in July 1863. British forces eventually numbered 14 000 (more than were available for the defence of England) but they had great difficulty pushing back Maori opponents who never numbered more than 2000 at any

one time. The territory occupied in the 'Waikato War', about 400 000 hectares, was confiscated but fighting was far from over. Imperial troops campaigned on the west coast while colonial units fought in the east.

The huge land confiscations were the basis for European expansion. In the North Island the population rose to 97 000 and in the South Island 159 000. Unequal growth brought political change and in 1865 the capital was moved to Wellington. The wars of the 1860s resulted in Maori unity as well as division. Co-operation and resistance continued to be the twin motifs of the Maori response to the pakeha. By 1892, however, less than one-sixth of the country was owned by Maoris and a quarter of that was leased to Europeans. Most Maori-owned land was now rugged and bush-clad and Maoris made up only 7 per cent of the population. Yet Maori society remained resilient and adaptable. 'Loyal' Maoris had been rewarded with four seats in the House of Representatives in 1867 and Maori MPs and other prominent Maori leaders have become increasingly skilled advocates of Maori rights.

# GEOGRAPHY AND CLIMATE

The total area of New Zealand is 268 000 square kilometres — about the same size as the British Isles or Japan. It consists of three main islands (North Island, South Island and Stewart Island) and a number of smaller islands, and lies in the south-west Pacific Ocean. The administrative boundaries extend from 33 degrees to 53 degrees south latitude and from 162 degrees east to 173 degrees west longitude. The length of the country is more than 1600 kilometres and its width at its widest point is 450 kilometres. Channels divide the three main islands — Cook Strait divides the North and South Islands and Fouveaux Strait divides the South Island and Stewart Island.

In geological terms New Zealand is not ancient when compared to the antiquity credited to the continental masses. However, there is irrefutable evidence in our rocks that the land goes back at least 600 million years and has existed as a more or less separate entity at least as far back as the early Tertiary — 50 million years or more.

Because it lies on the boundary between the Indian-Australian and the Pacific plates, the earthquakes and volcanic activity that formed the country still occur. However, compared with some other parts of the almost continuous belt of earthquake activity around the rim of the Pacific, the level of seismic activity is moderate. It may be compared roughly with that of California.

Much of the vegetation and wildlife is unique to this country and dates from the time when the huge Southern Hemisphere landmass (Gondwanaland) began to fragment. There are no endemic land mammals, apart from two species of bats, because they had not evolved before the Gondwana continent broke up. Because of a lack of predators, many flightless insects and birds have evolved, for example, the kiwi, weka and kakapo (the largest flightless parrot in the world). Some archaic elements in the land fauna are the reptile tuatara, the moa (now extinct) and the kiwi. The moa belonged to the group of large flightless birds that includes the Australian emu, the cassowary of New Guinea and the ostrich of South Africa.

The diversity of climatic conditions has led to New Zealand being classified into more than 260 ecological districts each with a distinct blend of topography, climate, vegetation and wildlife. Superimposed on natural diversity there has been 1000 years of human activity. Initially 80 per cent of the land was covered in forest but today only about 23 per cent remains, mainly in the mountainous hinterland.

Northern (subtropical), central (temperate) and southern (sub-antarctic) marine areas are all present around our coast, each with its own characteristic species.

New Zealand is a mountainous land with about 25 per cent lying below 200 metres above sea level. There are 223 named peaks rising above 2300 metres, the highest being Mt Cook or Aorangi (3764 m) in the Southern Alps, a range that runs almost the entire length of the South Island. The Tasman Glacier (29 km) is the longest of 360 glaciers in the Southern Alps.

New Zealand's rivers are mainly swift and difficult to navigate but they are important as

*Kaiteriteri Beach, near Motueka, South Island.*

sources of hydro-electric power. The longest is the Waikato River (425 km). There are many lakes of great scenic beauty, the largest being Lake Taupo in the central North Island.

## CLIMATE

Our country lies in the mid-latitude zone of westerly winds. The mountain chain extending the length of the country has a major effect on the climate and produces much sharper climatic contrasts from west to east than from north to south. The distribution of rainfall is mainly controlled by these mountain features. The average rainfall for the whole country is high but for the greater part lies between 600 mm and 1500 mm and is spread evenly throughout the year. The greatest contrast is found in the north where winter has twice as much rain as summer. Over most of the North Island there are at least 130 rain days a year; in the South Island rain days range between 80 and 200 (in Stewart Island and Fiordland).

Mean temperatures at sea level decrease steadily southward from 15°C in the far north to 9°C in the south of the South Island. January and February are the warmest months and July the coldest. The sunniest places are near Blenheim, the Nelson-Motueka area, and Whakatane where the average duration of bright sunshine exceeds 2350 hours a year. A large portion of the country has at least 2000 sunshine hours. A pleasant feature of our climate is the high proportion of sunshine hours during the winter months.

*Passengers on a Milford Sound Cruise.*

# GETTING OUT AND ABOUT

Holidays for New Zealanders are a fact of life. New Zealanders go on holiday for any number of reasons — relaxation, to 'get away from it all', nostalgia, to see friends and relatives, and to participate in sporting and other social events, or for a combination of these reasons.

In recent years there has been a trend towards more action-packed holidays. Holidaymakers want to be involved, to have new experiences, and overseas visitors want an insight into the New Zealand culture and lifestyle. Facilities have sprung up to cater for these new trends: souvenir, specialist and duty-free shops; cafes, restaurants, bars and nightclubs; guided tours and sightseeing trips by all means of transport including coach, taxi, jetboat, raft and plane; agricultural demonstrations and farm visits; large-scale heritage and theme parks; trips on river jetboats, helicopters, glacier excursions, steamer cruises, river rafting, hot air ballooning; guided hunting, fishing and tramping excursions; Maori traditions such as carving and weaving; visits to marae and Maori concert parties;

hiring of gear for outdoor pursuits such as diving, yacht charter, skiing, fishing, hunting, camping, horse riding and biking holidays; information centres in national parks and resort centres; and guided trips into caves, up rock faces and into the bush.

It is fortunate, with such a diversity of activities available, that New Zealand has a highly developed public transport system with scheduled air services to most areas and an extensive network of coach operations, rail transport, and passenger and vehicular ferry services. For greater flexibility more people are using campervans and making use of the many caravan parks and formal and informal camping grounds. Rental cars are used at some stage by 28 per cent of all visitors and there are several major rental car operators in the country. The use of private cars by overseas visitors has increased in recent years.

In order of use, private cars, rental cars and organised coach tours are the most popular ways of travel for international visitors. Holiday/vacation visitors favour rental cars or organised coach tours. Business travellers prefer private cars and rental cars and figure as the highest users of taxis. 28 per cent of travellers on working holidays prefer to hitchhike. Most visitors use several modes of transport, including bicycles.

# UNDERSTANDING ROAD SIGNS

In 1987 New Zealand began the changeover to an international 'symbolic' road sign system, which is used extensively overseas. Symbols are considered to be more easily understood than a written message, and less confusing to overseas visitors because they are used internationally.

The new system combines shape and colour with symbols to differentiate between classes of signs. They are reflectorised, which means they will be seen from a greater distance at night. The first signs to be phased out were signs that warn of temporary hazards such as roadworks, flooding or slips. Next were the permanent warning signs such as pedestrian crossings or curves in the road. In 1988 new GIVE WAY signs were introduced, followed

## PROHIBITORY

Speed limit 100 km/h

Speed Limit 50 km/h

Temporary Speed Limit 30 km/h

Road Closed

No Left Turn

No Right Turn

No Pedestrians

No U Turn

No Cycling

Stop

Give Way

No Entry

by all regulatory signs. Most regulatory signs are circular in shape, although there are some exceptions. The STOP sign is octagonal and the GIVE WAY sign is triangular. There are two types of regulatory signs — prohibitory and mandatory.

**Prohibitory signs** These have a white background, a wide red border and where appropriate a diagonal red bar across a white background. Prohibitory signs prohibit a driver from taking a particular action, for example, NO RIGHT TURN.

**Mandatory signs** These signs have a blue background with a white border and a symbol. They indicate that a driver must take a certain action, for example, TURN RIGHT.

**Permanent hazard warning signs** These are identified by yellow diamond-shaped signs.

**Temporary hazard warning signs** These are identified by orange diamond or oblong shapes.

# MANDATORY

No Turns

Turn

Turn Left

Turn Right

Pedestrians

Cycling —
Recommended Route

Keep Left

Low Clearance

Traffic
Signals Ahead

Winding Road

Greasy Surface

Lane Closed

# INDEX-MAJOR ITINERARIES

# SOUTH ISLAND